Censorship in Czech and Hungarian Academic Publishing, 1969–89

Censorship in Czech and Hungarian Academic Publishing, 1969–89

Snakes and Ladders

Libora Oates-Indruchová

BLOOMSBURY ACADEMIC
LONDON • NEW YORK • OXFORD • NEW DELHI • SYDNEY

BLOOMSBURY ACADEMIC
Bloomsbury Publishing Plc
50 Bedford Square, London, WC1B 3DP, UK
1385 Broadway, New York, NY 10018, USA
29 Earlsfort Terrace, Dublin 2, Ireland

BLOOMSBURY, BLOOMSBURY ACADEMIC and the Diana logo are trademarks of
Bloomsbury Publishing Plc

First published in Great Britain 2020
This paperback edition published in 2021

Copyright © Libora Oates-Indruchová, 2020

Chapters 3-7: English language translation of the Czech interview extracts © David Short 2010

Libora Oates-Indruchová has asserted her right under the Copyright, Designs and
Patents Act, 1988, to be identified as Author of this work.

Cover image: Snakes and Ladders
(© giochidelloca.it)

All rights reserved. No part of this publication may be reproduced or transmitted in any
form or by any means, electronic or mechanical, including photocopying, recording,
or any information storage or retrieval system, without prior permission in
writing from the publishers.

Bloomsbury Publishing Plc does not have any control over, or responsibility for, any
third-party websites referred to or in this book. All internet addresses given in this book
were correct at the time of going to press. The author and publisher regret any inconvenience
caused if addresses have changed or sites have ceased to exist, but can accept no
responsibility for any such changes.

Every effort has been made to trace copyright holders and to obtain their permissions
for the use of copyright material. The publisher apologizes for any errors or omissions
and would be grateful if notified of any corrections that should be incorporated
in future reprints or editions of this book.

Source of the epigraph: Luigi Ciompi & Adrian Seville, n.d. Giochi dell'Oca e di percorso.
With reference to:
Ayala García, Patricia, Carranza Flores, Antonio and Nicolini Pimazzoni, Davide:
'Serpientes y escaleras. Lecciones de expresión creativa y pautas de narrativa gráfica'.
ARTSEDUCA Núm. 9, septiembre de 2014 (Universidad de Colima, México, 2014).

A catalogue record for this book is available from the British Library.

A catalog record for this book is available from the Library of Congress.

ISBN: HB: 978-1-3501-0664-2
PB: 978-1-3502-5315-5
ePDF: 978-1-3501-0665-9
eBook: 978-1-3501-0666-6

Typeset by Deanta Global Publishing Services, Chennai, India

To find out more about our authors and books visit www.bloomsbury.com and
sign up for our newsletters.

To all those who shared their stories with me.

Snakes and ladders, or Chutes and ladders, is a classic children's board game. It is played between 2 or more players on a playing board with numbered grid squares. On certain squares on the grid are drawn a number of 'ladders' connecting two squares together, and a number of 'snakes' or 'chutes' also connecting squares together. […] The game was played widely in ancient India by the name of Moksha Patamu. […] Moksha Patamu was perhaps invented by Hindu spiritual teachers to teach children about the effects of good deeds as opposed to bad deeds. The ladders represented virtues such as generosity, faith, humility, etc., and the snakes represented vices such as lust, anger, murder, theft, etc. The moral of the game was that a person can attain salvation (Moksha) through performing good deeds whereas by doing evil one takes rebirth in lower forms of life (Patamu). The number of ladders was less than the number of snakes as a reminder that treading the path of good is very difficult compared to committing sins.

Luigi Ciompi and Adrian Seville, n.d. *Giochi dell'Oca e di percorso*. Available at: http://www.giochidelloca.it. Accessed 12 March 2019.

Contents

List of illustrations	viii
Acknowledgements	ix
Note on the translation	xi

1	Introduction	1
2	The limits: Regulation of Czechoslovak scholarly life in policy documents	47

Four Sheets of Stories: A visual metanarrative. 'The beginnings'	65
Dramatis personae	70

3	People and institutions: Surviving in normalized academia	73
4	The work: 'Driving' a manuscript on the highways and byways of state-socialist academic publishing	113
5	The author: Censoring and authoring under state socialism	147
6	The language: Research topics, vocabulary, writing in code	187
7	The review: Loss of memory, the ghosts of academia past in the present	215

Four Sheets of Stories: A visual metanarrative. 'The ends'	225

8	Snakes and ladders: A theory of state-socialist censorship	231
	Institutional personnel strategies and personal strategies of professional survival	231
	The highway code for getting published	259
	Acts of censorship, authors and their texts	270
	Politicization of research subjects, ideologized language and text coding	291
	The ghosts of academia past, their spectres haunting the present	312
	Conclusion	319
9	Coda	325

Bibliography	331
Index	352

Illustrations

Colour images

Four Sheets of Stories: A visual metanarrative. 'The beginnings'
1 The Prologue   66
2 The Inspiration   67
3 The Action   68
4 Anticipation   69

Four Sheets of Stories: A visual metanarrative. 'The ends'
5 The Prologue   226
6 The Inspiration   227
7 The Action   228
8 Anticlimax   229

Figure

1 The main components of the Communist Party's communication structure of science policies   56

Boxes

1 The construction of an 'imagined conversation'   34
2 The artwork   44

Acknowledgements

The research for this project and the writing of this book were supported by several funding schemes: The Czech Science Foundation, award no. GA 405/03/1056; Mellon Fellowship at the Institute for Advanced Study in the Humanities (IASH) of the University of Edinburgh; Marie Curie Intra-European Fellowship at the Collegium Budapest Institute for Advanced Study; Ludwig Boltzmann Gesellschaft; Aleksanteri Institute Visiting Fellowship, University of Helsinki; Short-Term Scientific Mission grant at the School of Slavonic and East European Studies (SSEES), University College London awarded by COST: European Cooperation in Science and Technology within its Action CA16213: New Exploratory Phase in Research on East European Cultures of Dissent (NEP4Dissent); and a publication grant from the University of Graz.

As the work on this project has taken a long time, the people that helped nudge it forward were many. My thanks go to all those I have been privileged to meet as participants and collaborators, to get to know as colleagues, to call my friends and to have as family over the many years of research and writing.

This work could not have even begun without the narrators whose voices are recorded here, and also Gábor Klaniczay, János Kornai and György Péteri, whose generous advice in the planning stage of the Hungarian part of the research was indispensable.

The fellows and staff at IASH, Collegium Budapest and Aleksanteri Institute created amazingly stimulating environments that nourished my work for months on end. György Szőnyi's effort to organize a truly professional discussion event in Szeged went beyond the call of duty. I would have been lost in translation without Gábor Halmai's research assistance in Budapest and David Short's incredible professional skills and dedication that helped preserve the immediacy of spoken Czech in the interview extracts as he rendered them into his playful literary English. Jeannette Goehring's photographer's eye captured the *Four Sheets of Stories* (still) on film.

Muriel Blaive, Barbara Falk, Padraic Kenney, James Krapfl, Lynne Pearce and Gerlinda Šmausová provided valuable comments on the drafts of the various parts of this work.

Sari Autio-Sarasmo introduced me to the Czechophiles at the Aleksanteri and took care that I always wanted to go back for more. Richard Dutton unwittingly planted the bug of censorship research great many years ago, and Peter Zusi, my host at SSEES, brainstormed the book title with me just a few months back.

The person-without-whom is, as in so many other instances, Merrill Oates, whose IT skills kept my gadgets in shipshape, but most importantly, whose companionship has helped me keep my feet on the ground, but not to too mundane a degree.

Finally, Rhodri Mogford, Laura Reeves and Sophie Campbell, my editors at Bloomsbury Academic, guided the manuscript through all the practical hoops to a book.

Note on the translation

The Czech interview material was translated by David Short.

The parts of the Hungarian interviews that were originally conducted in Hungarian were translated by Gábor Halmai.

The Czech postgraduate degree 'CSc.' (*Candidatus scientarium*) approximates a PhD and is translated as such where suitable.

The Czech advanced degree *habilitace*, for which a scholar receives the title of *Docent*, corresponds to either Readership (UK) or Associate Professorship (North America) and is translated as 'habilitation'.

1

Introduction

The annus mirabilis of 1989 brought an end to the communist surveillance of creative expression, media and knowledge production, although not all of the overseeing structures were dismantled immediately and some have perhaps never even been challenged. Fairly strict measures and legislation applied to the media and also to art in all of the countries of the former Eastern Bloc throughout the period of the communist rule. The production of knowledge, however, was not subjected to ideological restrictions in the same measure. Official censoring bodies overseeing science and scholarship existed only in some countries some of the time and were replaced by elaborate systems of negotiations and self-censorship at other times. Social sciences and humanities were placed in the 'ideological sphere' according to orthodox Marxist categorization and therefore more closely watched than sciences (Merton [1945] 1973). Yet, research institutes and university departments produced wagonloads of scholarly publications in all or at least most of the then existing disciplines. The argument that all that was worthless junk produced by stooges of communist ideology will not stand. It would imply that whole disciplines, research units and university departments would have to disappear overnight, unless they were filled by new personnel from 'the West' (which is what happened to a large degree in East Germany) or from the ranks of those who were educated in clandestine seminars on contemporary scholarly discussions. As to the latter, there were definitely such scholars, but the fact of the matter is that many – if not most – of the people teaching at universities and publishing scholarly work before 1989 continued to do so afterwards. Perhaps even more importantly, they produced cohorts of students who have peopled their disciplines in their home countries – and sometimes abroad – since. Instead of dismissing the knowledge produced under state socialism, we need to take it seriously and allow the authors, the researchers and the university lecturers, professional allegiance that came before loyalty to the Communist Party if they were members, and agency if they were not.

What was the life course of a thought under the politically repressive conditions of state socialism? What did the 'family' and social life of thoughts look like? Were thoughts perhaps communicated in a code shared by authors and their readers but inaccessible to censors? These are the questions this book explores: the rounds of permissions and other hoops through which a thought had to progress on its way from an author or a community of peers, through a publishing house, to book reviews; the handling of texts by their authors and in the contexts of scholarly institutions and communities; and how the scholars thought they communicated their ideas to readers.

The origins of this project go back to the late 1990s when I interviewed informally a former professor of mine in Prague to get help with collecting material for a chapter of my doctoral thesis that dealt with some Czech undergraduate textbooks written in the 1980s. I was trying to explain to the British audience, for whom the thesis was written, how the state-socialist ideology interfered in those texts (Oates-Indruchová 2003). I would not need this explanation for a Czech audience, everybody – or so I believed – would understand, because it was common knowledge; but the British needed printed evidence. I went first to my undergraduate faculty library that should have held plenty of textbooks and documents explaining the ideological grounds of the subject area about which I was writing. I ordered a dozen or so publications from the ancient card catalogue. They all boasted titles such as *Communist Education for the Teachers of* … , *Collected Documents of the Communist Party toward the Further Development of* … , *The Resolutions of the XIVth Communist Party Congress and* … or *Ideological Principles of the Methodology of* …

The next day I came to collect my 'catch'. The librarian handed the order slips back to me saying, 'I am sorry but none of these are available.'

Incredulous, I asked, 'Are you saying that they have become such popular reading that they are *all* out? Every one of the multiple copies?'

After a moment of – embarrassed, I wanted to believe – hesitation, he responded, 'No, the head librarian decided that these books were to be destroyed, because they were no longer needed. You see, they have no scholarly value.'

No doubt the head librarian's destructive zeal was motivated by a desire to purge the library of the books that were considered empty verbiage by generations of students and teachers, and who only read them because they were required reading in ideological courses. She probably did not realize that by this act she was also removing evidence of the ideological manipulation of Czech social sciences and education. The librarian at the counter saw my dismay and advised me to consult the National Library, which should hold one copy of all of these publications through legal deposit. I went – and drew a blank. These documents were all internal prints of that particular faculty, grey literature, and as such, were not kept in the National Library. They were gone.

And that is how I came to interview my former professor, let's call him Professor Horn. Not only did he not turn me out, but he *wanted* to talk and share his experience. He supplied me with the information I needed for the thesis chapter on the presence of the state-socialist ideology in textbooks, and then opened other questions – those that motivated the research leading to this book.

The question that triggered further questions in our conversation concerned the interweaving of the personal and the political: if the second-wave feminists declared that 'personal is political', during late state socialism in Czechoslovakia the political was always also personal.[1] Professor Horn himself was not able to say to what extent the harassment he received concerning his publications had to do with his person or with his subject matter. By association, he followed up with an example of how personal relations could also mitigate the ideological influence: 'We were writing an encyclopaedia and my boss insisted that we had to write an entry on the contribution of communism. Neither I, nor the editor, wanted to have anything to do with that entry. So, what did we do? We invited my boss to a pub, ordered drinks, and after a couple of those, she – the editor – said to him, "Honza, we don't give a shit about that entry." And that was the end of that.'

What was the relative power of 'the boss' at the department and 'the editor' at the publishing house? And where was the author? As to the latter, Professor Horn added still more complexity: 'When I wrote the history of one

---

[1] Jonathan Bolton observed that same parallel about the larger context, in which dissident intellectuals worked: 'If "the personal is political" was a feminist slogan of the 1970s in the West, dissidents were forced to take politics personally' (Bolton 2012: 17).

nineteenth-century Czech cultural movement, some passages in the published version were written by my boss, because I would have never written them in that way. If anybody reads that today they must think I am some Red-minded idiot.'

'Why did you agree with the publication?' I asked – naïvely, as it immediately became clear, for he answered simply, 'He was my boss and he told me to submit a manuscript.'

'But you had to give the final approval, you were the author, right? Or was he printed in the book as a co-author?'

'No to both questions. My approval and my being the author had nothing to do with it. He asked to read everything his staff members wanted to publish and made his decision about the suitability of the material. If he thought my work ought to be published, but required changes, that was "the law" and I had no say over whether I wanted to see it in print with his additions or not.'

Professor Horn just demolished my idea of the author with this statement – or at least a belief in some minimal autonomy of the creative process. Moreover, if one generally agrees with Pierre Macherey that the ideologies that govern the writer as a subject make it into her or his texts unknowingly, despite honest attempts at independent thought (Macherey 1978), Professor Horn's experience stood this theory on its head in the authoritarian conditions of state socialism. There, the official ideology asserted itself blatantly and consciously into what it allowed to be published. It happened in an act of manipulative creation that is familiar even today to spin doctors in public relations agencies: combining censorship, a restrictive action, with propaganda, a prescriptive action.

Professor Horn's revelation presented questions that concerned the author as much as the reader. How did the authors *personally* relate to their texts, what strategies did they have to employ to minimize the external ideological interference with the text? And where did all this leave the readers? Did they suspect that the author was not necessarily the one printed on the book cover, and did it change in any way the reading process? Did the reader perhaps approach a book published under state socialism with some sort of virtual reality glasses, which gave the text its 'true' shape? With a bow to reception theory, one must acknowledge the impossibility of any search of a 'true shape' of any text. Nevertheless, one can try and reconstruct the strategies the authors as creators employed to convey their ideas to the readers and, in turn, the authors as readers employed to learn what they wanted to learn in the state-socialist environment.

Moral dilemmas challenged the authors along the way: to withdraw into silence or to stay and speak, albeit with tongues tied by authority?[2]

Censorship in the Eastern Bloc

Even if we take only the later period of state socialism (Kádár or Ceaușescu years, period after the Prague Spring) rather than the whole era, we will find that scholarly publishing differed quite significantly in its relation to censorship across the Eastern Bloc. Some countries, such as Poland, had a formal censoring body, but small-circulation scholarly publications were expressly permitted greater freedoms than publications intended for public consumption (Schöpflin 1983: 32–102). Others, such as Czechoslovakia and Hungary, had no designated censoring institution regulating scholarship and science. The latter countries provide a better ground for the inquiry into intellectual communication and structures of text production under repressive conditions. Any restrictions on scholarly creation in countries without formalized censorship had to be 'dispersed' through various elements of the publishing process and 'displaced' away from the overseeing centre (Burt 1998: 17). A pattern of action following written rules of dos and don'ts and leading from one link to the next in the publishing chain was thus replaced with a pattern resulting from perception and anticipation. The perceptions were likely to be based on an idea of a *system* of state censorship that was countered by – possibly – a *system* of intellectual communication. The absence of a formal institution has methodological implications for the present research. Archival documentation is likely to be sparse and any 'perceptions' cannot be easily verified against a written record: the state that claimed it exercised no censorship was touchy about any suggestions of such practice and the word itself, a fact noted by researchers also on other state-socialist countries and beyond (Mihály 1993: 49; Coetzee 1996: 34; Klötzer and Lokatis 1999: 24; Dąbrowski 2017: 214).[3]

---

[2] This borrowing from Shakespeare's Sonnet 66 refers also to Janet Clare's work on Elizabethan censorship, with which state-socialist publishing has surprising parallels and to which I will occasionally refer. See (Clare 1990).

[3] Recently, Dmitry Kurakin argued that Soviet sociological community 'had a strong bias in favor of oral forms of communication' and therefore, 'important events, trends and facts were never documented' (Kurakin 2017: 398).

The element of perception is strongly represented in the pre-1989 works on censorship published either outside of the Eastern Bloc or in *samizdat*. They relied on testimonies of exiles or dissident and blacklisted authors giving accounts of their own experiences with censorship (Dewhirst and Farrell 1973; Siniavski 1989; Zipser 1990a). Testimony was also the flagship genre of articles in the magazine *Index on Censorship* (Gruša 1982; Šiklová 1983; Voslensky 1986; Demszky 1989). Occasionally, documents detailing censoring practices were smuggled through the Iron Curtain and supplemented the authors' perceptions with evidence from contemporary cultural policies, that is, with the perspective of the state. The so-called *Black Book of Polish Censorship* (Curry 1984) is an outstanding example of such a publication, and also George Schöpflin's collection of documents mainly on media censorship in Czechoslovakia, the GDR, Hungary, Poland and Yugoslavia (Schöpflin 1983). A surge of testimonies came out in the 1990s in the general atmosphere of hunger for 'witness accounts' of state repressions. Lidia Vianu was the first to collect systematically such testimonies in 1991–2. Her book, *Censorship in Romania*, contains twenty-six edited interviews with literary critics, poets and prose writers of several generations about their experience with getting their work published during the Ceaușescu regime (Vianu 1998). The narrators' detailed descriptions of the phases of the publishing process and the roles played by the various actors became a crucial inspiration for my project.

The opening of the archives in the 1990s stimulated document-based research of institutional processes (e.g. Wichner 1993; Tomášek 1994; Kaplan and Tomášek 1994; Kelly 1995; Lokatis 1996; Costabile-Heming 1997; Dobrenko 1997; Blium 1998; Šámal 2009; Romek 2010; Bock 2011). The researchers mined the archives for previously unknown details of institutional functioning, synthetized those into descriptions of censorship systems and proposed theoretical models of censorship. Reviewing the body of literature now, one finds that the details themselves did not bring any new *conceptual* information. All the pieces to construct models were available to researchers of censorship already in the *sum of the perceptions* articulated in the testimonials, which raises social interaction between the various actors into prominence. They rarely had access to the exact directives; they learned by doing and at least in the late phase of state socialism it is likely that together they also participated in the creation of the system of censorship and its practice.

Nevertheless, most of the testimonies or studies of documents focused on the repressive actions of institutions against the creative spirit and tried to build a taxonomy of state-socialist censorship.[4] The Hungarian blacklisted writer György Konrád, writing in 1983, considered censorship during the Stalinist period 'positive, aggressive' in contrast to the 'negative and defensive' kind of the 1980s (Konrád 1983: 449): 'At that time you were told what to say, now you're only advised what not to say.' The aim of this latter censorship that pervaded all state and social institutions was 'to discourage people from thinking' (Konrád 1983) and that made these 'state-owned citizens' who knew what not to say 'predictable, transparent' (Konrád 1983: 451). Another author, Richard A. Zipser, writing about literary censorship in the GDR in May 1989, distinguishes between self-censorship, editorial censorship (or *sanfte Zensur*, because it is mostly expressed as a 'friendly' recommendation), state ideological censorship and Party censorship that was conducted at every stage of the publication process by many actors (Zipser 1990b). Next, Robert Darnton carried out a comparative study between the *ancien régime* in France and the GDR, concluding that the former's operating principle was 'privilege', because the censors and authors came from the same milieu, shared the same values, while literary censorship in the GDR was based on 'planning'; state-socialist propaganda was inserted into every element of the publishing process, the task falling to the editors who thus had the upper hand over the authors (Darnton 1995). Darnton moved away from this position in his later work, placing emphasis on the dispersed nature of GDR censorship and the multiple points of negotiation between the various actors (Darnton 2014: 191).

Deployment at all levels was a defining feature of state-socialist censorship. Marianna Tax Choldin coined the term 'omnicensorship' for the way readers were moulded by library censorship in the Soviet era in contrast to the 'sovereign' censorship of Tzarist Russia (Choldin 1998: 26). The system moved from 'autocratic' to 'bureaucratic' and was defined 'sometimes by terror and always by secrecy and a remarkable degree of pervasiveness' (Choldin 1998: 26). Arlen Blyum develops on the concept and constructs a pyramid model of Soviet literary censorship: starting with self-censorship at the base, and progressing through editorial, Glavlit and secret political police censorship,

---

[4] The work on the GDR is exceptional in that already in the 1990s it considered agency and negotiation on the part of the authors (Lokatis 1996; Costabile-Heming 1997).

to the censorship exercised by the Department of Agitation and Propaganda of the Party Central Committee at the apex. The first three levels constituted 'preliminary' censorship, the fourth and fifth levels 'punitive' (Blyum 2003: 3–8). He then proceeds to articulate the 'repressive, regulatory, model-setting, ideological, selective, protective (…) [and] prescriptive' functions of censorship in 'totalitarian states' (Blyum 2003: 10–13) and argues that 'the prescriptive function appears to be an invention of the communist regime. (…) [censors were to] "educate" authors by prescribing what and how they should write' (Blyum 2003: 13). It needs to be said that Blyum focuses mainly on the period up to the 1950s and that is perhaps why he does not make a note of a change from the prescriptive to the proscriptive censorship.

These taxonomies rarely explore the reverse process of censorship: the various strategies of circumventing it. One such strategy, writing in an 'Aesopian language', was described by Lev Loseff in his now canonical work on Soviet literature (Loseff 1984). Writers used either 'screens' to hide the true meaning or 'markers' to draw attention to it (Loseff 1984: 50–2), in effect developing a system of communication with the reader. Kevin Moss elaborated on the idea of the code and argued that in the years before glasnost the Soviets mastered communication in a 'public' and a 'private' code, where certain words or phrases stood for something else, such as 'Ancient Russian Music' meant 'church music' (Moss 1995: 131). He then presents a range of stylistic devices employed to encode the intended meaning by Bulgagov in *Master and Margarita* (Moss 1995: 232–3). The most recent writer on Aesopian language, Irina Sandomirskaja, considers it an ambiguous strategy on several counts. She argues that the camouflaging produces 'a grey zone of uncertainty, vacillating between the mutually exclusive poles of resistance and collaboration, between challenging the power of censorship and conforming to it' (Sandomirskaja 2015: 64). Her perspective will be important for the inquiry into Aesopian language in this book.

As pointed out earlier, the taxonomies take a unidirectional perspective on censorship: the state and its agencies act on the writer and work together as a system. In recent years some scholars drew on the theoretical insights of New Censorship, to which I will return in the next section. They take a less totalizing view of late state-socialist censorship, emphasizing complicity, resistance and negotiation, such as Sara Jones in her study of three East German writers (Jones 2011) or Samantha Sherry in her study of Soviet literary translators

(Sherry 2015), thus foregrounding agency in the theoretical discussion. Jones shifts the research focus to the 'fluid boundaries between opposition and conformity' (Jones 2011: 21) and investigates how, and if, the writers, each of whom occupied a different political place, achieved a position of clarity in his or her relationship to the state power. Sherry also brings in the insidious consequence of the pervasiveness of censorship that Konrád articulated earlier and with reference to Pierre Bourdieu argues that 'censorial practices were governed both by the relation between representatives of power and literary actors and by the action of the habitus, as censorial norms were internalised and functioned unconsciously' (Sherry 2015: 7). This will also be a pivotal point in discussing the effects of censorship in the argument presented here.

Most work on state-socialist censorship has investigated literature. Censorship of scholarship and science has been much less in the focus. The pre-1989 work consists again largely of testimonials, such as Voslensky's in the *Index on Censorship* mentioned earlier, in which he observes how the choice of a research topic was already affected by censorship (Voslensky 1986: 28) or a brief account by Yuri Yarim-Agaev on his experience in Soviet science (Yarim-Agaev 1989). Once the archives and borders opened, analytical studies using both document analysis and interviews began to appear. Their scope is generally broader than censorship, covering various aspects of research conditions under state socialism or writing histories of individual disciplines. The former type of publications is of particular relevance to this project. Slava Gerovitch, for example, investigates discursive strategies in history writing that were developed in direct response to censoring pressures. He notes the development of a particular genre of history writing, 'internalist, factological, and discussion-avoiding', to which the censors could not object, because in the absence of analysis 'facts "spoke for themselves"' (Gerovitch 1998: 199–203). Even more interestingly, he sees this genre as being carried into the post-Soviet era as a legacy that would not go away easily. Sergei I. Zhuk, writing on American studies during the Brezhnev era, found that very same genre established in this research field also (Zhuk 2013: 322–3). The studies of particular institutions or disciplines are by now too numerous to list and, moreover, they touch on censorship and the publishing process only sporadically. So far the few exceptions include Siegfried Lokatis' perceptive and wry analysis of GDR academic publishing in the early 1960s (Lokatis 1996), partially also Jürgen Kocka's general outline of the interlocking of scholarship and politics in the GDR (Kocka 1998) and Zbygniew Romek's comprehensive study of Polish censorship of historiography before 1970 (Romek 2010). Of these, Lokatis and Romek allow for the peer, rather than exclusively censoring, function of editors and Lokatis brings forward the element of the authors' agency.

The GDR and Poland present two contrasting cases to the Czech and Hungarian scholarly publishing discussed here. The GDR system of censorship distinguished 'a significant push for codification' (Klötzer and Lokatis 1999: 256) from the early 1960s onwards. That included the regulation of academic production, which was dispersed, but at the same time fairly hierarchically structured (Costabile-Heming 1997: 54; Kocka 1998: 441–2), more so than Czech scholarly publishing, while both systems contained spaces for negotiation. The clearer and stricter hierarchization could have been the consequence of the unique feature of the GDR situation, namely, that 'the GDR's "class enemy" shared a common language' and, therefore, the censoring bodies had to be more precise and responsive in their methods than their Slavic or Hungarian counterparts (Klötzer and Lokatis 1999: 254). The Polish system had a centralized censoring body, but 'was based on the so-called delegation of censorship duties. In other words, the intention was to make sure that counsellors [i.e. the employees of the censoring agency] received only material which did not require any corrections' (Dąbrowski 2017: 215). The Main Office for Control of the Press, Publications, and Public Performance (GUKP) was established in July 1946 and abolished in April 1990, but as of July 1981, editors could challenge its decisions in court, while publications of the Academy of Sciences were exempt from its jurisdiction (Bates 2001: 1893). Although the censoring guidelines were secret, they defined the limits of permissibility relatively concretely for the censors, including the special status of scholarship already before 1981, as we know from the *Black Book of Polish Censorship* (Curry 1984). This created an environment of greater clarity for Polish academics. We will read the testimonies of Hungarian scholars in this book, describing their working conditions in similar terms, although Hungary as far as we know did not have any comparably formal rules. The similar experience stems from a different constellation of circumstances.

Three authors are important for the geographical focus of this book: György Péteri, John Connelly and Jiřina Šmejkalová. All three have been researching Czech or Hungarian state-socialist academia and publishing since the 1990s.

Péteri investigated the relationship of Hungarian scientists and scholars at the Academy of Sciences to the state power from the mid-1940s. He argued that not just the state, but also the early internal power struggles between scientists and scholars helped set the limits of social sciences in the subsequent decades. The state, however, needed the expertise of the economists to exercise power and in exchange for ideological compliance granted them relative autonomy: '[I]t made them the only group within Hungary's academic intelligentsia (…) with the privilege of being co-opted to the institutions with power over some restricted domains of policy-making' (Péteri 1998: 223–4). This work led Péteri logically to the study of patronage in academia, a system of mutual dependence that enabled serious research work to continue, although within limits (Péteri 2002, 2019). In other words, by showing the roles played by local actors and their interests, he implies that expertization mitigated centralization. That is roughly also the position at which Connelly arrived in his study of 'Sovietization' of East German, Czech and Polish universities from the end of the Second World War to de-Stalinization. He concludes that in the Czech case the 'Sovietization' was aided and abetted by internal dynamics, rather than conducted purely under Soviet tutelage (Connelly 2000). Somewhat in contrast, Šmejkalová's work on Czech book publishing maintains the top-down view and concentrates on the state interventions into the publishing process. Her work nevertheless brings a valuable description of measures and practices that were built into the structure of the publishing industry, such as paper quotas, which in effect acted as censoring mechanisms (Šmejkalová-Strickland 1994; Šmejkalová 2000, 2011).

Šmejkalová has also until recently been the only Czech researcher participating in international discussions on censorship. The rest of Czech scholarship on state-socialist censorship, and there is a respectable amount, has been directed at the audience reading in Czech. The early pioneering work of Karel Kaplan and Dušan Tomášek documents the day-to-day operations of the censoring office between 1945 and 1968 (Kaplan and Tomášek 1994; Tomášek 1994). Pavel Janáček shows how the Stalinist censorship practices towards popular literature and pulp fiction were to a degree a continuation from the 1930s and 1940s, rather than a new development (Janáček 2004). Petr Šámal outlines the chronology of censorship of public libraries in the early 1950s and supplies all known lists of proscribed books from the time. His particular focus is on the role of librarians as 'turners of human souls', tasked with the shaping of the socialist reader (Šámal 2009). The latest addition to this body of work is a two-volume encyclopaedic work mainly on literary censorship in Czech culture since 1749 to the present (Wögerbauer et al. 2015). It illustrates the long and obstinate history of unfreedom of creative expression in the Czech lands, implying pointedly that spells of creative freedom were few and far apart. As to the time periods covered by the Czech research on censorship, the post-1968 period is the subject only in Šmejkalová's research on book publishing, distribution and selling of books, and in two sections of the general outline of state-socialist literary censorship and several short case studies in the encyclopaedic collection. The core of Šámal's overview from the compendium has recently become available in English (Lauk, Šámal and Shek Brnardić 2018).

Studies of overall conditions in late Czech state-socialist scholarship and science have also until recently been directed at a Czech-reading audience with the notable exception of the work by the Finnish historian Riika Nisonen-Trnka, but most of its focus is on the 1960s (Nisonen-Trnka 2012). In Czech there are a number of autobiographies that also include the years between 1968 and 1989 (Komárek 1992; Potůček 1995; Wichterle 1996; Konopásek 1999), while studies proper cover mainly the years leading to the Prague Spring and the early days of its aftermath (Kostlán 2002; Sommer 2011). Initiatives to study the last twenty-year period of state socialism as a phenomenon in its own right have been fewer, but are gaining in interest. An early example in Czech literature and literary studies is a volume of conference proceedings (Wiendl 1996) and a special issue of *Sociologický časopis/Czech Sociological Review* (2004). The prevailing narrative in the 1990s as well as in the present has been that of rupture and discontinuity with the institutional and intellectual development of the 1960s (Prečan 1994; Nešpor 2014b). The studies tend to focus on repressions by the state and on the institutional conditions in various disciplines (Oates-Indruchová 2008; Urbášek 2008; Urbášek 2012; Voříšek 2008, 2012). In the present decade there has been a marked turn towards more layered perspectives and new questions, such as the legacies and continuities from state socialism (Skovajsa 2011; Skovajsa and Balon 2017b), niches of relative freedom within official institutions (Kabele 2011; Olšáková 2012; Nešpor 2014a), decentralization through expertization (Sommer 2015, 2016; Kopeček 2017) and gender aspects (Vohlídalová 2018).

This book draws on the previous research, but is attempting a more complex treatment of scholarly writing and publishing under the conditions of censorship. It looks at all stages of the writing process from the inception of an idea to post-publication reception and at the institutional and policy contexts surrounding this process. What strategies did the authors and their institutions use in the process of scholarly text production? It considers, in turn, a variety of actors participating in the process, while focusing on the self-perceptions of the authors themselves, in order to examine the relationship of the author-scholar to his or her text and the reader. How do the authors now perceive that intellectual communication between authors and readers worked then? The agency and negotiations of the creative actors, rather than their instrumentalization by censoring repressions of the state institutions stand at the centre of this inquiry. Of particular note is the choice of social sciences and humanities in the endeavour to understand the complexity and effectiveness of state-socialist censorship. The plurality of interpretations distinguishes literature or drama, but scholarly communication aims at precision and unambiguous interpretations. If censoring pressures motivate the writers and playwrights to invent new metaphors and language games to evade the watchful eye and ear of the censor, what significance do such Aesopian strategies have in scholarly texts?

Finally, a note on terminology: although I have been using the term 'censorship' in this introduction, I avoided it when talking to the scholars who worked under state socialism. As censorship officially did not exist, I was curious if the authors would contextualize their stories within censorship or not. If I used the term at all, I did so only after they did or in the latter part of the interview. This was the quest with which this book began: to reconstruct, from people's oral testimonies and also from written documents, an important part of the intellectual history of the Cold War, so that the scholarly texts written at that time did not lose their enigmas and substance and were not read as mere sad mementos of shackled ideas.

Theories of censorship

Censorship in state socialism has been largely conceived in terms of institutional regulatory processes, as 'the governmental suppression of discourse' (Cohen 2001: 8): how and for what reasons governmental agents controlled what could be spoken, written or shown. Mark Cohen, however, argues that this concept of censorship only emerged in the Enlightenment from its concerns with reason and individual rights. In his view, this is 'a much more specific version, a subset of the earlier one, for the government censorship of some work as a *negative* judgment of the work, backed up by the power to enforce that judgment' (Cohen 2001). He sees the problem with this narrower definition in that it does not adequately explain 'the relationship between power and control of discourse' (Cohen 2001: 5) and therefore proposes to return to the earlier understanding of censorship as an exercise of judgement:

> [C]ensorship is the exclusion of some discourse as the result of a judgment made by an authoritative agent based on some ideological predisposition. By an authoritative agent I mean someone with the power to enforce the judgment, whether it be a public agent, a private agent, or the producer of the discourse herself. (...) Censorship is the result of a mental activity in which the censor perceives and distinguishes relationships or alternatives with respect to the discourse being judged. (Cohen 2001: 15–16)

He joins the proponents of New Censorship, an approach arising from Foucault's work on discourse, power and resistance: power is present in every relationship and, in turn, 'points of resistance are present everywhere in the power network' (Foucault 1990: 95). Michael Holquist, most radically, asserted that as a property of discourse '[c]ensorship is' (Holquist cited in (Post 1998: 2)). Pierre Bourdieu is also often cited in this context, although he uses 'censorship' only as a metaphor to describe the dynamics of expression in the field: 'The metaphor of censorship should not mislead: it is the structure of the field itself which governs expression by governing both access to expression and the form of expression, and not some legal proceeding which has been specially adapted to designate and repress the transgression of a kind of linguistic code' (Bourdieu 1991: 138). Sue Curry Jansen, one of the early New Censorship scholars, calls this form of censorship 'constitutive' (as opposed to 'regulative') and defines its purpose as existing 'to create, secure, and maintain' the control of the powerful 'over the power to name' (Jansen 1991: 8). Thus, she further argues, in all human societies power and knowledge are 'bound together in an inextricable knot' (Jansen 1991: 4). The powerful transmit their version of social life and rules to the powerless, while the powerless use their 'knowledge of power to negotiate their own recipes for survival' (Jansen 1991: 8). Judith Butler then drives this point home, asserting that 'censorship is at once the condition for agency and its necessary limit' in the sense that it informs every 'decision of how to decide' (Butler 1998: 257). She borrows the psychoanalytical term 'foreclosure' to describe the proscriptive characteristic of discourse (Butler 1998: 258). This concept of censorship has been criticized in the context of state socialism as conflating all forms of social control with actions of authoritarian governments. Placing all forms of power at one level 'risks trivializing acts of violence and oppression' (Sherry 2015: 6) in this argumentation.[5]

I propose that a useful perspective on state-socialist scholarly censorship sits somewhere in the middle: the top-down instrumentalization of the creative mind does not allow for agency, while the 'censorship is' position does not capture the hierarchy of power present in state-socialist regimes of censorship. Significantly, the top-down perspective cannot explain the most elusive kind of censorship: self-censorship and its interrelatedness with all the other kinds of censorship. It cannot consider censorship 'as a system of control, which pervades institutions, colors human relations, and reaches into the hidden workings of the soul' (Darnton 2014: 243). Jansen's model of the 'power-knowledge knot' is a good starting point for considering the complexity of scholarly censorship under late state socialism in those countries that did not have a central supervisory authority. Although Jansen introduces 'constitutive censorship', she also identifies individual, hierarchically positioned agents – the powerful and the powerless. Helen Freshwater has critically assessed the New Censorship thought and called for greater emphasis on the relational nature of censorship and the involvement of multiple agents: '[C]ensorship is a process, realized through the relationships between censorious agents, rather than a series of actions carried out by a discrete or isolated authority' (Freshwater 2004: 1). Her definition presents the closest fit to the state-socialist situation. It accommodates Richard Burt's model of 'dispersed censorship' that he proposed instead of the traditional 'removal and replacement' model, that is, one that looked at the cuts made by the censor and replacement of the cut material by the author:

> By contrast, I offer a more complex and nuanced model of censorship involving *dispersal* and *displacement*. Early modern stage censorship (…) was dispersed among a variety of regulatory agents and practices; it was productive as well as prohibitive; it involved cultural legitimation as well

---

[5] See also (Müller 2004).

as delegitimation. Censorship was more than one thing, occurred at more than one place and at more than one time. (Burt 1998: 17; emphasis in the original)

Not surprisingly, this is the model adopted by Petr Šámal for his overall characterization of state-socialist censorship to get away from the top-down perspective (Šámal 2009; Lauk, Šámal and Shek Brnardić 2018). He further defines 'fields of censoring interactions' as those of the author, journal, publishing house, editorial plans and the process of their approval, pre-publication censorship, book distribution, the reader and parallel circulations (i.e. *samizdat*) (Šámal 2015). Šámal emphasizes the multiple phases of state-socialist censorship and 'the interconnectedness of the processes of planning, management and inspection' (Šámal 2015: 1102). I will add that the dispersal and chronological staging did not mean that the multiple censoring sites were all equal. To the contrary, the system was hierarchical, one censoring agent carrying more or less weight than another. Similarly, censorship at one stage of the writing and publishing process could have carried lesser or graver consequences than the same thing at another stage.

In this book, I will work with a model that is dispersed, multistaged, as well as hierarchical. In terms of the censoring sites and chronological stages, I follow the approach of Beate Müller, who proposed the classic communication model for the study of censorship: 'the sender of a message, its receiver, the message itself, the code employed, the channel (or medium), and the context' (Müller 2004: 15). I will look, in turn, into the institutional and policy contexts of scholarly publishing, the author, the receiver in the sense that the authors were also readers of scholarly texts, the publication venues and the language employed to write scholarly texts (i.e. the 'code'). The 'message', or the content of scholarly texts, will be my subject in so far as it concerns publishable and non-publishable areas, rather than textual analyses. Moreover, my treatment of censorship also incorporates the key aspect of Burt's model, namely, 'complicity and collaboration between censors, authors, and critics' (Burt 1998: 21) that pervaded all sites and all processes and was also a catalyst of self-censorship. The authors had to consider what and how to write also with regard to their 'partners' in the negotiation process, be it their colleagues, supervisors or editors. Self-censorship is elusive in the sense that it is difficult to document from published texts and also to articulate by the authors themselves. Authors writing under state socialism were aware of the dispersed system of censorship and they made concessions to it so as not to put their potential allies – typically, their editors – into an awkward position with *their* superiors. But, as Müller, who otherwise maintains the top-down approach to state-socialist censorship, also asks, 'Where does authorial revision end, and where does censorial excision start?' (Müller 2004: 25). Cohen doubts that self-censorship can always be traced to an authorial intention: '[I]t may also be unintentional: I may have so completely assimilated the values of society that my suppression of my opinion may be unthinking and automatic' (Cohen 2001: 14). In our case, it would be difficult to claim that 'society', rather than political mores, was the supreme censor, but the general idea of proscriptions having passed into the bloodstream holds.

That brings me to the final and crucial theoretical consideration of the end effect of censorship: Does the perennial strategizing to outwit the censor foster creativity and critical thinking, or does the potentially unintentional self-censorship lead ultimately to the detriment of thought? Before introducing the arguments supporting both positions, a caveat is in order: Janet Clare, working on Elizabethan stage censorship, cautioned about the very possibility to determine the exact influence of censorship. She argued that 'until we locate the text within the historical moment of production and reconstruct the precise preoccupations of the censor by way of evidence from censored texts, we cannot know – other than in the broadest terms – how censorship impinged on the working playwright' (Clare 1990: x). Her argument applies doubly to state-socialist scholarly censorship, where any textual evidence is thin on the ground and the best we can hope for is to bring together different types of sources, such as my sample that I will introduce in the next section. Theoretical work and personal testimonies provide arguments for both positions on the effects of censorship. Leo Strauss is perhaps the best-known proponent of the argument on the benefits of censorship. He argues that '[p]ersecution (…) gives rise to a peculiar technique of writing, and therewith to a peculiar type of literature, in which the truth about all crucial things is presented exclusively between the lines. That literature is addressed, not to all readers, but to trustworthy and intelligent readers only' (Strauss 1952: 25). According to him, the authors always have to be a step ahead of the censor and think of new ways to communicate their ideas and thus the authors and their readers mutually sharpen their critical and creative powers.

The other argument on the effect of censorship presents exactly the opposite view: censorship erodes creativity and critical thinking, because as the authors always have to think the way the censors do, they internalize the official discourse. Whatever innovations to expression they bring into their texts, they are always already a part of the official, or dominant, discourse. In other words, there is no such thing as writing between the lines, because any meaning implanted by authors or deciphered by readers has, in fact, already been incorporated into the official discourse. It was the prominent Hungarian dissident and post-1989 politician Miklós Haraszti who proposed this alternative view of censorship in his book on the role of the artist and writer in state socialism, *The Velvet Prison* (Haraszti 1987), that first came out in French in 1983. It resonates, however, also with other theorists and writers writing under the conditions of political constraints on communication. Blyum, for example, asserts unequivocally that '[c]ontinuous mimicry leads inevitably to the deformation and loss of talent' (Blyum 2003: 4). Jansen is equally sceptical about the usefulness of writing between the lines, calling the technique 'patois or slave-song': 'At best, it produces esoteric communication that can be decoded by an intellectual or conspiratorial vanguard. (...) However at its worst, equivocation is transmuted into a voice without an echo. If the cat-and-mouse game goes on too long, the cat usually gets the mouse' (Jansen 1991: 194). The salient point here is the absence of an 'echo', for what purpose does scholarly writing serve without reception? In testimonies of writers and scholars active during state socialism, however, both praise and castigation of the influence of censorship are present. In the introduction to her book on Romanian censorship, Vianu defends the romantic position on censorship with the following words:

> And yet, slowly but surely, creative minds found ways to outwit censorship. It required unusual energy, acquaintances in the right places, and *savoir faire*. A strong bond between writer and reader came into being, and the writer was eager to express what he was not allowed to say. The reader avidly waited for the least hint about how to read between the lines, an art perfected under communist censorship. (Vianu 1998: viii–ix)

Some of the writers and scholars she interviewed supported her position, others adhered strongly to the view of the corrosive effect of censorship. The literary scholar Vera Călin considered self-censorship particularly insidious, because it 'distorts not only the process of writing, but also the process of artistic thinking' (Călin in Vianu 1998: 24). She was thinking back to the state-socialist times, but the Hungarian writer and intellectual György Konrád assessed the effect of censorship in the same way as Călin while still writing during state socialism, when he characterized the effect as 'a slow wearing away' (Konrád 1983: 450).

The narrators interviewed for this book also expressed both polar views, which begs the question, why? The community of scholars is small, the time period short – two decades – and working conditions delimited by science policies similar across disciplines and institutions. It would be reasonable to expect consensus regarding the perspectives on the effect of censorship. What distinguished the authors in their responses to the system of censorship? One plausible area of difference could be their disciplinary expertise; another could be their professional trajectory. I will therefore look not only at the sites, chronological stages and agents of the communication process, but also at the concept of authorship and at the function of the 'code', that is, at the authors' attitudes to the purposeful use of particular language and textual strategies.

The people and the institutions

The first dip into literature on state-socialist publishing clarified the time period and, consequently, a narrower territorial focus. Kaplan and Tomášek covered the work of institutionalized censorship in Czechoslovakia up until 1968 already in the mid-1990s, but the last two decades of Communist rule, the so-called normalization period has received much less attention. Milan Otáhal explains the history and usage of the term 'normalization' as follows:

> The term normalization was introduced by the Communists, but they related it primarily to the beginnings of the period, for which one of the leading dissidents, Milan Šimečka, coined the term 'the restoration of order'. Post-1989 historians have adopted the term and use it usually to denote the whole period up to 1989 instead of the perhaps more fitting term 'real-existing socialism' in its second, 'static' phase. (Otáhal 2002: 6)

The period promised much more fertile ground for the research into the relationship between the author, his or her text and the reader, because there was no formal institution or legislation that would justify censorship in academic publishing. Censorship was legislatively abolished in June 1968. It was reintroduced by the Act No. 127/1968 Sb. of 13 September 1968, three weeks after the Soviet-led invasion of Czechoslovakia by the Warsaw Pact forces. The Act established the Bureau for Press and Information and the Slovak Bureau for Press and Information (Úřad pro tisk a informace and Slovenský úrad pro tisk a informace), but specifically stipulated that '[t]he freedom to publish the results of scientific and artistic work is not affected by this law'. The supposed absence of formal censorship prompted the broadening of my inquiry from institutions to all the key actors and stages of the writing and publishing process.

As to the territorial focus, the period between 1969 and 1989 coincided with the constitutional change that established Czechoslovakia as a federation, which meant separate ministries of culture and education; the Slovak Academy of Sciences being a separate institution since 1953. Even though the overall science policies applied to the federal state, the situation in Slovak academia differed to the extent that it would have necessitated a comparative approach. Jonathan Larson, for example, stresses the softer censorship of people. If the regime's dissidents in the Czech part of the federation were likely to be ousted into manual labour after 1968, their Slovak counterparts 'after much searching frequently found somewhat relevant employment hidden in a library, laboratory, archive, or museum' (Larson 2013: 123). Adam Hudek showed a certain continuity from the 1950s in this regard, when '[t]he representatives of the Slovak Academy actively supported its position as a refuge for proscribed Slovak scientists' (Hudek 2015: 180). If I were to do justice to the differences between the two parts of the state, the inquiry would have broadened beyond the possibilities of a single volume. I settled for research only on the Czech part on disciplinary grounds: my interest was not primarily historical, but theoretical, and for that it was better to start with one distinct publishing environment.

Most of the multilevelled censorship that had begun to emerge already from the brief talk with Professor Horn was not likely to be traceable in documents. First, no censoring institution meant no archive and, second, the general aversion at the time to leave behind written evidence of ideological influence was common knowledge. Paulina Bren, researching Czech television during normalization, commented on her frustration with the lack of archival documentation on her subject:

> Normalization's leadership was made up of communism's survivors, the very men who had managed to avoid or overcome the treason trials, purges, arrests, reforms, and counterreforms of the past twenty years; if they had learned anything by the 1970s, it was that they should leave nothing in writing. Theirs was a world of doublespeak, of endless speeches, with nothing but words piled on like verbal car wrecks. (Bren 2010: 5–6)

Therefore, oral history interviews constitute the backbone of the project, complemented by contemporary science-policy documents and the archive of the Editorial Board of the Czechoslovak Academy of Sciences. I drew on *Censorship in Romania* (Vianu 1998) in developing the interview structure, because Vianu had the same interest in the complex personal experience of her informants and because Romania also did not have a central supervisory authority in late state socialism. Her major advantage over me was that she had the brilliant idea to talk to people right after the change of the political climate, in 1991–2. The people had their experience still fresh in their minds and relatively 'unpolluted' by new experience. Also, the whole of the public discourse was rife with comparisons and memories of the recent past. I had the handicap of asking my questions a decade later, in 2002–3: ten years of 'getting on' with their professional lives for my narrators, ten years of living in totally changed conditions and ten years of a gradually changing public discourse – in short, ten years of intentional or unintentional forgetting. Public discourse was now increasingly disinclined to analysis and reconstruction of the past, while being more prone to packaging the past into the uncomplicated totalitarian paradigm. Martin Sabrow's criticism of this approach in research is directed at the use of 'totalitarianism' more or less for dramatic effect, when he writes that 'totalitarian approaches tend to shape dictatorship as states of emergency, and they cannot cope easily with everyday fascism and everyday communism' (Sabrow 2002: 73). Consequently, these approaches are severely limited in their analytical and knowledge-generating potential, or worse, they are deployed out of 'the desire to delegitimize the subject of study' (Lothar Fritze paraphrased by (Jones 2011: 3)). The social atmosphere meant that potential narrators would view my presence in the field and my motivations with suspicion.

Vianu's book still provided a good starting point. Detailed reading of the twenty-six edited interviews collected in her book yielded a preliminary typology of areas affected by the ideological dictate that I then refined into blocks of questions covering personal professional history, the publishing process and barriers to publication, self-censorship, text 'coding' and post-1989 reception of and reflection on earlier work. I tested this interview structure on five pilot interviews, adjusted it and continued with interviewing to the point of saturation, as the grounded theory method whose principles I followed in data analysis recommends (see below for more details). Or rather, I hit a dead end: no more conceptual information was emerging from further interviews, but a strong, yet puzzling theoretical category began to emerge: 'fear of publishing'. Most of the narratives shared descriptions of fear – of persecution, I supposed. Nevertheless, when I asked about concrete instances of retributions for something somebody wrote and published, only a couple of the narrators recounted some minor incidents – usually afflicting a colleague, not the narrator personally – but nothing that would explain the existential terror, with which the accounts teemed.

I had now twenty interviews, each lasting between one and two hours, with scholars in history, literary studies, philosophy and sociology, and with two former senior editors of academic and popular-science publishing houses. The 'pilot narrators' were people I knew and who enjoyed seniority and peer respect at the time of the interview. They then recommended other scholars, observing my two criteria: publishing activity in official venues during normalization and high current professional and peer status that derived already from their work during normalization. If scholars published during normalization, they would have to be competent in navigating the system, and if they enjoyed lasting respect from their peers, they had to be at least above-average researchers and their primary loyalty was likely to lie with their research rather than with the regime and the Party. To survive as professionals employed in state institutions, they had to have their feelers out for the limits of permissibility concerning what and whom they could write on, how to couch their arguments, where they could publish and what language they could – or had to, as the case may have been – use. In other words, I was looking for people from a broadly conceived 'grey zone', as the Czech sociologist and dissident Jiřina Šiklová called the people who may have been sympathizing with the ideas of the dissidents and even been meeting them socially, but did not express their opposition to the regime by withdrawing into the dissident circles and their *samizdat* publications.[6] Moreover, 'because their political involvement was minimal, they also had a lot more time for their own education and training, both personally and professionally' (Šiklová 1992: 183). She then goes on to identify this group as the leaders of their disciplines on the eve of the political change of 1989.

The final group of Czech narrators includes nine women and eleven men and spans several academic age cohorts: the youngest was a student in 1968; the oldest was already a reader or associate professor (*docent*) and an internationally recognized figure in his field at the time. Most of the narrators worked in Prague, because the majority of research institutes and universities were there, but some were employed in other Czech towns. Some started in the grey zone and later moved into *samizdat*, some were Party members during the whole time, some were struck off the Party membership list at the beginning of normalization, some never joined, and about some I cannot tell, because I never asked the question – I only know about the Party membership status of some of the narrators because they *chose* to tell me. I did not ask because I was investigating not their political pasts, but their involvement with their professions and, above all, with the works they wrote. Sadly, Professor Horn could not be in the group. By the time I finished the PhD thesis and was able to embark on this project, he had passed away and with him also his rich experience and depth of reflection.

The way to saturate a newly emergent category is by theoretical sampling: the researcher pursues new sources of information, focusing the search on that category instead of continuing with comprehensive questioning (Charmaz 2006: 96–122). Therefore, as soon as I could return to the field, in 2009, I took the 'fear of publishing' to Hungary, a country that shared many characteristics with Czechoslovakia: repressions followed the 1956 revolution and the invasion by Soviet troops, there was no designated censoring institution, scientific publishing enjoyed an elevated status vis-à-vis censorship, and a network of nonconformist intellectuals and *samizdat* publications was also in place. I followed the same interview structure, but giving more space to post-publication censorship, with three women and five men, whose collective

---

[6] On the history of the concept of a 'dissident' in the Czech context see (Bugge forthcoming).

profile in terms of generational spread, disciplinary background, seniority and peer respect matched that of the Czech researchers. I conducted the interviews mostly in English and in two cases in Czech and Hungarian. My meagre Hungarian allowed me to follow the gist of the narration, but Gábor Halmai, my trusted research assistant in Budapest, provided the full transcription and translation.

The oral history interviews of personal experience with state-socialist publishing necessarily contained a good deal of perceptions, rather than facts, of how the system worked. They covered the lived practice of academic publishing, but not the institutional dimensions and the official ideological discourse within which the practice took place. This is where document and archival research enters the scene to complement the oral material: science policies and Party propaganda concerning scholarship collected by Radio Free Europe/Radio Liberty Research Institute (RFE/RL) and housed in the Open Society Archives in Budapest, and holdings of the Editorial Board (EB) of the Czechoslovak Academy of Sciences (Ediční rada Československé akademie věd) collected in the Archives of the Czech Academy of Sciences in Prague and catalogued by Alena Míšková in 1990.

The choice of the RFE/RL collections requires an explanation, for the explicit ideological lenses and purpose of their origins do not make them an obvious source for this project. The RFE/RL needed official propaganda and other published material from Czechoslovakia and Hungary for its own analyses and critical commentaries on the situation in various areas of life under state socialism. To this end it conducted comprehensive media monitoring that also included social sciences and humanities, education and culture. It amassed articles and transcripts of radio programming from a wide range of sources: Communist Party documents regulating social sciences and universities and published in Party magazines and daily newspapers, news-wire reports and newspaper articles on the various regulatory measures of academic research and teaching, and articles from scholarly journals on the role of social sciences and humanities. In short, if one wants to illustrate the chronology and logic of the process of normalization that was to lead to the hegemonic power of the Party over academic life,[7] RFE/RL is the most comprehensive and systematic

---

[7] Others pursued a similar interest: Vilém Prečan, who documents in detail the period between 1968 and 1972 in Czechoslovak social sciences (Prečan 1994); Alena Míšková, who gives an account of

archive for this purpose. It cannot yield an exact and detailed historical record, but it can help in reconstructing an outline of the main tendencies in the Party's efforts to control scholarly research.

The advantage of consulting the EB holdings lies in that they cover, systematically and without gaps in chronology, a single institution, moreover one that oversaw academic publishing in the top Czechoslovak research institution. In her introduction to the archival inventory, Míšková provides a valuable summary of the function and activities of the Editorial Board. It was established in October 1961 by a decree of the Central Committee of the Communist Party of Czechoslovakia and held its first meeting in February 1962. Its mandate and scope of responsibilities were considerable: from the evaluation of publishing plans of books and the structure of the periodicals published by the Czechoslovak Academy of Sciences, the impact of the Academy's publications, through the decisions on all stages of the publishing process (approving publishing proposals and manuscripts, determining the length of publications and setting authors' honoraria), to essentially marketing issues, such as keeping an eye on sales, stock, and profit and losses of all publications. The EB reported to the Presidium of the Academy of Sciences, who also appointed senior academic managers (and trusted Party members) as its members. The Board held monthly meetings, whose agenda typically included discussion and decisions on publishing proposals and manuscripts submitted to the EB by the Scientific Committees (*vědecká kolegia*) for the various disciplines of the Academy, discussion of editorial issues with representatives of one or several Scientific Committees, and discussion of tasks assigned to the EB by the Presidium (Míšková 1990). The holdings of the archive of the EB contain the minutes from the meetings and the briefing materials provided to the Board members. The EB members found themselves in a double bind. They would have been essentially in the position of censors, but at the same time they were themselves creative individuals, scholars. As Board members they had to answer for their decisions to the institutions above them, as authors they were subject to the same ideologies into which they were streamlining others. I was interested in the balance between these two parts played by the EB, in order to gain an insight into the participation of smaller actors in the system of state-socialist academic publishing.

---

the Czechoslovak Academy of Sciences between 1970 and 1975 (Míšková 2002); and Pavel Urbášek, who researched the Czech university system during normalization (Urbášek 2002, 2008).

The three types of sources – interviews with Czech and Hungarian scholars, the records of the Editorial Board of the Czechoslovak Academy of Sciences, and science policies and policy-related documents – represent three different actors vis-à-vis state power: an individual researcher subjected to the state power, but having a degree of agency, an intermediary institution whose members are endowed with power by the state, but are subjected to it at the same time, and the Party state itself. They complement each other in providing material for constructing a picture of the institutional setting and structuring of social sciences and humanities in Czechoslovakia and, to a lesser extent, in Hungary. They inform on personal strategies of professional survival in these institutions, the stages of the publication process, and the relationship of authors to the production and circulation of knowledge under the politically repressive conditions of late state socialism. The stories told by the three sources often contradict each other. Bringing them together and relating the overall story in an ethical manner with regard to my interview partners turned out to be a methodological challenge. Its magnitude and the research process leading to its resolution would merit a separate chapter, but for reasons of space, I provide at least a short summary at this point.

Imagined conversations: A primary text on censorship in Czech and Hungarian academic publishing under state socialism, 1969–89

Coding for qualitative data analysis

The constructivist grounded theory method (Charmaz 2006) seemed to offer the most suitable guidance for data analysis in the given situation: to describe and structure a problem hitherto little known, and to hope to solve the puzzle within by developing theoretical categories from relating data to data. Kathy Charmaz belongs to the 'second generation' of grounded theorists (Morse et al. 2009), building primarily on the work of Anselm Strauss and Juliet Corbin (Strauss and Corbin 1990), but also on Pertti Alasuutari's adaptation of the method for cultural studies (Alasuutari 1995). All three sources motivated the analysis of the interview material in this project, with the document material brought in for additional confirmation and theoretical insight where necessary.

The constructivist approach retains the basic principle of the original formulation of the grounded theory method: open coding of the collected data – that is, naming a textual segment with a concept. To give an example:

[Question: 'How did you learn about these limits about what was acceptable and what wasn't?']

Professor Szebah: 'You live here, you just learn the language so that you know.'

The above short segment gets the name, that is, the 'code', 'Becoming sensitized to censorship: How did they come to know?' For easier manipulation, I also allocated a letter-number combination to each code. The one above became 'K5'.[8]

Constructivist grounded theorists depart from the original formulation in the next and further steps. Rather than investigating the relations between codes by gradually increasing the level of abstraction, they group the codes into categories with the aim of interpreting the relations within and between categories vis-à-vis concepts and processes (Corbin 2009: 42–50; Corbin and Strauss 2015: 76–7). Charmaz stresses the construction of the theory from the ground up, pyramid-like. She pursues as the main goal of the theory building the development of rich, saturated theoretical categories. She foregrounds the processual nature of the studied phenomenon: how things make sense, how they happen.

Grounded theory method was developed to research issues existing in the present. Although some researchers, such as Juliet Corbin herself in her work on the Vietnam War (Corbin and Strauss 2015), also took a historical perspective, it is not an obvious oral historical method. Pertti Alasuutari's work helps with this particular difficulty. He adapts the sociological toolbox of the early grounded theory to cultural studies, a discipline that counts history among its founding mothers. Alasuutari divides the process of handling qualitative data into two phases: the 'what' ('purification of observations', that is, a typology of an issue) and the 'why' ('unriddling' the issue), and notes that the two phases are likely to happen simultaneously rather than consecutively, because a researcher will always formulate and refine theories as new data emerge

---

[8] 'K5' has no meaning in itself. I labelled the codes sequentially, starting with individual letters; when I ran out of the alphabet I added the number '1' to the letter, '2' in the next round, and again, as long as needed.

(Alasuutari 1995: 13–18, 133–4). The raw observations, akin to Strauss and Corbin's open coding, are 'purified' by means of formulating propositions, or rules, about groups of coded segments. In practical terms, the researcher takes a group of segments with the same code and makes a generalized statement about them. The statement has to apply without exception to all segments in the group. That is because unlike quantitative research, qualitative research does not work with a statistically representative sample and, therefore, every text, every interview, every text segment is representative of a group of an unknown size and thus cannot be discounted as statistically insignificant. All segments are equal in significance and information value about the researched problem. If the proposition does not fit all the segments in the group, it has to be reformulated (Alasuutari 1995: 130–1). The typology will result from the sum of the concepts and throw light on how big the researched problem is; it presents a description of all elements included in the problem.

The 'unriddling' means an explanation of the relation between the elements in the typology and happens by relating the propositions to each other and to various contexts, such as, comparing with other cultures, research, texts or types of imagery (Alasuutari 1995: 133–42). This process leads to the gradual reduction of the amount of data for interpretation. The researcher proceeds to combine groups of propositions and formulate further rules about them. He or she continues the process until the data are reduced to what becomes the 'unriddling', the theoretical conceptualization of the researched problem. Each round of propositions means raising the level of abstraction – but in the way suggested by Charmaz, that is, by staying close to the data and aiming at understanding rather than explaining the problem under scrutiny (Charmaz 2006: 126–7).

A major advantage of this approach is that it allows the treatment of verifiable and unverifiable information together, because fictitious or unverifiable information is also a part of the researched problem – all pieces of information together present real or potential eventualities. Each segment is always confronted with other segments and incorporated into the 'unriddling'. It is a laborious process, marked with many cul-de-sacs and retracing of one's steps, but an ideal model for this project that comprised such heterogeneous material. The archival documents recorded in equal measure facts, ideological discourse and descriptions of events rendered in propagandist language. The personal accounts were created in the present moment and were filled to the brim with guesses, assumptions, resentment, pain, nostalgia, vested interests, self-stylization and romanticization, as well as dotted with anecdotes, memory gaps and captivating detail of personal experience.

The skeleton typology of scholarly publishing and censorship that is the subject of this book derived from Vianu's work and formed the base for the semi-structured interviews. My own open coding of the interviews expanded the typology into 119 codes-concepts. I then employed Strauss and Corbin's axial coding to consolidate the now fragmented data 'into components of an organizing scheme' (Charmaz 2006: 61). The resulting matrix comprised four large categories of institutions, text, author and language, with the supplementary fifth category 'assessment of the past', each divided into subgroups.

The records of the Editorial Board of the Academy of Sciences were a different matter in this respect. These did describe concrete instances of the publishing practice alongside the 'ideologese'. They relate to the first three categories – institutions, text, author – and they link the subjective experience constructed from memory and formulated in the interviews with the abstract language and generic framework of the policies. As I consulted this archive only after I completed the interviews, I read the records for any new codes, but none emerged. That confirmed the saturation of the interview sample with respect to the three categories and also provided a cross-check of the degree of subjective distortion of the information in the interviews.

Textual presentation of the data: Post-academic writing

While both kinds of archival materials rendered themselves to written presentation in a straightforward manner, the interview material resisted. The argument supplemented with interview quotations always sounded partial and inadequate, not doing justice to the material. If I introduced a scholar who claimed not to have been subjected to any censoring constraints, it made another look like wallowing in self-pity. At the same time, the first scholar's optimism was clearly skewed by a specific bias and the second narrator's pain was real, even if I disagreed with his moral position. Each time I let one voice speak, others began to talk over it. Additionally, from what place in time did these voices speak and to whom? Were they recounting events deeply ingrained in memory, well-rehearsed stories of the past, or reflections on past experiences, but co-created in the course of our interview and constructed through the prism of the current public discourse? Did they speak to a junior colleague, to a young woman, or to a member of a generation presumed untainted by the state-socialist past and to whom they were appealing for understanding? It became obvious that '[i]f an author or researcher simply pours data into an existing analytical or writing format, the work feels artificial, forced, and lacking in impact' (Pillow 2012: 1990). A conventional academic writing approach made the story I wanted to tell sterile, it flattened the richness of contextual layers and contradictions. In other words, the material called for what had since become known as 'post-academic writing', where '"post" may be used to mean "to carry on" but differently' (Badley 2019: 188).

The inspiration for the written representation of the interview data came from feminist methodology and from literary studies. Feminist methodology has had an enormous impact on qualitative research also outside the focus on gender. Its principles include, among others, the following: making visible the lives and experiences of women; reflexivity of structures and assumptions underlying the research and its categories, including relations of power and privilege; ethics of research; and legitimization of the subjective and the emotional as important parts of women's experience and also of research ethics (see, for example, (Fonow and Cook 1991; Reinharz 1992; DeVault 1996; McCorkel and Myers 2003; Fonow and Cook 2005). Correspondingly, I aimed at such a mode of written presentation that would make visible the lives and experiences of my narrators, treat them ethically by allowing them to represent themselves to the greatest possible degree, make visible the power relationship of the research situation and lay the research process bare, while not shunning the emotional and the subjective. Only such an approach would stand a chance of preserving as many as possible of the often contradictory, and sometimes questionable, even doubtful, intricacies of the individual stories of themselves that the narrators shared with me. Bringing out the subjective helps 'situate' the experience of producing knowledge (Haraway 1991: 183–201) under state socialism and adds finer grain to the theoretical grasp of censorship.

Making more of the research process visible is, primarily, an ethical measure that is to keep the reader aware of the manipulating presence of the author-researcher, because '[t]he "account" cannot be objective. It is a political product, its construction comprising a set of explicitly ideological moves. To put it briefly, *representations* are *interpretations*. They can never be pure mirror images. Rather, they employ a whole set of selective devices, such as highlighting, editing, cutting, transcribing and inflecting' (McRobbie 1982: 51, emphasis in the original). The presentation of the interview material in this book should constantly remind the reader that the narrative was constructed by the researcher – and how it was done.

I decided to present the interviews in two stages corresponding to Alasuutari's typology and 'unriddling'. First, I would create what literary terminology calls a 'primary text', a story complete with characters and a dialogue; or, a typology of scholarly publishing under state socialism. In the second stage, I would conduct a textual analysis of the narrative part – 'unriddle' the typology – and build a theory of state-socialist censorship in the pyramid-like way proposed by Charmaz and employing the process of formulating tiers of propositions outlined by Alasuutari.

The purpose of the primary text is to preserve the polyphony of the material and to evoke the atmosphere of doing scholarly research and publishing under state socialism, before supplying the explanatory commentary and theorizing. Padraic Kenney called the early 1990s in East Central Europe in a proper Bakhtinian fashion 'a carnival of revolution' that disrupted the 'incessant monologue' of pre-1989 discourse 'with a cacophony of insistent and derisive voices' (Kenney 2002: 3). These voices are still heard in the narratives of the researchers participating in this project and are given prominence by means of 'imagined conversations', which the primary text consists of. The text follows loosely the form of a quest narrative, with the narrator as the novice and the interviewees as the guides, who lead the novice through the realms of state-socialist academic publishing, all the time mentoring her and conversing with each other. Several of these terms now require further explanation.

Mikhail Bakhtin's concept of polyphony was a response to censorship, which reinforces the importance of preserving the polyphony in this case, too.[9] He developed the concept on Dostoevsky's novels that contain 'contradictory philosophical stances' (Bakhtin cited by Pearce 1994: 45) within one text, which is 'the direct result of one of the primary criteria of the polyphonic text: the independence of characters from their narrator. The multiple voices and characters of Dostoevsky's novels are not subsumed in the worldview of the author-narrator: they are fully independent and, as Bakhtin puts it, "equally valid"' (Pearce 1994: 45). Polyphony refers not merely to the

---

[9] I am grateful to Lynne Pearce for reminding me of the contextual origin of Bakhtin's theory.

presence of multiple perspectives, but also to 'the registering of different points of views in multiple voices' (Marcus and Fischer, *Anthropology as Cultural Critique*, 1986, cited in (Fontana 2003: 54).[10] It is a principle that is difficult if not impossible to achieve in conventional academic writing, because there the convention dictates that no matter how many perspectives the author includes, the *voice* of the entire article or book has to be single. I specifically wanted to avoid the presentation of the material in one voice on two grounds: (1) to minimize a 'colonization' of the narrators' voices and (2) to distance myself from voices with which I disagreed, but without passing a judgement. Carolyn Ellis and Leigh Berger propose the use of narrative form for such occasions: 'narrative's openness to multiple perspectives can successfully communicate the difficulties and dilemmas of studying those with whom we do not connect as well as those we do' (Ellis and Berger 2003: 165). Capturing and presenting the multiple voices first and only afterwards trying to make theoretical sense of the polyphony offers the possibility to bring the whole spectrum of perspectives into mutual interaction and unpick its discursive layering, overlaps and clashes.

The impulse to elect specifically the quest narrative as the organizing principle for this undertaking came from my adopted positioning in the interview situation and also from the nature of research itself. Every research is a quest not with the ambition to arrive at the ultimate knowledge but, to borrow Derrida's words, 'to understand enough to understand more' (Smith 1998), to move the horizon of what we know by generating further questions, although some of the original ones may have remained partially unanswered. The Czech theorist Daniela Hodrová defines literary quest narratives as 'initiation' narratives in that the novice learns during the journey that the goal is something larger than originally presumed, not a material object, but a greater knowledge, including self-knowledge: 'the novice finds the Philosophers' Stone in himself' (Hodrová 1993: 173).[11] In this project, knowledge beyond the original quest for a description of publishing conditions included the understanding that personal dilemmas, self-justifications, fears and emotions were all integral parts of the system of scholarly publishing during normalization. They were equally present in the process of giving shape to the experience in an interview, perhaps because the narrators felt themselves 'under implicit pressure to communicate a personalized self – a self

---

[10] Andrea Fontana writes about his own application of polyphony when he co-authored a polyphonic play constructed from in-depth interviews with a lap dancer (Fontana 2003: 61).

[11] Incidentally, we will encounter the journey of Hodrová's own manuscript in Chapter 4 in the archival materials of the Editorial Board of the Czechoslovak Academy of Sciences.

that cannot be derived simply from public discourse. In a context where there is clearly dominant public discourse, such as in revolutionary times, arguing with some aspect of it can be a way of meeting the personalization requirement' (Andrle 2000: 218). The personalized self that existed before the interview was, by definition, shaped also during its course. Molly Andrews points out the difficulty in recreating East German life histories for today's audiences:

> [T]he political climate has changed, and is still changing, to such a degree that what constitutes the memorable – at both the collective and individual level – is itself in acute transformation. One can reasonably suggest then that the stories that people tell, even, and perhaps most importantly, to themselves about themselves and their past, have been and continue to be in dramatic flux. (Andrews 2000: 187)

Unlike Andrews, I was not looking at the transformation process from the outside, but was living in it, in the memory-making and stories in flux, as much as those I was researching. Qualitative researchers, like the novices, are changed by their subject and acquire self-knowledge. In this case it came from two sources: first, from the realization that the narrators and I were only partially spectators in the storying of the past, we were also its agents, and second, from reflections on the continuing legacy of state-socialist practices in academia. For I too have been a participant, willing or not, in the inherited practice. Having gone through my undergraduate education still under state socialism makes me 'an associate member', so to speak, of the community I was researching.

The narrators constituted 'an imagined community' in the sense that they all belonged to academia, they all shared in the participation in the state-socialist system and were oppressed by it, and many were colleagues from within one discipline. Moreover, they also formed a certain 'horizontal comradeship' (Anderson 1991: 6), they did not necessarily know each other in person, but related themselves to the boundaries of 'us' (academics who, during normalization, remained loyal to the discipline) and 'them' (those whose loyalty was primarily to the Party). The commonalities were, nevertheless, contrasted with the many voices and perspectives. Hence the presentation of the interview transcripts through 'imagined conversations', a textual strategy I developed to capture both the community and the polyphonic aspects. The conversations are 'imagined' because they never took place, they are constructed by me from segments of interviews conducted one-to-one.

The construction of the conversations follows a particular set of rules. First, the conversations had to include *all* information once, but only once, in order to present a typology of the studied problem. That meant that once I pre-sorted the coded interview segments into the five categories of institutions, text, author, language and 'assessment of the past', any 'repeats' had to go. In the next step I grouped the segments into sub-categories, organized these into sequences with a story potential and, finally, joined them into a narrative (see Box 1). The final text presented in this book includes a pruned version of the original at the publisher's request to shorten the manuscript. All the material that did not find its way into the analytical Chapter 8 was edited out, unless it was needed for continuity.

Box 1: The construction of an 'imagined conversation'

Part of the organized interview segments coded as:

K5: Becoming sensitized to censorship: How did they come to know?

[LI: 'How did one know what one might and might not write? What was and was not possible?'[12]]

Professor Stachys: *(Pause)* 'I don't know. Mmm, I can't, hard to say.'

Doctor Helianthus: 'Actually that was an advantage – us not knowing exactly. It was determined by the upper echelons at academic journals and other such. They [drew up] a kind of directive, which of course never [interested] me in the slightest, 'cos I never strayed into areas that would have to chime with speeches by the country's political leaders.'

Professor Lilius: 'That's a very hard question for me, 'cos it's all so far in the past when I was writing that I can't really bring it to mind – and sometimes you don't even realize these things quite rationally. Yet you do them 'cos you know the pressures are there, and if you want your book to come out, then … in the later one there are certainly some signs. The possibility of its being published was looming, so I'm sure I must have done the odd trick with it.'

Final text (Chapter 5):

I waited for the group to assemble back around the table and asked my first question, 'How did one know what one might and might not write? What was and was not possible?'

---

[12] The English utterances presented here are not the raw transcripts, but translations of the edited Czech segments.

> Silence. Then Professor Stachys said, 'I don't know. Mmm, I can't, hard to say.'
>
> 'Actually that was an advantage – us not knowing exactly,' Doctor Helianthus maintained. 'It was determined by the upper echelons at academic journals and other such. They [drew up] a kind of directive, which of course never [interested] me in the slightest, 'cos I never strayed into areas that would chime with speeches by the country's political leaders.'
>
> There was again a brief silence, before Professor Lilius spoke.
>
> 'That's a very hard question for me, 'cos it's all so far in the past when I was writing that I can't really bring it to mind – and sometimes you don't even realize these things quite rationally. Yet you do them 'cos you know the pressures are there, and if you want your book to come out, then … ' He broke off, suggestively.
>
> 'In my later book there are certainly some signs. The possibility of its being published was looming, so I'm sure I must have done the odd trick with it.' (See also p. 169 below).

Ethical principles of qualitative research demanded anonymization of people and places and editing the cumbersome prose of raw interview transcripts without altering the meaning. Naturally, when David Short, the excellent English literary translator, rendered the interview material into English, he had greater licence in word choice and syntax than I had with the Czech original, but we worked in tandem, consulting the original, so as to remain as close to it as possible. Anonymizing the narrators themselves required a systematic approach in choosing pseudonyms, because I wanted to preserve their individualities as 'characters' and also signpost their other 'demographic' characteristics: sex, rank, discipline and country (Czech Republic or Hungary). I settled on names consisting of the real-life academic title of the narrator at the time of the interview and a surname inspired by Latin botanical names for the Czech 'characters' and Dacian plant names for the Hungarians, although I took liberties with the originals (see Dramatis personae for details).[13]

---

[13] https://en.wikipedia.org/wiki/List_of_Dacian_plant_names (accessed 15 August 2017). The anthropologist Nigel Rapport developed a similar method of written presentation of his research on violent discourse in a Newfoundland city. The key difference between his and my technique lies in the identifiability of the characters as distinct individuals. Rapport constructs his 'scenes' from many conversations to which he listened or that he recorded, meaning that utterances attributed to one 'character' were not necessarily originally spoken by the same person (Rapport 1987: 21).

The final result reads like a narrative rich in dialogue, yet when one reflects on the process of its construction, it is not that distant from conventional handling of interview data: advancing one's argument by including a quotation, commenting on it and moving to the next point of the argument. Here, quotations are accompanied by other quotations, rather than by a commentary. What is the gain in this writing method? For one, it is – I hope – more engaging to read. More importantly, though, it allows for the coexistence of the multitude of voices and facets of the personal experience of writing and publishing under state socialism: struggles for personal and professional integrity, defiance of the restrictive system, as well as self-romanticizing and self-fashioning, which were all often present within the response to one question by one narrator. It also enables the preservation of the intimacy shared in the interview situation that would be lost in the conventional approach. In short, it ought to paint a fuller picture of the subject and of the research process, although one must be mindful that '[a]ny story we construct is partial, privileged, and rhetorically crafted for an audience' (Adams, Jones and Ellis 2015: 82). Most important of all, the imagined conversations are an attempt to 'take responsibility for representing those who participate in ways that do not reproduce harmful stereotypes' (DeVault paraphrasing Bhavnani's 'Tracing the Contours: Feminist Research and Feminist Objectivity', DeVault 1996: 42). The stereotype in this case would mean writing about the dehumanizing and instrumentalizing pressures of the state-socialist regime and the complicity of those working in its institutions. Such an *a priori* perspective would not further our knowledge of the regime. Presenting the imagined conversations before their analysis allows the narrators to state their case in their own words first, and then begin to weave the reader's conceptual understanding from them. In the language of research methods, the snippets that form the imagined conversations constitute *all* of the raw data used in the subsequent analysis and theory building.

The outcome: Snakes and ladders

This whole 'quest' began with the interest in the structures and workings of censorship and scholarly communication during late state socialism on the example of the Czech normalization period. The search for answers to the four initial main questions on, first, the institutional context and the personnel relations within it; second, the trajectory of a manuscript through institutions towards publication and post-publication reception; third, the concept of an author and the authors' relation to their own texts; and, fourth, the language and 'code' of communication, quickly yielded the fifth and theoretically most interesting question: the simultaneous occurrence of the two opposite views on the effect of censorship on intellectual thought – detrimental and beneficial – in the fairly homogenous sample of the Czech scholars.

Very early on, it became conspicuous that the documentation originating in the circles of state power, the policy documents and Party decrees, told a different story from the one the scholars shared about the functioning of censorship in Czech academia and how they dealt with it in a country that did not have a formal censoring institution covering scholarly and scientific pursuits. The two stories remind one of James C. Scott's 'public' and 'hidden transcripts', where the former refers to 'the open interaction between subordinates and those who dominate' (Scott 1990: 2), while the latter 'represents a critique of power spoken behind the back of the dominant' (Scott 1990: xii). The 'public transcript' is therefore 'unlikely to tell the whole story about power relations' (Scott 1990: 2). In our case, the story of 'power' presents a linear narrative of centralized and increasing control over scholarly life. The story of the 'subjects of power' weaves a much more complex storyline. Theirs sounds more like a game of snakes and ladders, albeit with the researcher having a bit more agency than deciding whether to cast a die or not. One cast an idea into the institutional environment and its progress depended on whether it landed on a square with a ladder that helped it up to the next level of approval, or slithered down a level or two if it landed on a snake. Answers to the five questions lay in bringing the stories of the 'power' and of the 'subjects' together, including the re-examination of these two actors as each other's opposites, and contrasting the Czech experience with the Hungarian, in order to saturate the theoretical category of 'fear of publishing'.

Looking at the two stories as not separate, but as two sides of the same coin, three characteristics of normalization in academia become identifiable: a gradual tightening of ideological control from 1969 onwards, a divide in political positioning among scholars according to where they stood in relation to the reform process of the Prague Spring and a generational change that had implications for the scholars' perceptions of the process of normalization in research institutions. The first characteristic unequivocally emerges from the policy documents, the second and third from the juxtapositions of the interviews and of the policy discourse.

The political positions among academics were fairly clear in the aftermath of the Prague Spring, when academic institutions were purged of the sympathizers of the reform process, but the line between 'us' and 'them' blurred increasingly with the passing years. This process was linked to a generational change. Those with a personal political history of 1968 (Generation 1968) spoke about academic institutions as 'being normalized', that is, they articulated the distancing of academic institutions from the ideas and spirit of the Prague Spring in the first years of normalization.[14] Inevitably, however, the age cohort that entered academia in the 1970s did not note these changes. The working conditions in their institutions seemed 'normal' rather than 'normalized' to them.

Normalization's rulers, unlike the totalitarians of Stalinism, did not demand their 'subjects' to be true believers, but like Václav Havel's greengrocer who dutifully displays ideological slogans in his shop-window without really believing in them (Havel 1992), they disciplined participants in a ritual of adoration and submission. Both the 'power' documents and the interviews imply that, with progressing normalization, the Party moved away from pushing for ideologically correct *content* of research to an ideologically correct *form* of framing it. In other words, the scrutiny of the *real convictions* of academics was replaced with insistence on an *appearance of ideological loyalty*. There is no doubt that ideological regulation of scholarly research, publishing and university teaching formed a tight and highly restrictive framework, which, however, suffered from *overcentralization* (Kornai [1959] 1994) – and that opened manoeuvring spaces for individuals working within the system. The stifling fear produced by the vague yet potentially crushing directives created a seedbed for a variety of censoring practices and self-censorship on the one hand, but aided and abetted the cultivation of a plethora of personal strategies of professional survival on the other. The researchers' accounts suggest that the Hungarian scholarly environment was less vague than the Czech, with a clearer separation of rules that applied to the Academy of Sciences and to universities. The Hungarian narrators also imply a higher

---

[14] I use the label 'Generation 1968' merely to distinguish between the two groups of academic interviewees in my sample. For a much more nuanced and different generational perspective in political thought please see (Andělová 2019).

degree of solidarity among scholars and greater academic freedom, although sanctions for ideological transgressions seem to have been harder there than in the Czech case.

Early normalization targeted people and institutions, rather than specific content of scholarly texts. Those who expected persecution for the part they played during the Prague Spring or because of their research orientation strategized either to keep any form of professional existence, to continue in their area of research, or later, when the worst years were over, aimed at professional development. The latter marks a generational shift as it appears only in the narratives of Generation 1968: they were persecuted in the early years of normalization, but perceived the 1980s as the time that offered certain openings of intellectual spaces within state institutions.

Unclear directives meant that every actor on the social side of the publishing process – the author, his or her superior, editors – guessed at and, occasionally, negotiated the boundaries of permissibility. It follows that any publication constituted a potential risk for all involved in terms of their professional future and further publication opportunities. Some manuscripts were sent for an ideological review, but the authors typically did not know that in advance and were not necessarily informed even after the fact. Indeed, if censorship officially did not exist, a manuscript could hardly be rejected on political grounds and such rejection procedures lacked due process. Needless to say that this practice subordinated scholarly content to ideological propriety, and that institute and department heads worried more about drawing undue attention to their workplace than about research results. 'Publish *and* perish' was the order of the day, discouraging rather than motivating publication productivity and making publishing a privilege, rather than a professional necessity. This placed the editors in the publishing houses in the situation not unlike that of the Elizabethan Master of the Revels: they were responsible for not giving offence to whoever had the power to persecute them, while at the same time they needed manuscripts to publish (Dutton 1991: 7, 1999: 388). They cultivated personal relationships with both authors and ideological reviewers in order to push manuscripts up ladders and avoid snakes. Inevitably, personal relationships took precedence over the professional standards of a review process. The need brought together groups of trusted friends and acquaintances that formed 'gated' communities, publishing spaces designed to keep out outsiders. A shortage of resources – paper quotas, limited number of publishing venues, and within those further quotas on proportions of content by subject or geopolitical representation – further exacerbated the importance of personal alliances. In short, written and unwritten rules, modified by exemptions and complications, regulated every step of a manuscript towards publication: who, and under what conditions, could write and publish; who, where and how often, supervised the process; to whom, and under what circumstances, the regulations did not apply; and what the sanctions for transgressions were.

The conditions kept changing over the period: spells of relative ideological relaxation alternated with ideological turns of the screw in response to the overall political situation, such as *perestroika* or activism around the Charter 77. The narrators differed in the amount of personal experience with censorship. Most frequently, they listed examples of various forms of preventive censorship and self-censorship, less frequently post-publication censorship, and some even insisted that they had never been subjected to any act of censorship. Reports of actual textual censorship, that is, when an author would be told to remove this or that part of a text, were relatively rare. If they did occur, then they were usually accounts of 'friendly' censorship, a form of censorship half way between preventive censorship and self-censorship. A colleague or the publisher's editor would *verbally* advise them to change the wording or some parts of the argument. Even then, the advice included additions rather than omissions to make the text politically palatable, such as, boosting the argument with citations of Marxist classics or Soviet authors or with the use of stock Marxist–Leninist vocabulary.

Authors were not entirely at the mercy of the system in resisting censorship. The lack of clear boundaries allowed for their varying interpretations and for negotiation. Authors, line managers and editors could then exercise agency as individuals, even if that agency took the form of self-censorship. The general awareness that constraints did exist made self-censorship pervasive, but also elusive, because it did not necessarily have to be conscious, but passed into the bloodstream, so to speak. Peer communities provided further support to researchers in their plight with censorship. Some of these communities created alternative spaces within the system, for example, annual seminars by invitation only, which provided forums for freer discussion.

The Czech scholars reported much less frequent and less dramatic personal or second-hand experience with post-publication censorship than the Hungarian narrators. Yet some of their accounts were saturated with memories of fear, while the Hungarians often spoke of enjoying a considerable degree of academic freedom, despite having colleagues and friends who lost their jobs in retaliation for something they wrote or, in extreme instances, went to prison. The crux of this difference seems to lie in the far less systematic preventive censorship in Hungary than in the Czech academia, where the foggy rules further exacerbated the anxiety. They kept everybody at all levels alert, even over-sensitized, to textual minutiae before a text was printed, so that post-publication censorship became almost superfluous. The proactive censorship resulting from the guessing game of the hypothetical objections the reader at the next level might raise made everybody at different stages of the publishing process both a censor and the censored and, consequently, inclined to censoring perhaps more than was necessary.[15]

A side effect of the counteracting mechanisms of surveillance and resistance was attrition of the category of authorship. The authors' control over their texts diminished and they themselves undermined the concept of an 'author' by resorting to publishing under the anonymous 'et al.', pen names and allonyms (*s pokrývačem*).[16] In this book I will call the latter strategy 'ghost-authoring'. A 'ghost-author', unlike a 'ghost-writer', is not a person who lends his or her narrative skills to a person who may have an idea for a story, but has little ability in turning a phrase or no time for writing. Rather, it is someone with little or no relationship to the text published under his or her name, but possesses the impeccable political credentials and shields a text written by a person in political disgrace. It was also usually the person who handled contacts with the publisher.

Politicization plagued not only people and epistemological grounding, but also research subjects and certain words or concepts. The subjects of research ranged from desirable and acceptable to sensitive or deemed downright unsuitable for socialist reality. This categorization went hand in hand with the use of language that reflected the Cold War division of the world into 'good' and 'bad', each side being often associated with particular schools of thought or research topics.[17] A second binary, one that resulted

---

[15] Šmejkalová made the observation about the guessing game by authors of the objections to their texts at next level in her early work (Šmejkalová-Strickland 1994: 204).
[16] *Pokrývač* in the literal sense of the word means a roofer, that is, the handworker who tiles the roof of your house.
[17] Petr Fidelius, to my knowledge the only Czech scholar researching the area of the language of normalization as it was developing, calls the strict division of the language use the 'principle of the great axe' (*princip velké sekyry*) (Fidelius 1998).

from the political positionings in relation to the Prague Spring, developed in the Czech environment. The authors either felt compelled to write on *any* research subject with regard to and only in these binaries, or tried to transform the research areas that found themselves on the 'bad' side of the political divide in such a way that they became presentable on the 'good' side. Research on 'lifestyle' is a case in point: after 1968 it metamorphosed into 'a socialist way of life'. 'A language of attributive phrases' (*přívlastkový jazyk*), as one of the narrators termed it, that emerged by this process could lead either to an increased sensitivity to language or to a loss of attention to language. The latter was described by Alexei Yurchak as a 'citational' language: catchwords and phrases circulating in the authoritative discourse could be inserted into texts to signal ideological correctness and importance, but the words themselves became empty of meaning (Yurchak 2006: 63–73). The linguistic sensitivities differed according to the audience of the given text. The smaller and more specialized the audience, the greater the liberty of word choice. There seemed to be, in fact, two parallel academic worlds in both countries: scholars at the Czechoslovak Academy of Sciences and at universities had to exercise more caution than researchers in applied research institutes, while in Hungary the dividing line ran between the Academy of Sciences and universities.

The need to write only on certain subjects and in a particular way, by definition, produced a debate in the interviews on the possible existence of a certain *code* of communication between the author and the reader, or an Aesopian language. The implication is that 'coding' honed critical reading and creativity. If at all the authors acknowledged that such a practice existed, they tended to see its importance in imaginative literature and in poetry, but much less in scholarly writing. In the latter, they conceded that perhaps it rested in 'layering the text' (*vrstevnatost textu*) and in stylistics. The former involved a complex textual strategy, creating a Bakhtinian dialogic text rich in intertextual references, which required that the readers be 'in' and on the same wavelength. It relied on the reader's capability of '"active understanding" enabling the dialogic encounter of historically determinate utterances, each of which not only takes account of what has already been said about its object, but is also always oriented towards and shaped by an anticipated response' (Shepherd 1989: 92). It is the 'anticipated response', in particular, that invited misinterpretations, misunderstandings or just 'not getting it' – a serious problem in research writing. In contrast, 'stylistics' may not have signified 'encryption' by employing a range of interconnected textual strategies in the way described by Loseff (1984), but merely the existence of a set and limited vocabulary.[18] A reader who knew the vocabulary did not need to have 'to decode' but 'to translate' or transpose expressions, a fairly mechanical skill. Arguably, this manner of 'translating' would have more likely led to decreased attention to the precise meanings of words, rather than to critical and creative thinking. This brings us to the answer to the question of why the two contrary views on the effect of censorship appeared in this small and relatively homogenous sample. It was a matter of erroneous interpretation of textual practices: 'layering' was not an effective communication strategy and the informants defending stylistic strategies as a form of coding mistook 'translation/transposition' for 'coding'. Consequently, the situation in which the communication between the author and the reader fails and the failure is not compensated by another gain, such as cultivating critical reading and formulation skills, indicates that the effect of censorship is unequivocally detrimental – which begs the question of the legacy the state-socialist practices in scholarly publishing left behind.

Ideologically based dualistic approach to research problems or interpretation of history has burdened post-socialist scholarly work and public discussions. One of the narrators went so far as to say that all that had happened after the fall of the regime was a reversal of whose voice was now legitimate and whose was not, but that the practices remained the same. If true, it could be at least partially explained by the post-socialist strength of the symbolism of oppression and resistance that left little space for the development of a greater variety of discourses. Another and logical part of the problem, however, lies in the defence mechanisms originally devised by the various actors to counter the political power: the importance of personal relationships, reluctance to describe processes of consequence in writing, smokescreen strategies, sliding over the precise meanings of words. In the 1990s these may have become defence mechanisms of old actors in new positions of power against newcomers from the ranks of people, subjects, schools of thought, methodologies or emergent publishing communities. Add to that a culture of insecurity and lack of clear

---

[18] Loseff creates a whole 'typology of Aesopian means' employed by Russian and Soviet writers. They operated on three different levels (genre and plot, intended audience and utterance) and included, among others, emotional colouring, such as pathos, polemics or irony, and various other devices, such as allegory, parody, parable, ellipsis, quotations and shifts (Loseff 1984: 53–121).

rules as the operating environment and it will become apparent what obstacles may have stood in the way of a change towards a more open and merit-based system of scholarly research and publishing – a system that would benefit the production of knowledge first of all, rather than require that new authors continue to learn and play the game of snakes and ladders.

Organization of the book

The next chapter outlines the framework of science policies and Communist Party directives from 1968 to 1989 from the RFL/RL holdings and published research. Chapters 3 through 7 contain the 'primary text', composed of what I termed 'imagined conversations', on five themes: institutional and personal strategizing; the journey of the physical text through institutional structures; acts of censorship, self-censorship and the overall relationship of the author to his or her text; the language of scholarly texts of normalization; and the assessment of the past by the narrators. Chapter 8 develops a theory of state-socialist censorship in five stages corresponding to the preceding five chapters. Direct quotations from the 'primary text' of Chapters 3 through 7 are referenced in the margin throughout the chapter. Readers for whom theory holds no interest may want to skip this chapter and draw their own conclusions on the functioning of the various levels and kinds of censorship in social sciences and humanities during Czech normalization from the preceding chapters. Finally, the Coda reflects on the relevance of the normalization experience for the present.

Box 2: The artwork

Four Sheets of Stories: A visual metanarrative

The eight photographs included in this book were created in the early stages of the project as an exercise in research pedagogy, namely, at the point when I was thinking through the forms of the written presentation of the interviews. I opted for manual rather than computer-assisted coding of the transcript printouts, following the view of some social scientists that 'the use of technology may destroy the intimacy between researcher and data' (Hesse-Biber cited in Bryant and Charmaz 2007: 24).

I printed each interview in a different colour for ease of orientation: historians on paper in the shades of blue; literary scholars green; philosophers red; sociologists yellow and orange; editors grey; and women on lighter shades than men. Then I cut up the transcripts into strips by codes, divided them into the five categories of institutions, text, author, language and 'assessment of the past' and pinned them up on old bed sheets. I hung these on curtain rods, that is, against windows. The sheets were only four, the small number of strips pertaining to the last category, fitted on one sheet together with another category.

Sunlight shone through the colourful fragments and transformed them into stained-glass window patterns – or stories, old stained-glass windows often portrayed stories after all. An exploration of the associations between pattern and story led to four pairs of installations about how stories are told and, by extension, about moments in the research process.

Beginnings and ends of a story:

1. 'The Prologue': a table set for dinner / a table with remnants of a dinner;
2. 'The Inspiration': a made-up bed / a clothes line with the bedding drying on it;
3. 'The Action': a desk with a computer / a desk with a book;
4. 'Anticipation and Anticlimax': a scrambled jigsaw puzzle and the completed puzzle – with two pieces missing, because no research ever answers all the questions.

'Story' versus 'plot':

'Beginnings': the background sheet of transcript excerpts has them organized by interview, so that they form blocks of colour on the sheet; or a 'story' as a chronological sequence of events in narratological terminology (Rimmon-Kenan 1983: 14–16).

'Ends': these contain less text, as some elements always get subtracted in the process of telling a story. Consequently, the snippets are reordered into the 'imagined conversations', the technique born of this exercise; or, the 'plot'.

A metanarrative:

The photographs act as a *commentary* on the researcher's journey through the research material. At the same time, they are *reflections* on the narrators' constructions of their own lives as stories and their images of themselves in the past.

Photo: Jeannette Goehring and Libora Oates-Indruchová

2

The limits[1]

Regulation of Czechoslovak scholarly life in policy documents

In the Czechoslovak context it is relatively unsurprising that humanities and social sciences became a primary focus of the ideological pressure in the aftermath of the Soviet-led invasion in 1968. The mobilizing power of Czech and Slovak intellectuals has been noted by scholars as being a political force at least since the nineteenth-century national movement (Pynsent 1994; Hroch 1999). Therefore, after the communists came to power in 1948, intellectuals and their work had to be harnessed so that they would be effective for, and not against, the ruling ideology. In this context, the humanities and social sciences were seen as politically important, because they provided interpretations of social – and hence also political – reality with the potential to influence public opinion. Sociology – seen as a 'bourgeois pseudo-science' – was considered especially dangerous and thus was abolished as a university discipline in 1950. It was re-established in 1965, as part of the political thaw of the 1960s (Petrusek 2004: 598–601; Voříšek 2008, 2012), when critical inquiry in other scholarly disciplines began to develop anew, only to become subject to sanctions and restrictions post 1968. The severity of repressions among academic staff at universities and in the research institutes of the Academy of Sciences provided a telling testimony to the process of heightened ideological surveillance of the time: numerous job losses, publication bans and transfers to a different type of work. This chapter outlines the ideological and policy framework designed to enable the dramatic upheaval of academia. It then examines the subsequent

---

[1] An earlier version of this chapter was published as Oates-Indruchová (2008). This text is here used with the permission of *Europe–Asia Studies*.

stages that set the limits in the humanities and social sciences within which research, publishing and university teaching had to manoeuvre. Its subject is the realm of officially documented instruments of control, regulations, policies and measures used by the governing institutions.

While the scope of normalization in relation to academia was all-encompassing, its pace was uneven. The Communist Party asserted its influence by means of a top-down process: it started with the top layers of institutional hierarchy and gradually spread its controlling directives further down the ladder of academic institutions, from the academic 'centre' to its 'significant periphery', by various repressive, preventive and structural means. The main parts of the process were completed within a year of the beginning of normalization in academia (between May 1969 and June 1970) and further substantial measures followed by the mid-1970s. After that and until the demise of state socialism in 1989, however, the speed and force of ideological control seemed to have slackened. I will propose that this slowing down of normalization was a manifestation of a shift in the Party's focus from an emphasis on ideologically correct content of research (including its theoretical and methodological underpinnings) to ideologically correct form. That is, a shift from concern about the real convictions of academics, as demonstrated by their creative approach to Marxist–Leninist theory and method, to a concern with the appearance of ideological loyalty, as demonstrated by scholars keeping within set doctrinaire boundaries. I will further propose that the centralized system of power over scholarly life was inherently inefficient in communicating the Party directives and supervising their implementation in all academic institutions.

The intellectual community in 1968: An irritant in the eye of normalization

The Warsaw Pact invasion in August 1968 opened the way for the anti-reformist forces in the Communist Party to reclaim the power positions they had lost and to introduce measures to regain control over all spheres of social life. A directive issued following the plenary session of the Central Committee of the Communist Party of Czechoslovakia (Ústřední výbor Komunistické strany Československa, ÚV KSČ; henceforth Central Committee) in May 1969 identified the priority areas for renewing the influence of the anti-reformists.[2] According to the summary in the subsequent Progress Report these included the following goals:[3] 'to renew the unity of the Party on the principles of teachings of Marxism–Leninism', 'to increase the operational ability and fitness for revolutionary action of the whole party', and 'to renew the leading role of the Communist Party in society'. All three goals resonate with Peter G. Ingram's argument on justifications for censorship:

> The protection of truth and the suppression of error have from time to time been major grounds for policies of censorship. (…) The maintenance of right opinion is thus justified in two ways: by its conceptual connection with what are believed to be truths, and by its teleological connection with the preservation of society. (…) In particular [censorship] is believed to protect a society against the social fragmentation that may be brought about by a generally free access to competitive ideas. (Ingram 2000: 17–20)

The Communist Party considered itself the bearer and protector of truth, whose leading role in society stemmed from the need to lead the working classes to the fulfilment of their historical role. That required that society and the Party itself be consolidated and any threatening 'fragmentation' resulting from allowing a voice to group interests be nipped in the bud. With regard to social sciences and humanities, the relatively vague statements of the goals began to take a concrete shape in a confidential document of the Ideology Commission of the Central Committee (Ideologická komise ÚV KSČ) discussed at the meeting of the commission in June 1970. The document outlined the main tasks for the whole area of scholarly research. Primary importance was given to 'the completion of the cleansing of the top executive bodies of the Czechoslovak Academy of Sciences and academic institutions of right-wing opportunist and anti-socialist elements'. Two further tasks were the 'drafting of an Act stipulating a unified control over and coordination of the development of scholarly and scientific research, technology and investments' and 'calling a plenary session of the Central Committee on the further

---

[2] 'Realizační směrnice květnového pléna ÚV KSČ pro další postup strany v příštím období' (The Executive Directions of the May Plenary of the ÚV KSČ toward Further Party Actions in the Upcoming Period).

[3] 'Zpráva o plnění Realizační směrnice a další úkoly ideologické činnosti strany' (Progress Report on the Executive Directions and Further Tasks of the Ideological Activities of the Party) available in (Otáhal, Nosková and Bolomský 1993: 119).

development of scholarly and scientific research and technology' ('Progress Report', available in (Otáhal, Nosková and Bolomský 1993: 49). While social sciences and humanities were 'a tool from the realm of ideology for acquiring knowledge of social reality and for the class struggle',[4] university lecturers posed a threat as 'ideological conspirators and organizers of anti-socialist and anti-Soviet demonstrations' (Tůma 2002: 22). The 'normalizing executive' in the Party leadership clearly realized that scholarly disciplines were the terrain on which intellectuals honed their potential for the expression of independent thought, social action and civic consciousness raising.[5] Scholars and scholarship needed to be reined in and then used for the promotion of the ideology of normalization.

The first step in the renewal of the 'unity of the Party' was a thorough vetting of all Party members (*prověrky*) between 1969 and 1970. This was carried out through 'the replacement of Party ID cards' following a formal interview in front of a committee at one's workplace.[6] The goal was the elimination of politically unacceptable Party members – those who actively participated in the reform process or did not express their full support for the normalizing developments. In a purely technical respect, the process meant issuing new Party ID cards to members; however, being or not being issued the new ID card carried enormous consequences for every individual member. Vilém Prečan characterizes the implications of being placed into one of the three categories – 'expulsion, striking off the Party membership list and positive vetting result (*vyloučení, vyškrtnutí, prověření*)' – for an individual's career prospects as follows:[7] 'They were dealt with accordingly at their workplaces: contract termination, transfer to a less qualified job at the workplace, transfer to a less ideologically "demanding" workplace but still being able to use one's qualifications; or, on the other hand, transfer to a higher post, a cushy seat on a gravy train' (Prečan 1994: 298). According to Oldřich Tůma the Party removed a total of 28 per cent or almost half a million of its members in this vetting

---

[4] Antonín Dolina (1972), 'Fakta k zamyšlení', [Radio programme] Praha, 4 January, OSA 300-30-6, box 44.
[5] The 'normalizing executive' or 'normalizing forces' here refer to the complex power dynamics of political directives and the individuals appointed to executive posts, where the personal motivations ranged from ideological zeal to personal ambitions.
[6] For details on the process see (Konopásek and Kusá 2006) and, in Czech, (Černá 2012).
[7] Being 'struck off' the Party membership list meant that the person's Party ID card was not renewed; their membership ceased by this procedural step, rather than by the retributive act of expulsion.

process (Tůma 2002: 21). He further argues that academics were affected by the vetting more than other professions: 'Academics were represented among those expelled from the Party two-and-a-half times more than would correspond to their ratio in the overall membership before the vetting' (Tůma 2002: 22). Alena Míšková has confirmed this finding and concluded that the Czechoslovak Academy of Sciences showed a 61.5 per cent decrease in its Party membership (Míšková 2002: 164).[8] The blacklisting of people from jobs, professions and publishing did not stop in 1970. A list of persons who were to be removed from public life and whose professional activities were to be restricted was compiled in early 1971 and included numerous scholars (Hradecká and Koudelka 1998: 221–34 cited in Šámal 2015: 1173). Šámal further documents, based on oral testimonies, that the list was periodically updated; however, the actual text has so far not been recovered (Šámal 2015: 1182). Nevertheless, the blacklisting gradually subsided by 1973 or 1974, when it became possible even for those who had been dismissed as politically undesirable to find some form of professional existence, but no formal rehabilitation was possible until after the fall of the regime in 1989.

The first year of normalization: In sweeping strides or faltering steps?

Reading through Party documents one cannot help but admire the ingenuity of the normalizing forces and the thoroughness of the whole process of power centralization. The 'executive' of normalization knew that in 1968 they had been in the minority, hence the intention, first, to cleanse the Party and, then, to encroach on the minds and freedoms of 'the masses'. They employed a top-down approach. The 'Progress Report' from June 1970 stated plainly that 'right-wing opportunist elements still prevail' among the intelligentsia and that they exerted an influence over the majority of 'our academic and intellectual front' (Otáhal, Nosková and Bolomský 1993: 4). The orchestrators

---

[8] František Morkeš describes the form of the vetting at universities and provides details of some of the questions asked at the interviews (Morkeš 2002). Ladislav Prokůpek details the normalization process in the Institute of Philosophy and Sociology of the Czechoslovak Academy of Sciences and outlines also the process of similar interviews with non-Party members at the Institute that began in autumn 1970 (Prokůpek 2002).

of normalization knew only too well that if, in this situation, they tried to assert their influence in every research institute, university classroom or on every piece of published research from the start, they would encounter massive resistance. Thus it was necessary to weave the web of hegemonic power from the centre, from the key positions and spaces.[9] After that, they could gradually co-opt wider and wider circles, all the way through the hierarchy of intellectual institutions and their staff. The operational ability of the Party would thus increase and the Party's leading role in society would be renewed and secured.

The 'Progress Report' summarized the accomplishments of the Party over the first year after the issuance of 'The Executive Directions', and these accomplishments were certainly impressive.[10] The Party managed, among other things, to conduct most of the vetting; to draft and pass the amendment to the Bill on the Czechoslovak Academy of Sciences, which 'fully respected the demands of the Party' (Otáhal, Nosková and Bolomský 1993: 86); to assemble a new leadership of the Academy of Sciences; to close down, merge (in the case of the Institutes of Philosophy and Sociology) or re-structure institutes of the Academy of Sciences and to dismiss their directors if they were deemed to have a blot on their political history; to deprive politically compromised researchers of their membership in the Academy or dismiss them from their jobs there; to do the same with university professors; to re-structure the teaching of Marxism–Leninism at universities through newly established institutes of Marxism–Leninism;[11] to sign new contracts for research visits to socialist countries, with an emphasis on the Soviet Union, in order to replace similar contracts with capitalist countries signed during the reform process; and to draft the state plan of research for 1971–5 with three telling thematic areas for social sciences – 'the social and human context

---

[9] Alena Míšková also arrived at this conclusion in her case study of the Czechoslovak Academy of Sciences (Míšková 2002: 164).

[10] The list of measures implemented by June 1970 in the whole 'ideological sphere', as it was officially termed, and which included scholarly research, education, mass media, culture and art, and the measures planned for the next year are all listed and commented on in the 'Progress Report on the Executive Directions'. The document is reprinted in full in (Otáhal, Nosková and Bolomský 1993: 35–105).

[11] Apart from 'The Executive Directions' and the amendment to the Bill on the Czechoslovak Academy of Sciences, Vilém Prečan also lists the amendment to the Bill on universities as the third key document from the early stages of normalization. The Bill gave the Minister of Education the power to establish and abolish university departments, and to conclude and terminate employment contracts with academic employees (Prečan 1994). This amendment, nevertheless, came into force in August 1970, that is, after the 'Progress Report', which is discussed here.

of the scientific and technological revolution in the CSSR; the critique of the ideology of contemporary anti-communism; and the communist education of the population of the CSSR' (Otáhal, Nosková and Bolomský 1993: 88). Petr Šámal outlined the measures in an area of particular relevance to print censorship: the book industry. He researched that the Union of Publishers (Svaz nakladatelských, vydavatelských a knihkupeckých podniků) was dissolved as of 1 April 1970 and its responsibilities were transferred to the Division of Book Culture (Odbor knižní kultury) at the Ministry of Culture, 'the institution authorized throughout normalization to approve publishing plans, allocations of paper to publishers, or amendments to the competencies of individual publishers' (Šámal 2015: 1168). These measures affected in varying degrees the publishing of scholarly books, too: the Academy of Sciences had its own publishing house, Academia, and did not fall under the authority of the Ministry of Culture, but other publishers that published books on social sciences and humanities subjects for a more general audience did.

This process gave the Party control over the upper layers of the intellectual hierarchy and direction over all research in the social sciences and humanities, as well as over professional communication. New directors of research institutes and heads of university departments would now make sure that their institutions and staff followed Party directives; Party-defined research themes determined what research would be funded; and the new agreements about research visits would orient academic professionals towards the socialist countries and away from the West.[12]

At least that is how it was supposed to work in theory. In practice, the Party lost crucial time in spreading its 'normalizing' influence between the invasion in August 1968 and the beginning of the actual vetting in mid-1969. It admitted as much in the 'Progress Report': 'The situation in social sciences remained practically unchanged until the end of 1969. The process of

---

[12] Prokůpek has written about the isolation and Sovietization of Czech science from the onset of normalization, giving the reorienting of professional travel towards the East as an example of the process (Prokůpek 2002: 215). Marek Skovajsa and Jan Balon have recently provided an illustration of the impact of this reorientation on their analysis of references in *Sociologický časopis* between the mid-1970s and mid-1980s: 'a sharp drop in the number of references to Western sociological literature after 1969, complemented by an equally brusque increase in the number of references to publications from the Soviet Bloc, especially the Soviet Union itself; a clear focus on the national literature; high, though oscillating levels of references to classical Marxist–Leninist authors; similarly cyclical reference frequencies for Communist Party documents, which reach a peak every 5 years in a rhythm determined by the schedule of the party congresses; and sparse references to pre-1948 and 1960s national sociology' (Skovajsa and Balon 2017a: 85–6).

differentiation between social science professionals was virtually impossible as long as the leading positions in the institutes were held by the right-wing powers' (Otáhal, Nosková and Bolomský: 84). During this period, 'endangered' scholars had time to close ranks in solidarity, prepare themselves for sanctions and perhaps even organize some minor, but important, acts of resistance, as the contemporaries themselves will narrate in the next chapter.[13]

With the vetting process underway, it was possible to implement normalization more fully. Once the leadership of the academic community was consolidated according to the new ideology of the Party, all researchers in the Academy of Sciences were put on probation. In June 1970 editorial boards of all academic journals were disbanded and editors-in-chief fired, to be replaced by those the Party now trusted. Furthermore, the new law on the Czechoslovak Academy of Sciences enabled the newly appointed directors of research institutes to sign new contracts with all academic employees – the main feature being that these were now temporary contracts of a maximum duration of four years. Additionally, in the spring of 1970, the main supervisory body of the Party for the whole sphere of education, academic research and culture, the Ideology Commission of the Central Committee, began its activities.[14] It worked in cooperation with the Department of the Central Committee for Education, Scientific and Scholarly Research and Culture. Their joint responsibilities were to translate the Party directives into practice, to oversee their implementation and to report their findings to the Central Committee. The chairman was a secretary of the Central Committee and the members were recruited from the Central Committee ranks and top executives of the media and research institutes of the Czechoslovak Academy of Sciences. The Commission reported directly and exclusively to the Central

---

[13] In this context, it is interesting to note the analogous view of Vilém Prečan on the inner strategies of the Party: 'The intelligentsia could be attacked only after it was deprived of its public tribune and its connections to the wider public had been severed. To form consolidation groups and factions within the various areas of culture and its institutions including the educational system also required time' (Prečan 1994: 283). Prečan wrote his article as a direct participant and a person persecuted in the vetting process; however, it has to be noted that he wrote it in 1973, that is, at the time when the disastrous curtailment of Czech scholarly life was acutely felt, but when he could not have access to the text of the 'Progress Report', which was a confidential Party document, so he could not have known that the Party leadership was itself dissatisfied with the progress of normalization.

[14] The Commission was established in May 1969, but its members never convened until a new commission was appointed in 1970 and met for the first time in March. See (Otáhal, Nosková and Bolomský 1993: 20–1 and 131), respectively, for a detailed account of the activities of the Commission, and for a description of the general scope of responsibilities of all commissions of the Central Committee.

Committee and was therefore the main channel for bringing Party directives to research and educational institutions and, conversely, for reporting on these institutions to the Party itself.

The last thing that remained to be done in this initial stage of normalization was to codify the supervisory structure in legislation: the Party prepared a law on 'The Unified Management and Coordination of the Development of Scientific and Scholarly Research, Technology and Investments' ('Zákon o jednotném řízení a koordinaci rozvoje vědy, techniky a investic') (Otáhal, Nosková and Bolomský 1993: 91). The Party, although it was the 'leading force in society', was not a legislative body, but in this way it ensured that its recommendations on the directions of academic research would now find support in law.

Advanced normalization: Reaching further into the rank and file

The Party developed a methodical sequence for directing scholarly institutions. It began by raising its concerns and demands at Party Congresses and plenary sessions of the Central Committee. Next, it worked these into framework ideological policy documents. Top executives in research institutes and Party media then wrote articles for key scholarly journals and Party mouthpieces on the basis of these documents to provide guidelines for the 'behaviour' of the scholarly community. The notable print media outlets included *Rudé právo, Tvorba, Život strany, Nová mysl,* or *Tribuna,* and the academic journals *Sociologický časopis, Filozofický časopis* and *Český časopis historický*. In parallel efforts, the Ideology Commission of the Central Committee made practical suggestions to influence institutional processes (Figure 1).

The document 'The Lessons Learned from the Crisis Development in the Party and Society since the 13th Congress' (Poučení z krizového vývoje ve straně a společnosti od XIII. sjezdu) declared the Party's position to the public. Paulina Bren maintains that 'one of the central lessons of *The Lesson* was the untrustworthiness of intellectuals' (Bren 2010: 68). According to a secretary of the Central Committee, Jan Fojtík, 'this document is a foundation for critical analyses of individual academic areas, and it provides clear guidance for the assessment of the situation in institutional social science units, as well as for

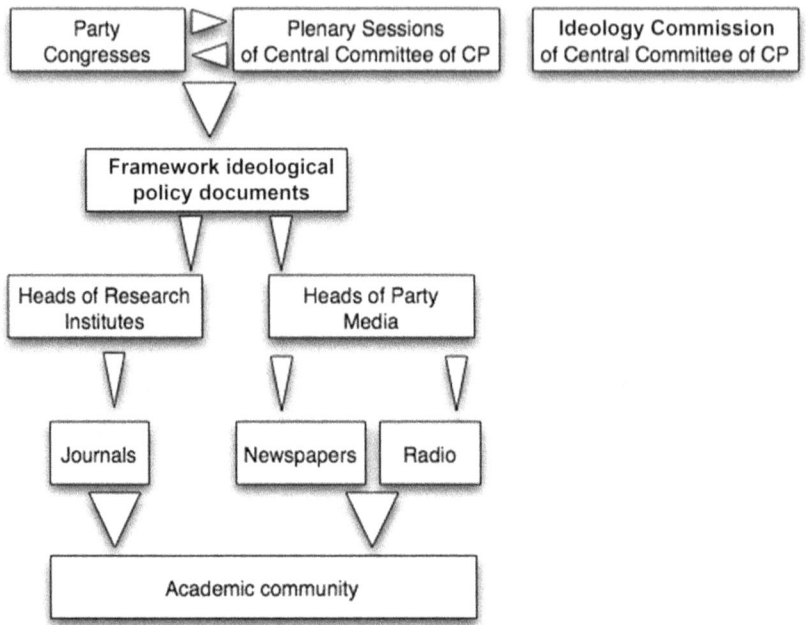

Figure 1 The main components of the Communist Party's communication structure of science policies.
Source: Libora Oates-Indruchová.

identifying and setting the future agenda of these units' (Fojtík 1972a: 147). The 'critical analysis' of social sciences as a whole was published in an internal Party document in May 1971.[15] The Central Committee appointed work groups that were to produce similar 'critical analyses' for each discipline.[16] From then on the Party produced such policy documents periodically, evaluating scholarly disciplines in terms of their adherence to the Party priorities and setting research agendas for them. The titles of these documents are self-explanatory: 'The Development, Current State and the Tasks of Social Sciences' (Vývoj, současný stav a úkoly společenských věd), produced in 1974;[17] 'The Unified Program of Social Sciences after the 15th Congress of the CPCz' (Jednotný program společenských věd po XV. sjezdu KSČ) released in 1977 (Pecen 1977); and 'Partisan Work at the Czechoslovak Academy of Sciences and Slovak Academy of Sciences' (Stranická práce v ČSAV a SAV) issued in

---

[15] 'Nástin kritické analýzy společenských věd zejména v ČSAV', published by the Central Committee in May 1971 and comprising 167 pages. These data are cited in (XYZ (Praha) 1977). Humanities are usually subsumed under social sciences in the policy documents of normalization.
[16] The process of producing 'critical analyses' is described in (XYZ (Praha) 1977).
[17] *Rudé právo* (1974).

1978 (Kubánek and Lacina 1980).¹⁸ The document 'Further Development of the Czechoslovak Educational System' (Další rozvoj československé výchovně vzdělávací soustavy) published in 1976 focused on ideological work and the social sciences and humanities content in schools (Janovský 1979). Scholarly journals under the helm of the new, vetted editorial boards lauded these achievements: 'The revisionism and right-wing opportunism defeated, literature, including its appreciation in criticism and theory, now develops on the renewed Marxist–Leninist foundations of the cultural politics of the Party' (Miko 1981).

The document of 1974, 'The Development, Current State and the Tasks of Social Sciences' serves as a typical example of how the Party communicated its ideological directives to the lower echelons of academic hierarchy and to the public. Its origins can be traced to Fojtík's article on the 'tasks' of social sciences after the 14th Party Congress in *Nová mysl* in February 1972 (Fojtík 1972a). In March he presented an overview of the article at the General Assembly of the Czechoslovak Academy of Sciences (Fojtík 1972b). This material then reappeared in an article published in *Tvorba* in November (Hrzal 1972). Throughout 1973 the Party organized seminars, in which it consulted researchers and university faculty before formulating the final version of the document.¹⁹ That was then published whole or in part, for example, in *Rudé právo* and *Nová mysl*, on the Czech Press Agency wire service, and it was also broadcast on the radio.²⁰

Further guidance was given by Ladislav Hrzal, the chairman of the Scientific Committee for Philosophy and Sociology of the Czechoslovak Academy of Sciences and a Vice-Rector of the Political College of the Central Committee, in a prescriptive article on the tasks of philosophy and sociology in *Sociologický časopis* in September (Hrzal 1974). It is a prime example of the not merely authoritarian, but also uncreative approach of 'normalizers'

---

[18] The variety of media outlets in which these documents were cited provides a good overview of the communication channels for Party directives.

[19] Fojtík first announced the seminars in 1972 (Fojtík 1972a). Míšková's study of the Academy records seven such seminars for 'academic employees–Communists' also in 1972 and 1973. They were held following the 'recommendations of the Presidium of the Central Committee on country-wide seminars for social scientists of 11 February 1972' (Míšková 2002: 165). According to Míšková, the strategy was an effort towards re-education of the communist research corps and considers it as the second phase of normalization (Míšková 2002).

[20] *Rudé právo* (1974); 'Social Sciences' (1974), [Press release] ČTK, 20 June, OSA 300-30-6, box 44; (Filipec and Rohan 1973); Josef Závada and Marie Sulková-Zítková (1974), 'Fakta k zamyšlení', [Radio programme], Praha, 27 June, OSA 300-30-6, box 44.

in executive positions. Hrzal did not bother, or was not able, to elaborate on the Party document 'The Development, Current State and the Tasks of Social Sciences' and come up with a research agenda specific to 'his' two disciplines. His article outlined the agenda of philosophy and sociology, but it was merely a compilation of the tasks set out in the framework Party document for all scholarly disciplines. That document was formally introduced to the academic community in September 1974, again by Fojtík, at an agitation seminar for social science employees in managerial positions in the Academy and at universities.[21] The aim of this thorough and lengthy process was to secure the transfer of the message about the Party's decisions from the 'centre' at the Central Committee of the Party to the 'significant periphery', that is, to the heads of research institutes and university departments, who were then personally responsible for ensuring that their employees did not, and effectively could not, step out of line.

Interestingly, the bulk of the variety of media, scholarly and propaganda materials stored in the Open Society Archives did not turn up the traces of any major propagandist and science-policy documents after 1976. Later general articles on the role of the social sciences refer to the State Plan of Basic Research, but do not cite any new policies. For example, 'The Main Tasks of the Social Sciences', an article by Vladislav Mokošín, an employee of the Central Committee, refers to the State Plan of Basic Research, but not to any expressly ideological documents (Mokošín 1986: 17 and passim). While umbrella research themes continued to be set down in each Five-Year State Research Plan, the accompanying policy documents outlining the ideological foundations of all research seem to have been discontinued.

A change in the direction of the Party's ideological focus from the content of scholarly research to its form might be a likely explanation. If, in the 1972 document 'the ideological plenary' set out as the primary task of social sciences 'the principled criticism of inimical ideology with simultaneous creative development of Marxism–Leninism and positive solutions to theoretical problems' (Hrzal and Matouš 1972), by 1977 the Party, in a similar document, declared: 'We will gradually increase the extent of the Party influence in the social science area' (Majcharčík 1977: 9). In other words, the aim was no longer even to maintain the appearance of developing a theoretical foundation

[21] *Nová mysl* (1974).

of Party-directed scholarship, and hence, still adhering to the principles of scientific inquiry, but to exert unbridled ideological influence. We can also see this as a move from a dynamic to a static approach to ideological regulation of intellectual work: creativity and development of Marxist–Leninist theory and method were no longer required or needed, only a preservation of the ideological status quo – a diagnosis pronounced already at the time by Václav Havel, as Barbara Falk reminds us. She adds that in contrast to Marx, for whom ideology is 'a mobilizational call to arms', '[u]nder authoritarian communism, ideology is not a call to action, but a convenient excuse for passivity' (Falk 2003: 218).

One possible interpretation of this development is that, as the years went by and the Party took control over the layers of scholarly institutions further and further from the centre, it could now afford to drop any remaining regard for professional scholarly standards and concerns that social science research be directed towards society's needs. The second explanation is that by the end of the 1970s the Party knew that its ambition for ideological persuasion was falling short of the mark. Therefore, its attempts at ideological control were increasingly desperate manoeuvres to save face, while, in fact, the Party was retreating from its positions in the actual management of research. In other words, the Party was now concentrating on the surface and was satisfied if it met with an appearance of ideological compliance on the part of scholarly institutions and their researchers. It ceased to examine their real convictions, for which it may have been aiming at the beginning of normalization.

The second explanation finds support in commentaries by high-ranking Communist officials in contemporary Party press, suggesting that the Party was not happy with the overall implementation of normalization. In 1972 Fojtík expressed his satisfaction that 'the management of [social science research] was entrusted to people who have proved their loyalty to the Communist Party, the politics of the Party, and their creative Marxist–Leninist abilities to contribute to the understanding of social practice' (Fojtík 1972a: 168). In contrast, commentaries on Party statistics in the 1980s expressed open displeasure at the percentages of Party members at universities and in research institutes. One of the main Party mouthpieces, *Život strany*, stated in 1980 that the target numbers of membership were not met at universities and, even, that 'the representation of Communists in many departments does not guarantee the leading role of the Party at those workplaces' (Kašparová 1980). Similarly, in 1986 *Život strany* acknowledged failure in increasing the membership percentages in the Czechoslovak Academy of Sciences (Mokošín 1986).

The Party implemented a variety of practical measures to gain maximum control over scholarly research and university education. The agitation seminars taught by members of the Central Committee were a regular activity, in which the Party members employed in academia had to participate and, in the 1980s, some non-Party members also took part. Other similar events included regular meetings of the Academies of Sciences and scholarly publishing houses in socialist countries. The latter resulted, for example, in the project for the book series 'Criticism of the Bourgeois Ideology of Anti-Communism and Revisionism' (Kritika buržoazní ideologie antikomunismu a revizionismu) in 1974, in which the Pravda publishing house participated.[22] In 1980 the Party took yet another step, namely, to have the local Party cells in the ten 'most important' social science institutes of the Academy of Sciences report directly to the Department of Education and Scientific Research of the Central Committee.[23]

The Party paid particular attention to universities. Already in 1974 it had issued a request to the Czech and Slovak State Committee for Academic Degrees to oversee the selection of PhD candidates, 'so that they met the necessary moral, political and professional requirements, as well as had appropriate previous experience and creative thinking'.[24] In 1976 the Cabinet for Political Education and Agitation (Kabinet politické výchovy a agitace) was created at Charles University in Prague for ideological education of the university faculty. It organized the Evening University of Marxism–Leninism (Večerní univerzita marxismu–leninismu, VUML) (Češka 1976) and in 1978 the Party set down the goal that every faculty member should complete VUML (Konicková 1978). Also in 1978, the Party cells at universities were restructured to make them more effective (Majcharčík 1979). A year later, a new exchange of Party identity cards was carried out at universities based on an assessment

---

[22] 'Politická aktualita' (1974), [Radio programme], Hviezda, 5 August, OSA 300-30-6, box 39.
[23] The ten institutes included the Institute for Philosophy and Sociology, the Economic Institute, the Institute of Czechoslovak and World History, the Czechoslovak–Soviet Institute, the Institute of the State and Law, the Institute for Czech and World Literatures, the Institute of the Theory and History of Art, the Institute for the Czech Language, the Oriental Institute, and the Office of the Presidium (Kubánek and Lacina 1980).
[24] *Nová mysl* (1974). The term PhD refers to the postgraduate degree of CSc. (*Candidatus scientarium*), as it was then called.

of the faculty members' attitudes to the initiative 'Further Development of the Czechoslovak Educational System' (Bareš 1979: 24).

Apart from these structural and organizational measures, the Party also implemented some conceptual and some blatantly restrictive mechanisms. Conceptually, for example, in 1972 it declared the need to narrow down the number of research topics in social sciences (Fojtík 1972a: 156), and throughout normalization it always set research foci for each Five-Year Plan. The openly restrictive measures included the proscription of authors who did not pass the vetting procedures at the onset of normalization, a screening of translators and the imposition of quotas on paper allocation for publishing houses in 1970.[25] A later measure, in 1986, assigned to the directors of research institutes the unpleasant task of dismissing academics who did not have sufficient publication output (Mokošín 1986): 20). This meant that people could be dismissed not only for their professional incompetence, but also for low levels of academic production due to their refusal to participate in fettered scholarly discussion or because they were punished for their earlier political sins with a publication ban.[26]

The above is not an exhaustive list of the steps taken by the Party towards gaining overall hegemony, but it gives an idea of the conditions in which academics whose loyalty was to their disciplines rather than to the Party had to conduct research, write and, indeed, survive professionally, and perhaps most importantly, teach further generations of university students. The alternative was to resign from their posts and vacate the field of intellectual instruction to normalization supporters and those academics who used politics primarily as a vehicle for their own career advancement. It also gives an idea of the conditions into which new generations – those without a 1968 political and academic past – entered when beginning their research and teaching careers.

---

[25] Vladimír Solecký, 'Komentář' (1972), [Radio programme], Praha, 1 September 1972, OSA 300-30-6, box 38. For more details on the restrictions on publishing houses see (Šmejkalová-Strickland 1994) and (Šmejkalová 2011).

[26] Skovajsa and Balon list further actors in the Party state control mechanism that exerted influence on the professional existence of individual academics: 'the omnipresent Communist Party units that operated on multiple levels simultaneously (on the departmental, faculty, university, district, city, regional or the national level, but also within the neighborhood of one's residence), and on the relevant local trade union, the Socialist Youth Union, the Czechoslovak–Soviet Friendship Union and other organizations within the spurious public sphere of the authoritarian state' (Skovajsa and Balon 2017a: 79–80).

The complexity and thoroughness of the system of intellectual regulation created a highly restrictive framework for scholarly research, publishing and university teaching, but at the same time its emphasis on central control was just as cumbersome and, consequently, as destructive to the system of management of scholarship as was central planning for the economy. The Hungarian economist János Kornai wrote: '[Excessive centralization] seeks to regulate everything with instructions, a goal that is impossible. It sets out to centralize everything, an aim that is unattainable' (Kornai 2007: 90). The Party's attempt to control all aspects of scholarly life was inherently inflexible. It simply took far too long to send a message from the 'centre' to the 'periphery' and back with feedback. Jiří Trávníček studied restrictions to library holdings during normalization and came to the same conclusion – that despite developing a machinery of blanket vetting of libraries and placing certain books into closed depositories, motivated readers found a way of accessing them: 'The regime had to introduce restrictive regulations, but it was not able to ensure their implementation. Those who were to execute them, did that with great displeasure: in some places they ignored if not sabotaged them' (Trávníček 2015: 1319). The Party leadership was hampered by its own procedures and could not respond to real-time developments, whether in order to increase its ideological influence or to curb minor resistances among academics that may have been taking place.[27] It overextended itself. While it focused on one area and tried to watch several others out of the corners of its eyes, tiny resistance activities crept behind its back, opening alternative spaces for intellectual communication.

The picture assembled in this chapter from official decrees and directives tells the story of only one element, even if it is the dominant element, in the complex discursive landscape of scholarly research, teaching and publishing. It should not be mistaken for a confirmation of the dichotomy of the oppressor and the oppressed, as the conditions of research under state socialism are often viewed in popular perception, for it cannot provide information on the

---

[27] Interestingly, John Connelly arrives at a parallel conclusion concerning overcentralization in his analysis of the Sovietization of the Czech, Polish and German higher education systems between 1948 and 1954. He maintains that an emphasis on ideological micro-management on the part of both the Soviet and East Central European decision-making bodies hampered the creation of Soviet-type models of higher education in East Central Europe. For example, each visit of a Soviet professor to another socialist country had to be approved at multiple levels by both sides; thus, it sometimes took several years before the visit took place (Connelly 2000: 160).

actual practice of scholarly life and on the agency of its various participants. The science policies discussed here represent the 'public transcript', but to be able to unpick 'the impact of domination on public discourse', one needs to investigate the 'discrepancy *between* the hidden transcript and the public transcript' (Scott 1990: 5, emphasis in the original). That will be the subject of the next five chapters narrated as 'imagined conversations' among contemporaries. The narrators in this book were not ruled by the powerful in the same way Scott's slaves and untouchables were, but their accounts carry some of the features of the hidden transcript in that they speak of strategies employed 'behind the back of the dominant' (Scott 1990: xii). The picture drawn on the preceding pages is necessary as a background to what follows and also for further study of the effects of the dominant agent's actions and of the negotiations conducted by the other agents within the given discursive limits. It illustrates the mechanisms of control the Party used towards social sciences and humanities and delineates the contours of the constraints placed on scholarly research.

Four Sheets of Stories: A visual metanarrative

'The beginnings'

1. The Prologue
Photo: Jeannette Goehring and Libora Oates-Indruchová.

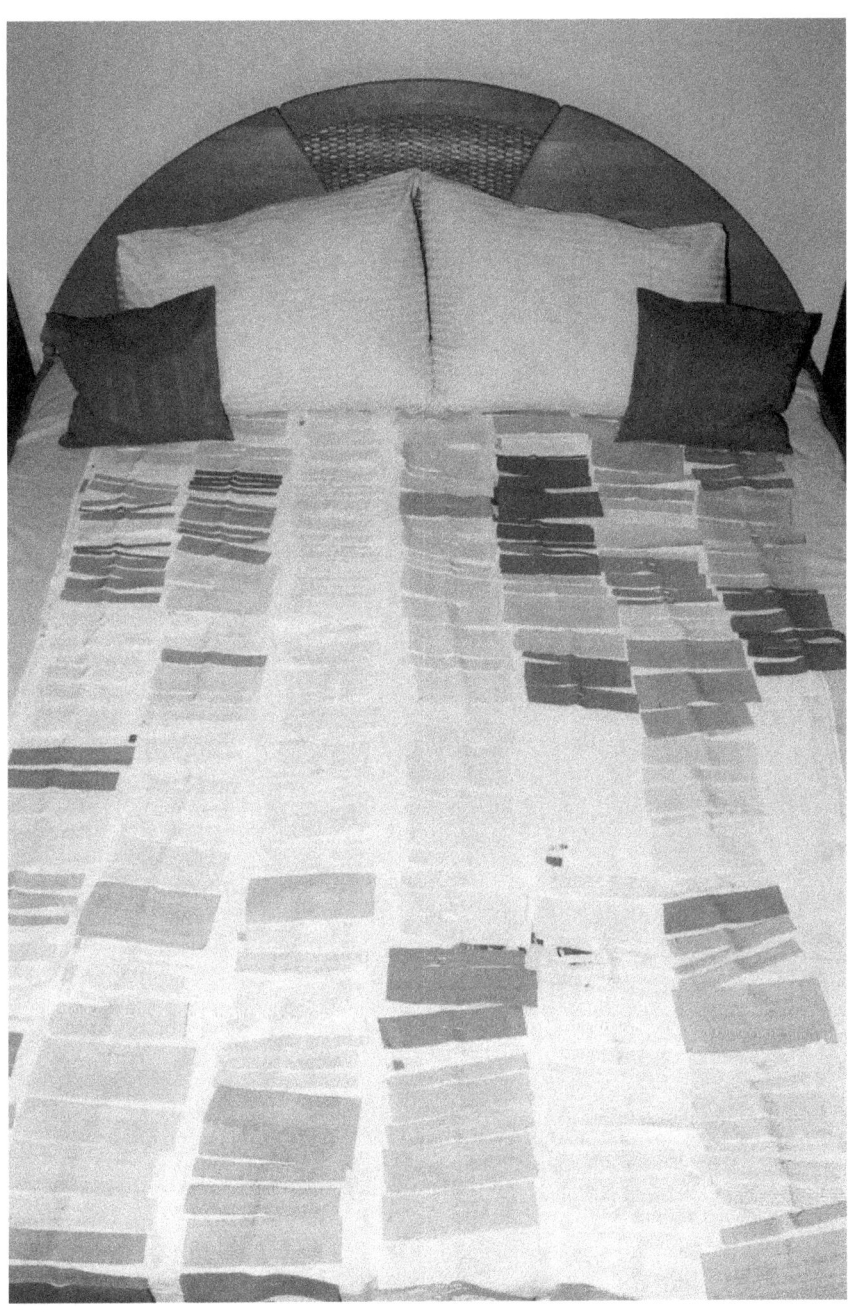

2. The Inspiration
Photo: Jeannette Goehring and Libora Oates-Indruchová.

3. The Action
Photo: Jeannette Goehring and Libora Oates-Indruchová.

4. Anticipation
Photo: Jeannette Goehring and Libora Oates-Indruchová.

Dramatis personae

Novice: the story's narrator; somewhat similar to the author; she identifies as Generation 1989 – not in the academic workforce during normalization, but a university student then.
Mentors: the first phoneme of the name identifies the academic discipline; for example, Lilius is a *li*terary scholar, Fragaria a *ph*ilosopher and *S*ztipoah a *so*ciologist.
The Czechs: they sit around the table in a nondescript conference room; their names are inspired by Latin botanical names, their academic titles are those at the time of the interview; they represent two age cohorts distinguished in the text by the script used in their names:

- *Regular script*: Generation *1968* – they were already in the academic workforce at the time; they were born in the 1920s and 1930s, for example, Hedera.
- *CamelCase*: students or postgraduates in 1968, and therefore, *not in the academic workforce during the Prague Spring*; they were born in the 1940s – corresponds roughly to the Hungarian generation born in the 1950s – for example, LoTus.

Grammatical gender of the names:
Stellari*a* ('a' ending, feminine); Sambucu*s* ('s' ending, masculine)

Editors:
Mrs Euphrasia, 1920s–30s, Prague, Academy of Sciences (1970s), popular-science publishing house (1980s).
Mr ErIgerus, 1940s, Prague, the Academy (late 1970s), then with a popular-science publisher.

Historians:
Professor Hedera, 1920s–30s, Prague, Academy of Sciences, retired in the early 1980s.
Professor Helleborus, 1920–30s, Prague, university lecturer.
Doctor Helianthus, 1920s–30s, Prague, lost his job at the Academy in 1969–70, then freelanced for several years, from the mid-1970s worked on short-term contracts at various research units.
Doctor Hepatica, 1920–30s, Prague, fired from the Academy in 1969–70, freelanced (early 1970s), then part-time and short-term contracts at a university, from the 1980s on a disability pension.
Doctor Hyacintha, 1920s–30s, Prague, left her university appointment in 1969–70 and moved to an institute of applied research.

Literary scholars:
Professor Laburnus, 1920s–30s, at a regional university, teaching restrictions after 1969–70.
Professor Lilius, 1920s–30s, Prague, university lecturer, transferred to a non-teaching position in 1969–70.
Doctor LoTus, 1940s, lecturer at a Slovak university.
Doctor LupiNus, 1940s, lecturer at a regional university.

Philosophers:
Professor Fragaria, 1920s–30s, Prague, university lecturer, transferred in the 1980s to a unit with a different disciplinary focus than her subject.
Doctor ForSythia, 1940s, Prague, university lecturer.

Sociologists/social scientists:
DOCTOR SAMBUCUS, 1920s–30s, Prague, Academy of Sciences.
PROFESSOR SINAPIS, 1920s–30s, Prague, lost his university appointment in 1969–70, was banned from teaching, moved to an institute of applied research.
PROFESSOR STACHYS, 1920s–30s, Prague, lost his job at the Academy in 1969–70, was banned from teaching several years later, although he remained at the university.
DOCTOR STELLARIA, 1920s–30s, Prague, lost her university appointment in 1969–70, but worked in applied research for most of the period of normalization.
PROFESSOR SALVIA, 1940s, Prague, institute of applied research.
DOCTOR SILENA, 1940s, Prague, applied research institute (1970s), the Academy (1980s).
PROFESSOR SORBUS, 1940s, lecturer at a regional university.

The Hungarians: they have their icons / room interiors projected on the wall and join the conversation here and there from the virtual space; their names derive from Dacian botanical names, their titles are those at the time of the interview; they represent three age cohorts, grouped into two generations for simplification and distinguished in the text by the script used in their names:

- *Regular script*: those born in the 1920s and 1930s (Generation *1956*) – in the academic workforce at the time of the Hungarian revolution, in their experience of political repressions they are close to the Czech Generation 1968; and also the age cohort born in the *1940s* – too young to be in the academic workforce during the Hungarian revolution or even the general amnesty of 1963, but in the workforce in the early 1970s, the time of the reprisals in Hungarian academia linked to the invasion of Czechoslovakia, for example, Sztipoah.
- *CamelCase*: the generation born in the *early 1950s*, like the Czech generation of the 1940s, too young to be in the academic workforce at the time of the reprisals linked to 1968, for example, HorMi.

Grammatical gender of the names:
Szandili*ah* ('h' ending as in 'Hannah', feminine); Lustan*i* (the Hungarian adjectival 'i' ending, masculine)

Historians:
PROFESSOR HORMI, 1950s, Budapest, worked in a governmental research unit (1970s), then at the Academy.

Literary scholars:
PROFESSOR LAXI, 1940s, Budapest, worked at a regional university, then at the Academy of Sciences, faced a teaching ban from around the late 1970s.
PROFESSOR LUSTANI, 1940s, worked at the Academy of Sciences, but was transferred to another institute for political reasons in the mid-1960s.

Sociologists/social scientists:
PROFESSOR SZANDILIAH, 1920s–1930s, Budapest, worked at an applied research institute in the 1950s, then at the Academy of Sciences, with occasional university teaching.
PROFESSOR SZTIPOAH, 1920s–1930s, Budapest, a governmental research unit (1950s), then at the Academy from the late 1960s, part-time university lecturer from the mid-1960s.
PROFESSOR SZEBAH, 1940s, Budapest, the Academy, part-time university lecturer from the mid-1970s.
PROFESSOR SZKIARI, 1950s, Budapest, teaching ban until 1977, then a university lecturer.
DOCTOR SZOLPI, 1950s, Budapest, worked at a Party research institute.

3

People and institutions
Surviving in normalized academia

Let us now set the written records aside and immerse in the memories of those who were members of the scholarly community in Czechoslovakia and Hungary in the 1970s and the 1980s and who continued to enjoy the respect of their peers also at the beginning of the new millennium. Let them be our guides and mentors on our quest to find how ideas travelled from their authors through the various formal and informal channels to reach the readers in (state-controlled) print. What transformations did ideas go through and who affected them? We know from the previous chapter that the Party exerted growing and relentless pressure on institutions to rid themselves of people politically compromised by participating in the Prague Spring reform process. The picture assembled from the various propaganda documents, science policies and post-1989 research illustrated the legalizing framework that enabled the Party to place its own trusted people in leadership and decision-making positions. But what did these processes, whose aim was the 'renewal of the leading role of the Party in society', feel like and look like to the individual researcher in a research team or a lecturer at a university department? What were the pressures and restrictions on employment – and on other kinds of participation in the academic community?

*

I listened to almost thirty individual voices, telling me of this experience, opening new vistas, revealing twists in the road, arousing emotion. In the following five chapters, I will take on the role of the novice on a quest and, in the process, try and bring to life the scholarly world that the owners of these voices inhabited and recalled in their memories. It is an intellectual, not a physical, journey, so a single, anonymous space will do. It is also a space in which language barriers do not exist. I imagine that I am sitting in a room, probably a conference room, large enough for the twenty Czech guides and mentors to converse comfortably. I cannot always see all of them with equal clarity; they drift in and out of my mind's focus. There is a soft whirring sound from the video projector above our heads. It projects on the wall an image of webcam shots of empty rooms and frozen portraits of the eight other mentors who will be joining our quest journey here and there from Hungary.

I

I introduce myself and thank everybody for coming to this two-day symposium on personal experience with scholarly publishing in the last two decades of state socialism. Armed with the knowledge gained from the archival documents, I ask first about how personnel politics worked in these particular researchers' professional circles during normalization.

Professor Helleborus opened with a simple statement, 'In the social sciences, nobody could get to the top unless they were also a Party member.'

'And even on the committees of professional associations, for instance, there had to be a certain number of Party members,' Professor Hedera added. 'On our one there was five. The list of candidates had to go to the Central Committee, 'cos these committees had to be approved, right? And it became a right problem to keep things up, so this or that association, they might pay someone's subscription just to keep them in, 'cos they might want him on the committee at any time. We'd just circle their name in red then bung it in for approval and that was that. Obviously our association wasn't at all prominent politically. If it had been, they'd have taken a closer look at the names on the list. But with us, since they didn't know anybody, at least they could see the five circles, so we'd done what was expected. That Central Committee lot, they never even saw our association at close quarters, so we freely went on with our meetings that entire time.'

There was a pause, while the others pondered whether camouflage was all it took to hoodwink the watchers and continue one's work as if no machinery of restrictions existed, or whether professional associations would have perhaps found themselves under lesser surveillance than research institutes and university departments. Finally, Doctor SiLena looked timidly – perhaps defensively – at Professor Hedera and returned the discussion from the politics of a meeting room to the hard reality of employment contracts.

'When my department – incidentally, quite a successful one – was shut down in '77, I found myself job-hunting again. It wasn't that hard. Obviously there were still no openings in academia, because for that they demanded a Party card, and I even went to two places where they actually told me, "Get yourself a Party membership card and come back." And then I applied for a post advertised at a certain university and got it, despite not having a Party card. They told me my application had succeeded, but next day they phoned to say I hadn't got the job because I was a woman. Except in those days there was nothing you could do about it, because these things were never put in writing, see? You'd won, but nothing came of it. Then I applied to several academic institutions, universities, but, really and truly, without a Party card there was nothing doing.'

Professor SorBus nodded in agreement, although perhaps not with Doctor SiLena's revealing comment that political and gender discrimination existed side by side in state-socialist academia. Rather, he seemed to share her scepticism about the powers of camouflage, for he said, 'Entrance exams [at our faculty], as a case in point, were a nightmare. Because you got sent a document, the list of applicants, and on the Dean's version there were some red and black dots. The black dots were by names that mustn't be let in, and red dots were for those who had to be. And the rest, they had no dots. Which meant we fought for the ones without dots and for the odd one with a black dot. And the Dean, who a lot of people curse today, though he himself did nothing bad, well, what he used to do was go to the Regional Committee of the Communist Party and say, "Look here, you need these four people, but I need these two here." Now and again we did salvage someone.'

This description of barter trade at entrance exams would have been comical, had it not concerned the futures of many young people who were excluded from putting in their 'bid' – their currency of knowledge and academic merit were clearly inferior on this market. On the other hand, however, they had a 'broker' in the person of Professor SorBus and the dean, which was perhaps more than other people and students had elsewhere.

As the conversation continued, the memories of more people seemed to suggest that the surveillance in Czech academia was worse at universities than in research institutes, because the Party was afraid of the influence pedagogues could have on the young generation. Professor Fragaria recounted her own story: 'In 1970, after I left the Party, I couldn't teach properly, could I? I even had it set out that I should teach up to Marx, but that I wasn't allowed to teach beyond Marx, 'cos I might not give it the proper ideological slant. And I couldn't rise up the pay scale. My options were either simply to be fed up, or to kind of make the best of whatever was going. So I became mainly concerned with teaching my subject wherever it was taught, even if no students were taking it as a major.'

'I know that they also banned one colleague in the Department of Slovak Language and Literature, who was a writer himself,' Doctor LoTus added another example. 'He's not very well known here in Bohemia, but the simple truth is that in Slovakia he is well known as a writer. Anyway, they banned him as a non-Party member from lecturing on literature. That probably came under the proviso that as non-Party member he mustn't lecture on literature, any literature, because lectures on literature could only be given by the politically maturest of the mature, and obviously non-Party members were not that. So he, a Slovak literary figure, couldn't give lectures on Slovak literature. After that they let him lecture on literary theory and lead seminars, but he wasn't allowed to give [literature] lectures.'

Doctor Hyacintha, who herself had to change employment after the vetting, introduced another perspective. 'The big break didn't come straight away in '69, but not till around '74 or '75. With every change, individual departments came to be headed by more compliant individuals. On the other hand, they did have a measure of integrity so that when people's moral fibre was being assailed and the Anti-Charter was meant to be signed, the chairman of the Party branch and the chairman of the trade-union branch went off to city hall where, with the authority vested in them, they signed on behalf of everyone, say 200 employees, without bothering them or even informing them about it.[1] They took it as something they had to deal with as part of the job.'

---

[1] Anti-Charter (Anticharta) was a media campaign in 1977 directed against the signatories of Charter 77; personages in the public eye, including academics, were forced to sign the text (without having read the text they were supposed to be refuting, that is Charter 77). 'Anticharta' (2009), Ústav pro studium totalitních režimů. Available online: https://www.ustrcr.cz/uvod/antologie-ideologickych-textu/anticharta/ (accessed 30 April 2019).

Mrs Euphrasia thought back to that time and added, 'At my institute, I don't know if it was an internal directive for getting rid of inconvenient people. Anyway, everybody, I'm not sure if it was at 65, everyone had to retire. Whether at institutes of the Academy of Science or universities. So people of an age when they still had something to offer to students. The official reason was that you were too old, so out you go, right? It's obvious, for another thing, that these people were also not Party members. Then when our institute got a new director, the first thing to happen was he banned anyone not employed there from using the library. This obviously affected those who had to leave allegedly on the grounds of age. These were people who'd been scholars all their life and suddenly they were done for, because they'd got no access to the latest literature. But you had cases like this one professor who became night porter at the university library and that gave him access to it.'

'It was all down to some personnel management measure that anyone who wasn't in the Party, whether ever, or given they'd been expelled, they all had to leave the department around the start of the eighties, that's right,' Professor Fragaria concurred. 'So one colleague went to the university archive and I switched to a different discipline.'

All this seemed to support what I deduced from the policy documents: the orchestrators of normalization were reaching deeper with every passing year, subjecting further and further layers of institutional structures to the centralizing power. But most of these memories also contained a 'but' that presented a small token of resistance or a tiny alliance against this power – be it the alliance of Professor SorBus and the dean with the students, the resistance by camouflage in Professor Hedera's professional association or the stubborn strategies of Professor Fragaria and the professor-turned-night-watchman to carve a niche for their work within the boundaries imposed on them. The new, Party-appointed, 'pliable' administrators mentioned by Doctor Hyacintha also seemed to have played an intriguing role that, in effect, lightened the professional existence of those under them at least of some ideological ballast, even if it may not have been intended in that way.

We can even consider how much the obedience of these administrators of the Party *enabled* their employees to maintain a higher *moral* ground by not always forcing them into manifestations of conformity with the ideology. Doctor Hyacintha, who was forced out of her academic job, banned from teaching and left with minimal publication venues after the vetting, came to a surprising defence of her managers, but also pointed out their lack of professional principles.

'I can't imagine anyone today trying to resist that kind of pressure, if it were pressure of a financial kind. But back then it was still technocrats in office, and they were pretty far-sighted and pretty courageous. It was only over time that our institute was joined by people linked more to the apparatus of the city Party committee. At the end of the seventies a member of the city Party committee joined the management and at the same time he was ex-director of a big company, so all these things were functionally interconnected and people like this weren't really interested in the prospects for development or any alternative ways of dealing with things. This new management was more interested in demonstrating how efficient it was.'

'What mattered most for working in the seventies and eighties, though it varied quite a bit, was what the boss was like, yes,' Doctor Helianthus, agreed. 'Though you can't always put your finger on it for certain. In our history department, as everyone knows, when one of the most energetic normalizers became head of department, well, he did throw certain people out, but on the other hand he defended one of his opponents, insisting he was a competent historian. But it has to be said they weren't actually ploughing the same furrow. So it was always far more complex, since the selfsame person might keep one individual on while scuppering another. Though now we're talking about personal, or more precisely, competitive interests. Opportunities to publish were also affected by competition among those who were in power, but were afraid they might be attacked by younger people, because not even the bosses on the history front were sure of being there forever. They knew what had happened to their predecessors, right, so they saw to it that there was no new talent rising in their quarter. In one such case, the individual concerned, in order to attack a competitor, used his own student, who willingly played ball.'

'In my field there was some very interesting movement across the generations,' Professor Stachys added. 'Instead of the normal rotation, now older generations were replacing the younger. The younger generation had replaced the previous generation, but after the vetting, what happened was that the younger generation was struck out and the even older generation, which had completely failed to get their way here in the sixties by reason of utter intellectual impotence, now did get their way. My boss: a total nonentity who became a professor and dean of faculty.[2] An utter nonentity in the field, who not only knew nothing about the field, but he didn't even understand it. We were screwed for having secretly made fun of these people. We found them ridiculous because they were so dim. And they replaced us. We were suddenly the nonentities and they simply held the positions of power. They couldn't decide our fate anymore, it was too late for that, wasn't it? That was done and dusted, but they could make life unpleasant for us in various ways. So this was the most interesting change, our place being taken by a generation that was older than ourselves. And they were extremely dangerous, being just unintelligent boors.'

I knew that Professor Stachys could not publish for a while, so I asked, 'Was your publication ban more to do with certain thorny topics you dealt with or your own person?'

'My person,' Professor Stachys said without hesitation. 'The explanation's here in this basic scheme. It was simply pushing out one generation that had taken control of sociology, that was us, the promising young line-up that had to be got rid of. And they did get rid of us, in the manner of us getting struck off and expelled from the Party, didn't they? They either left us in our jobs or they chucked us out. But the stigma was there and this country is too small for it not to be known who was who in the field.'

He gazed at his hands for a moment. He must have been reflecting on the thorniness of his person in the political side, because he finally said, 'In the last year before November I got into the institute of the Academy of Sciences. For them to be able to take me on, my boss had to have a statement from the secretary of the Central Committee. I, a mere nobody, was an item for the most supreme body just so as I could join the Academy. That was in '88, but who was to know how different it would all be in a year's time?'

'Sociology was always very suspicious and sociologists were always suspicious,' Professor Sztipoah, so far the only Hungarian participant present in the virtual space, chimed in from the wall. '*They* were afraid of sociology, because sociologists would uncover the real.'

'We were branded as people who – to use the period terminology – wanted to replace the class-based viewpoint with the viewpoint of bourgeois sociology,'

---

[2] Jonathan Bolton equally concludes that 'the purges (…) cleared the way for a new class of people – those who valued advancement above consistency and principle. (…) The early 1970s saw a widespread replacement of talent by mediocrity' (Bolton 2012: 64).

Professor Stachys continued, pointing out the special status of his circle. 'You can read as much in many places. Until about the middle of the seventies we were an object of fierce criticism. It was the people, especially our one-time great pal, who wrote with such militancy against Machonin's team. And then Machonin voiced a very wise thought: "As long as they're spitting at us, let's be thankful. The worst will come when they realize it's better to keep quiet." And then they actually did keep quiet and we duly fell into the abyss of oblivion, because after that who remembered there'd been a Machonin team? Who remembered the Richta team, the Mlynář team?[3] But we who'd been there became stigmatized forever. But those teams, they've all vanished, eh? The stigma had remained. That was one thing, the professional aspect. But otherwise it was a power struggle, a fight for positions.'

If it was so clear who bore what stigma, I could not help asking how the fact became known, if some people did not even try to get their work published in some places or nobody talked about them.

'But what form did the ban take?'

'None at all,' Professor SorBus replied. 'That was the nastiest thing about it, because in essence no bans actually existed. It was always down to some secretary for ideology or whoever. At university faculties as well, though it wasn't quite that bad here: six people [at our faculty] were affected, but even they eventually had the odd chance to write something about Comenius and the like. If it wasn't anything likely to be seen as provocative, then it was all right. So it was never formalized, but those organs had the power to say no.'

'My organization got a tip-off from them not to employ me,' Doctor Stellaria contributed her own bitter experience. 'I'd started and two days later *someone* phoned from the Central Committee or the City Committee, not sure exactly who, and they advised me I couldn't stay, higher powers had intervened. So I applied for a job with deaf–mute children. There they said in advance it was all right for me to start working with that kind of kids because they didn't have any abstract thinking. I must have been there about three times and then they

---

[3] Pavel Machonin (1927–2008) was a Czech sociologist who in the 1960s led a research project on the stratification of Czechoslovak Society. Radovan Richta (1924–83) was the head of the Institute of Philosophy and Sociology of the Czechoslovak Academy of Sciences between 1969 and 1982. He edited the collective volume *Civilization at the Crossroads* (*Civilizace na rozcestí*) (Richta et al. 1966, 1969), from which the term 'socialism with a human face', the motto of the Prague Spring, developed. Zdeněk Mlynář (1930–97) was a Czech political scientist; after signing Charter 77, he was forced to emigrate to Austria. He later became a professor at the University of Innsbruck.

advised me that "We can't allow you to be here anyway, because there's a lot of young teachers here who'd be influenced by you." And again I got it from my employers, *never* from the Communist Party, that's why there's not a shred of evidence, right? The Party were never so direct as to put a piece of paper in your hand, see?'

Professor Hedera pointed out that such pressure could have been systematically applied not only with respect to stigmatized individuals like Doctor Stellaria, but also to whole research units. 'You even had to go to the Central Committee to be sort of screened. Everyone had to, always three in the morning and another three after lunch, everybody separate. No one said a word against anyone, it was always: "You're great scholars", right, and of course, the contract. The contract was actually signed by the institution, not the Central Committee. I went there once, even though I'd nothing at all to do with the Party. They were so terribly nice, so terribly sort of smarmy: "But comrade, you're really first-rate." On the other hand, they'd always shout like mad at … , you know … ? But then I've no idea what this business, what their policy was. Though otherwise nothing happened, they extended one's contract and that was that. Then again, the institute didn't do what the Central Committee would have ordered them to regarding signing contracts. They [at the institute] were terribly nervous, they had to think what to do so as to please that body. And so as to let it have things in a form it would like, right? But if, say, they slipped to the Central Committee someone the latter might not want … ,' she left the sentence unfinished, then continued, 'The problem was that they [at the Central Committee] only knew the top names. Of course they didn't know others personally, so, at institutions, who was to be shooed in depended entirely on personal relations. So they were kind of afraid [in the institute] they'd be risking a hard time, because there was always all that spying: "Well, who knows what he's like, he supports that there reactionary." So they were afraid.'

'At one university they still didn't know how to set about it,' Doctor Hepatica elaborated on the stigmatization. 'How to take me on, when everything was subject to approval by the powers at the top and I've got that kind of [political] handicap. So some thought went into it and I said I wasn't going to answer any questionnaires, I just wouldn't. By then I was settled, because I was translating and interpreting and I also had this trifling pension of a thousand crowns a month and I said to myself, "I don't need this, having to argue the toss with someone, when I'm not going to be approved anyway." So, I wasn't allowed to teach, but I was giving dissertation tutorials anyway, tutoring postgraduates, working on textbooks, I was fully occupied and still got a thousand crowns a month, but things were a little bit different after all. When my first book came out and was well received, I just carried on doing research and published another book in the mid-eighties, also successful, and since people were now aware of me, since I'd been published by Svoboda, well, who was going to start asking me questions about anything and nothing?[4] By now I was publishing articles; was approached by *Politická ekonomie* and other journals; had conducted vivas in Slovakia and had publications in another socialist country and what not. To cut a long story short, when the '89 revolution was behind us, in 1990 I ran into the editor I'd left my things with – he was very pleased not only that it was first-rate, but also that I wrote well and he hadn't had much to do on it and I asked him: "Do tell me, how was it possible that you could publish me when I'd never filled in any forms?" I'd not signed any bits of paper. And he says: "That's precisely why I could publish you, because there was no paper at the publishing house [to say otherwise] and so I sort of didn't know. It reached me with so-and-so's recommendation and I didn't ask any questions and so it worked out all right." They held no record of the author. I had a contract, but in the card index of authors there was no card of mine.'

She seemed to be saying that in the immediate aftermath of the vetting, the ideological spotlight was on *demonstrable* 'black marks'. If, like in her case, written evidence was simply missing, some individuals may have been overlooked, providing nobody was motivated to drag them out to light. Paradoxically and at least until the pressure that came later on institutions to *increase* the proportion of Party members as opposed to *removing* the compromised members, this may have meant an opening of some limited opportunities also for non-Party members, such as Professor Hedera.

'Even after '69 I had a few years co-editing a major journal in my field,' she recollected. 'The reason they put me on the journal's new board was sort of because the editor proper had been my professor at university, he had a very soft spot for me and didn't much like the new people, though basically he was a hard-line normalizer, but with him it was a matter of deep conviction, but

---

[4] Svoboda was a publishing house of the Communist Party of Czechoslovakia and published literature in social sciences and philosophy. For details see the entry 'Svoboda' by Burget (2013).

I never once talked politics with him. He wanted to maintain the journal's standard of scholarship and they kept trying to agree who could do it, who couldn't, until it finally dawned on them that I'd been neither expelled from the Party nor struck off, I'd stayed on at the Institute because nobody could think of anything against me, because my subject was economic and social history and historical demography, which never got bogged down in any kind of political context, so for that reason to all intents and purposes no one actually knew anything that went against me. So I became an editor, but under constant pressure from certain quarters, as is to be expected in scholarly circles: matters of personal relationships, friends, enemies, that kind of thing. Those pressures were there for quite some time until finally the editor said: "You've got to join the Party." Well, I was in no mind to join the Party during the normalization period. So, I was replaced by another editor who taught at the Evening College of Marxism–Leninism,[5] but she was good enough for the academic quality of the journal.'

'So as not to spoil the statistics at the place I was working, which had about two and a half thousand employees, they always gave me a short-term contract,' Doctor Stellaria recounted her own absurd employment situation. 'So every three months I was fired and every three months I was re-hired. That went on for ten years, up to about 1980. That was because otherwise I'd have to show up on the books, whereas if you're there only up to three months, you don't have to show. Which is a quite interesting proceeding, and I wasn't the only one. It's fair to say that in comparison with other people who were thrown out of the Faulty of Arts I was one of those who came off best, because we'd been thrown out and were looking for jobs at a time when there was great solidarity among people and when people saw you as one of their own who'd got into a spot of bother. Whereas the people who were thrown out later, in '74 or '75, they came off much worse, because by then people were afraid. At that earlier stage, they hadn't been afraid to take me on, see?'

'They thought long and hard what to do with me so I could be taken on,' Doctor Hepatica continued on the subject of employment strategizing. 'Then someone came up with the idea that they could hire me as a disability pensioner for a year, just to help out, on a one-third contract, and that didn't

---

[5] Generally known by its acronym VUML, which will be used later in the dialogues.

have to be approved by any district Party committee and so on. The point being that pensioners couldn't be in permanent employment. It wasn't subject to approval, so that's how it was resolved.'

Professor Stachys concluded the discussion with his own rather gruesome story.

'After I'd had a heart attack, the doctors altered my capacity-for-work status, thereby making it impossible for the faculty to dismiss me. So they had to keep me on. In that respect, the normalization regime might not have been legitimate, but it did have laws. And it respected them. They knew that, say, going to court, that the Labour Statutes did do …'

He did not need to finish to get his meaning across.

'So they may have demeaned me so far as they could, see? But they couldn't throw me out of the Faculty,' he added.

'They fired us on the instant,' Doctor Hepatica countered, but then picked up the thread of moral support and solidarity from people who kept their institutional positions unthreatened.

'That guy from the university who knew me well and knew my predicament, he comes next day and he says: "I don't want to hear all the whys and wherefores of what's happened, that doesn't concern me right now, but I'd like you to review this book." So, I wrote the review and my review was published in the nick of time before all those checks started. That way he gave me some encouragement to know I wasn't a complete has-been, do you see? The moral support of these people was terribly important. So I can honestly state, hand on heart, that I didn't compromise myself in my books, because I was being supported by people who were completely to one side, and the books remain topical and I'm not ashamed of them; on the contrary, I can pride myself on them and when I read them today I'm amazed how bright I was back then, like I'm perhaps not nearly so now.'

Doctor Helianthus wanted to continue the solidarity theme.

'I was at one institution, and gradually what they did with contracts for work was contrived so flexibly that one time the institute – 'cos it was in collaboration with others – so sometimes I'd get my money here, sometimes I'd get my money there, so it wasn't quite so concentrated at the beginning. In large measure it was also a question of agreement, so I wouldn't be on the payroll at one institution all the time.'

'There were obviously some places where I couldn't go at all,' Professor Sinapis said. 'Like the Academia publishing house; there it was practically out of the question. But at Svoboda, for instance, there was a degree of momentum at the start, because actually even that series we published in carried on and we were well in with the women editors, and once I was banned from publishing, we agreed on translations, so I translated, or my wife, who *is* a translator, also translated some pretty decent things for them.'

Doctor LupiNus, whose publication opportunities were not affected by a political stigma, said, 'Look, at *World Literature* we basically always found a way round. That was a huge help with my budget. Every year, they'd fill over a year a good part of one issue with stuff of mine. That gave me six thousand, which was a massive sum in those days, as much as two months of my salary. But it got up my nose when they said: "Come on, you've got a fixed income."'

A touch of sarcasm crept into his voice, as he proceeded to explain that the publisher was referring to those who had to rely on acts of solidarity.

'So you'd got this well-known freelance translator and those poor guys, yeah, they'd publish something in instalments in *World Literature*, two months later it would be out as a book, so they got paid twice over. I once got a sight of the fees. Think of it, they were living hand-to-mouth on a hundred, hundred and fifty thousand a year. And how much was I making? Forty.'

From almost the opposite end of the opportunities spectrum, Doctor Stellaria offered an insight into the situation of scholars who needed solidarity to gain any, not just academic, employment.

'Factories would give these people jobs, they could be sort of buried away there. I managed to get dozens of people into ČKD Semi-conductors. Though again, with this kind of thing it was about who knew who, personal contacts. So at ČKD Semi-conductors, they had a section that employed the disabled, well, one case was a member of the opposition who was there as a programmer, nominally on health grounds, see? But somebody had to vouch for his health condition, and that was people at the hospital where I was working. It was the contacts between the hospital and the factory, because in those days we were in what was called "work toward a rapprochement between the intelligentsia and the workers":[6] in other words, it was where preventive medicals were carried out, and I was specifically tasked with a round of preventive medicals for ČKD Semi-conductors employees, so I knew *loads* of people there.'

---

[6] The doctrine of 'rapprochement between the social classes' (Gagyi and Éber 2015: 601).

Professor HorMi strolled into the picture on the wall. He had apparently overheard the end of our conversation, because he began to recount a contrasting experience from Hungary.

'[Miklós Szabó] who later became a liberal MP, was a fellow here [at the institute of the Academy] since the late fifties. He was known to hold Free University lectures[7] – the Free University lectures were the most famous ones in Budapest at that time [1980s]. And he was one of the most well-known dissident figures who belonged to the official world, as well as to the underground, because he had a legal employment here at the institute, he was not fired. There were pressures from the Communist leadership, from the Central Committee, in the late eighties that Miklós Szabó be fired, but the managers of the institute, who were Communists, defended him. There were several signs of solidarity shown in this direction. For instance, several notable scholars, fellows of the institute, also undertook presenting lectures at the Free University to express their solidarity with Miklós Szabó when it was complained that he was involved in dissident [activities]. They were official personalities, historians who were previously Party historians. One of them, a well-known Party historian, also held a lecture in the framework of Free University to show his solidarity toward Miklós Szabó. This was a typically and specifically Hungarian way of transforming the system from within, making it more and more liberal, flexible. Accepted personalities, bosses, leaders at the academic level, were always engaged, not in explicit dissident activity, but in partly defending it.'

Professor SalVia was shaking her head. She could not relate to professional solidarity among colleagues within an official institution.

'In all this the seventies were messy, unpleasant. A case in point, one thing that offended me deeply and was truly wounding was when a group of my close colleagues at work, where we were all fond of each other and got along well together as we were dolling up what we'd written so as to suit and making fun of this self-censorship, and I thought of them as my friends and still do – the ones who are still alive – well, when it came to it and I failed to sign the Anti-charter, it all stopped. That week when I was waiting to see whether or not I'd

---

[7] Miklós Szabó (1935–2000) was a Hungarian historian. 'Free University' was an underground university set up in Budapest in 1978 (Falk 2003: 128–9). For more on Miklós Szabó and his involvement in the activity see ('Recordings of Miklós Szabó's Lectures Donated to OSA' 2013).

be fired, it was these people who said, "You put us in jeopardy," and suddenly they were like my worst enemies. And I told myself: "Aha, I seem to have got things a bit wrong." Then it turned out all right for me, so everything changed again, but it left a nasty taste in my mouth and an edginess and other odd things … I don't know. I believe all this shaped and distorted relationships, it distorted a lot of other things, on the other hand I should have thought about how many people I'd harmed.'

'My boss told me, "Well at least promise me that once you've gathered your wits together you'll hand in your notice," and I said, "All right,"' Doctor Stellaria reminisced about the response of her superior to an instance of pressure from the Party. 'You see? So again it's psychological pressure: you don't want to make trouble for him and in effect he actually manoeuvres you into agreeing with him so you're not actually a victim – you're just playing along with these people. So I handed in my notice myself and that was also quite interesting because several other employees told me: "That was so nice of you, to have taken the pressure off us, you're really kind." See that? How appreciative they were that I'd handed in my notice and so not made life difficult for them? This sort of thing was hugely appreciated by the people around one. And that was in '88.'

Everybody fell silent as if waiting for more.

'Though to say it was the regime and this kind of thing was par for the course, no, no,' she continued, 'I'm sure my boss had a guilty conscience over it. He wasn't a shit, just scared. No more than that, see? He had under him a bunch of people for the chop, so he couldn't be a shit who wouldn't want to give them a job. It was a kind of collaboration with the centre of power: If I'd been ruled by my principles, I'd have refused to hand in my notice, and it would have been hard for them to throw me out. But I was thinking that I couldn't make life difficult for those people, could I? If I'd been approached by someone from the Party Central Committee, I'd have dug my heels in and said: "Not bloody likely, never!" But the way power was fragmented downwards bit by bit, I actually quit voluntarily because I didn't want to be awkward. And that's what makes it so stupid to compare that regime with others out there in Peru, Chile or Salvador. Because this wasn't physical pressure, nor was there any economic pressure, see? It was psychological pressure pure and simple – or not even that: you went into it voluntarily, that was it. I even handed in my notice as of the twenty-second or thereabouts, but he wanted it right away, see? And I'd said: "Could you give me at least to the end of the month?" And he said: "'Fraid not, they'd have been here again." By *they* he, a member of the Party and the People's Militia, meant the secret police.'

Professor SorBus contributed a 'provincial' perspective, his view on solidarity at institutions outside Prague.

'When the vetting process was going on at our faculty,[8] six people paid the price, which is an incredibly low number for an "ideological" faculty. Several others paid the price as well in due course, though they were then assigned to research posts with no teaching element. The faculty held together. To put it bluntly, the sons of bitches woke up too late. Popular resentment was still in the air so those who might have immediately risen to the top in exchange for acting as informers, well they only woke up sometime after the vettings were all over, by which time there was a measure of resistance among the community, along the lines, "We need to discuss it, then we'll see," and all in all nothing came of it, you see. Whereas if they'd come along at the outset, they could have done whatever they wanted. I know things were pretty drastic at the Faculty of Natural Sciences. Surprising as that might seem. I'm not a natural scientist and I only know because people of my generation either fled to the West or told horror stories about being slung out by their own teachers. And to me that was beyond comprehension, but it was a political struggle, well not political, but a fight by those noisy intellectual thugs who'd been scared that with the arrival of Dubčekism they'd lose what they'd achieved and almost did lose it, and then they were out for revenge. It's sort of simple, because I can't imagine it was all over some problem in maths or physics. Or maybe it was? I don't know, but I don't think so. In Prague things were different. It might have been tougher at the Arts Faculty in Prague. But out here in the provinces we've got the edge; bad times are easier to survive. Of course there were groups of people and individuals who hated each other's guts, but that's just human, though I don't think they'd go with finger-pointing and saying, "This one here, he's a saboteur of socialism." It was never that brutal. Though maybe only here, at the Academy [of Sciences] things might have been much worse. Here we had the advantage that the people were sort of ever so young, but I did appreciate that we were sheltered by the institution

---

[8] That is, Faculty of Arts; in 1969–70.

and having to teach; or again that, in the provinces, it wasn't so easy to sling people out and replace them.'

The measure of solidarity clearly depended on the immediate political climate. Professor Sinapis placed his own professional trajectory in that context.

'Between '78, when I had to leave my place of work and move to an outpost of it somewhere completely different, several hundred kilometres away, and about '83 or '84, for those five years or so I basically couldn't publish. For one thing, in these circles everything's known, meaning my bosses also knew I'd had a spot of trouble at work, and that a Soviet delegation had come out against the results of our project, and that I was once more classified as not terribly reliable, so all I was allowed to do was write up reports or arrange internal conferences, you know the kind of thing, I was allowed to take part in those, or seminars [= colloquia or workshops]. And the other thing was that my own energies hit rock-bottom. Now I think about it, [the change came] probably due to the climate change in the second half of the eighties, when even ideological concerns passed, and up to a point it was also the fact that that cock-up with *Rudé právo* ended in the long grass, nothing actually came of it, and its author was even criticized later by the boss of the ideology section – as I heard – for treating our scientists insensitively.'

'There were objective turning points in the world of politics and there were divisions due to personalities – in my case due to conditions prevailing at the Faculty or within the publishing house,' Professor Helleborus agreed. 'In any event, what I felt as critical moments in history and the social sciences, though, thinking about it, it was also general, it came after Charter 77. At that point things took a major turn for the worse, suddenly surveillance was ratcheted up. Previously they'd have ignored this or that bit of writing – not that it would be approved as a matter of course, but it was just let through, see? But from the end of the seventies the criticizing started, they started laying into people, several book reviews of the kind came out. This kind of thing admittedly passed me by, but it obviously had an effect on the whole atmosphere. It was plain to see I reckon in '78, '79 through to 1980, but after that, things started to ease up a bit. So then it starts to ease up a bit, you can't pinpoint what year, but anyway the eighties and then pretty much from Gorbachev on.'

The mention of the individuality of cases provoked several responses from others.

Professor Stachys said, 'In essence, my head of department kept me in post as a kind of loophole for himself. So I simply survived out of sight. He chucked Doctor Stellaria out at once, didn't he! She went with the first wave, we were the second. How people's fortunes unfolded was a measure of their courage. Doctor Stellaria was very courageous because she'd no option.'

'Party members who were in charge somewhere, usually their way was to foster the folk who'd been struck off [the Party membership list],' Mrs Euphrasia confirmed. 'They had no chance of advancement, no entitlements or expectations, they were just the busy little bees whose work kept their bosses in post.'

'In a way these were feudal relationships,' Doctor Sambucus explained. 'This means that sociology departments had their institutional leading lights. These were people who had to fit certain political and ideological parameters so as to hold those positions at all. And that means they obviously had to be demonstrably and functionally conformist within the terms of the official ideology, they had to produce things along those lines, and on top of that they had to have connections in political high places, usually at the ideology section of the Central Committee. And up there they generally had certain benefactors who guaranteed their positions. That was the period elite and a coterie that one was no part of and that sat up there at the top. They were an institute's "upper class", and department heads were also part of it – in various degrees, not all to the same degree. And some needed to have under them certain handymen and handmaidens with whom they formed kinds of coalitions – unwritten coalitions, of course – and these coalitions took on different forms. My unwritten coalition agreement meant that I was the guy involved in practice and anything to do with quantitative matters, and I wouldn't meddle in anything else. On the other hand, I wouldn't be prevented from doing my own thing. In other cases the alliance was formulated differently. So they might write the [ideologically] higher-profile things and any relevant [i.e. ideological] passages and the boss in question would see to it that they could publish it. The thing worked in different ways with different groups, and between different pairings the "contracts" might take on different forms.'

'It's all about social capital,' Doctor SiLena added a sociological interpretation of the practice. 'Provided your social capital is somehow respected or recognized, you may acquire a kind of advantage within the field, if you're offered it, and that's how people treated each other. To be a bit more precise, and so it doesn't sound so bad, then actually, those people who'd been labelled "normalizers", they had personal relationships with some people who'd come off badly and they offered them some small opportunities when they could. But not other people. They didn't do it generally, just for anyone they had a personal tie to. So they might enable someone to earn something on the basis of its being put under someone else's name. But none of this applied to young people at all, absolutely not, because young people going into sociology in the seventies couldn't have any such [social] capital. They couldn't have any personal ties, social contacts, to draw on. So we were pretty much excluded from the thing.'

'The Institute's director took one on as a kind of censor, sort of, but he set him up in a section that was pretty much sidelined,' Mrs Euphrasia offered another category, into which social capital could sometimes take its beneficiaries. 'He was a philosopher, bright, but struck off, might possibly have even been expelled [from the Party]. He, by being held on to, was ridiculously indebted to the director and always did his bidding. Yet he was a good philosopher. He kind of made sure the director got into as little hot water as possible, because he knew that the things that mattered most kept changing. So the director would hold on to people like that. That chap was hard-working, well-versed in his specialism, and certainly what he proofread, was all perfectly in order. Obviously "scientific communism" and all that stuff was blown up to ludicrous proportions.'

Several others were prompted into recollections of instances of exploitation by their superiors in exchange for what the superiors saw as 'favours'.

'There was this conference at the university,' Professor Fragaria began, '[and the Dean told me], "You've got to write a paper for me and a paper for yourself on mediaeval philosophy." I'm not mediaeval, I do modern philosophy, and for me it's a bit, well ... . [To which he said:] "You're in no position to choose, you can have a month off, here's a topic for two papers and there's an end of it."'

'I was in that category of people employed on one-off contracts where basically I got jobs set me that I usually had to do within some broader framework,' Doctor Helianthus confirmed the no-choice position on his own example. 'It was quite common practice for those at the top to give the orders and the rest did their job for them and they just added their own signature, see? Of course the great advantage of this state of affairs was that you did get money and you would be engaged in specialist work, though you weren't always alone, or rather you were hardly ever a sole author, usually there'd be other co-authors who either did nothing or just took care of the most important thing of all – money. So you have to see things from this angle as well, because without the one-off contracts, *de facto* you couldn't exist.'

'In some instances we did translations,' Professor Sinapis added, 'but they came out under other names, for which we duly had to pay the authors in question something.'

'It all depended on who was where at this or that publishing house, who dared, who had the guts to let something through,' Doctor Hepatica described the situation in publishing, 'and obviously it also depended on the authors. One close colleague of mine, who stayed on at the Institute – they didn't throw him out the way they did me – and we stayed in touch and then he, poor guy – he wrote sensible stuff, things I agree with, but just now and again he had to pay the odd small tribute so as to be able to stay on. Because it was about history, he was at that Institute and the Institute had to approve what he wrote, so there was a tribute to be paid. But at some institutions it wasn't like that. He had to cite, I don't know, Husák, or say that the Party and the Government had resolved ... , and the fourteenth Party Congress ... or some other such thing. Personally, I never once mentioned the fourteenth Party Congress, or the fifteenth.'[9]

'[One colleague, a specialist on mediaeval literature,] transferred to the Academy,' Doctor LupiNus joined in. 'Well, he couldn't pick and choose there, that's where the biggest Party henchmen of all were. In short, he hadn't done himself any favours. Along comes '78 and their boss forced them to write about what February[10] meant to them personally, right? My colleague who worked there told me, "I told the boss: 'But I was only two at the time.' 'Never mind that. It must have appealed to you ideologically.'" That was a colleague for whom its appeal was such that he fled with his family to France.'

'One place where there was fear was Communist meetings,' Doctor ForSythia contributed a surprising reflection. 'That was tough! Like whenever there were joint meetings of the Department of Marxism, where I was, and then comrades from other disciplines, and you'd get this sudden sense of the

---

[9] After the winning faction of the Communist Party deleted the XIVth 'Extraordinary' Congress held in the Prague quarter Vysočany on 22 August 1968 from the Party history, it renumbered the Party congresses and held the 'Ordinary' XIVth Congress in May 1971, the Congress at which Gustáv Husák was elected the general secretary.

[10] That is, the Communist coup d'état of February 1948.

terrible fear gripping those pedagogues, right? Each one distrustful of the next. Lots of people felt impelled to become visible by having a say, in case anyone got funny ideas about them, so they ended up talking utter codswallop. Everyone pretended it wasn't codswallop, but everyone knew it was. Quite a drama it was, actually. You could tell who was with who, who was against and who was having kittens. It was really easy to tell.'

Professor Stachys replied that the problem of the need to pay 'tribute' was a generational issue. 'The generation that embarked on its professional career after '68, that was the most problematical group of course. They didn't have a choice, did they? Basically, we did have a choice, given us by the Party in 1970, when the vetting process was on.'

I turned back to Doctor ForSythia and asked, 'You've spoken of an atmosphere of fear, but is there any specific example of someone actually being sanctioned for what they'd written?'

'You mean if someone specifically wrote something and paid a price for it politically? Wait, let me think ...'

She paused and then said, 'But of course, there was Professor Fragaria, she had problems of that kind. Then members of the Department of Philosophy at the Arts Faculty, though not all of them. And one colleague at my faculty. He was dead scared of the head of department. There was something personal about it, too, but I didn't know what, but whatever it was it had trickled down from the political plane. It was there and I remember him saying he couldn't write. The numbers of people kept from writing by fear were huge. These were people who'd had a knuckle-rapping perhaps before something had come out, right? And for whom it was a sort of hint that if they carried on in the same way, they'd hit a brick wall. So mostly those folk took the precaution of not even trying. One woman who did have a go is Professor Fragaria, she got a knuckle-rapping, and that colleague at the Department of Philosophy of the Prague Arts Faculty, he did as well. They couldn't hold any office. They weren't thrown out, they simply became creatures under constant surveillance.'

I thought I'd ask Professor HorMi, who was now the only one from among the Hungarian scholars visibly following the conversation, about how different the situation was in Hungary.

'Did you ever encounter a case of someone being sanctioned for overstepping the boundaries, for publishing something they shouldn't have?'

'There were several. There were campaigns. The calculation of when they would occur was not possible. Let's see the eighties, for example: in the mid-eighties there was a conservative turn, it was a period when Kádár started to decline and the new conservative, would-be Communist leaders appeared on the scene not too long before. In '85–'86 there were several measures taken by the Communists against the freedom of intellectual life: banning journals, articles and such, because they stepped over the boundaries [with] a topic, a theme. For example, literary journals like *Fatáj* published in Szeged, *Alföld* published in Debrecen dared to say more than had been approved by the then political leadership. Maybe that one or two years earlier these articles would not even be noticed. But at that time there were wars, struggles within the Communist leadership and that produced a cause, the image that the articles were dangerous. I want to demonstrate that there was no permanent logic of how the leadership, the political elites, reacted to the incidents of intellectual life. There was a dialectic, a dynamics, whose unpredictable characteristics depended on the internal dynamism. Those articles which produced angry reaction at that time were unimportant two years before.'

Professor Hedera suggested that, in a situation where one could not find set down anywhere what was permitted and what was not, there still was a way of getting ahead and doing something interesting.

'The main thing was not to start having doubts about whether a thing was permitted or not. Like for many years I'd been a member, actually I'm still on the committee, of my discipline's professional association – from '64 right up to the present day. Through that entire time, right through the period of "normalization". All our undertakings were guided by the desire to be sort of acting [openly]. If we wanted to do something that needed people from abroad brought in, our chairman would write to the Ministry of Education about it. They didn't reply, because they'd no idea what to do about it; since they hadn't replied, he took it as read that the thing hadn't been banned. And it was also then that we set up a private foundation with the hundred thousand crowns – a lot of money back then – the association inherited from a certain professor, whose express wish was that we'd award an annual prize to the best work by rising stars in our field.'

Mrs Euphrasia completed the picture of institutional strategies by remarking that if the political pressures applied to managers in academic institutions generated persecution, resistance, solidarity and exploitation, they also opened opportunities for seeking personal profit.

'[Jaromír] Obzina's section of the Central Committee oversaw science [and education],[11] the lads there each had charge of a different institute of the Academy. And our Director – I don't know if it was his idea or the guy from the Central Committee's – anyway our Director gave him a contract that meant that he was with us, either part-time or in some sort of consultative capacity, I don't know. So he had a regular income from us on top of what he was getting from his Central Committee job, which was no small sum, seven or eight thousand a month. It's true he was there quite often, but my point is that he did have that income, right? And then when I told my husband about it, he said: "Blimey! He's at our place as well. I'll have to check." And he found that the guy had the same part-salary at that other Academy institute. How many other institutes he was in charge of I've no idea. That's the way things worked, that's how the Central Committee handled the institutes of the Academy [of Sciences].'

I was not sure that I understood correctly that a repressive and directly censoring measure could, paradoxically, have the opposite effect.

'Does that mean that the Central Committee's approval was secured by offering people a place at the trough and in that case they'd let it lie? So they weren't there to spy on it, but to be bought over?'

'Maybe in the fifties people were in earnest, but in the seventies it was more and more of a farce, done deals really. Previously people might have been let into the Party on the basis of a kind of conviction, but now it was all about snouts in troughs.'

II

After the coffee break that followed this insight into the possibilities of subverting surveillance, I wanted to know more about the personal negotiations with power. With the institutional terrain so difficult to navigate and woven with few marked paths, with the constant need for alliances and with the

---

[11] Jaromír Obzina (1929–2003) was a member of the Central Committee and during normalization headed its variously named departments for tertiary education and science. He was also the Minister of the Interior for a good part of the period.

surveillance of unknown extent by the Party, the rank-and-file academics must have treaded carefully every step of their way to survive as professionals. Mere *survival* within an institution would have been the primary goal of many immediately after the vetting in 1969–70. The personal issue everybody had to solve next was at what cost one could *continue* one's work, for the political conditions did require everyone to make adjustments.

'Somehow I managed to stay on at the Institute. It was at a price though, understandably,' Doctor Sambucus began, 'you had to hunker down sometimes and attend meetings that were not at all nice. Then one time I had some trouble with the secret police, but I survived somehow.'

'You only need to look at *Sociologický časopis* in the seventies and eighties and see the things being written,' Professor Stachys took the subject onto the ground of concrete scholarly production. 'Either it was harmless, but utterly flat, with no originality, no spark, or there was a battle going on. 1970 was the centenary of the birth of Lenin. That caused a huge battle over who was going to produce an article on "Lenin as Sociologist" for *Sociologický časopis*; you understand, it was like buying an indulgence. "Me, me!" So *Sociologický časopis* had five articles come in on "Lenin as Sociologist". And look who won! Did him no earthly good at all.'[12]

Professor Fragaria shrugged. 'Under the past regime, the way things were was that a bias towards the natural sciences and technology was a direction that seemed to mean not getting soiled by contact with the regime, whereas a bias towards the humanities did mean getting soiled by the regime,' she explained. 'Which is why many people steered clear of the humanities, which in turn meant lower levels of remuneration and fewer opportunities in humanities teaching or research, and that explains why we were left with women, because for them it's a cheaper job. For them it's pin money, and men, well, they ruled the roost in technology and the natural sciences.'

'The burden was that decent folk could not go in for a proper career. Whether in politics, or in scholarship either,' Professor SorBus confirmed. 'Really, if you were let down by a partner, or, I don't know, there was actual infidelity, such catastrophes were vastly greater than they'd be normally because in those years this was the only realm where we could live in dignity and meet people

---

[12] *Sociologický časopis* has the following article by a member of the journal's then editorial board with a title similar to the one given by Professor Stachys in 1970: (Urbánek 1970).

without needing to ask if they'd been expelled from the Party or just struck off or how things stood generally, see? Everything worked along personal, friendly lines, so on the one hand it was a huge boon to experience, because any one of us could have spilled the beans on our friends twenty times over, but it didn't happen. It might have happened elsewhere, I'm not suggesting that people were always fantastic, but that private realm counted for a great deal, but equally, when something in it blew up, it was a much greater tragedy than it might be normally. It's an experience of a completely different order. Although … it's said, for instance, that one's children were hostages of the state, which was obviously so.'

Doctor Hyacintha remarked that she herself had to change her academic environment in order to stay employed as a professional. She elaborated, 'As late as the summer of '69 I was still teaching the course [which related national history to the history of art], but in the summer of '69 it was clear it was the end, the course didn't stand a chance. When I heard the then minister Hrbek's speech on reinstating departments of Marxism–Leninism and the role they were going to play, I gave in my notice and I was very fortunate, because a friend told me about a sociologist's job going at some planning body.[13] So I switched to a completely different field and a completely different kind of work. I started working in an office, with a job as a planner. Unlike my previous situation, the hours were fixed, we sat there from morning till evening, and every time we got to our feet, we had to log where we were going, where we'd been, and they even kept a close eye on what we were actually doing, like really working or just reading. That "just reading" looked rather suspicious, but at the planning institute I had a constant urge to learn things that might come in handy. I imagined that in, I don't know, three to five years I'd be able to go back to the university and that by then I'd have a better understanding of certain things, I mean things like lifestyle or how a place is run and stuff like that, and that I'd have got some useful terminology under my belt; that I'd simply bone up on things that might well prove useful at the university. I kept visualizing a return to teaching, given that I'd found it hugely enjoyable the last two years. I'd had a real sense of the students' interest, how attentive they were.'

---

[13] Jaromír Hrbek (1914–92) was the Minister of Education of the Czech Socialist Republic between August 1969 and July 1971, that is, during the period of the normalization vetting.

'I don't want to appear defensive, or be thought to be making excuses for myself or whatever,' Doctor Hepatica interjected, 'but it was important to make any change of direction in good time. Changing to another subject than one based on ideology, since the economy was functioning normally and you could describe it without having to say that Husák or the 14th or 15th [Party] Congress had passed this or that resolution.'

Professor Helleborus, who also changed his research direction at the time, looked at her and said, 'If I'd insisted and carried on with, carried on writing, I might well have been able to do it through [the theme of nations]. That's certainly possible. But I thought, why should I bother arguing the toss with anyone over it?'

Assuming that people either managed to stay in their jobs by changing their research topics or managed to find new jobs outside the community in which they and their political involvement were known, the need for caution would not necessarily have gone away. As we already know, the political conditions in academic institutions kept changing. Professor SorBus suggested that making oneself invisible was a useful strategy in later years.

'The first thing [the head of the Prague department] asked when we met up was: "How was the case of Comrade Z resolved?" I said: "The case of Comrade Z was resolved by the regional Party committee." Officially he wasn't allowed to teach. [Now and again] all the sociologists from the three departments would meet for an awayday somewhere and he would harangue us. Those inevitable three-hour lectures of his wherever it was. But we always left Z and some of the expellees at home, with "flu", in case something cropped up that might lead to their instant destruction.'

I turned to Professor SalVia, who described her working environment as a marginalized group, although she was too young to have any political stain on her employment record traceable to the Prague Spring, 'Were you in a marginalized group deliberately, voluntarily, because of wanting to avoid positions that were or might be exposed politically?'

'[I'd have avoided] anything at all involving a political, I don't know, way of thinking or employment or anything, so being where I was was perfectly tolerable, because I didn't mind it, having chosen it myself. I did mind, who wouldn't? And if I wanted to, I expect I'd have found a way, but at the same time, because you can never be too sure of yourself, I always contrived some sort of safeguard deliberately, so as not to sink into complacency. So for me it was an odd sort of time …' She paused and added, 'I was pretty much unaffected and I had nothing to complain about, whereas those colleagues [of mine] did have a bad time of it.'

'We did have problems around the time of the vetting, or later, if someone somewhere wanted to progress,' Doctor Hepatica began to sum up. 'If you were after a habilitation (*docentura*), they'd start poking their noses into the kind of things you wrote and how they were written. But if you didn't want anything and got on quietly with being a pensioner, and an invalidity pensioner at that, nobody poked their nose in at all.'

Professor Helleborus added, 'The issue was always the rules of the game, and you had to know what the rules were, and there's the question of who did or didn't abide by them. But if you did know the rules of the game and kept to them, then actually your bounds were pretty clearly defined, and they weren't even that small, I reckon. But the rules of the game had to be known.'

'How did you find out what the rules were?' I asked.

'For a start, a worm keeps crawling back down the same hole, but human intelligence is better than that. In other words, you discover when you've hit an obstacle, or where someone else has. The basic rule was not to go on the attack, not launch into any kind of offensive actions, just not be provocative. That's one thing, but the other is that within any discipline there were things that were sometimes more possible, sometimes less. I wouldn't dare claim you could put some kind of time-frame on it.'

'Sociology got round it partly,' Doctor SiLena pitched in, 'and that's a problem that besets us here to this day. I'm more into empirical stuff. That was simply one way out, because with empirical data – like when you've established that, I don't know, 30 per cent this and 50 per cent that – there was nothing they could say against it. So by that token there weren't those areas of friction. In empirical sociology areas of friction are fewer.'

I was not satisfied with this somewhat static description of the ideological environment and wanted to hear more about how the researchers adjusted their research interests, the language of their texts or the structure of their argumentation to the conditions in their fields that I knew were changing.

Doctor Sambucus must have sensed my thoughts, because he said, 'Well, there were articles, and then there were the special measures the Party took – ideological conferences – where the social sciences were discussed, so I found the right part and tried to get a sense of what it might mean. Because there were stages when, for instance, it was the declared intention that the only social scientists who'd be allowed to stay at the Institute and in the Academy [of Sciences] generally would be those who were Party members. So to me that was relevant, because it would mean I'd have to start looking for something else before it was too late. So of course I was alert to developments and to whether things were going to go off in that direction or not. But was I vastly seized by the problems that figured there …? You could always find something lurking in the background, but you'd have to be an insider, because you'd need to know what currents were flowing inside the Ideology Commission and what that meant for other things. But that was often beyond my powers of discrimination.'

Doctor Stellaria agreed that one had to pay attention to the political discourse of the time. 'For one thing, I always followed politics, obviously, here *and* there. So I'd simply leave a chapter out, not write about it. I knew you couldn't write, for instance, about the Catholic case against abortion, so I just didn't touch the subject. It wasn't there, so it couldn't get anyone thinking, because I knew I could be compromising people who were actually on my side. It's really a mechanism of voluntary collaboration, you might say. It even showed up in things like this. I'd be silly to stick in a quotation from some, some papal what's-it … and so put [the editor] on the spot.'

'I didn't suppress anyone, not even Orwell,' Professor Lilius disagreed with the strategy of omission, 'but it was a critical element, that's for sure. But it was good in that I was at least giving some information about them, so the students had that information. I expected [the regime] to last a bit longer, true, but there was definitely no one I deliberately avoided.'

He brought the discussion round to the subject of self-censorship and so I asked everybody, 'Do you think that your texts were affected more by censorship or self-censorship?'

'Censorship,' Doctor ForSythia responded promptly, 'that's for sure.'

'Self-censorship was so powerful that …,' Professor Stachys began to disagree, but unable to find the right words, said instead, 'And not just self-censorship, but also friendly censorship, of one another. Things like: "You're mad! That's pure suicide! You can't write that!" I think it probably worked.'

Doctor LoTus also did not think that he encountered much actual censorship. 'Nobody made cuts in anything of mine. With my first book, that was the first instance [of censorship], I expect that conditioned me for the later ones, so in future I'd know what not to do. What I was told was less about what was in it – we were all sort of aware of the limits of what could be published – and more about what wasn't. Like it was a bit short on Marxism, so I tacked on a page or so of Marxist literary theory.'

If pre-publication textual censorship was so rare, I wondered, how about post-publication censorship? I asked Professor SalVia if she knew of any case among sociologists of sanctions for something someone had written that they should not have.

She shook her head, 'I don't think so. Given there'd already been the self-censorship and censorship. So it couldn't even have appeared. It simply couldn't have come out. The editors – subject editors, editors in charge or whatever they were ...' She seemed puzzled. 'I don't quite remember.'[14]

I didn't try and prompt.

There was a lull in the conversation. I realized that my mentors were waiting for me to ask about the obvious: their personal involvement with the Communist Party as a strategy or compromise at the nexus of their personal ambition to continue their work and the various institutional pressures. I had no intention to ask the question, out of tact. Yet, this was the direction Doctor SiLena now took.

'It was probably expected that the people who'd been taken on [to be employed at the Institute in the years after the vetting] without a Party card would gradually set about getting one. A failed expectation in my case. With some colleagues the department did get its way. And others later left because of the stress.'

Doctor LupiNus nodded, 'In about four years, I made it up to [the approximate equivalent of] senior lecturer. In '74 I was summoned in to be told I had to up my profile. There were three options and I had to decide on the spot: join the Party – ah, sorry, *joining* the Party, that was a problem because at the time there had to be one member of the intelligentsia to three workers, and not many workers were rushing to join – *apply* to join the Party, take a course at VUML, or start work on a CSc. thesis.[15] I took the CSc. option. So in '74 or '75 I started work on that. In '83 I submitted my thesis – that was a big problem

---

[14] Chapter 5 will pursue the issue of the various forms of textual censorship in greater detail.
[15] CSc. stands for '*Candidatus scientiarum*', roughly an equivalent of a PhD.

at the time, the lack of submissions: those who could write weren't allowed to, and the young ones either wrote rubbish, if they were functionaries, or they couldn't be bothered, so I ended up waiting ten months – that was against the law, by law the deadline for approval was three months – before the board met. Despite that, what turned up was: "Comrade, where's your VUML certificate?" In short: "If you're doing a CSc., don't miss out on VUML." So I had to take a VUML course. What a joke they were! So I'd kept getting by, getting by, until the Department was being reorganized in '86 and there wasn't a single Party member to become Head. And I'd, like, already submitted my application, backed up by the VUML thing. This was *perestroika* time, I gave the nod, put my application in and thought, they won't … because it was never that simple, more like a title fight, see?' He paused a fraction of a second and added, 'They got me into the Party in '86.'

Professor SalVia did not look at him, when she said, 'I'd lived through a ban on my further education, and that left me with a lifelong sense of gross injustice, and the main reason I was determined never to join the Party was that at some stage in life one might start feeling accustomed to enjoying certain benefits, which were unquestionably there, and start seeing oneself as something special, someone special, who's entitled to decide about others – like how others had decided about me back then. Ultimately, viewing things at a greater remove, you have to conclude that, basically anybody's capable of anything, to coin a phrase, because all those stories from the Soviet Union – it's utterly horrendous and to this day I really do think anybody's capable of anything.'

Nobody seemed to want to break the silence that followed her words. I suggested a short break to let some air into the room and to stretch our legs a bit.

III

When everybody settled back around the table, we tackled the last aspect of survival strategies in institutions: not just how to *keep* an academic job in the vetting of 1969–70 or how to *continue* one's scholarly work if one passed the vetting, but how to *develop* one's research interests *meaningfully*.

Professor Sinapis was the first to speak.

'I admit that any manoeuvring that went on was less at the textual level and more on the level of personal relationships. After '69, the upper echelons, including the professions, were filled with lots of people I'd also known previously and who were in a way conscience-stricken. They felt that something had happened that had put them on top, with a career, and a salary, and I don't know what else. And later on I did exploit a few of these people and they were a bit like battering-rams, helping to push through the work as a whole rather than me having to think about how I should write or amend something. So like I say, I didn't bother too much about the wording of a thing, I mean getting it into a shape that would sort of pass muster, it was more that I made these people my tools and was convinced it was a good thing. I would just go along and see them and they'd say: "Okay, I'll see what I can do." And that peculiar coalition here of friends and enemies from various quarters, it really was quite an interesting sub-system, inaccurately described as the "grey zone". Because there it was a case of what I believe is to be found anywhere, that there are certain "schools", certain communities, that give priority to their own people. And I'd left my community and gone elsewhere, though the community was sort of still, up to a point, inclined to get such people involved and back in the fold, though they could never admit as much officially.'

Doctor Stellaria, who could not publish under her own name, identified one such place, where she could continue some of her work thanks to personal relations. '[One] editor at Svoboda – her husband, they got divorced later, he was a piece work, [there were] about four of them like him, Party henchmen who wrote the worst articles[16] – she also had to be in the Party, working at Svoboda, and she knew I was one of their authors.'

'She was an editor-in-chief [at Svoboda], very fond of literature, and she had the extra asset of feeling pretty secure, with an ex-husband in the Culture section,[17] Mrs Euphrasia also recalled that same editor. 'Her current husband was [high up] at one of the institutes of the Academy. To a large extent it was she who made the decisions and she was someone you could talk to.'

Authors' textual strategies were on the programme the following day, but I thought we could at least touch on them briefly now, as they related to the networking strategies we were discussing.

---

[16] She probably means newspaper articles, which in turn would imply the *Rudé právo*, the Party daily and therefore a newspaper with the largest print run.
[17] That is, of the Central Committee.

Professor Helleborus began by explaining his approach to composing research and publication proposals. 'You made the case somehow. Then within the work itself it didn't matter that much, but in making the case for any proposal to be submitted, you always got it in there somehow. It might be something along the lines of "developing the theories of Marxism–Leninism". Sounds wonderful, eh? There can be no objection to developing theories.'

'I created my own sort of [vocabulary], not that I'd ever been forced to, because the nature of our work didn't demand it, since we were writing technical things, analyses, but in the preamble we always had a suitably worded paragraph on the successes of socialist agriculture,' Professor SalVia added about her use of a similar strategy in research reports. 'We treated it as something of a joke, we were more like having a bit of fun, but for me personally it didn't mean a thing.'

'I had to include commie sentences like that for instance in my CSc. thesis, and to this day I'm ashamed of them,' Doctor ForSythia insisted how acutely personal her own use of the ideological language still felt today. 'In the Conclusion, I had to have them there. What's worse, they came from some Soviet Communist Party conference and they were totally stupid quotes uttered, I think, by Andropov, who was only at the top for a few months before they removed him.'[18]

'What kind of things did the editors or other readers of your texts ask you to change before it was found acceptable for publication?' I prompted Doctor Stellaria, who struck me as more specific than the others about the nuances of scholarly language of the time.

'Well at one time you couldn't quote Fromm, another time you could,' she replied. 'Or this, for instance: "Hey, you ought to have 'socialist society' here." To which I said, "Look, but that's silly; I'll put 'our society', okay?" "All right then." That happened all the time, or: "Stick in a few quotes from some Ameri ...", she corrected herself, "'Soviet." So in went the quotes, or footnotes referencing to Soviet sources. Such was the requirement that there was.'

Her response suggested that although one had to 'learn' the ideological language, its function or that of politically appropriate citations was really

---

[18] Yuri Andropov was, of course, not 'removed', but died in February 1984 after a mere 15 months in the post of the General Secretary of the Communist Party of the Soviet Union, most of which time he spent in hospital.

to keep up an appearance of ideological compliance.[19] Authors saw these 'implants' as separate – and by implication, separ*able* – from the content of their texts. Already the policy-related documents allowed this conclusion. I now wondered where else the strategy of keeping up appearances may have been used.

'People at the institutes would write the kind of stuff described by some as "Christmas science", Professor Stachys chipped in with a mischievous smile. 'They'd start on something in November because bonuses were paid out in December, see? In November you'd write a two-hundred-page research report – on research that basically hadn't even taken place. It was just so much hot air. And three years later, you'd take it out of the drawer, dust it off and do a re-write, get it? There'd be nothing on topics that were taboo, generally it was prescribed topics. Smart folk, of course, managed to find a niche to suit them.'

Doctor Hyacintha continued by pointing out that even the ideologized language could be put to practical use.

'That narrow circle of specialist readers would appreciate the fact that certain overlooked entitlements, or some imbalance, got an airing. On the whole, the case being made was more important than any form of words. The more telling the argument – like when someone was able to spell out how crime prevention was better value for money than caring for jailbirds, once young people had lapsed into that adverse stage – if they could calculate that. If they could make the case for certain expectations of how the disabled be perceived, in the sense that in Japan it took, I don't know, under two years for all barriers to wheelchair-users to be removed, so there's no doubt that in our own socialist society … and so on, you see? Really, on the whole, what mattered more was that the case being made should be in some way useable, because the assumption was that – it's a lovely expression, they called them *decizní orgány* [i.e. decision-making bodies, an inelegant neologism in Czech] – these decision-making bodies needed a well-constructed case so as to be able to get whatever sensible objective through. They needed it to be as intelligible as possible, they had to get their heads round it as quickly as possible, and it had to be nice and easy to grasp so that they could reproduce it and so push it

---

[19] This point has been frequently made in memoirs and also by other researchers, e.g., (Voslensky 1986: 28–9; Filipkowski et al. 2017: 148). Marek Skovajsa and Jan Balon call the practice 'ritualistic citations' (Skovajsa and Balon 2017a: 74).

through. You were aware you were no spokesperson, but that you could offer someone an argument that might produce a change – and that even that was a success, for someone to repeat it somewhere and perhaps drive it through.'

*

This game of perceptions and appearances implies an important feature of state-socialist academic life: the necessity and even the priority of ideological appeasement over scholarly content. How this integrated into the stages of the actual publishing process will be our subject in the next chapter. Still later, we shall take on the subject of how the participants in this process continue to maintain that their work *was* scholarly and that they are regarded *as* scholars by their peers today. Nevertheless, before we get into those discussions, several researchers will have more to say about strategies – intentional, born of necessity or thrust upon them – of moving on with their work that went a fair bit beyond personal relations and keeping up appearances: turning a discriminatory measure into a professional advantage, creating alternative professional spaces and in few rare instances also bypassing the system by publishing under a pen name and by confronting the system's restrictions directly.

*

Professor Stachys responded to the bullying of the system (and his supervisor) with a buttock-clenching stubbornness to outlast them all and to keep abreast of his discipline by exploiting the resources that remained available.

'Throughout that time we still got the main sociology journals. At one o'clock I got up, went for lunch and at two sat myself down in the university library. At that hour I still had strength left to work and I did work happily until six. On my desk I had a little sign that said "Don't lose your head!" Because that was their objective, wasn't it? How they wished to see us take to drink, start neglecting ourselves, give up reading and stop caring about anything. That was exactly where they wanted you. That was their line of attack.'

Unprompted, Doctor ForSythia added her own experience with discrimination of another kind – gender discrimination. 'I have to say that always, even as a teacher, I've always felt a bit like – but it's still the same even now – like that I have to be cautious, and that I'm a woman as well, right? It *is* a disadvantage.'

I did not understand. 'In what way did you feel it, the fact that you're a woman?'

'For example, when the timetable was being set up, well, somehow, whatever was left over was given to a woman, see? Men contrived to choose what suited them. If someone had to go somewhere, an outside lecture, or like when we had to go and see students in their hall, it was the women who did it. When someone *had* to be sent to Moscow say, on a compulsory study visit – it *was* compulsory, someone *had* to go – it was me who went. I'd got three small children and I had to go. I was there for two months and it was also interesting, those two months were great, because I used to go to the INION – that's the library for *inostrantsy*, foreigners – and it was there that I read up on Husserl, 'cos they had him there.[20] On proper open access in German. They'd got everything. But only for foreigners, not for Russians. That was where I prepared everything I needed. While here I'd had awful problems. I might phone the Patočkas at home, hoping for access to his works.[21] I'd found out where his descendants lived and asked them if they'd mind lending me the books. They wouldn't, they didn't trust me. I don't think they trusted anyone. And in Russia, at the INION, I could read it all. The file I brought back with me was huge, all the things I needed, you see? There at the INION they even had books by Czech philosophers who were banned [at home], and I could take them out and read them – just like that, in Czech!'

'So in the end, being a woman turned out to be an advantage.'

'It turned out to be an advantage! But I had to go, 'cos the men weren't going anywhere, so I *had* to go.'

In the case of Professor Stachys (who was struck off the Party membership list during the vetting), as in that of Doctor ForSythia (who was a Party member), however, the superior intellectual gain of this discrimination-turned-advantage could take the material form of publications for the most part only after 1989. Still, it helped them not only not to get rusty, but also to get ahead in their disciplines – albeit as 'intellectual reserves', so to speak, for the time after the regime change.

---

[20] Institute of Scientific Information on Social Sciences of the Russian Academy of Sciences (INION) was founded in 1969 and still exists today. Homepage: http://inion.ru.
[21] Jan Patočka (1907–77) was a notable Czech philosopher and one of the first spokespersons of Charter 77. He died after having endured hours of police interrogation after his signature of the Charter.

Today, we can read several accounts based on memoirs and also on archival findings on the most remarkable and significant strategy of professional development: the creation of alternative intellectual spaces.[22] This is also where my mentors took me next.

Professor Fragaria recollected, 'We would go there [to Jan Patočka's flat] every week to have seminars of a kind all those years, right up to Charter 77. A number of groups used to go, turn and turn about. And there was a lot ... Me and [Martin] Potůček, who's now a professor at the Faculty of Social Sciences, and many others, we'd meet up there from time to time and, together with folk from Brno who were at the Economics – there is a Faculty of Economics there somewhere, isn't there? – we'd work on grant applications, as they'd be called today – in those days they were like project plans – on the economy, economic development and suchlike.[23] Afterwards we'd hang out at the wellness facility of Prádelny [approx. United Laundries] or something like that – Osvobozená domácnost [approx. Home-help Services], who rented it out – and we'd spend the Friday, Saturday and Sunday chatting about various topics of interest.'

Doctor Sambucus pointed out that the alternative fora were also organized wholly within the official, that is state-funded, structures.

'With various twists and turns things gradually eased up,' he explained, 'and then you could operate within various sort of lateral contexts, like the Society for Science and Technology,[24] where I reckon I did, under their roof, some fairly interesting things. The Pardubice Dům techniky, we had a brilliant lot there. And then there was the Biology Association,[25] of which I was a member, with its environmental section, which was obviously also non-conformist. These were the kind of circles that gradually emerged, up to say 1980 at the latest. They had their occasional problems, 'cos of course they were being watched, but by then it was tolerated. In reality I functioned mostly not in the context of the Institute, but within those groupings, which brought together people from different institutions, mostly, I think, from institutes of applied research.'[26]

---

[22] For details on some of those see (Kabele 2011; Olšáková 2012; Nešpor 2014a).
[23] Potůček offered his and others' perspectives on scholarly life during normalization in (Potůček 1995).
[24] Vědecko technická společnost.
[25] Biologická společnost.
[26] That is, research institutes that reported to various ministries rather than to the Academy of Sciences which covered basic research.

'It could be that I didn't make enough effort, so I've no sense that [the journal *Sociologický časopis*] was closed to me,' said Professor SorBus, in consideration of his own publication possibilities in mainstream titles. He thought for a moment and continued with further examples of alternative communities.

'Look, someone like Professor Stachys didn't come a cropper in connection with '68, he was zapped by his head of department. So for instance, he published in Slovakia. Every two years, we had a symposium at our department, under the heading "The socialist way of life as a social reality". That "as a reality" was of the essence, because of necessity it involved empirical works. If someone produced a screed on what "socialist man" would be like in the future, we didn't take it. And in this forum Professor Stachys could do his thing. Obviously, it wasn't very public. Then we put out proceedings, but it was a faculty publication, so it was accessible, it was in libraries everywhere, but it didn't count for much in reality.[27] Then there was one brilliant thing that gradually moulded us, and actually it disintegrated after the revolution [i.e. November 1989] – by which time we were better off anyway – and that was Pilsen. It was brilliant, it was an invitation-only symposium, and a place where we would meet in large numbers. There were some there who were banned from appearing at any kind of conference, not allowed to say a single word, see? And that [ban] got scrubbed. Every time they said it would be banned next time around, but because it was in Pilsen it got sorted out somehow. I don't know how they did it.'[28]

Professor HorMi joined us again and offered a perspective from Hungary.

'I met several friends of mine with the same direction of scholarly interest, social history. It was the second half of the seventies, turn of the seventies and eighties, friends of informal circles, political scholars and many young "inners", so to speak, were to unite and ask differently several issues: how to outweigh Marxism [and find an approach] that was not oriented to labour history or state

---

[27] *Socialistický způsob života jako sociální realita* (1982, 1984, 1986, 1988). A participant in the seminar, the Brno sociologist Ivo Možný (1932–2016) recollected that the title was formulated as an intentional confrontation with the section of the Sociological Institute of the Academy of Sciences dedicated to researching the socialist way of life. The section 'did not research anything and (...) produced a normative ideological picture of life in a country with advanced socialism. The title, nevertheless, could not well be attacked for being polemical, because calling the socialist way of life a reality was irrefutably politically correct' (Možný 2004: 621).
[28] Smetanovské dny, first held in 1980, then annually till today. For details see http://www.smetanovskedny.cz/en/history-p30.html (accessed 28 February 2017). The catalogue of the National Library of the Czech Republic lists altogether eight volumes of the proceedings from the period between 1980 and 1989; the last volume from the event held still during normalization being ([1989] 1991).

history, one that didn't have any connection to the mainstream – to the then mainstream – which was to some extent a version of the Marxist [approach]. Not the most dogmatic, but still. It was a very important phase not just in my own life, but in the lives of several of my friends and fellows. A decade later we first established ourselves institutionally, establishing – even before the political change – the first Hungarian social history association, an alternative to the Historical Society. These guys from the informal circles – there were several – made up the core of the staff who managed to establish a new type of historical scholarship in Hungary, social history. This institutionalization happened officially in the late eighties when a minor circle of social history was successfully established and started to organize conferences, publications, research projects.'

A quiet chuckle came in response from the virtual space. Professor Laxi must have been listening in for some time. He may have been thinking back to the times of his own adventures with state publishing houses whose doors were closed to him for several years during the Kádár regime. I turned to him, 'Now you're laughing at this, but how did you respond then when they told you that you couldn't publish?'

'I could write for myself, so there was no problem. What I did was that I typed up my unpublished material and showed it to my colleagues here at the institute every Wednesday. They would have a good laugh at it, so it was an in-house journal kind of thing, then I printed it – here, you can have a look.' He held up a thin volume to the camera.

'Personally I didn't contribute [to *samizdat*],' Professor HorMi said. 'I was not an author in *samizdat* journals – journal form being the most important, because very few books were published. I published only once, in the eighties. But from the late seventies I had an active part in *samizdat*: this room [my office at the Academy of Sciences] being the main disseminator in this part of the city. A friend of mine brought copies of these journals here, so this was the centre for this.'

'How did that work?' I asked. 'For me, from what I know about the Czech environment, it's quite incomprehensible that these things were actually stored in an institute of the Academy of Sciences. Did you encounter any political pressure or harassment?'

'No, there was none. Everybody knew, our bosses knew as well that we were sellers of *samizdat*, but they didn't do anything against it. It was not officially, but unofficially approved. [It was] this very specific Hungarian atmosphere characterizing the late Kádárism, meaning the period from the mid-late seventies until the late eighties.'

His recollections did not seem to resonate with any of the Czech researchers. They had to resort to other tricks within their institutions to access literature in their fields. So far we have talked about strategies for navigating the ideological quagmire at home. I wondered how the authors dealt with publishing abroad. Only Doctor Helianthus offered a personal (rather than textual) strategy.

'I failed to get anything published abroad, my boss would never have permitted it. Except I did publish two things, but pseudonymously. In 1968–9 I had a longish stay abroad, and while there I got to know a leading economic historian, and when a volume was in preparation to mark the Keynes centenary, and because that was something I'd done in the past, as I did again later, they recommended I write something for it. So I did, though it came out under an acronym of my name in reverse.'

Nobody has touched on the most obvious approach to push at the limits of official professional *creative* existence: asking the direct question of the appropriate bureaucratic body. Finally, Professor SorBus recalled at least a second-hand instance.

'Tonda [Přidal] went to see the local Party committee – in that respect,[29] Zlín was always on a plane a couple of notches higher when it came to IQ, while at Jihlava it was disastrous – anyway, Tonda went there and told them he'd like to have in writing what he could and couldn't do, and why he couldn't do it, with the result that he got a letter saying there was no reason why he couldn't publish under his own name. Thereafter he did publish things and that was that. I'm not suggesting by this that if everybody had done the same thing it would mean there was freedom, oh no. And that was later anyway, around '79, and Tonda wasn't … you know … worst off were those who'd been struck off or expelled from the Party, they were, like, stigmatized.'

As we made our way to lunch, I reflected on how overwhelming my induction into the setting of my quest to find what is largely absent from the paper highway left behind by the communist regime was. The institutions and people in managerial positions within them functioned within the basic

---

[29] Antonín Přidal (1935–2017) was a Czech literary translator, author and critic.

framework outlined in the policy and policy-like documents produced by the Party leadership. This outline, however, was fleshed out by solidarity and rivalry, by loopholes and games of hide-and-seek, by opportunities of the moment and alibism, and by profiteering and alms handouts. The researchers and editors of scholarly books whose voices are recorded on these pages – my mentors and guides on the quest – illuminated for me three stages of negotiating personal professional survival within the normalized academia: elementary 'survival' (i.e. keeping *a* job in research), survival and continuation in one's profession (continuing to publish and/or teach), and continuation paired with professional and intellectual development (i.e. venturing into new research areas, expanding one's capacity by continued self-education in professional literature). At every stage it was necessary to balance the effort put into achieving one's goal with maintaining one's dignity, with environment and topic changes, with bypassing and appeasing, and with making oneself invisible or confrontational.

*

Now the quest journey can begin in earnest. The mentors will guide the story's novice-narrator through the highways and byways of state-socialist academic publishing, explaining the routes along which articles, research reports and book manuscripts had to travel from the moment the author got an idea, through that idea's materialization in writing, and to that writing's reception.

4

The work

'Driving' a manuscript on the highways and byways of state-socialist academic publishing[1]

I

Walking back from lunch, I visualized the landscape that the policy documents outlined and that now the mentors brought to life: a labyrinth of roads through a dark forest. Scholars were supposed to write and publishing houses to produce academic texts in a maze of institutional personnel politics and oblique policy statements on the 'tasks' of social sciences and humanities. We are not puzzling here over the academic top brass, or 'the normalizers'. Those would have been vetted and trusted Party members with privileged access to publication venues. Their primary loyalty lay with the Party, rather than with the advancement of their disciplines. Our interest is in those who were loyal first of all to their academic disciplines and professions. The respect in which all of the researchers who were now returning to their seats around the conference table were still held by their peers years after the regime change implies that they did, indeed, belong to this latter category. So my first question concerned the navigation device they needed to steer their works towards publication.

'What were an article's fortunes, from the moment of conceiving an idea to write about to the moment of its publication and critical reception? Did you have to abide by a particular procedure, taking certain things into account, did it have to be read and approved by someone, or did the text have to undergo any modifications?'

---

[1] An account of the archival story that is here relegated to the footnotes was published in (Oates-Indruchová 2019). This text is here used with the permission of Bloomsbury Academic.

'Well, someone probably did read it. In the case of academic things, then obviously the editors would sometimes read it and maybe make the odd correction,' began Professor SorBus with an uncomplicated, if indeterminate, recollection of the approval hierarchy.

'And the head of department? Did he have to read it?'

'Maybe he was supposed to, but he didn't. Nobody bothered much really.'

'At that time it was quite easy,' Doctor SzolPi's image announced to the room, 'there was no peer review, somebody wrote something and it was published. It was quite rare that something came back.'

'There was no process that somebody would have to read the work that you submitted, or that you would have to have something like a reader's report?'

'I don't think there were any particular rules except that everything you wrote had to go through the director of your institute. You had to show what you wanted to publish,' Professor Szandiliah corrected the over-optimistic view on academic freedom in Hungary. 'When Penguin published my book, which was, I don't know, three hundred pages in English, who could go through that? He just looked at one page and saw I used the word "'56 revolution" and told me not to use the word "revolution" and that was all the critique I got. Because who could read fifty pages of French or [English]?'

Doctor LupiNus also thought that at least when it came to publishing scholarly translations, the process was fairly uncomplicated and rather dependent on establishing personal trust with the publishing house.

'At the outset, my contributions [translations for a literary review] were passed to the publisher's chief editor for review. My first two. Then it was left to the copy editors. I think because they knew me by then. There was a kind of tacit agreement.' But then he added, 'Original scholarly works were different, they always went through the regular process of external appraisal.'

I turned to Doctor Hyacintha and asked her about publishing research reports in her institute, 'What happened to the text? Did it have to be approved by someone, for instance?'

'Surprisingly not, and I think it was much the same at, say, the Institute of Economic Forecasting.[2] Things always bore the name of the senior person responsible, and that person might have read them or not. He was liable more

---

[2] Prognostický ústav of the Czechoslovak Academy of Sciences (1984–93).

for ensuring timely delivery, for full and proper coverage. That it had all the trimmings, maps and suchlike, but there was no ideological monitoring. It took various different forms. Like in the case of summarizing one of those grand conceptual works on various types of urban development, there had to be an introductory section referring to the objectives of development, and that was supposed to include something along the lines …', she searched for the right word, 'what my colleagues in architecture called "a bit of salad dressing to go with it". I asked how open one was permitted to be, and they said: "I'm sure you know really." And they didn't suggest any great trumpet-blowing was called for.'

Perhaps I had asked the wrong question, it all sounded way too straightforward. Professor Szandiliah had piqued my attention earlier by the offhand mention of Penguin, so I tried a different tack with her younger colleague Professor Szebah whose image pinged to indicate that she had joined us.

'What kind of process was there when you wanted to publish in the West? Did you simply send the article or did you need somebody's approval?'

'In the 1970s, as far as I remember, we first had to get permission from the director, but not in the 1980s, then we were quite free just to submit.'

'You just reported afterwards that you had published?'

'Yes.'

'If you sent something [to the West],' elaborated Professor Szandiliah, 'it was very hilarious in a sense, because you took your writing and had to go through a process of meeting in secret, you had to envelope [the writing] in three different layers of paper and each paper had to be stamped by the official person in the institute. Everybody knew that you knew what you took with you and as soon as you left the country you would open it. It was ridiculous.'

For a while now, Mrs Euphrasia had been shaking her head in disagreement at the idyllic picture of Czech academic publishing. Finally, this former editor in an institute of the Academy of Sciences interjected, 'People who'd been struck off [the Party membership list] or those who were out of favour, they – I'm not sure of the exact details – they were supposed to report what they were publishing to their head of department. It could actually be justified on the grounds of its falling within the discipline or something, so the HoD was entitled to see it, to check it for any snags. People who'd been struck off had to get special permission from their HoD.[3] Once things had got that far, they mostly appeared in academic journals. But people expelled from the Party, they weren't allowed to publish at all. This was applied rigorously and everybody knew who it applied to.' She made it clear that her editorial office had to observe a chain of command.

'Getting up and setting off to a publisher and submitting a manuscript, that was hardly on,' Doctor Hepatica instructed me. 'The way it was with research was that the outcomes of a research paper were also always assessed – there were dozens of research papers, but only one was published, because it depended on what it was and who had recommended it. So ours was a serious organization, doing serious research and subject to regular peer review. A work would be submitted, and a group would convene to assess it. And provided that group – additionally they had to be credible individuals or whatever, people you knew and suchlike – if they recommended your manuscript, then the publisher's door was open to you, more or less. Though they obviously took account of like whether it wasn't off message, in any way. So, if it had been a work involving history, they'd have turned me down, because historians would have taken a different view of it; I'd have to have sung the Party's praises, glorified its history and stuff like that. But in this sphere I had nothing at all to do with the Party and its history, just the functioning of the economy. So if they recommended it, and I've got personal experience of this, the way it worked institutionally was that academic works could only be on the basis of the recommendation of some board or certain competent individuals and suchlike. Say it had been just me, if I'd wanted to produce something for publication, then I'd have been ignored all round, nobody would even have read it. But given it had been assessed as a research assignment, then the HoD was also at the meeting, where he heard about it and where the written reviews were also tabled, so then it could go straight to the publishers. I drafted a proposal – obviously what I submitted was smaller, later the work was bigger, because between whiles I'd worked it up into a book. Then perhaps the same people who'd been at the board wrote again, so I submitted it to them as a proposal to be submitted for editing. What

---

[3] The request for a written review of a proposed publication by the Head of Department (HoD) 'in justified cases' was formalized in the Academia publishing house in 1976. However, the minutes of the Editorial Board of the Academy of Sciences (EB in the text, or EBAS in the references) do not list the criteria for this justification (Minutes from the 43rd session of the 2nd EB, 29 January 1976, EBAS, box 11).

processes it went through there I've no idea. All I did then was submit the manuscript. The man who'd recommended me submitted the proposal. So the arrangement was simply that I'd turn up bringing it with me. I took it along and told them who they might approach for reviews if required. Beyond that I don't know anything about anything.'

I was sceptical about whether an author could be so much in the dark regarding what happened to her manuscript in the publishing house, but before I could verbalize my doubts, Doctor LoTus said, 'Officially things were submitted to the HoD. Ours wasn't a department of English, but Germanic and Romance Studies. So I submitted it to my Head, who was a Germanicist. And he said: "I'll see to it that someone goes through it to see whether it's any good or not." I didn't try to worm out of him who'd been through it, though I guessed and I think I guessed right. I don't know if anyone read it with a view to putting me right somehow, but I don't really think so. At least I had no sense of anyone looking me in the eye and saying: "Comrade ..."' He tapped his finger on the book lying on the conference table before him. 'The reviewers are stated here. I assume it was a formality on their part, and I assume somebody else read it as well, which might well explain the three, nearly four years it lay around, ready to go, at the publishers.'[4]

'And no one told you what was happening to the manuscript?'

'No, they didn't do that, basically it was all secret. I wasn't told and even now, after so many years, I'd dearly like to know what went on during those four years.'

---

[4] Although the experience of Doctor LoTus was with another publisher, in the Academia publishing house a three- to four-year production time after the manuscript had been accepted would have been usual, rather than exceptional, and would not necessarily imply political difficulties. The delays were caused by at least three structural factors, functioning as censoring mechanisms: fixing the publishing plan a long time ahead, backlog in the printing house and paper quotas. Academia's publishing plan was fixed two years in advance (Minutes from the 33rd session of the 2nd EB, 19 December 1974, EBAS, box 11) and had to be approved by the Presidium of the Academy, while the Editorial Board merely proposed it (Minutes from the 9th session of the 2nd EB, 28 September 1971, EBAS, box 9), and at the beginning of normalization also by high Party 'bodies' (*orgány*) (Minutes from the 14th session of the 2nd EB, 7 April 1972, EBAS, box 10). Academia's contractual printing house had at least a three-year backlog (Minutes from the 3rd session of the 1st EB, 24 March 1970, EBAS, box 9). If the annual reports on the activities of Academia call the situation at the printers' 'unfavourable' (*nepříznivá*) in 1972 (Minutes from the 14th session of the 2nd EB, 7 April 1972, EBAS, box 10), by 1989 they use the attributive 'catastrophic' (*havarijní*) (Minutes from the 52nd session of the 4th EB, 16 March 1989, EBAS, box 17). Finally, Academia had the same paper quota for books in 1953 as it did in 1983 (Minutes from the 108th session of the 3rd EB, 24 March 1983, EBAS, box 14).

His response raised the issue of the connection – or disconnection – between a professional and a political peer review. I asked Professor Szebah whether she was aware of the two review processes in her time in Hungary.

'It wasn't formalized, but it happened from time to time and it was case dependent. Formally, I submitted a publication to one of the Hungarian journals and they did some partly political reviewing, so it was not always professional, but that was their internal matter, I never got any review as feedback like in Western journals. What you learned was just the end result: if it was going to be published or not, but you never knew who reviewed your piece.'

I wondered how far this lack of transparency went and asked Mr ErIgerus, who worked as an editor at the Academy of Sciences before he transferred to a publisher of popular science, to comment on what Doctor LoTus and Professor Szebah had said.

'It all started with a publishing plan, and that had to go of course to the Ministry of Culture, Division III, the division responsible for books, for approval. Nominally, they were there to coordinate matters so that different publishing houses didn't put out books on the same subject. To what extent they allocated paper, I don't know. And I expect it was the case that if something [untoward] caught their eye, then ultimately what happened, when the publishing plan was given final approval, was that the book simply vanished. But as I say, I don't know how the various levers worked, so I can't say. I didn't have anything more to do with it until the moment they informed me that my publishing plan for the coming year had been approved.'

In other words, not even the editors had a clear picture of the reviewing process.

'Officially, approval was given by the chief editor, but some levering did go on. After that, well, it looks as if they only bothered checking after a thing had come out – at least on the evidence of one case, when a reaction came from the Central Committee only after the book was out. The assumption was that we'd exercise self-discipline,' Mr ErIgerus drove the point home.

If Doctor LoTus puzzled over the existence and identity of the political reviewer, Professor Lilius felt that in his case there were no such mysteries.

'I was writing this massive tome and I didn't get it finished and submitted to the Academy of Sciences until '85 or thereabouts. By then things were getting a little easier, it has to be said, and yet there was a professor there as chief editor, and then two others: a woman and alongside her on my book another editor, who was that utterly vicious kind of ideologue, an avowed, staunch Stalinist, whose job was to check it out for any "ideological" failings.'

Professor Helleborus threw his hands open, as he asserted, 'There were two academic reviewers, right? And the way it was done was largely formal. There was no problem about that. The moment you moved into the 19th century, there was a special rule, and now I realize it wasn't really quite free of censorship, that things about the 19th and 20th centuries were basically political – it was never said in so many words, from when till when – but such things had to be read by someone from the Institute of Marxism–Leninism of the Central Committee. They weren't censors, more like the most seasoned ideologues. And there was one brilliant lad there to cover history who'd really deserve …' A shadow of a smile passed over his face in reminiscence. 'He was our shield, as they say, he did read things.'

Political approval then played a part in certain subjects but not in others, which was immediately confirmed by Mrs Euphrasia, who offered an insight into the higher echelons of editorial work on a politically charged scholarly work.

'Look, [the manuscript of an encyclopaedia] was sort of sifted, screened more than once: first there was the chief editor, he was accountable for everything. He then appointed a kind of liaison officer who was really the main sieve and he had lots of others to cooperate on all the different areas.'

She compared this practice with her later experience in an editorial office for popular science. 'There were some topics that they [the Division for Book Culture of the Ministry of Culture] had reservations about as possibly troublesome. In such cases they'd insist on a particular reviewer. Sometimes by name, sometimes from a particular institution – mainly that meant the Institute [of Marxism–Leninism] of the Central Committee.'[5]

---

[5] The Academia publishing house had a special body, the College of Peer Reviewers (*lektorský sbor*), instituted in 1972 and revised in 1978, from among whose midst were recruited all peer reviewers (Minutes from the 14th session of the 2nd EB, 7 April 1972, EBAS, box 10; and 35th session of the 4th EB, 14 May 1987, EBAS, box 16). Every member of this list had to have an approval from his or her HoD and be vetted by the Party, as well as by the appropriate Scientific Committee of the Academy of Sciences. In social sciences and humanities almost all of the reviewers were Party members, only the lists of the Scientific Committees for fine arts and linguistics included a significant proportion of non-members (Minutes from the 35th session of the 4nd EB, 14 May 1987, EBAS, box 16). The Scientific Committee for the particular discipline could appoint a peer reviewer outside of the list only when it argued that the regular list did not include a specialist in the field of the publication in question; the nomination was subject to the consent of this reviewer's

'The way the system worked was that people would come in from outside offering titles [to an editorial office for popular science],' Mr ErIgerus added. 'Any manuscript that was slightly controversial in period terms, which was anything that fell within the social sciences, had to have the blessing of the Institute of Marxism–Leninism. Officially, if memory serves, these papers were signed by the Director of that Institute, but we had our own kind of contact man there, we called him the Forgotten Devil, and he was a really super guy who, now I weigh it up with hindsight, took amazing risks and helped ease the passage of our manuscripts. We'd always take a manuscript to him at the Institute of Marxism–Leninism, or he'd come and collect it if we phoned, and it would remain in his charge as reviewer for a time. In the end he'd just take a sheet of headed paper, write that he recommended it for publication, possibly after certain amendments which he indicated, or which he would specifically go through with us, but it was signed by his Director.'

The projection wall suddenly went blank. A power outage. We took a short break while I used the mobile phone to call our Hungarian participants and ask them for patience. In the meantime, we had to continue without them.

II

In 'driving' their manuscripts towards publication, the authors and editors showed a good deal of reactive resourcefulness in their confrontations with communist 'highway patrols'. But did they also act proactively? Did they try to push on by finding byways in anticipation of the roadblocks that *might* lie ahead across the main roads?

'In the eighties things were more or less strung together in such a way that it was possible for you to publish your first book,' Doctor Helianthus assessed his own trajectory of publishing difficulties after 1968. 'That was when I openly published mine on the economic history of the first half of the 20th century,

---

HoD. The implication of this mechanism is that – for better or for worse – a relatively small group of people (several dozen, depending on the particular Scientific Committee) acted as both scholarly and ideological gatekeepers at Academia. If an author or a manuscript aroused the ire of a particular individual, there was little chance of seeing the manuscript in print in this publishing house. On the reverse side, however, if a Scientific Committee befriended a peer reviewer from the list, it acquired a channel through which manuscripts could be shepherded towards successful publication.

'cos I reckoned the topic was tolerable enough to permit it. Though even then it was the case that I had to find "acceptable" people of note to recommend it for me, 'cos even in 1980 it was unthinkable for Academia to publish a purely academic work without it being reviewed by the right kind of people, properly vetted.'

'In my own case, if the editors were at all edgy, I might hope to take it to someone who'd rubber-stamp it in his own name,' Doctor Sambucus agreed. Seeking out favourable reviews even before these were asked for was apparently definitely useful.

'Institutes and institutions had their research assignments. For those assignments to be evaluated, for institutes to be seen to be active, they had to be published,' Doctor Helianthus argued. 'That way you were gradually – this was my case as well as others' – slotted in: I began in '74 with my first major publication, when, as part of a research project on the economic history of the first half of the 20th century, I worked up the sub-topic of the 1920s, which was published in-house as part of the overall project in the form of a short-run print. Of course, even that was a complicated matter, because my superior, who I'd done it for, didn't want to sign it off himself for printing, but said plainly: "If you can find someone kosher who'll review it for you, it'll come out. If not, it'll end up on ice." In other words, there were two things that mattered, and they were general: first, people who, in the parlance of the time, weren't "kosher", couldn't publish for general consumption, but only as in-house prints. The second condition was that you had to find reviewers who were recognized authorities in the field, but were also kosher and could endorse it for you. So, once you'd achieved that much, you'd crossed that most perilous hurdle, that is, being pronounced to be actively publishing, if only in specialist terms and for internal purposes. Then other developments followed. Invariably, even later, when it was [possible to publish] in such journals as *Český časopis historický* or have your own book published, which I didn't manage until the eighties, though I'd had it ready long before, I still had to find people, not so much the publishers, but individuals, who'd act as your reviewers, that is, vouch for you and bear the brunt of any trouble that might arise – which didn't happen often, but there were cases.'

Mrs Euphrasia grinned, 'Thing is, institutions [that is, institutes of the Academy of Sciences] had vast sums available to pay for reviews, and we could buy a reviewer, right? I mean in a good sense of the word. Everybody needed money and those folk might even get the thing done overnight, knowing they'd get paid in a couple of days' time.'[6]

'Obviously things varied from case to case,' Professor Sinapis agreed. 'When I submitted a manuscript, that's where you get those strokes of luck, I chanced on responsive copy-editors. That an editor was responsive showed in how she simply said: "Yes, I'll do everything I can to ensure it comes out." And then the ordeal began. I mean the readers' reports. They were always devastating. They would ask the Political College and the like to provide them.[7] But I would always take some initiative of my own as well. Like, having a director who'd once been on the Central Committee and was a person of note, as a philosopher in inverted commas, a professor and Lord knows what else besides, I put the problem to him quite openly: "I've got such and such a thing to be published and I need a review or reader's report." Obviously he was very tough, but he *did recommend* the thing; "tough" in the sense that he had to have his reservations, about me being off-message ideologically and other stuff like that. In other words I always got what I was after. My initiative, with the aid of friends, [amounted to] swaying certain reviewers, or they might just suggest the kind of reviewers who were high up in officialdom, and though they might be known to lack integrity, they did know their way around the subject, so everything balanced out. So some kind of recommendation was

---

[6] Briefing materials for the EB meeting in December 1985 suggest that peer reviewing could, indeed, be a lucrative side job. They include an analysis of the implications of a new Academy of Sciences internal regulation for the peer review process of books and articles. The internal regulation itself was to implement the Governmental Decree no. 298 (Usnesení vlády č. 298) issued at the end of 1983. The Decree and the internal regulation put a limit on the number of hours an employee could work outside his or her main contract under simplified tax conditions: a total of 90 hours per year for all employers combined. Anything above that and up to a half-time equivalent required a regular employment contract, which was subject to the main employer's consent and to full taxation. The practice in publishing houses, and not just in Academia, was (and, largely, still is today, at least for book manuscripts) to contract peer reviewers under the simplified arrangement, stipulating the number of hours per item. Often, as the briefing materials state, journals made only a verbal agreement for article reviews and paid the authors summarily for all such work once or twice a year. The complaints noted in the briefing materials were that the new obligation of formal written contracts exponentially increased administrative load in the publishing house, put in danger the quality of the peer review process and discriminated against peer reviewers from the Academy of Sciences, with whom now these additional contracts at Academia could not be signed, because they were employees of the mother institution, while legally, the option that they would do the work for free was complicated. The intriguing part of the argumentation is that peer reviewers often exceeded the 90-hours-per-year limit. That was perhaps natural, given that Academia could approach only those listed in the College of Peer Reviewers, but testifies to the not-insignificant financial incentive to oblige the publishing house (Minutes from the 19th session of the 4nd EB, 17 October 1985, EBAS, box 15).

[7] The Political College of the Central Committee of the Communist Party of Czechoslovakia (Vysoká škola politická ÚV KSČ).

always there, if with a recommendation for some reworking. Then came the reworking stage, a bit akin to walking a tightrope: deleting certain sentences, altering certain words, inserting certain words, so honour could be satisfied both ways, yes, but there was always a limit beyond which you couldn't go. So, that was the second stage. Then there was the third stage, re-submission, this time it went to the editor-in-chief. He knew it was a delicate issue. And in one instance here I had a huge stroke of luck, because I was writing about a subject that had a considerable bearing on the editor's private life. He was having a major problem at home and I was writing about that very problem, albeit from other angles, but in one chapter I showed how it all connected up. It engaged his interest in the extreme, so he invited me in and we had a most obliging chat together. He treated me most obligingly, like: "In some respects you've been an eye-opener. We have to get your book published. But it'll take a while." And that while was three years – which wasn't bad going. With my second book it took six years, and believe me, that was a real test of who'd hold out longest. One time later, I bumped into a certain post-November [1989] minister and we compared notes, because we'd used to meet in the same corridor of the same publishers with the same problem. His book had taken seven years as well. Hard science. And even that took that long.'

I noticed an ironical smile on Mrs Euphrasia's face and turned to her for an account of power games played by the Ministry of Culture regarding reviewers.

'I phoned the reviewer demanded by the ministry and told him I'd got this manuscript and needed a reader's report on it, and I expect I said something along the lines of how good it was, I'm not sure now. I took it along to him and he took it from me in the doorway and everything went quiet. In due course our chief editor called me in and she was laughing like crazy. She said: "I've got this glorious letter." It's a good thing she was laughing, otherwise they'd have thrown me out, you get it? The letter wasn't addressed to us, but to the Division of Book Culture [of the culture ministry]. It said: "I've been asked to read and review a manuscript by Mahler on Smetana, which I find unacceptable, and since, having spoken to the editor, I have formed the impression that she is of an uncritical bent, I am sending my report to you."[8] Because he was afraid I might bury it somehow. My boss said at the time:

---

[8] Probably (Mahler 1989). The book was republished in 2004 (Mahler 2004).

"Right, now we've got reason to be annoyed. We've been bypassed and he's charging us with hushing things up." So we were grossly offended. But that business went on for three or four years! We got in some more reports, but all to no avail, because the Ministry said that unless we got a positive report from that particular reviewer, it couldn't be published.[9] The author and I decided we'd have to rely solely on biology working in our favour and that it would all be resolved biologically, because the reviewer was over eighty, and he did actually die, see?' She paused, then added, 'But he could have been only forty.'

Professor Hedera took this as a cue to share her own editorial clashes with power.

'One time, the editorial office had a manuscript by a certain historian, a Party member who'd never got himself into hot water, he hadn't been expelled, they'd kept him in the Party and in his job at the institute, and the manuscript had even reached the proof stage, because we'd put it in the journal. Well, some economic historian – still alive – and a member of the editorial board and a powerful man, felt he was a rival within economic history. He was peed off with him because of some conferences where they'd clashed, in short, he was furious at the man, so he trotted round to the editor-in-chief, without asking the board, and had a kind of word in his ear to the effect that we couldn't possibly publish that author, there'd be a terrible hoo-ha if we did, because of whatever it was he accused him of. It was not at the behest of the government or Party or whoever, but just

---

[9] The case of Daniela Hodrová's manuscript of *Pohyb románu* offers a glimpse of a rather shady instance of peer reviewing – shady by today's standards, but hard to tell how routine it was at that time. The manuscript was based on the author's doctoral (i.e. CSc.) thesis from 1980 and submitted as a publishing proposal to Academia in 1982. The EB approved the proposal in November 1982, but subsequently withdrew its approval in May 1983. What happened was that the lead of the two reviewers declined the job (citing other commitments and health issues) and the manuscript was given for a preliminary assessment to the chair of the Fine Arts Scientific Committee of the Academy (Vědecké kolegium věd o umění). The briefing materials for the EB meeting quoted from his negative assessment – one of the rare instances of providing a quote from any reader's reports in the briefing materials or, indeed, any fragments of these reports preserved in the EB archive: 'This is certainly not a step ahead in the sense of Marxist research, but in the opposite direction. I consider the work as ideologically and methodologically very harmful, it would lead literary interpretation toward a relapse into total ahistoricity and deideologizing'. The EB scrapped the proposal on the basis of this assessment, but was aware that rejecting a proposal on the grounds of a preliminary assessment was at odds with legal procedures. Therefore, it made a foolproof decision to satisfy these: first, a new lead reviewer had to be appointed, second, a formal peer review had to be written and third, the author was to be acquainted with the peer review and given the chance to rewrite (Minutes from the 110th session of the 3rd EB, 26 May 1983, EBAS, box 14). Perhaps predictably, the author of the negative preliminary assessment was appointed the lead reviewer in November 1983 (Minutes from the 2nd session of the 4nd EB, 17 November 1983, EBAS, box 15). The work was not published until ten years later, after the regime change (Hodrová 1993).

because the author had done something to this chap, or done something presented as damaging, and for that reason shouldn't be getting things published. The editor was scared witless. I got to thinking: "Well, there's no point getting our whiskers singed unnecessarily, so what to do about it?" The way they did it was, at the next board meeting, the colleague who invariably carried the can for all messes the editor got himself into and dealt with the Party, though the Party actually despised him, said that he apologized for having admittedly produced a positive report on this here article, but that he'd re-read it and was withdrawing his report. He took it on himself so that the individual wouldn't go and take the matter upstairs to complain about them publishing a damaging article. It was only damaging in being in competition with that historian. There wasn't a shred of ideology to it and he didn't even use that kind of argument. He argued that the author had done Lord knows what somewhere or other and was definitely heading for trouble, and we were too for having published him.'

She fell silent. 'So that's how things went,' she concluded what I took to be her scepticism about whether ideological purity was necessarily always the real reason for preventing someone from publishing.

Professor SalVia's face grew darker during this exchange and now she said, 'We would read each other's stuff and suggest changes. At one stage we had a boss of whom we used to say everything depended on whether he woke up a Sokol or a comrade.[10] Because he could either be a super guy or suddenly get the urge to run everything. So one day he came up with something that was supposed to be thoroughly demeaning for my older colleagues, the ones struck off: that I, a mere fledgling sociologist, would check everything they wrote to see it wasn't unsound – at the time it was still reckoned I'd be joining the Party sometime. My older colleagues found it hilarious and said: "Ok, we'll just run things by you." I found the whole thing hugely offensive and kept crying until the idea was scrapped. Because I felt that they felt humiliated and insulted, that there was no other point to it. Otherwise, final research reports were second-read for us by assessors from the Ministry. They were interested to see if anything had any practical applications.'

---

[10] That is, a member of the physical educational and nationalist movement Sokol, founded in the nineteenth century, suppressed during the German occupation between 1938 and 1945, disbanded by the Communist government in 1948, and briefly renewed in 1968–9.

Uneasiness settled around the room as the memories shifted from the authors' struggle with political constraints in institutions, to, essentially, jostling against each other for a better spot in a traffic jam. To brighten the atmosphere, I returned the talk back to the publishing houses and asked if they were all the same or if procedures were different at different publishers.

Professor Hedera was the first the respond, 'The Academy of Sciences was an institution, it had its own publishing house and the point was to keep that publishing house supplied. The state plan for scientific research was meant to secure manuscripts for it, which means that it was, in a manner of speaking, an internal matter. I mean, whenever it was, whether in the sixties or during normalization, all manuscripts had to be submitted through, so approved by, an institute's management. Though I'm talking about those employed at the institution. Both I and my husband have always been employed at a scientific institution, each of us at a different institute of the Academy, so I don't know [what would have happened] if someone turned up out of the blue at a publishers bearing a manuscript.[11] You'd have to ask some copy-editors, there's plenty of them still alive, how it was handled, at Mladá fronta, for instance, somewhere like that.'

Doctor SiLena was not to be roused from gloom as yet and presented a counterview from university publishing. 'No sociology textbooks were published, and coursebooks were produced by the faculties themselves, edited by the normalizers, who had a what-d'you-call-it, *emprimatum* [imprimatur], for the purpose. It was a no-hope situation. The whole field was split, really split, with huge gulfs between.'

---

[11] It is difficult to reconstruct reliably the exact practice of the hierarchy of approvals at Academia from the archival holdings of the EB, because these procedures are not consistently recorded and, anyway, social sciences and humanities were always placed into a separate category, to which exemptions from a general rule applied. What is clear, however, is that Academia had little publishing autonomy: it was a service to the Academy of Sciences that executed the decisions of its Scientific Committees and the Editorial Board, rather than a publisher with even so much decision-making independence as other state publishing houses – a complaint expressed already in 1971 (Minutes from the 9th session of the 2nd EB, 28 September 1971, EBAS, box 9). At that same meeting, Academia was requesting – in vain – a share in the formulation and implementation of the editorial policy of the Academy (Minutes from the 9th session of the 2nd EB, 28 September 1971, EBAS, box 9). Only as late as in May 1987 did the EB discuss the possibility that editors-in-chief of Academia's publishing departments could be entrusted with appointing peer reviewers from the approved College of Peer Reviewers independently of the Editorial Board (Minutes from the 35th session of the 4th EB, 14 May 1987, EBAS, box 16).

'But as you wrote and had to think about what could and couldn't be written, did the process ever vary in any way, according to the publisher, the year or the period?'

'According to the year *and* the publisher,' Doctor Stellaria asserted. 'For instance, in the early seventies there was no problem at all. It was actually worst after Charter 77, it's basically all down to the "chartists", it was them who messed things up, you see. So that was the worst period, up to say '84 or '85, a really tough time, then things eased up and almost anything was possible again. Now the publisher side of things: publishing houses had far fewer problems and less censorship, and the people there were nicer than at, say, the daily papers. The dailies had the closest watch on them. At Mladá fronta it was easier, but again as a book publisher [i.e. not an academic journal – and not of the eponymous daily paper].'

I wanted to object that she strayed into the area of non-academic publishing, but Professor Helleborus preceded me and returned the conversation back on track.

'It was better when [the reviewers] were Party members. It was always better if they were. On the other hand, it varied from place to place. If it was a publishing house that was under the Party's thumb, like Svoboda – I published with Svoboda precisely because it was hiding in plain sight – things came out there that couldn't elsewhere. Those guys could take greater liberties than anywhere else, you see.'

'I never tried to publish anywhere where I wouldn't be allowed to,' Professor Fragaria joined in. 'We were part of a particular group of people who published what they thought important. We had a kind of community of philosophers and humanities specialists and there were things in which we wouldn't have published and there were doors we wouldn't push at.'

'The Nakladatelství politický literatury [Political Literature Publishers] in Revolution Street,[12] I never got in there, despite all the people I knew who I tried to …' Doctor Helianthus hastened with his own example. He broke off and proceeded to explain why one should even try to publish in such a place. ''Cos the whole problem was that at Academia, for one thing, they paid

---

[12] He is talking about the Svoboda publishing house; it went under the above name for a few years until 1965. Doctor Helianthus must be referring to an earlier period than is our concern here, because the last book published by Nakladatelství politické literatury and registered in the catalogue of the National Library in Prague was published in 1966.

peanuts, and for another, if you were an Academy employee, you got no fee anyway, so it was both an advantage and a disadvantage. An advantage in that those who were after money were not pushing and shoving to get in and so your turn would eventually come, and the disadvantage was that you didn't get paid anything. Whereas at Nakladatelství politický literatury they paid 1,800 crowns per manuscript fascicle [*autorský arch*].'[13]

'That was a lot.'

'You're telling me! But that was only for high-ups. Otherwise it was more like a thousand or so. I never managed to get in there.'

'I never tried placing anything with *Sociologický časopis*, because I knew it would never get through,' Doctor SiLena said. 'There things were different again: they had quite a flood of stuff coming in, people being invited to submit things, and it being a journal reserved for the comradely elite. You couldn't get in there ...' She paused and corrected herself, 'Though obviously if you were involved in methodology, you could. That other lot were in there all the time, with their accounts of correlation coefficients. But with a scholarly article I could never get into it at all, because I'd never been invited to offer one. The way it worked was that you were invited personally, and they only ever invited heads of sections – because those section heads published there non-stop. It was a censorship mechanism, because no ordinary person could publish in it. I did publish something at the end of '86 or thereabouts, but it was only a research report thing, which isn't seen as a proper article. So yes, but certainly not an article. Truth to tell, I wasn't even bothered.'

'For my part, I wasn't so active as to have that kind of [overview] of the various publishing houses,' Doctor Sambucus agreed with the 'not bothered' bit, 'so it's beyond my purview. I think most of what I wrote during that time, they weren't articles for *Sociologický časopis*, or books, but whole heaps of, you know, [papers] in various collective volumes from various seminars – today

[13] A manuscript fascicle (*autorský arch*) consists of 20 standardized pages; 1 standardized page is 1,800 characters including spaces; 1 manuscript fascicle unit is then 36,000 characters including spaces. The records of the Academia EB do not frequently mention actual figures, but record the pay grade for each approved publication (at the beginning of normalization there were 8 pay grades), if not the criteria by which the authors were rated. In Academia 1,800 crowns was an honorarium for pay grade 2 in 1970, so the second highest (Minutes from the 1st–9th session of the 1st EB, January–June 1970, EBAS, box 9). The recommendation to favour authors who were also employees of the Academy was issued in November 1972 as an economizing measure and became a regular ground for declining publishing proposals towards the end of the decade (Minutes from the 17th and 70th session of the 2nd EB, 23 November 1972 and 22 February 1979, EBAS, box 10 and 13).

they'd be called "workshops", we called them "seminars" – all about, I don't know, social development, or management of some kind, or, I don't know, migrations. There were huge quantities of these things, things that were printed in just fifty copies, mimeographed, then bound after a fashion or stitched. So today when I look at the list I've got somewhere, I see there's six times as many of those things as things that came out in other forms. They weren't monitored, and may not even have been archived. You didn't have your hands tied with this kind of thing, and so any scholarly [discourse] actually mostly went on in these spheres of publication.'

The discussion on political territorial divisions made me wonder, how full of twists and turns the byways must have been, to get past all the roadblocks.[14] Doctor SiLena straightened in her chair and I knew she was going to add yet another twist.

'Paradoxically, I got my hands on foreign sources via the Political College, which produced translations of [works by] Western sociologists for its own needs. So, given the chance, I seized it and copied things out – Bourdieu for instance. You couldn't cite them, having got hold of them illicitly.'

Obviously, such a politically trustworthy institution could be allowed to publish texts in this 'sanctified *samizdat*', a mechanism that bypassed standard procedures and provided a privileged access to knowledge. Production for general scholarly consumption had to be funnelled through checkpoints to simplify the task of patrolling it.

As if she could read my thoughts, Doctor SiLena continued, 'Our boss didn't solve the problem with cuts in texts; it was solved by them not including your thing in the [collective publication]. You see, I never got the chance to work, or prepare anything, completely independently, that was another part of how they went about things: there were ten to fifteen people in the section and each one wrote [separate] chapters. Things even went so far that some were banned from writing chapters at all, because they weren't trusted – I was, that's not the point – but only some could do the writing and the rest were there to

---

[14] As with everything in a centrally planned economy, the territory of scholarly publishing also was divided into specializations by a directive from above, in this case in 1972: Academia was to publish basic research and, selectively, also textbooks, manuals, popular science and encyclopaedias, while Svoboda and Pravda were to focus on the history of the Communist parties and labour movement, as well as political literature (Minutes from the 108th session of the 3rd EB, 24 March 1983, EBAS, box 14).

help. Then, if this or that chapter failed to gain approval, they just left it out, out of the book in question. First they'd give it back to you for reworking, but clearly that wasn't on, given that reworking could end up with the text being degraded, and I refused to re-do anything, so that's how it then ended.'

Just then the power came back on. I tried to call the Hungarians, but reached only Professor HorMi.

III

I had barely hung up when Mr ErIgerus began to describe a whole new set of traffic barriers set by the ideological patrols.

'Then of course there was all that wrangling: in the eighties we started to take over a number of Western encyclopaedias and the condition was that we had to translate also a Soviet children's encyclopaedia. And then came the boycott on the part of the staff, so we portioned up the encyclopaedia and handed it out to various experts to translate and adapt the entries, and it dragged on for so long that by the time three volumes of the Western encyclopaedia were out, there still wasn't one bit of the Soviet one to be seen. Basically, so we could publish certain books that were at the outer edge of what was possible at the time, the editorial office had essentially been commanded to do one or two propaganda books a year for schools, marking various anniversaries: February [1948], the October Revolution, I don't know, the Duchcov railway bridge incident[15] and suchlike. Basically we were also under orders to do translations of Soviet popular science books, and I think that, with few exceptions, we always managed to choose things that at least weren't too rubbishy.'

Doctor LupiNus added that a similar practice existed in the field of literary translations too. He said, 'At the time, [the journal] *Světová literatura* [World literature] had a policy: one-third communist bloc, one-third developing world – where they also put Chinese classics – and one-third West.[16] So it was

---

[15] A bloody encounter on 4 February 1931 between the demonstrating unemployed led by a Communist senator and the gendarmerie.

[16] This practice is quite possible, because the content of journals was more carefully monitored than the content of books. The EB evaluated the journals published by the Academy of Sciences every year as to their scientific and ideological content and their structure was closely watched. The Academy published 67 journals throughout normalization, all of which had a strictly defined size, which means that their editors did not have any flexibility as to the number of pages of individual

hard to get things accepted, 'cos with [all the] English, French, Italian prose, verse [and so on] – see? So later on I'd talk to them first and gave up doing things on the off chance. Of my early attempts, I gradually managed to lodge maybe a third of the things I offered them.'

Somewhat to my surprise, because I did not think this point was relevant to Hungary, Professor HorMi spoke up.

'The idea [of a new journal] came from several of us, mainly historians, working here in the 1980s. We started to organize ourselves in a much wider circle, integrating philosophers, sciences …' He paused for reflection. 'We wanted to make it an official, legitimate [journal], but it was not successful in the long run. There were several attempts. First, there was a law in the socialist period that a journal was allowed to be published only by an officially accepted organization. Therefore, we proposed to the leaders of the Historical Society, to establish a separate section within it, a youth section or social history section, which would be able to publish a journal under its own name. We started to negotiate with the leadership of the society in the 1980s, it took years but it turned out that they were disinclined to allow the establishment of this separate section. So this idea of the "king's road" at the end of which we would be able to publish a journal of our own was an illusion. There were other attempts, but until the second half of the 1980s, due to the rigid attitude of those privileged and deciding these issues, they all proved to be failed attempts.'

'There were production deadlines, plans and this and that,' Professor Sinapis tackled the issue from another angle. 'Whenever something didn't get into the

---

issues. The paper allocation and, therefore, also the decision on the structure of the journals came from outside of the Academy, from the Czech Office for Press and Information (Český úřad pro tisk a informace, ČÚTI), although the Academy had its representative there (Minutes from the 25th session of the 2nd EB, 28 March 1974, EBAS, box 11). As in other instances, here also the dual pressure of structural censoring mechanisms and ideological censorship cannot be separated: when the EB recommended in 1977 that articles by international authors be allocated a maximum of 15–20 per cent of the overall journal content, was it motivated by increasing budgetary and paper quota difficulties, or by the increased political pressure after Charter 77? The former concerns can be traced in the archives of the EB throughout normalization, while one of the most salient instances of the latter is recorded in 1977: in the name of making the 'activities of the Academy of Sciences toward ideological and propagandist work more effective', the EB assigned the Academia publishing house to compile a list of topics 'suitable for ideoeducational uses'; these should have included political anniversaries and Academia was to recruit authors (Minutes from the 56th session of the 2nd EB, 23 July 1977, EBAS, box 12). To be fair, the EB issued recommendations concerning the scientific quality of the journals also, such as in 1980 the criterion that Academia's journals published in foreign languages should not be accepting articles by Czech authors that had been rejected by international journals (Minutes from the 81st session of the 3rd EB, 22 May 1980, EBAS, box 14).

following year's plan, it got delayed by a year, and it didn't get into the plan because something else wasn't ready, some reader's report, or the editor-in-chief might say: "No, we'll reschedule it." So those were the official [reasons]. The unofficial ones were always simply the fact that the publishing house itself kept a sensitive eye on what was and wasn't possible. A publishing house would have people who were keen to publish decent books, and they'd watch for the right moment when a book could come out.'

This assessment was reminiscent of the work of the Master of the Revels in Elizabethan theatre. He, too, had to keep a watchful eye that no inappropriate play was performed either at the court (although there, more licence was possible) or for the vulgar public, but at the same time had to maintain a steady supply of entertainment.[17] Editors were the state socialism's Masters of the Revels and the discussion now turned to them.

I asked Mr ErIgerus, 'What kinds of editorial amendments did you have to make in copy?'

'Well, according to my contract I was responsible for "linguistic, factual and ideological correctness". To this day I can remember that ghastly sentence. Obviously I tried to keep my edits as painless as possible.'

'It's interesting that in the production of textbooks, and I hadn't appreciated this before, so much depended on the copy-editor,' Professor Laburnus was quick to confirm Mr ErIgerus's claim as to the importance of editors. 'I found that copy-editors, male or female, were good Czechs and not much inclined to promote the regime. So my hands weren't particularly tied, and when I was worried that my editor might take her red pen to it, I handed her two versions and she said: "Look, Doctor Laburnus, whenever you try to put in a good word for the regime, it ends up sounding quite wrong. Better leave it out and we'll hope it'll pass muster."'

He clearly saw the issue of acceptability as revolving around concrete words, which presumed meticulous attention to all published texts at all approval levels. I doubted that was always the case.

Professor Helleborus confirmed my suspicions. 'The English translation of my book wasn't published entirely legally. Only now, in the 1990s, have I learned how the editor did it. The point was this: everything had to go

---

[17] See (Dutton 1991: 7).

through Dilia and Dilia demanded a reference from the employer.[18] The way I did it was this: I had a letter from the Faculty agreeing that I could publish it provided the manuscript would be read and reviewed at the Faculty. But then I "forgot" to have it reviewed at the Faculty, and gave them the text straight off. They cheerfully sent it on without demanding any review from me. Later on I told the copy-editor at Dilia, "I'm so very grateful to you for that oversight." And she says, "I know." And that happened more than once, them just sending a thing on. Though if anyone had happened to start poking about, well, I'd actually got a publication that hadn't been through the proper approvals process. So that's why I played cautious and tried to hedge my bets in other ways.'

Doctor Hepatica broke in with her view on the editor's motivations to take such potential risks, 'My book sold out fast and the editor said, "I publish plenty of bad things and I am keen to publish good things as well." That was his interpretation to me.'

But Professor Helleborus did not think that was all there was to it and elaborated on editors' strategies with another example. 'I was on the editorial board [for academic publications], I don't know what its proper name was, at Svoboda, and the chief editor for history was Kotek – it was thanks to him – no one else had published them – that that huge series of mediaeval chronicles came out: in a Party publishing house, right, because they'd got money and so could bear the cost, and he made the case for it somehow.[19] The series on Czech history was based there and the editor-in-chief asked me: "Do you know anyone to do the second half of the nineteenth century, I need to move things on?" I said: "Otto Urban does it, he lectures on it." So then I went and told Otto about it [to which he said]: "I've got them in a drawer, the lectures, so why not?" It went into the editorial plan and there was this editorial meeting with various bigwigs, history bigwigs, sitting on it – they're mostly dead now – and one of them kicked up quite a stink saying that Urban was a structuralist. (It was from that milieu that a review

---

[18] Dilia (1949–present) was then the agency negotiating international copyrights; it was also a publishing house. The EB minutes confirm Professor Helleborus's description. Moreover, an author, at least if employed at the Academy of Sciences, could offer a manuscript to a foreign publisher only if Academia was not interested in publishing it (Minutes from the 35th session of the 2nd EB, 27 February 1975, EBAS, box 11).
[19] Ludvík Kotek; the chronicles included, for example, *Ze starých českých kronik* (1975), *Zbraslavská kronika* (1976) and *Husitská kronika* (1979).

later came out, saying how dreadful it was and the like.) My heart sank and I told myself that the whole thing was scuppered. I asked Kotek – he was just sitting there: "Should I say something?" And he says: "Leave it, just leave it." They let the big cheese have his say and left the book in the plan and it came out.[20] If three or four others had chimed in it might have been called into question, but with only one shouting his mouth off and everyone else sitting there and saying nothing, the editor concluded there was just the one dissenting voice and all the others agreed. Then it had to go before the Central Committee, but there you had former fellow students and drinking buddies. One of them wrote how excellent and Marxist and everything it was, and it was published. Which goes to show how boundaries could be shifted.'

Professor Sinapis openly disagreed that copy editors would have held that much sway and said, 'The manuscript of my book was still lying about at the publisher's and I'd go round there now and again and I'd take the copy-editor out for a coffee, over which she'd tell me what was what. And invariably she'd say: "Well, it looks as if we'll have to wait a while longer." Really, the most important thing there was the position of editor-in-chief. He was the decision-maker, and these people were pretty faint-hearted, because he was sort of accountable as supreme censor. So my editor could be as accommodating as she might, but – I don't know about the inner workings – every time, like I said: "The editor-in-chief's still unsure, he's still wavering." When they did finally approve it, it was another two years before it hit the bookshops. So actually we were publishing historical works.'

'It was down to the editors-in-chief which manuscripts never even reached the history editorial office,' agreed Professor Hedera. 'At the journal, I did try with this or that author who knew himself that he did have a chance of getting in. The problem was that a decision had always been taken behind closed doors somewhere where the executive editor had no say.' A split second later, she added, 'Any more than the editor-in-chief even, more or less. The oracle always appeared from somewhere, so the editor-in-chief made life easier for himself by trying to eliminate more rather than less, if you understand.'

---

[20] Probably (Urban 1982).

This last remark stirred Doctor SiLena's resentment and she exclaimed, 'I switched to the Institute of Sociology, and what a shock that was! There the head of section censored every sentence, every article, every word.'

Heads of sections in research institutes would have a similar gatekeeping function as the editors-in-chief in journals and publishing houses – and probably without the redeeming necessity to cooperate with the authors, because they did not have to worry about any yearly publishing plans. They were responsible that the institute produced work according to the state research plan and that the results were duly reported – where and in what form, that was another matter as we have already learned.

'We carried out sociological projects and every year there was a final report on the empirical research, and we each contributed a chapter to the final report. It was a collective job, but mostly it was signed by our boss alone,' Professor SalVia expanded on the list of abuses committed by the 'bosses'. 'It invariably bore the name of the boss "et al.", and while mostly there might have been the ten names of the people involved listed on the title page, bosses were quite resistant to having individual chapters attributed to their authors, because that would show that the boss hadn't actually done any part of it. And that was very widespread, I think it went on almost everywhere. Bosses were busy running things and didn't have time for research, but they needed publications. It wasn't till '76, I think, that we won the right to be identified in our chapters – otherwise, come '89 we'd probably not have had a single publication to our names.'

A fleeting and somewhat bitter smile of recognition passed over Doctor ForSythia's face. She said, 'Connected with one of my scholarly articles, I translated about sixty pages of the philosopher I was writing about, and because it was translated, it could be printed and published. But it only came out on condition that the head of department wrote a foreword.'

'What got published was mostly books by people who were someone's friend or acquaintance, or who came recommended,' Mr ErIgerus summarized laconically an editor's perspective. 'Someone could simply turn up at the publishing house and I'd get a phone call or some message from my superiors that the person in question should be accommodated. So that was the other way round, but to me basically another form of censorship, because publishing a book by someone like that, when I was ninety per cent convinced there was no need for it, meant scratching something from the plan that one would have been glad to publish. So in effect censorship worked that way too. Restricting a publisher's scope through the paper allocation, forcing inclusions in the publishing plan, in part for ideological reasons – like those translations from Russian. Hmm, and then there were the friends who needed some extra income. One interesting thing was the different royalty rates. Most fees were actually calculated by the number of sheets, because only exceptional authors had a contract that gave them a lump-sum payment, rather than a percentage from sales. But besides that there were different rates for "Meritorious" (*zasloužilý/á*) and "National Artists" (*národní umělec/umělkyně*)[21] and they fell into completely different categories of remuneration.'

The room was brimming with the energy of righteous outrage. It was time to unwind over afternoon coffee.

IV

Refreshed and in a much better mood, perhaps we could explore a more positive side of the system of fast lanes, that is, personal favours. Professor SorBus seemed to share my view, because he said, 'I did a rave review [for the publishers]: that we'd be missing out, so they should all think hard about it. There were those turns of phrase like if we wanted to let bourgeois literary scholarship have the edge on us, so be it, then we'd better not publish the thing, though it would be a terrible shame not to. Of course, it wasn't a magic formula that would always do the trick, I'm not saying that, but the [woman] editor deserves to have a monument put up to her, and the editor[-in-chief] as well.'

On occasion, the political capital of those in positions of power provided an opportunity for expressions of individual solidarity, as Professor Lilius remembered fondly. 'On the verge of the 1970s I'd gone to the GDR and a colleague of mine, who I knew, was there, heading the Soviet delegation. After dinner, he invited me for a vodka. We went to his room, he took a bottle of vodka out of this old suitcase he had and poured out two *stakan*s, as they call them, we downed the vodka, then he pointed up at the chandelier: "Let's go for

---

[21] These were titles arising from awards, distantly akin to MBEs and OBEs in the arts. – Translator's note.

a stroll." So he, as leader of the Soviet delegation, had his suspicions – probably rightly – that his room was bugged. So we went to the park, where he shook my hand and apologized for the invasion [of the Warsaw Pact into Czechoslovakia in 1968], which for him had been a terrible day. And then [much later] he wrote to the Academy of Sciences, which was actually what enabled me to get my book published.'

'In our environment articles would appear in a completely different way,' Doctor Stellaria dismissed such sentimental recollections. 'For instance, I was in jail and needed to assign my copyright for a book – it came out in Svoboda in the first half of the eighties – and I was a contributing author, but obviously not named. I sent the copyright via a fellow prisoner, inside her genitals, because as a "mere" prostitute and petty criminal she had access to a normal lawyer.'[22]

'Obviously not named'? She apparently saw the removal of the author's name as a facilitating measure, rather than as coercion, although it was a concession to the ideological power all right and she could receive no credit for this publication. I was going to press her on this, but Doctor Hepatica was quicker.

She leaned forward and declared, 'With the very first one it was like this: some man was preparing a volume and he knew I was interested in the subject, so someone approached me on his behalf to get me to write something for it. Well, I did, and there were no names given. The man who published it took [the whole volume] on himself and I've never ever spoken to the other people who also contributed.'

I had to concede that at least some of the time, when editors and publishers removed authors' names, they did not do it for personal gain, but in the interest of the publication itself – and perhaps also as a gesture of solidarity.

---

[22] 'Copyright', an English (i.e. 'capitalist') word, is an unlikely expression to have been used during normalization, although as the EB minutes document, even a state-socialist publishing house cared about the authors' consent to publication. How consistently and whether only in politically sensitive cases, such as in this one, that cannot be established from my sources. The EB minutes record one case from early normalization when a co-author who emigrated in 1965 threatened to file a lawsuit if the botany book to which he had contributed about 30 per cent (and some other authors had also made minor contributions) was going to be published without his name. The EB feared the legal issues and, therefore, it first put the publication on hold in order to seek a solution and later assigned the chairman of the EB to submit the publication to the President of the Academy of Sciences for approval (Minutes from the 3rd and 5th sessions of the 2nd EB, 13 January 1971 and 24 March 1971, EBAS, box 9). The book was published the same year, citing a collective authorship (*kol.*); even the lead author was removed and listed only as the author of the Introduction (kol. 1971).

For a change, our connection dropped and the projection wall stared blankly at us once more. I sent text messages to everyone in Hungary and summoned a technician. While she tinkered with the modem, we continued from where we had left off.

V

It no longer felt like a quest for knowledge, but like being inside a spy novel. Every step along the way of an article or a book to print surrounded mysteries, concealments, strategic spins on facts or downright misinformation. I asked Mr ErIgerus what sort of a navigational aid the ideological gurus supplied.

'When people at the Institute for Marxism–Leninism wrote their reader's reports, what was their case for recommending that something be published?'

'They never made out a case. Mostly there was no more than a curt statement saying "we recommend that such and such a work by such and such an author be published".'[23]

---

[23] The record of decisions about publication approvals and rejections mirrors the tendency observed already in the policy documents in Chapter 2: from concrete to vague, from more information to less as the years went by. At the very beginning of normalization, the EB minutes relatively honestly record emigration or ideological reasons for withdrawing a book from publication or rejecting a proposal or manuscript, and the grounds for the decision are detailed in the briefing materials. Roughly from the late 1970s, political grounds are no longer recorded, the decisions in the minutes are listed as plain 'approved', 'rejected' or 'put on hold, pending such and such supplementary information.' Only at the first sight non-political reasons continued to be given, such as budgetary reasons and the division of spheres among the publishing houses that I mentioned earlier. From 1977 new grounds for rejecting proposals appear. They could be categorized as 'recycling' (a substantial part of the proposed manuscript has already been published in journals), 'per author allocation' (the author has already published a book recently either in Academia or elsewhere), 'not ours' (the authors are not employed at the Academy of Sciences, but at another research institute or university that also has a publishing house), 'market saturation' (a publication on a similar topic is already available), 'no PhD dissertations, new editions or studies not resulting from the projects within the State Plan of Basic Research' (Minutes from the 56th, 63rd–64th, and 69th–71st sessions of the 2nd EB, 23 June 1977, 18 May 1978, 29 June 1978, 25 January 1979, 22 February 1979, and 22 March 1979, EBAS, boxes 12 and 13). Political reasoning, if it ever appears, is shrouded in vague formulations, typically, that such and such proposal has to be consulted with 'bodies' (Minutes from the 77th session of the 2nd EB, 20 December 1979, EBAS, box 13). A direct request for ideological conformity seldom appears. One example is a manuscript on ecology whose printing was postponed until the authors rewrote the text so that it 'was consistent with the Marxist understanding of the substance of the ecological issue and its conceptual solution based in the Marxist–Leninist scientific world view, as well as in the practice of building a socialist society'. This rare concreteness, however, may not have been what was presented in the official record, because the formulation appears only in a draft and is crossed out in pencil, while the finalized minutes were not preserved in the archives (Minutes from the 12th session of the 4th EB, 24 January 1985, EBAS, box 15). As to the amount of information on the proceedings of the EB sessions, between 1979 and 1982, the briefing materials are not at all or only occasionally preserved.

I tried another tack, 'How were the authors informed that their work could not be published?'

This time it was Professor Hedera who responded.

'At *Český časopis historický* they had a manuscript by Josef Macek.[24] I said: "Here's Macek's manuscript, so let's put it in." Because Macek might have been deposed as director, but the Academy hadn't thrown him out altogether, merely transferring him to the Institute for the Czech Language somewhere. So: "Macek's a rank-and-file researcher, so this article here's no problem." The point here was that if nobody had the guts to say "this could be put in", it was to the general satisfaction of those in power whose responsibility it was because they didn't have to concern themselves with it. But as soon I'd raised the question, telling the editor-in-chief that we could put the Macek piece in, he said: "Wait though, I'm not absolutely against it, but we must go and ask." And there you have it. Where exactly they went to ask I don't know, because they went, as they said, "to the department", which was a department of the Central Committee down there by the river, but which department they meant I obviously don't know, because I wasn't a Party member. It could have been because Macek was too high up – he was also a former member of the Central Committee – so could he or couldn't he? Of course the editor didn't go there himself, he sent a member of the editorial board, his minion who did all his dirty work for him. In this respect the editor was pretty idle, but basically he would send this particular guy everywhere. Whether he really did ask that time or not I've no idea, but the editor came to me and said: "We can't do this. It's got to go back to him." And I said: "All well and good, but how do we get it back to him?" I was thinking they might send him a letter, see? I'd have written to him, I'd have got the message to him, because we did actually meet up from time to time and I could have found a way to get it across. At which point he said: "Hmm, let's keep it here." And they sort of filed it away. When our secretary – who'd previously been Macek's secretary and they'd kept her on at the institute because she knew everything there and still took various materials to him – when she took the materials to him, I said to her: "Look, take it to him and tell him they're refusing to publish

---

[24] Josef Macek (1922–91), Director of the Historical Institute of the Czechoslovak Academy of Sciences at the time of the Soviet-led invasion and a Communist functionary. As the Director of the Historical Institute, he was ultimately responsible for that institution's '*magnum opus*' of the invasion, the 'Black Book' (*Sedm pražských dnů* 1968). For his negative position on the invasion he was expelled from the Party and transferred to the Institute for Czech Language in 1970.

it." So he'd get to know, so he'd know what was what, see? Except the secretary was probably too scared, because my impression is that she didn't tell him in so many words, she just gave him back the materials. She did claim to have told him, but I wasn't there to see. Because I later met Macek and he immediately let fly at me: "For God's sake, woman, is it your role to play the censor there?" I said: "Please, Josef, did our secretary tell you what the matter was?" And he said: "Of course! You tossed it back at me like a bone to a dog!"'

Professor Stachys nodded with sad recognition and said, 'Somewhere about 1985 it was, I did an experiment, an attempt to tweak the devil's tail, a deliberate experiment when I wrote this thing and wanted to test – today it sounds ridiculously naïve – to see if they'd give me a bit of paper saying it was being rejected, my text. It was a book, about two hundred pages. I took it round to Svoboda, Jarmila Oborská was still there, she knew me from our previous collaboration, so I went to see her and she says: "For goodness sake, you must be mad! This really isn't on." I said: "No, I'll leave it with you and you'll let me have a piece of paper saying that the Comrades have assessed it and rejected it." "But that's not on. Surely you can understand …" It was simply a game where for some reason I dug my heels in and insisted I wanted that confirmation in writing. It could have been from a sense of being powerless, like wanting to be able to prove to my offspring that I wasn't a complete buffoon, but that I really had been prevented, you understand? But no proof was to be had.'

He brought the conversation to the authors' own assessment of the quantity of their written work. Doctor ForSythia added immediately her own, quite different perspective.

'I always sensed I was at a disadvantage because I was a woman. I just had this sense, all my life, and it's still with me today. Not so much these days, but I do sense it. Take publishing: for instance, at our institute all such matters were argued out in pubs. I couldn't do that. I did look in from time to time and it even felt quite good. You have a pint and you feel good. But I couldn't keep going there and it was there that all major decisions were taken. So as a woman you went to work and from work and that left you isolated, with no part to play in those discussions, which were vitally important. That was one thing. And then I felt it in an odd way during formal decision-making processes, that as a woman you were simply expected to cope, right?'

We heard Doctor SiLena mention earlier her own share of gender discrimination in hiring procedures and that she was finally hired from her applied research institute by the Academy of Sciences. I thought she was going to return to that now, but her thoughts were apparently running in another direction for her mouth twisted as she said, 'You have to appreciate that I was operating within empirical sociology. In other words not your top-flight, scholarly sociology, not until I arrived here at the Academy institute. But the standard was so shocking, so low that when you had to submit a mere twenty pages a year, well, it came as a shock and I started looking for extra work. Can you imagine what it was like, given I could write twenty pages over three days? What were you meant to do with the other 250 days? A rotten place to work in every sense of the word.'

Her every syllable dripped contempt. 'These days I understand it in terms that the greater your output, the more problems you had. So they had one sociology journal and all they ever did was tasks assigned by the state. A state project might be for two years and the only outcome was one miserable little book. Can you imagine that? That one little book involved thirty or forty people.'

The mention of sociology prompted Doctor Hyacintha's memory. 'In the seventies a colleague and I had a long-term research project, with Pavel Machonin in the background behind us, though his name couldn't figure anywhere. With this three-year project completed, we hoped to publish [the results] in *Sociologický časopis*, but suddenly that was a no-no, because certain names within the social sciences were taboo. I don't know if this was due to an excess of "zeal" on the part of some of the editors at *Sociologický časopis*; they did say they'd take the report, but without attribution beyond the fact that the research was carried out at our institution. That way it was all right. After that we never attempted to get our researches published. There were always just reports that went into the institute archive, or perhaps to the relevant department at city hall, but never intended for public consumption.'

'Scholarly writing, that was quite modest, you know,' Professor SorBus agreed. 'Most of our output here was for the [various series, *Acta*, of the] university. I had the odd thing come out, but there was very little of it, for instance in *Filozofický časopis*, *Sociologický* [*časopis*] – really only ever when the crunch came and you needed an item for your bibliography, so we'd cook something up, but I wasn't really bothered because it got you nowhere. And the prospect …' He left the end of his thought hang in the air.

'If I were Einstein, I might have fought to gain …' He paused again. 'There was no [academic] debate. To an extent I might write the odd book review, but more if I was pressured into it or in response to a request. That was why we didn't write much, at least in my case. Because our main concern was survival in our private lives. That was our shield and a confirmation that there was nothing amiss with us, but there was no chance of any upward mobility.'

Professor Helleborus inclined his head to one side, as if he was trying to reconstruct something in his memory and said, 'I didn't have anything published in the West. No one raised the question, or rather, it was more that I didn't dare try. I can't remember now if anyone showed any interest or not. But I also didn't want to draw attention to myself. I'd have to rack my brains now to piece together how things were, because I know there were things, that someone showed an interest, but somehow it always kind of …' He broke off. 'It was nothing that even I would have taken as being in any sense central, you see.'

It was again one of our editors, Mrs Euphrasia, who supplied a coda to the round of explanations of low publication numbers.

'I was at the Academy institute from the mid-sixties to the mid-seventies. In that period a new director came in, and he knew that as long as a large, multi-author work was in preparation, everything was okay, everybody would eat out of his hand, because he had plenty of money for editorial meetings, all manner of consultations, anything, but as soon as it appeared, the idyll would be over. Everybody would pounce on it and start criticizing. So the whole time I was there nothing at all appeared. All the time it was preparatory tasks, which is the absurdity to end all absurdities when you realize it was ten years.'

The technician finally succeeded in restoring our connection to the virtual world. I tried to call our Hungarian participants again to join us for the last segment of today's discussion. I reached Professors HorMi and Szandiliah.

VI

We have 'driven' the abstract collective manuscript almost to its destination: the printing house. What happened to it there, at the proofs stage? What kinds of criticisms, if any, were raised after it came out?

Doctor Helianthus had a response ready, but gestured that he needed to go back a step, to the reviews. 'In the eighties, or earlier, in the second half of the seventies, the general trend was that if those who would end up accountable maybe thought it wasn't Marxist enough, they'd write that this or that needed pointing up more. Then most of them never checked if it was there and signed on the dotted line. So that's how it should be viewed, because without someone vouching for it, we couldn't have published. Later, at the first stage, there were the [comments] that such and such should have been emphasized in the introduction and that such and such wasn't mentioned, and it was usually sorted out by the addition – or not – of a sentence or two. In my own area, economic history with a marked bias towards statistics and factuality, it was more a question of certain broader conclusions that you had or hadn't drawn. Or all it was about was the kind of tribute you paid to the gods and nothing else, I believe. Which is why these works, and this doesn't apply just to me, but also those by anyone else who was publishing at the time, are of huge value as regards facts and of a demonstrable worth analytically. Of course you couldn't have any conclusions in them, that was something I avoided and I found the perfect weapon for the purpose: if someone recommended I [change] something, I'd correct it on the galleys, then when the page proofs came I changed it back to the original [wording], and I don't think I was alone in this.'

Doctor Helianthus's successful manoeuvring should not lead us to thinking, though, that once an article or a book reached the printing house, that was the end of checkpoints and the destination was reached. The journey of every manuscript, one would normally hope, does not end at the printers', but at the readers. For a state-socialist scholar, readers would be another checkpoint – and not, of course, only in the sense of the scholarly contribution of the work, but also in that of its ideological merits and failures.

Doctor Sambucus gave an example of this post-publication patrolling.

'*De facto* I had a fairly free hand in the area of statistical indices. I think that was really because perhaps hardly any of the people who might have raised objections actually read it. The institute's director once called me in and said how surprised he was that it had come out, seeing it was a positivist work. He said that the subject, its handling, wasn't the least bit Marxist: "All you've got is a few sticking plasters so they'd publish it." On the whole he was [right], but the book was out. It's possible he'd had his say on the manuscript, but he'd let it go anyway. I couldn't say. He definitely called me in – and I really doubt I could have sent it off without his consent. So I expect he said it beforehand.'

We could now embark on the details of the variety and extent of censorship, but that was on the programme for the following day. Instead, I asked my mentors and guides to look back on the whole period from the 1960s, if they saw any decisive turning points in it that affected their own work and scholarly publishing in general.

'There were watershed turning points, but I don't think they coincided with any political or more fundamental changes,' Professor Sinapis summed up his personal trajectory. 'For instance 1977 is seen here as one such turning point – because that's when hold-ups started happening in publishing.[25] Like, I had a book with one publisher for six years before it came out. That entire time went on all the whats and hows. Then when it did appear, it seems to have fitted into a particular period, so there *was* somehow a kind of turning point, but it really was no big deal. So the only big turning point is the time of *perestroika*, say '85, '86, because that's when I went into *samizdat* in a big way.'[26]

No other Czech researcher felt like continuing, but Professors Szandiliah and HorMi wanted to share their Hungarian perspective. Professor Szandiliah began, 'There were waves of more liberalism and less liberalism and a very bad period. I don't think that I published anything in this period. It's sort of instinctive that you know that it is something serious.'

'There was a cyclical movement,' Professor HorMi agreed, 'fluctuation of liberalism – conservatism – liberalism – conservatism, but the inherent attribute of the Kádár regime was not to be so rigid as the Romanian, Czech or Bulgarian [regimes]. At the end of the 1980s, the atmosphere, politically

---

[25] The rejection grounds for publishing proposals in the minutes from the EB sessions suggest that 1977 was, indeed, a turning point in scholarly publishing, when budgetary issues including paper quotas and ideological pressure worked in concert with each other, resulting in stricter limitations on who and what was published.

[26] Looking through the EB archive, one cannot discern any dramatic changes in *perestroika*. Rather, some minor reform tendencies starting already in the early 1980s that did not necessarily point to any ideological relaxation, but to the opening of new, if tentative and limited, spaces for scholarship begin to emerge: in 1982, the idea from above to invite proposals for new journals appears for the first time since the onset of normalization (Minutes from the 97th session of the 3rd EB, 18 February 1982, EBAS, box 14), although nothing came of it till the regime change; in 1987 a reform of the peer-review system that would delegate the authority to choose peer reviewers from the EB to the editors-in-chief was proposed and in 1988 approved, although social sciences and humanities were exempt and the EB retained its authority to appoint peer reviewers for those disciplines (Minutes from the 35th and 41st sessions of the 4th EB, 14 May 1987 and 18 February 1988, EBAS, boxes 16 and 17).

and otherwise, became so unstable in Hungary that the power, the communist power, the central power, power of reform, academic power et cetera, became insecurer and more flexible. I think that this is why it's very difficult to talk about this because there were so many factors working here in parallel and contradictory ways. These instabilities and flexibilities, weaknesses shown by the reformed Communist leadership, including academic and university [leadership], started to show less and less essence of their previous authority.'

The time was up, I thanked everybody for the rich discussion and in a few moments I was alone in the room. As I proceeded to turn off the projection equipment, I recapitulated the gains of the quest so far. The policy documents together with the accounts of personnel politics conjured up the image of a labyrinth of roads in a dark forest. That has only intensified as I listened to the researchers' understanding of the journey of an idea to publication and reception.

Patrols and checkpoints now crowd the image. The authors and editors were sometimes aware of their presence, sometimes only suspected it. What is more, there did not seem to be any magnetic north to provide compass bearings, let alone a map of the winding highways and byways. One had to resort to orientation by stars and tree bark, so to speak. Yet, there was considerable traffic in this labyrinth and the following day we were to talk about the diverse encounters and 'crashes', as the case may have been, in this streaming traffic: about the acts of censorship and about the very concept of authorship in state-socialist academic publishing.

5

The author

Censoring and authoring under state socialism

Despite the black-and-white polarity of good and bad guys implied in the chapter title, 'censorship' here subsumes a rainbow-like range of memories, assumptions, conjectures and ponderings of what happened to the words on a page before they were typeset and after. I tried to avoid the word 'censorship' in the questions I asked in the original interviews. If I did use it, then either only towards the end of our talk or after the researchers themselves spoke about it, so as not to cast their experience *a priori* as censorship. I wanted them to teach me how they themselves looked back on their lives as academic authors under state socialism. We already know that they had to relate their *texts* constantly to the 'highway code' of the publishing process that our imagined discussion group tried collectively to recreate in the previous chapter. We also know that they had to manoeuvre their *physical selves* within the institutional constraints described in the chapters before that. Hence, our next concern is, logically, the *authorial self*.

I

People begin to arrive, help themselves to a hot drink from the side table and take their seats. I had checked the connection to our Hungarian participants earlier, so we could get down to tackling the key questions of the full morning programme right away: How did the scholars think about the texts they were creating and about themselves as their authors? To put it differently, who participated in and was responsible for the words as they were finally printed? What constituted the authorial persona and how much agency did 'it' have?

Professor Hedera did not think censorship was an issue, because she said, 'I worked on topics that I needed. I can't say I was ever restricted either as to topic or ideology.'

'[Final reports from research projects] were very open, there was no censorship there,' Doctor SiLena specified the free arena. 'We were under no influence, it was quite unrestricted. Quite the reverse: directors [of factories], it's quite odd, but this is how it was, they wanted to know what people thought about their factories. I never once encountered having to amend a report in any way. As for volumes of papers [from colloquia], you didn't have to adopt any pose, you really could write what you wanted.'

Professor Fragaria gave them both a sceptical look and said, 'I gave a paper at a conference on the Middle Ages and my fellow medievalists from the Institute of Philosophy, non-Party members, came running along to say: "Goodness, you can't go into print saying it's nothing to do with the Hussite tradition following on into the next period. You just can't, because they wouldn't give the Academy our research funding and we need to research the Hussite period as a progressive tradition so we can do medieval philosophy and the 17th century." So I self-censored out the, as it were, "inappropriate" advice that in scholarly terms things are quite different from how they were presented in school textbooks.'

Professor Szebah, who I only just noticed had joined us, smiled reminiscently at this example of 'friendly censorship' and added her own case.

'[In the 1980s] I discovered that unemployment existed in a very strange form much before [the end of state socialism] and I wrote something on that and I tried to publish it in the formal sphere. Again, unemployment was an issue that you wouldn't write about. And then, it was a very strange experience, in the publishing house where I wanted to publish, one of the main editors there read this piece and then invited me for a [meeting]. He first sat in one room, but then in another room it was just he and I. He said that it was very interesting and shocking, but that he imagined that it could not be published in Hungary. It wasn't published, but it happens you know, so I published it in the underground within a year.'

'I'd be interested to know if you were involved in *samizdat* while being simultaneously employed at the Academy of Sciences, and what effect working in *samizdat* had on your job.'

Before she could respond, Professor Lustani chimed in, 'I was publishing the same in *samizdat*. I put this essay also into one of my edited volumes in 1970, this article was selected for a volume of my writing in an official publishing house. I gave the manuscript to the publisher in 1970, but it came out without this article in 1983. The rest of the volume, which also had politically very blunt articles, came out without a change of one letter officially. So, for me, there was no separate [publishing]. I used to say that if they threw me out of my job it would not be important because I could always translate, I would get by, but they didn't dare touch me because I was protected by all my knowledge of languages: I was the only one who knew some of the languages.'

This dual-track strategy never came up among the Czech researchers as an option. For them, it was state publishing house *or samizdat*. It is then not surprising that they mentioned 'friendly censorship' as a part of preparing their texts for publication. Doctor Sambucus now returned to it.

'Where it was articles, I don't recall ever having any major problems with reviewers, but I did get some important, but fatherly, comments from one *docent*. He said, "Hmm, if you want it published, you should take out this bit and this bit." I don't know what it was about, whether it was the sources I cited or some reference. But it sounded friendly.'

'For instance I couldn't write that a woman's attitude to abortion could be bound up with her religious beliefs, so I wouldn't put the poor copy-editor in the embarrassing situation of having to tell me, "you know, I've got to delete this",' Doctor Stellaria presented another perspective on the 'friendliness'. 'These were the sops to Cerberus I gave in essence voluntarily so as to simplify things for the editors.'

Doctor SzolPi's image unfroze and he picked up on the element of self-censorship.

'Self-censorship in Hungary probably worked somehow that people knew the system enough, and also, sociology is a relatively small group and people knew each other – this is still the case: even in the anonymous reviewer system, of course I know who is the author. We probably didn't want to cause any problem to anybody, so if I wrote something and I knew it would be a difficult thing and submitted it, then I would put the editor in a difficult situation, he would have to tell me that I couldn't publish it. We did not want to harm anybody.'

I could tell that Doctor ForSythia didn't quite agree with this vision of symbiotic harmony as being responsible for censorship and encouraged her to share her experience.

She said, 'The problems were like this: in philosophy, people who ran into a brick wall were usually those who came along with a subject that most people didn't understand. But that's the same today, isn't it? And in order to discredit someone like that, political grounds were advanced. That doesn't happen today, today it's done differently, but it does happen. Those political reasons were usually expressed by someone getting up – for instance I remember – the man shall be nameless – he did philosophy, and of course he knew Marx extremely well, but he found phenomenology an affront – so he got up after I'd spoken about Husserl: "Husserl's philosophy is a philosophy of the elite, a closed community, in 1968 I wanted to attend in person one of Patočka's lectures, and I was told I had no place there." Which can't even be true, that someone couldn't go to a Patočka lecture, they were always open and public. Phenomenological philosophy was simply viewed as a means by which a tiny elite made itself out to be better than the rest, and the reasons given were these: it's an elitist, bourgeois philosophy, a dead-end street from which no change in society can be achieved, because this philosophy actually seeks only to explain, while our aim is to change society. I was extremely lucky that my work and that whole department of philosophers was led by an eminent sociologist. If he hadn't been in charge, I'd have got nowhere with my work.'

Personal insecurities and rivalries appeared to be lurking behind the overt ideological objections reported in Doctor ForSythia's account. Doctor Helianthus seemed to be thinking the same, because he now said, '[After 1989] I had a huge advantage in that I had a drawerful, as we used to say, of material and things ready to go. I hadn't published them before because there'd been problems and [when you were] in our category it was quite tricky to go publishing more than your superior.'

'Actually, the main signature on the final reports from our research projects was our sheriff's,' Professor SalVia added another twist. 'We then had our names on our respective chapters.' She gave a little grunt of exasperation and continued, by association, on our earlier subject.

'He would read the whole thing, so that was the first stage of censorship; already at that stage it [i.e. anything "improper"] wouldn't have got through. And there might be the reviewer acting for the Ministry.' She reflected for a second and said, 'I can't recall.'

'For a text to be published,' Professor Helleborus declared, 'then for one thing it hadn't to contain any open attacks on socialism, could it, or against any authors who were sacrosanct. The other aspect was, I think, that by some means or other it had to be shown to be of some use socially. It had to be socially justifiable somehow, be shown to be beneficial.'

'Did you have any successful strategies to fight the censors?' I asked. 'If they said, "you're not putting that in," did you try to get them to backtrack, and did you ever succeed?'

'In various ways,' Doctor SiLena answered. 'Sometimes what happened was that I realized I'd expressed myself ineptly and tried to change it precisely because it was ineptly expressed and sounded silly. I mean, why not admit it? Then another way: I might refuse absolutely to do anything at all with it, because I was sure of myself, and it got through. And then there was the way whereby they said, "no way." So with each way my own response was different. I didn't really come up hard against censorship until I joined an institute of the Academy of Sciences. I also found something else there: that utterly banal sentences were simply misunderstood and misinterpreted. I was shocked at how they were given a political interpretation. It was explained to me that a banal sentence like "A person is walking along a street" could imply some political problem, and I was not inclined to accept that, seeing it as paranoid.'

A series of pings sounded, signalling that more of the Hungarian participants had come online. I wanted to have a more thorough discussion of self-censorship later, but it seemed the right moment to ask the general question, 'What do you think had the greater effect on your works, censorship or self-censorship?'

'Self-censorship,' Professor SorBus said decidedly, 'I reckon, because censorship was practically non-existent. It did exist, but in the sense that it was people who were censored, not what they wrote. That if you mightn't write, you mightn't. You might pen a paean to Stalin, but it would get you nowhere. And there were such cases.'

Professor Sztipoah immediately followed up with a Hungarian perspective.

'There was this policy of culture and policy of science, Aczél type:[1] three words, TTT, you know, *tiltani, turni, támogatni,* prohibit, tolerate, support. I was tolerated in a certain sense. First of all, music was not so interesting at

---

[1] György Aczél (1917–91) was a high-ranking Hungarian cultural politician in Kádár's government, holding the posts of the Minister of Culture and Deputy Prime Minister.

the beginning for great policy. Music wasn't so rigid, so sectarian, it was more open and that was one of my lucky [turns], to begin as a music sociologist.'

'From the ideological perspective, I would always navigate on the edges of tolerance and prohibition,' Professor Lustani categorized himself.

'I was never invited to the university to teach, never,' Professor Sztipoah continued her recollections. 'Sometimes somebody, Professor Szandiliah, for instance, or somebody else would invite me for one or two lectures at ELTE[2] or at the [Karl] Marx University of Economics, but I was never invited as a professor.[3] I was a Doctor of the Academy, high, but never [a university professor]. It was the same for [János] Kornai and others. They were never invited, we could do research when we had the money or we needed no money, we could write manuscripts, but with the publishing, it depended on the situation. And we couldn't go to the youth, to university people.'

Professor Szandiliah, encouraged perhaps by the mention of her name, came in with a clarification of her situation. 'From the sixties on two universities wanted to invite me as a professor. I knew it because the rector or the head of department who wanted to invite me told me later that they didn't succeed – Berend Iván[4], I think, told me that he had wanted to invite me three times to the University of Economics, but he was always rejected because I wasn't a Party member, but I wasn't a Party member because I didn't want to adjust to ...'

She trailed off, then concluded, 'So I was really accepted to the university as a professor in '89, in '87, until then I was just a senior researcher, but the deal was fine by me.'

It seemed to be an opportune moment to ask her about the censorship cases that were well known and that occurred to people from her professional circles.

'What was the reaction at your workplace when a case of persecution, like those of István Kemény or Iván Szelényi happened?'[5]

---

[2] That is, Eötvös Loránd Tudományegyetem, Eötvös Loránd University, in Budapest.
[3] The meaning here, I think, is to be appointed full professor, a practice common enough then and now for senior researchers at the Academy of Sciences, rather than not to be invited to teach the occasional course or give a guest lecture. Such invitations mean that the person holds the professorial rank and usually teaches something, but his or her main employment remains at the Academy.
[4] Iván T. Berend (born 1930), a historian, the Rector of the Karl Marx University of Economic Sciences in Budapest from 1973 to 1979, the President of the Hungarian Academy of Sciences (1985-90), Distinguished Professor at the UCLA History Department since 1990.
[5] These two cases acquired the status of legends. István Kemény (1925-2008) was a Hungarian sociologist. He was imprisoned after the 1956 Hungarian revolution. After his release he worked in marginalized academic jobs including as a researcher at the Hungarian Statistical Office. There he conducted research on poverty in Hungary and reported on his results in a lecture at the Academy

'Let's say, we revolted. These were usually very critical things, but impotent. Impotent in the sense that Kemény was expelled from the Statistical Office but the Institute of the Academy, which as in the Soviet Union was a sort of an asylum, invited him to do research. The Central Statistical Office was a government agency, the institute was an academic agency. My feeling is that [in the Soviet Union] the function of the Novosibirsk Sociology Institute was a sort of an asylum for those intellectuals who [the state] didn't want to kill or deport or whatever, so they went there. [Tatyana] Zaslavskaya and others went to Novosibirsk, they were distanced from the students, couldn't "infect" the students, but could work.[6] In a sense, symbolically, the Institute of Sociology in Budapest was situated on the top of the Royal Palace hill, as far from the university [as possible], and more or less, in sociology it played this role of an asylum.'

Professor Szandiliah articulated something I had not heard from any of the Czech researchers: a clear dividing line between the Academy of Sciences and universities along political sensitivities as to the amount of academic freedom and access to resources.[7] The Czech situation seemed to be much muddier. Therefore, I now wanted to learn about the experience of the Czech scholars with a variety of structural censoring measures.

'In the seventies it was like …,' Professor SalVia began and immediately reflected, 'I think that it's more transparent nowadays …'

She fell silent, before she recollected with perceptible gloom, 'And then the fear. On the one hand we sensed we'd nothing to fear, that not that much could happen to us. In addition, if you weren't ambitious, what could happen to you? If I wrote one article more or less, that really made no difference. And again, in the case of such unimportant people as I was, I'd find some job or other. I was not in danger of starvation. Not a bit. And yet the fear was there. A friend

---

of Sciences in 1970, after which he had to leave the Institute. In 1977 he left Hungary and lived and researched in France. He returned to Hungary after 1989 and worked at the Institute of Sociology of the Hungarian Academy of Sciences, including as its director (https://de.wikipedia.org/wiki/István_Kemény_(Soziologe) (accessed 8 March 2017). István Szelényi (born 1938) is also a Hungarian sociologist. In 1974, a manuscript of the book *The Intellectuals on the Road to Class Power* that he co-authored with the writer György Konrád (1933–2019) was taken to the West (Konrád and Szelényi 1979). Both authors were subsequently arrested. After their release, Szelényi emigrated, while Konrád remained in internal exile, blacklisted as an author. Szelényi then taught at several US universities, including UCLA and Yale, as Professor of Sociology. For details on Szelényi and Konrád see (Takács 2016).

[6] Tatyana Zaslavskaya (1927–2013) was a notable Soviet/Russian economic sociologist.
[7] György Péteri documented the emergence of the dividing line as an official policy (Péteri 1998).

and I got to musing that it's because humans are endowed with imagination so they imagine all the things, things that might …' She left the verb unspoken. 'And it didn't happen and I don't think that realistically it would have even then. I don't know. It was a time of every kind of lost illusions, because while our older colleagues cleaved to the Party and ideology as something that might lead somewhere, we didn't have this anymore. To us it was plain that there's no such ideology. That there's no certainty either, nothing of the kind. One thing is, and this was odd, that we were forbidden contact with all foreign teams, including those in the people's democracies, so the Poles were too avant-garde for us. This also meant that all kinds of contact with abroad – not that there was the money for them anyway, so no one travelled anywhere – had to go through our admin, but there wasn't the interest because it only meant something else they had to worry about. So nobody prevented us, but it was impossible anyway. People from abroad invariably needed a document to say it was an institutional matter, and if it wasn't, contacts with outside were simply not possible.'

'I started to travel abroad in 1985–6, mostly to the West,' Doctor SzolPi commented.

'That is actually a story,' he went on. 'I think that for Eastern conferences, if there was a conference in Bulgaria, East Germany or the Soviet Union, the Hungarian participants were better selected, because at these conferences it was clear that if you went there you had to be careful what you said, because there were Russian, Bulgarian, East German sociologists there. If you went to a conference in Frankfurt you could say whatever you wanted.'

Professor HorMi seemed to be listening carefully, because he now picked up the strand of structural hurdles and opportunities to make his first contribution of the day.

'In the 1970s, we wanted to be informed widely about new trends in the Western world, from France – *Annales* – through England, to the United States, where there were so many new schools, new efforts, among historians in economic history, urban history,' he began. 'How could that have been possible? A good question. We had a relatively free access to books and journals, secondly, there were some possibilities for travelling, especially for the elite, but with the time passing this provision was offered even to us. I first travelled to the West in 1980. Later when I was here [at the institute] I got an even longer fellowship to the United States in 1984. In this matter, the Soros

Foundation, the earlier form of the Foundation as it existed at the time, not the present-day form, had been a great help in providing the financial assistance to many average people like me – I didn't belong to the elite and this possibility was formally a privilege.'

To the Czech scholars this reversed political logic of travel permissions must have sounded tragicomic. Mrs Euphrasia, at least, joined in with an anecdote in the genre of drama of the absurd.

'With China it was complicated. One of our researchers had contacts there, professors and others. If he was after some book, the Chinese would always reply elegantly: "We'd love to be able to assist, but the library is undergoing reconstruction." "The book is out on loan." You know, the kind of excuses that no one would ever believe. He might write five times, and then his powers failed him because he never got the book. So people like him, there were plenty more at the institute. And what were they to do? In essence they were in service to the Central Committee. Doing summaries from the press. They knew exactly what to focus on. So that was their research.'

Mrs Euphrasia has related already in the chapter on personnel politics the devious ways in which institutions kept control over access to research resources, and the ingenuous ways some researchers invented to circumvent the obstacles. I thought Doctor Helianthus had a similar experience, so I asked him, 'You said you also worked on your own account, besides working on state research assignments. Were you working on an entirely different topic?'

'No, no. You couldn't very well do that at work because at the time there was also the problem of authorizations and things. Although archive applications and authorizations were devised in very broad terms, it was quite impossible to contemplate doing political or cultural history if you were assigned a task within the state plan on economic history.'

'That's an interesting thing,' Professor Sztipoah responded from overhead to Doctor Helianthus's last point. 'It was not a question to publish something. I was employed here in the institute, but I never got [funding] from central funds. At that time I could not find out why I didn't get funding.'

She obviously opted for alternative sources of funding. Doctor LupiNus must have concluded that, because he proceeded to explain why he did not resort to some of the alternative resources in his field.

'Through the entire seventies and eighties I never went near the British Council, or the American Cultural Center. They did send me *Dialogue*, if you remember it. And I got called in by the secret police to check up on what it was I was getting.'

The picture that was gradually emerging from our conversation began to explain why some of the researchers denied any existence of censorship. Every step of who published and where, of the text's journey from a research institute or university department to the printing house, as well as access to resources was peppered with barriers and checkpoints. Those who published within the state structures had to take them into account, but they also perceived them simply as parts of the system. Certain circumstances needed to be factored in, but the researchers did not necessarily feel them as acute limitations to their creativity. I wanted to know more about what kinds of interventions into their actual texts they did perceive as limiting.

'What words, names or topics did you have to omit from your writings?' I asked.

Silence. Then Mrs Euphrasia seized on the second of the three items.

'The problems related to individuals. This one was a pessimist, that one was a bourgeois historian, this one was an anti-Semite, that one had emigrated, and so on. Mostly it was the Chartists, if anyone did append their name [to a civic proclamation]. As a second category, if you were a ballet dancer or the leader of an orchestra and had been expelled [from the Party] you couldn't be named either.'

'Hungarians were okay,' Doctor Stellaria remembered. 'Though again you had to check whether someone like [András] Hegedüs hadn't become undesirable in between whiles, without you knowing he was undesirable.[8] They'd cross it out and say: "Let's get rid of this [Hegedüs], he's a bit passé over there." *Again* that feeling of voluntary collaboration: when all's said and done, I didn't have to publish the book, did I? I could show you three books and how they differ: the Czech edition, the Slovak, the second Czech edition – and then it came out in Bulgaria and Poland, the same book, but any changes in it they did those themselves, because the publishers sorted that out between

---

[8] András Hegedüs (1922–99) was a pre-1956 Hungarian Communist politician. He had to flee to the Soviet Union during the Hungarian revolution, but after his return he worked as a sociologist. In the 1960s he founded the Institute of Sociology of the Hungarian Academy of Sciences, but was later dismissed for his criticism of the 1968 invasion of Czechoslovakia. For more details on his biography and thought see (Péteri 2016) and (Takács 2016).

them. And because they knew you were hidden under a ghost-author (*pod pokrývačem*) anyway, they never came to me about it at all.'

I phrased Doctor Stellaria's experience into a question, 'Did it ever happen that you published an article, and then when you saw it in print the text was different from the one you'd approved at the proofing stage?'

Professor Sinapis exclaimed, 'No, never. Whenever I'd had the proofs, it was always identical.'

'And did anyone ever make you put something in or tell you: "Insert this passage here"?'

'Yes, yes,' he responded with equal vehemence, 'and I have it in writing in those reviews, that on such and such a page it would be appropriate to say such and such, or add this or that source. It was well-meaning on the whole, in support, so as to prevent or blunt possible criticism, and in some cases the recommendation came from conviction. Some peer reviewers were simply convinced I was wrong and that I couldn't write such and such there, and it was put quite strictly.'

'And did you put the things in as demanded?'

'Not usually. Mostly the adjustments I made were just formal things.'

Doctor ForSythia bounced in her chair and interjected, 'The supervisor on my PhD dissertation was great, he let me complete it. The problem was defending it afterwards. To get through the viva I had to put in an extra Soviet neo-positivist. Then I had to put two extra quotes in the Conclusion, from I don't know what resolution of the Soviet Central Committee. It had to be done, or it wouldn't have got through. It cost me huge lot of effort, but the work, on this topic, did come out. But I had no end of problems, not to put too fine a point on it, getting it published. The fact is that I'd originally wanted to write about phenomenology only, but I also had to write about neo-positivism. So I conceived it as two opposites, kind of. And then they also made me, "forced" really wouldn't be too strong a word, to write about their conceptual apparatuses, 'cos it was something akin to dialectical materialism, where the conceptual baggage of Marxism was worked through. So when I employed the phrase "conceptual apparatus", it was as you might say digestible at the time, see? In other words, I occasionally had to use the kind of expressions that had the right ring to them.'

'I'd finished a certain coursebook and they sent it back, complaining that the foreword failed to stress the advantages of socialism in that particular sphere,' Doctor LupiNus added a similar example. 'So I had to put in a couple of sentences that I recalled from some leaflet issued by the relevant ministry. I put one sentence in further on, and in the introduction I said that the matters described evidence the merits of the socialist system. Those were my only little sops to Cerberus.'

'I was lucky in that I didn't write about socialist society, so there was no point in any of that, though it's true that in some cases inevitably ... ,' Professor Helleborus began with some relief. 'For example, when I was working on that Czech book, I'd got a survey of the earlier criticism in it, and then they persuaded me I needed a separate chapter on the classics of Marxism and Leninism, see? I'd got them in as part of the overall context, but it was, like, I ought to highlight them. Which I duly did. Today I'm thinking, when younger people read it, they must think: "He must have been losing his grip!" Ah well, that's the way it is. Interventions like that.'

'I don't recall any particular obstructions,' Doctor LoTus continued on the same subject. 'Though there was that thing with my book, when I was told it wasn't Marxist enough and I ought to have more pages devoted to Marxist-Leninist literary theory. So I added two or three pages of Marxist–Leninist literary theory, which among all the literature textbooks appearing in this country at the time was second to none in how little there was. And given that I'd made doing the book a [socialist] pledge ([*socialistický*] *závazek*),⁹ I was advised by colleagues in the department that the Party congress was taking place, so I could do something with the introduction: "Since you've made it a pledge, shove in a sentence to say you're publishing it in honour of the Congress." So I think the Party congress does get a mention in the introduction. I took it a bit like when Mrs Müller was pushing Schweik in his wheelchair to the draft board and shouting: "To Belgrade, to Belgrade!"¹⁰ So I thought, why not put the Party congress in? Regrettably, but I can't change it, what's done's done. In my mind was: "To Belgrade, published in honour of the Party!" At the time, I don't think I sensed it might act as a brake or was at all significant,

---

⁹ A socialist pledge was a concept usual in the so-called Brigades of Socialist Work (Brigády socialistické práce), workplace collectives that by adopting the label participated in the state-socialist form of competition. It meant making a pledge to deliver some work performance above the usual or contractual quota (i.e. unpaid hours of work). Doctor LoTus's experience suggests that the pledge could have also been individual.

¹⁰ The words are spoken by Schweik himself, not by Mrs Müller, in *The Good Soldier Schweik* by Jaroslav Hašek. In the scene, Schweik, being pushed along in a wheelchair, brandishes his crutches as he shouts the patriotic exclamation on the way to the Austro-Hungarian draft board that will send him to fight in the First World War.

that I could find myself in a heart attack territory. Logically, you exercised a degree of self-censorship, obviously. If you wanted to get something published, I don't think you gave too much thought to what might or might not be okay. But in any case, there probably wasn't much trust in the intelligence or ability of authors to judge what was permitted and what wasn't. So that book, I was simply told it was not very mature ideologically. That was always an argument they could use.'

I wondered whether everybody shared this experience and asked, 'Did the people who read your texts at any of the stages of approval do anything about the empty phraseology, terminology, that was meant to be there?'

Professor SorBus shook his head resolutely, 'No, no. That's the thing about the amplifier of terror: when you're scared, you'll put the empty phrases in yourself.'

In a way, it was a devastating admission of authorial compromise – and, I expect, it must have cost Professor SorBus a great deal to make it. But were there instances when one drew the line of compromise and fought back in an attempt to reverse a censorial act?

'In what way could you gain more space?' I asked.

'General discussion,' Professor Helleborus responded promptly. 'You've got a tough review that says a thing is structuralist or whatever, then you convene a meeting to discuss it, a gathering dedicated to that sole subject, and all those present or a number of relevant authors say that it doesn't strike them that way, that it isn't structuralist – it *is* structuralist – but that it isn't structuralist and that in a nutshell it's quite useful; well, that amounts to a broadening of space.'

Professor Szebah took over from him, 'If they required corrections of things, then I was ready to make them. If they wanted a topic or a part of the writing, then I said "No, I withdraw." There were always people like me who were always on the borderline. I was in the official sphere and worked without a real break in what I was doing, so it was not an interest to push me or people like me into the dissident groups very much. I knew that there was some instance of these negotiations on both sides, so if I say "OK, then I don't publish," then they'd probably give up something, so this was the pattern of negotiations.'

She again brought up that clearly defined perception of limits and options in the Hungarian experience. A brief pensive silence followed. Then Professor Fragaria began to tell her own story.

'In 1974 I was writing a coursebook and, basically, these problems, including the structure of materialism, went in because people found it useful in terms of being able to use it afterwards in explications of, I don't know, literature or history and so forth. There were always ideas floating about for how to get such issues across, in a respectable manner, but without running into trouble. So, I'd written this coursebook and along comes this colleague who'd found a reason for getting rid of our department. His ambition was to wind up as dean or some such, so he persuaded people, in the department too, that my coursebook should be written off and I should quit the faculty because of it. Clearly, if I quit, as one who'd been struck off [the Party membership list], others would follow and so there'd be more space available. I said I was having none of it. And then they all said: "Look, it's done and dusted, he told us." He really was an educated man, so they all had a kind of enduring faith in him, like old pals, so it never occurred to them, his coevals, that this was an unspeakably dirty trick. And at the time I thought: "This is one way to prevent publication of anything that's not quite orthodox, and also, if they chuck me out, they'll chuck other non-Party members out as well, and the game'll be over." Anyway, I found myself a couple of Party members – fair-minded, honourable people – and I said: "Come to the discussion, I won't appeal to you, but depending what comes up, we'll see if there's anything to be done about it." That was to be a [departmental] discussion of my coursebook, which was supposed to damn me for a revisionist. I went to see the Dean and told him: "This isn't something, Dean, that concerns me, it concerns you, because I've discovered that five people have simultaneously labelled me revisionist because of pages x, y and z, in other words, those pages were pre-targeted. Are you going to tell me what to do? Because I'm not going to fight on my own behalf – it's your problem." And he said: "You know your subject, so have some serious answers to the objections ready, and I'll convene Prague colleagues in the field and we'll carry out an enquiry." Well, the colleagues from Prague, irrespective of whether they were members of the Party or not, they all, with the exception of the two I'd invited, who were admittedly unobtrusive, ordinary, folk, said they would agree with me, but that they didn't have the time to come and be present. And they said: "Look, it's not as if we wouldn't support the issue at stake, but someone could take advantage of it. But if we're not there, that's that." So the discussion began. He [the primary objector] rambled on, 'cos it wasn't really his field at all, I showed he was wrong, and finally he said: "Well, clearly these are interesting problems and we shall come back to them." And so [the whole hoo-ha] was nipped in the bud.'

She sat back in her chair and the others pondered the weight of what she had said. Then Professor Sinapis spoke.

'I wrote an article, it had a pretty neutral title, but it was an attempt to give a tough, critical appraisal of the state of our discipline, which had totally collapsed. Of course it came under what was called SPEV – I'm sure you've no idea what that is – the State Plan for Research in Economics,[11] which was overseen at the time by a certain *docent*, who didn't know much about it, but she trusted us and so remained there as guarantor. We produced a volume of papers arising from our seminars, and it included six or seven quite important ones, and one of our circle – we didn't know – but he proved to be a spy, who immediately reported it first to the Institute of Economics, then to the Central Committee, and that's where it was dealt with. At the Central Committee it was decided, on an initiative from that professor-spy, that a series of articles [under the heading] "They're raising their heads" [Zvedají hlavu] should be issued, claiming that there was a danger, at the end of the 1980s, that "our" enemies were regrouping and suchlike. It was meant to be a series, but only the first part came out. And at that time we undertook a massive campaign through various channels to sway the leadership of the ideology section of the Central Committee, and we succeeded.'

The recollections by Professors Fragaria and Sinapis brought the discussion to the type of censorship that comes last in the trajectory of a text: post-publication censorship. Doctor Helianthus seemed to be shaking his head at either the daring or the folly of Professor Sinapis – and, by implication, of his editors, for he now said, 'I always met "responsible editors", that's to say either an "executive editor" or the chairman of the editorial board or publishing house, and they didn't interfere with my text much. What tended to matter more was when someone gave, as we used to say, a "tip-off" to the ideology department of the Central Committee, to the effect that this or that …' He expected me to make an educated guess and complete the sentence. 'That invariably produced horrendous complications all round. Though perhaps less for the person affected, 'cos always, from that moment, all aspects were

---

[11] Státní plán ekonomického výzkumu.

toughened up again. It mightn't go on for too long, but always six months or a year at least.'

Doctor Helianthus put his finger on the pitfall of post-publication censorship: when it occurred, its fallout could reach way beyond the author and editor concerned and affect a whole community or field. I thought I saw Doctor ForSythia shudder at the prospect of such a portent and turned to her inquiringly. She began to narrate, apparently from the middle of a thought.

'Before it was published the article was read by my supervisor, who had me re-work it several times over, but finally he let it go. But although he'd let it go, once he saw it in print with his own eyes, he got scared. Scared of the unseen and unexpected bombshell that would often land back then. These were the kind of bombshells you never expected and from quarters where you least expected them, and suddenly one came and you had to come to terms with it. And once you'd had this happen to you two or three times in a row, you got quite scared, didn't you? During my lectures I never guarded my tongue, 'cos philosophy always got me going. I knew there were informers among the students. I don't know why, I never suffered any come-back for that. The only come-backs I had were for things I'd written. Partly it was the criticisms, and then it was things my colleagues said that had a drastic effect on my confidence: "Ha, you've gone and done it again." Just that. And if you asked: "What have I gone and done, what have I done wrong, what's wrong with what I wrote?", the other party would say: "Come on, enough said, you can't not know." But I didn't know a thing. And that's how my fears grew and grew. Fear was a terrible thing.'

'You said you'd got heaps and heaps of stuff written. Did you try to get any of it printed?'

'Yes, and I was scared. You can't imagine the horrors I went through when the first criticism of my little article turned up. I've still got it at home. It was terrible. I was in a cold sweat because I knew it would be read by A, B and C. Afterwards when you write something and you're seeing it through the eyes of critics and when you know the critics a bit, the text gets sort of recast into something different. Recast into something they'd be able to accept. Well, I'd taken an awfully long time over that article; it only had about four pages. I'd tried so hard to express the ideas in it simply, I mean so as not to upset anyone. Then when it came out and I was talking to my supervisor, he said: "When I opened the journal and saw phenomenology in it, I went all hot and cold." He was scared as well. He was afraid what the response was going to be. When the response came, it was ugly: describing it as having missed the point. Not at all pleasant.'

The gloom in the room could be ladled into buckets. I pressed on, 'So the risk of publishing something was not necessarily that those people were associated with someone personally, but with a publication that had had an unfavourable reception?'

'Hmm, for a long time [possibility of] publication was linked to a person who for one reason or another might not have been acceptable,' Doctor Helianthus thought. 'Over time, nothing ever happened in ninety per cent of cases – though there was for example that case of František Kutnar's *České dějepisectví* [Czech Historiography], or another well-known major case was Otto Urban and his *Kapitalismus a česká společnost* [Capitalism and Czech society].[12] You'd got people who – this was the commonest pattern – raised a query at the Ideology Commission of the Central Committee how such and such a work by such and such a person could be published when that person hadn't conducted themselves properly. Or later there were those notorious critical reviews that created a lot more trouble for the work and the people involved.'

'The review of that excellent book, *Capitalism and Czech Society*, was signed by some guy who was admittedly an historian, but he'd been put up to it by his bosses, and it was vile,' Professor SorBus explained. 'It wasn't signed by some … ,' apparently, the meaning he wanted to communicate was 'one of scholarly stature'. Unable to find the right word, he gave up and continued, 'but by some research fellow. In the end it didn't do Urban any harm. In short it revealed that there were misgivings about him and he could live with that, but it was the end of the eighties by then.'[13]

---

[12] (Urban 1978). Antoon de Baets says the following of Kutnar's case: 'A two-volume work by historian František Kutnar, *Survey of the History of Czech and Slovak Historiography* (Prague 1973–7), and especially volume two, *From the Beginning of Positivist Historiography to the Threshold of Marxist History-Writing*, was severely criticized by J. Haubelt in *Československý časopis historický*. Subsequently, the book was withdrawn from the market and from use in the universities. The Historický klub (Historians' Club) in Prague, a group of historians under Kutnar's presidency who produced politically independent studies, was temporarily interrupted in the mid-1980s' (Baets 2002: 183). The original publication of the two volumes: (Kutnar 1973, 1978).

[13] There are two possible explanations of the confusion of dates: first, Professor SorBus confuses *Capitalism and Czech Society* (1978) with Urban's later work, *Czech Society 1848-1918* (Urban 1982), although that would still be only the early, not the late, 1980s; second, in his memory, he is unable to associate a case of a successful breakthrough against censorship with one of the most repressive periods of normalization, namely the years following the campaigns against Charter 77.

Professor Fragaria was shaking her head, suggesting that the *perestroika* years were not necessarily and unambiguously more permissive.

'We had a motley company of about 15–20 people of every hue – Bohemians, Moravians and Slovaks. In 1988 we held a conference to appraise and analyze the book *Civilizace na rozcestí* [Civilization at a Crossroads], which in '68 had been a kind of project for the future, still half in the spirit of '68; it saw more than one edition and was gradually expanded and still appearing even after '68.[14] And at the conference some people were saying they'd known how bad things were for quite some time. And we and others said: "No you didn't, because the problem hadn't been opened up and wasn't clear." A report on it came out in one economics journal and as soon as it appeared the whole discussion was brought to a halt – by then it was 1988.'

'One bit of unpleasantness concerned a book on heraldry,' Mr ErIgerus recalled. 'Fortunately, that too had actually been reviewed and accepted by our man at the Institute of Marxism–Leninism. Anyway, when it appeared, there was a great commotion. I think something even got into the papers because the author blithely criticized the arms of the Czechoslovak Socialist Republic. I think his actual words were that it was a heraldic pig's ear, because the lion had been deprived of its crown and given a star instead, it had been given a hair-cut and even set on a Hussite pavise, which is ridiculous in heraldic terms. And the book also had some passages about ecclesiastical heraldry. But the only upshot was that we as a department all lost our bonuses or whatever, and it was recommended that the book shouldn't be re-issued, even though it had sold out.'

'I don't know of any particularly fierce sanction,' Professor Sinapis said. 'I only know about the kind of sanctions that led to people leaving their jobs themselves, having decided they weren't going to carry on working at such and such a place. There *were* those pressures, but if there was any case of immediate denunciation ... ?'

He pondered for a moment.

'I got the run-of-the-mill sanctions, like having my bonuses taken away for doing something that led to serious reservations at the reviewing stage. But in my eyes those are quite normal, ordinary things and I don't view them as

---

[14] The talk is of (Richta 1966 [2nd edn. 1967, 3rd edn. 1969]; English translation (Richta 1969).

particularly significant. Though a real sanction did loom over me in one case, and that was the case of that big [condemnatory] article in *Rudé právo*, where only an intervention from on high saved me from ...' He left the consequences to my imagination and said, 'Because I was in danger of being thrown out of my job, and my boss told me not to count on being there much longer. In which event I'd never have got another job in my field, actually. That was the only such potentially life-changing moment that came my way.'

The icons overhead of several of the Hungarian researchers flickered to life during this last exchange. Post-publication censorship was evidently something they could relate to. I asked the projection screen, 'Were there any consequences at your workplace when they learned that you published in the underground?'

It was Professor Szebah who responded, 'No, it's quite a protected institute, so that's why I said that I was quite lucky that I started to work here and I remained here. Somehow it was considered a half dissident place, many dissidents worked here and we worked together or otherwise were part of what we did here. In this sense it was very protected. But what happened is that I started teaching in the seventies regularly, I taught at ELTE from 1977 onwards and I never got a regular contract there and it was promised – the director there was much attached to the Party – he promised me several times that I would have a job there, but somehow it never happened. It was in 1990, after thirteen years, that it happened.'

Professor Laxi continued with his experience, 'I was a committed, but politically rather uninterested anti-communist. I hated them like shit but I didn't have any political ambition. I simply wrote about it wherever I could and this was the problem: [after] my first volume of studies, because of an event, my own professor at the university gave me up and my scholarship was taken away. I was lucky not to have been kicked out. Here at the institute there were cases when I wasn't even allowed to attend the 20th century meetings, so that I don't bark there or do some political mischief. My first volume of studies, which was already in the press, was cancelled. A friend of mine, who was under constant police surveillance, and I did together a book series. It was banned, so we were stigmatized. I signed the Czech *Charta*,[15] for this I was

---

[15] That is, Charter 77. Jiří Gruntorád explains the multiple difficulties in tracking down all the signatories from the original set to the fall of the communist regime: there are several lists, only some names were originally made public, many not, either as an oversight or deliberately to protect the signatories (Gruntorád 2011). Barbara Falk cites a total of thirty-five Hungarian signatories (Falk 2003: 128).

banned from the Radio for two years, I couldn't lecture anywhere or publish but I wasn't thrown out of the institute, that's already something, isn't it? I was teaching for a while at a provincial university in secret, because the Interior [ministry] put pressure [on universities] that I be removed because I would contaminate the youth. I didn't get paid [as a lecturer], but under some other title – for cleaning. Then they took me back. So more or less the reprisal for the Czech *Charta* lasted for two years, then they would allow me to speak on the Radio again and such.'

Professor Szebah indicated that she wanted to speak.

'In a somewhat more liberal period in 1977 I published something in the underground and therefore my passport was taken away and I couldn't travel for a year.'

'Because you published it under your own name?' I asked for clarification.

'Yes. But clearly the piece I published was the least harmful ever. It was a critical analysis on the basis of a survey that I ran. So the content was not the problem, but the fact that I published in [the underground] that was the drama. The reaction was very harsh, because I was ...,' she hesitated, wondering how best to explain it. 'I was not sent away from my workplace, but at least I couldn't travel. The uncertainties on these issues always came, but that is common sense. It was always very hectic what would happen to you and you couldn't forecast what would follow.'

'There was great difference in premiums[16] and salary and in the possibility to travel,' Professor Sztipoah summed up the situation. 'Professor Szebah at the time didn't get a passport. It was explicit in salary, explicit in the premium, explicit in the travel possibilities, in decorations. But I am a gentle lady and I don't like ... '

She paused and then continued haltingly. 'When last summer I got a high decoration I was very embarrassed. ... I don't like [these things], it was not a measure for anybody. Decorations are the keys to politics and to power, it's not my business, it's their business, but it is very typical. ... I belonged to the tolerated people.'

I addressed Professor Lustani, 'When you said you couldn't publish for a while, what do you think was the problem: your political views, the topic of your research, or some text that you'd written?'

---

[16] That is, a salary bonus.

'All three. I had texts which were published abroad without any sort of censorship, so I got a disciplinary warning. Also my political views. Hungarian intelligentsia had a major undertaking in 1979, a commemoratory volume on Bibó.[17] This was an illegal publication. I was given a final warning and was almost thrown out of my job, but there were lots who were actually fired. Just like in the Czech Republic. It was hard to fire me, but that was only my case, others, who were not in my situation, were indeed fired. Those were more careful. I wasn't so careful and I looked courageous. I wasn't more courageous than the others, but my position was better because I was dealing with a lot of these small literatures, cultures. I had a degree of indemnity due to being the only one familiar with these cultures and the slogan was always about the brotherly friendship between socialist peoples and about socialist cultures having to get to know each other. Who would have [fired *me*] who made friends with the [other] peoples? There were literatures that they could only get to know through me. That had protected me.'

'So let me list the sanctions,' Professor Laxi interjected. 'For a while I was officially removed from the provincial university, banned from the Radio and was under a publication ban in journals for two years. These were the ones, but not too horrible, I wasn't fired from my job.'

A few moments of silence followed this unsentimental pronouncement.

'There were ups and downs as the political climate changed,' Professor Szebah resumed the discussion with a summary of the overall situation.

'There was a tough period around 1973 when the Lukács School was expelled. We reacted to that and there was a political scandal that we went against the Party, but in the end they decided that nothing would happen to us, we [just] got some *ejnye-bejnye* [scolding]. Me and my husband were young researchers and we thought that we would try and write the chief secretary of the Hungarian Academy of Sciences asking for an explanation: that we learned a lot from these people and we didn't understand why they were anti-Marxist, because we learned Marxism from them, so we were asking for an explanation – we, as young researchers. We sent this letter to the chief secretary of the Academy and

---

[17] István Bibó (1911–79) was a Hungarian political scientist and sociologist. During the 1956 revolution, he was a minister in the government of Imre Nagy. After the defeat of the revolution, he was arrested, and sentenced to life imprisonment, but was released in the amnesty of 1963. The *István Bibó Memorial Book* (Bence et al. 1980) became a rallying point of Hungarian opposition and a legend in the history of Hungarian *samizdat*. See for example, (Falk 2003: 136–7).

obviously he never answered, but the director of our institute called us to report [to him] and he was blackmailing us, but then nothing really happened.'

'We demonstrated, we wrote letters, we signed [petitions], we tried to do something, but with mixed success,' Professor Sztipoah picked up on the idea of a mild revolt against sanctions.

'You wrote petitions? To whom?' I asked, incredulous after what I had heard so far.

'To the Academy, a letter, I don't know, maybe I can [still] find it somewhere. We wrote in [Ágnes] Heller's case, [András] Hegedüs' case,[18] we always tried to, not everybody, but some of my colleagues. Every institution was divided, different types of colleagues: there were, for instance, those who were '56 revolutionaries, those who were really religious and against socialism, and there was the Party secretary or the Party members among academics – different types of people.'

'What was the reaction at the Academy to your participation in those petitions in support of the colleagues who were persecuted or censored?'

'We didn't get money for research, it was difficult to publish something.'

The drooping heads around the table reminded me how long we had gone without a break, but Professor Szandiliah gestured that she would like to make a concluding remark on post-publication censorship as she had experienced it.

'When the term "poverty" was banished, [the poor] had to be called "low-income people", but nonetheless the research was done. It was also presented, then I was sent away from the office and István Kemény took over the research. He made a public presentation and used the term "poverty" and that was enough to expel him from the Statistical Office and not to publish the research. Kemény was always a thorn in the flesh, he was imprisoned after '56. He started to organize I don't know quite when [the research on poverty]. He was a very clear case for the powers-that-may-be to demonstrate that they were there. It's not really censorship, it is a sort of demonstration ... ,' she considered for a moment, 'yes, of censorship. It was a pretext to get rid of István Kemény in the Statistical Office. [Not using the word "poverty" in public presentations] was a

---

[18] Ágnes Heller (1929–2019) was a notable Hungarian philosopher. She was a student of György Lukács and a member of the Budapest, or Lukács, School that formed in the 1960s and was persecuted for their criticism of the 1968 invasion of Czechoslovakia. Heller emigrated to Australia in 1977 and later took up professorship at the New School in the USA. For a brief summary of Hegedüs's career see note no. 8 and also (Falk 2003: 430).

ridiculous compromise, because in [scholarly] writings we used the term, so it was just a … ,' she hesitated, 'but if you want to use the term "censorship" you can. It was, as I see it, much more and much less.'

II

During the break, I was thinking how odd it was that everybody had something to say about avoiding certain topics or language that might give political offence, but as far as I could remember the pile of policy and Party documents that I had read only ever said what was desirable to research and how. There was nothing about subjects or expressions being unsuitable. How did the authors become sensitized to what was subject to censorship? The question is inextricably bound with the issue of authorial agency, which in turn raises questions about the very concept of authorship. These would be the problems that we would try and unpick before lunch.

Professors HorMi and Lustani were already online, and we needed to begin. I scanned the room and could see that everybody looked more cheerful after they had had a chance to drink a cup of coffee and munch on a biscuit. I waited for the group to assemble back around the table and asked my first question, 'How did one know what one might and might not write? What was and was not possible?'

Silence. Then Professor Stachys said, 'I don't know. Mmm, I can't, hard to say.'

'Actually that was an advantage – us not knowing exactly,' Doctor Helianthus maintained. 'It was determined by the upper echelons at academic journals and other such. They [drew up] a kind of directive, which of course never [interested] me in the slightest, 'cos I never strayed into areas that would chime with speeches by the country's political leaders.'

There was again a brief silence, before Professor Lilius spoke.

'That's a very hard question for me, 'cos it's all so far in the past when I was writing that I can't really bring it to mind – and sometimes you don't even realize these things quite rationally. Yet you do them 'cos you know the pressures are there, and if you want your book to come out, then … ' He broke off, suggestively.

'In my later book there are certainly some signs. The possibility of its being published was looming, so I'm sure I must have done the odd trick with it.'

I was not getting very far with my question, so I rephrased it, 'How did you learn about these limits to what was acceptable and what wasn't?'

'Official social science did define them, yes,' Doctor Sambucus said firmly. 'It defined what constituted bourgeois sociology: anything to do with social stratification or a historical view of the life of society, so Marxism crept into the discipline all round, and *de facto* not even its conceptual apparatus was really sociological, or the discourse in these areas might have been declared to be sociology, but *de facto* it often didn't even use the conceptual apparatus of sociology. You could easily tell, and you knew who was behind these things. So there was no problem there.'

'There was not a fixed border, it was very flexible,' Professor HorMi opined. 'It was something not defined from above. There were suggestions, at the same time there were negotiations, time to time, from occasion to occasion. But the task of realizing what is to be allowed or not was imposed on the editors, it was local, decentralized. There wasn't a central censorship office that would decide over these issues. [After] the very liberal turn of Hungarian intellectual life, especially since the late seventies, the limits were very wide. For example, when you published an article – I published – in which you could talk about the non-existence of the class theory as a relevant guiding principle, there was not any censorship barring you in publishing it. *Valóság* (Reality) was the name of a very interesting journal for several decades, it was established following the sixties. It was the most liberal Hungarian journal – meaning it was the maximum that could appear here. It was marking the limit.'

I wondered if any of the Czech researchers could be so specific about the limits in their disciplines.

'I think it must have been pretty deep-seated,' Professor SalVia offered. 'I don't remember ever having looked for them; I expect I realized as soon as something cropped up about something not working, or about a setback or other snag, that it was off limits.'

'Intuition told us there were things you mustn't write about,' Professor Stachys agreed. 'I didn't have a problem with that in the sense that I wasn't publishing for general consumption anyway, so there was no problem for me to deal with. But I know from colleagues, yes …' He paused for reflection. 'Sure there were differences, but that went with the passage of time. In the eighties it started to ease up.'

'It was in the air,' Doctor LupiNus diagnosed, as if talking about an epidemic. 'I used to read the cultural press: *Literární měsíčník*, *Tvorba*. There it was easy to see. And in the eighties they even got to arguing among themselves, see? I used to read reviews and suchlike. What I never read was any of those political resolutions.'

Doctor LoTus picked up at the mention of specialized publications, 'I kept an eye on what was coming out in Czech, and Slovak, the regular official things in my field and in the broader context of literary studies. It was so obvious the games some people were playing: they'd staked all on normalization, and every second sentence was a fine display of Marxism–Leninism and I don't know what. So there was no point, 'cos I never wanted to get into that position and never did. And then I saw there were others, who were patently resorting to camouflage, just like me. Anybody could tell they meant to say something else and that maybe they were actually saying it, but not as plainly as they would if they could. There'd be random camouflage in the shape of references to Marx or Lenin. That kind of thing. I think if you compared the surroundings, you got some idea of what could be said, how far you could go without getting your fingers burned.'

I said, 'When I was preparing for this [symposium], I read a number of editorials and such from *Sociologický časopis* and various Party publications that I found in the archives. At one time their titles were almost identical: some Party document came out and then found its way to research institutes and journals to become the basis of articles on, say, the role of the social sciences under socialism or their importance for socialist ideology and the like. Did you ever read things like that?'

'Goodness, that was the last thing I'd ever have done to amuse myself,' Doctor Helianthus exclaimed, but then continued less categorically, 'Though I did take an occasional look at the papers to get some idea of what was, as they say, "flavour of the month", but beyond that I wasn't interested. But there were no real discipline-specific interventions in my field in the eighties. There it was more about individuals and individual topics. Of course there were some politically charged areas: political history, or where myths had been created around [Julius] Fučík and suchlike.[19] There it was about voicing an opinion: when someone got up and protested about it or described it as erroneous.

---

[19] Julius Fučík (1903–43) was a Communist journalist executed by the Nazis and an iconic communist hero.

Invariably whether there'd be anyone to stir things up mattered most from the mid-seventies onwards. That was absolutely when it mattered most.'

I considered the researchers' position towards the professional and political discourse from the perspective of today's competitive publishing. We are now always pressured to *have* a research project – preferably one that falls within some declared national or European priorities – and to publish the results as quickly and prestigiously as possible. That often implies sticking to the discursive conventions hallowed by usage and not stepping on the wrong toes. Just before the break Professor Szandiliah mentioned that the term 'poverty' was unacceptable to use in public presentations of research and I remembered that I had heard something similar also in the Czech context. So how did the contemporaries think of the relations between research and publishing during normalization in a general sense?

I said, 'We've heard that at the time one couldn't write about poverty for instance.'

'Not that I couldn't write,' Professor Hedera responded. 'When I'd completed an investigation, I thought it reasonable to write about it. It was more a question of what not to launch into. It would never have occurred to me, really not …' She paused to give an example, 'For instance, I'd been doing something on working-class culture in forties and fifties Prague. I had lots of papers in those in-house collections at the Institute, so to say that I couldn't carry on or couldn't …' She hesitated. 'It's not really right to say "I couldn't" [write]. That I'd have liked to, but couldn't.'

Professor SorBus clearly did not miss the implied self-censorship in what Professor Hedera said, for he now reflected, 'That self-censorship business, I reckon, had a positive side to it, it stopped us parading ourselves too much as apparently sanctioned, "official". Sure there was self-censorship from the other angle, arising out of caution about what to write, but it's hard to say. It might have been because I didn't write much and was quite young that I didn't have the same problem as historians ten-fifteen years older at the Academy, who weren't exactly forbidden to publish, but were so got at that …'

He did not complete the sentence, as Professor Sinapis interjected, 'To my mind, self-censorship represented two things: one's personal limits – individual aptitudes – and what could be written. So no matter how much I might want to, there's some things I'm just not capable of doing any better. But when I did write, it was invariably without regard to what the end impression would be. That means that the juice of an article, study or whatever was always the same. Interventions that amounted more or less to censorship, or the recommendations, or this other thing here,' he pointed to a volume in front of him, 'only got in so as to make a thing acceptable to officialdom. It's quite different in the case of research reports, which were done in the knowledge that they'd be officially reviewed, because they were [research] assignments that had to be carried out. That's quite a different type of text. Mostly we did them more or less collectively, so it was tremendous fun. I mean, writing a study about a project in such a way as to contain all the empirical data and *at the same time* the claptrap that was part of the big deal of securing funds for research.'

'Have you also written such research reports?' I asked Professor Stachys.

'But of course,' he replied without hesitation, 'though I've suppressed it since and forgotten all about it. I made quite a reasonable living doing all sorts of research, different things …' He paused and added, 'But I couldn't tell you now whether any of it was before sixty-eight.'

Doctor LupiNus sat back in his chair and said placidly, 'Well, I haven't lost my enthusiasm. At the beginning I tried to get my own things accepted and in the second phase I was more looking to find my real metier. In the seventies I tried to come up with something original, and in the eighties I gave up throwing myself into …'

He didn't say what, but continued, 'So I took Sylvia Plath along to a publisher and they told me: "Nobody knows it." I just kept being unlucky like that. So back in the eighties I was looking for security. Now I'm back to trying to get my own things accepted. You could say I've never been so well off in publishing terms as I am today. Finally I can get on with doing what I want. I'd say that in '92 I was young again, starting out a second time.'

'How much did you get published up to 1989?' I asked at large.

'Only two things,' Doctor ForSythia was the first to answer. 'I had awful problems. Let me put it like this: for me philosophy isn't like a shovel you just pick up and put down again, it's my life, I absolutely love it.'

'You have to accept the same responsibility for what you elected not to do in the name of your character as for however things done in the name of your character ended up: so that, within the constraints afforded you, you'd given whatever you could,' Professor Fragaria came to her colleague's defence.

'It's a matter of individual decision and we told Patočka roughly as much when Charter 77 happened along, and he said: "Don't sign as long as you're in a position to teach. What's important is that you teach." As long as we were at the faculty, that is. So we attended the seminars at his place, and later, after it became impossible, we remained in written contact anonymously and by all manner of devices, but we thought: "Right, given we're in this position, we have to teach."[20] We concluded that it wasn't possible to allow the nation to be primitivized for twenty years, maybe more, maybe less, just because there were constraints. Since that was where we are, we had to, within the limits possible, give children and young people the maximum we could.'

Professor Fragaria raised the subject of service to one's profession. I wondered how that tied with almost the opposite of the decision not to publish: the 'glory' of authorship.

As if on cue, Doctor Stellaria said, 'It took huge libations for something to come out. But I didn't feel the least bit aggrieved, because I thought: "Thank God it's coming out." Ludvík Vaculík was one who knew plenty about such things, he was hugely supportive and said: "If, without prostituting yourself, you find a loophole and the chance to say something positive, go ahead and say it."'[21]

Professor Lustani's image came to life as he was nodding in agreement. He said, 'I published translations of structuralism in a collection I edited at the end of the 1970s, I think. It was in the making for years, it was very good, the best studies on Russian formalism, Czech and Polish structuralism and phenomenology. There I would publish the essays under a pseudonym, because it was with the most official academic publishing house and I didn't want to risk it, it wasn't worth it. I was translating under an assumed name, because I was then the structuralist enemy. I couldn't publish under my own name, and I couldn't even publish translations, let alone translations of structuralist writers under my own name, but I could select and edit texts.'

A reflective pause followed, after which Professor Sinapis said somewhat tangentially, but obviously on the subject of the quantity of his oeuvre, 'I also ran out of energy because that time I was writing a book and didn't know

---

[20] The implied chronology is probably incorrect: Jan Patočka died in March 1977, three months after he signed and became one of the spokespersons of Charter 77, so Professor Fragaria most likely speaks about the seminars that took place between Patočka's retirement in the early 1970s and his signing of Charter 77.
[21] Ludvík Vaculík (1926–2015) was a Czech writer and a *samizdat* publisher. He is also known for authoring the petition 'Two Thousand Words' in June 1968.

whether it would come out, and throughout I was focussed entirely on it. It took me three or four years to write and consequently I didn't feel like publishing anything at all. I knew the kind of problems I'd be up against, so I thought: "Right, my lad, you'll write your book and here it can stay, and all will be well."'

I wanted to go back to the subject of authorship. I knew that Doctor Stellaria published exclusively under pen names, so I asked her, 'When you wrote under a pseudonym, what steps did you have to take toward publication?'

'Look, I had to find myself a "ghost-author" (*pokrývače*),' she explained patiently. 'That's what everyone did. Someone who'd officially be the one to approach the publisher. I couldn't go [to them]. Or they could come – in my case – to find me at work. Anybody could come there, couldn't they? Of course, I bowed to whatever they wanted. So it made no sense to write about, what for example … ?'

She rummaged in her bag. 'This book here: it came out later in Slovakia, they had different criteria there, they wanted me to get rid of different quotations. I'd got some from Fromm for instance: in one edition they're there and in the other they're not, because they didn't want them, the quotations, any more.'

'How was it with the pseudonym? Did you go round to the publishers saying you'd got an idea for a book … ?'

'Yes, a proposal I wanted to do. Someone would go there instead of me, or mostly we met up on neutral ground somewhere.'

'And was any written record kept?'

'Yes, about the proposal. Very often it was a colleague, male or female, who took the proposal along for me. They had to be well known and … ,' she considered.

'Hmm, actually it was done as a project: usually, when you do a book proposal, you write two or three chapters to see if they like it. And then they signed the contract with that person, who then became the official author. If it was an article and not very long, it was said not to matter; even if it came out that it was you, no one would be fussed. Whereas, if it was a book, that was too much bother for the publishers. They'd want some guarantee that the other person was of the right background in case it came out, so as it wouldn't come out.'

The researchers spoke about escaping to teaching and concealing authorship as moves to avoid censorship in publishing. Did they also use other measures?

'I published both at home and abroad, but the articles that meant most to me came out abroad,' Doctor Stellaria offered one alternative.

'In the second half of the 1980s things got a bit easier, but after that I more or less felt, you might say, progressively freer, which finally led to us publishing and writing *samizdat*,' Professor Sinapis described his final strategy. 'That was hugely liberating, and after that I lost all interest in pursuing any kind of official standing.'

'Obviously, those were the best things I ever wrote,' Professor Stachys said with reference to his publishing in *samizdat*. 'I had no inhibitions, either political or institutional. I really couldn't care less. I just wrote about things that interested me and that I knew about. So we just had a field day.'

'There were journals I didn't want to be in – up to a certain time,' Professor Helleborus introduced a strategy practicable within official publishing. 'Then in a single instance *perestroika* did get the better of me, but that's a different story.'

He laughed and continued, 'I wouldn't have published in any political journal. At one time, because this was connected with the seventies, I mean the end of the seventies, I didn't publish at all in *Český časopis historický*. I simply decided that I wouldn't write for it. But that was my decision to make, see?'

I took it to mean that he did not feel censored, but developed his own form of resistance to ideological pressures.

Doctor LoTus nodded enthusiastically, 'Before the nineties I published dozens of reviews, mostly in Slovak literary journals. I didn't put things in any of the Czech ones. *Literární měsíčník* struck me as pretty awful, and then, hmm, well, *Tvorba*.'

His remark seemed a condemnation not only of the content of these journals, but also of their language. We planned to spend the afternoon on the subject, but we could look into it now briefly in general terms.

'Had you also established your own expressions that you preferred to those demanded by officialdom?'

'In that regard I think I was quite irresponsible,' Professor Sinapis reflected self-critically. 'I just didn't think it that important. To me the end result and all the other stuff was more important than the handful of banalities that might appear somewhere. Of course I see things differently today when I pick something up in a fit of nostalgia: "For God's sake, how could you write that?" But judging with hindsight, in a different situation, that's something else of course. I'd rather try thinking what it was like back then.'

'I think it was second nature by then,' admitted Doctor Helianthus, 'but the main thing was that I'd retreated to subjects that lacked political topicality and so weren't being monitored. And wherever it did run all too clearly counter to current pronouncements I tried to avoid drawing conclusions, or I put them in a form which left no room at all for doubt, and I left it to see if anyone would pop up and attack it. I can tell you that after '75 there weren't so many people like that.'

Mrs Euphrasia turned to me and said with some emphasis, 'You have to realize that, in an encyclopaedic work, those [phrases demanded by the age] were just ballast. Our main concern was with getting facts in. Giving it some kind of direction, right? Also, the editor had some things of her own in it. I always thought it was like a Modigliani. That it had its particular distortions and they might even be beautiful – but it shouldn't become a monstrosity.'

She reminded me of why I had set out on this quest. I asked, 'As a student before 1989 I remember that we would always read various things between the lines. Do you think that kind of thing existed at the time, or is it silly to think that?'

'I don't think it was so much reading between the lines,' Doctor Helianthus dismissed the idea. 'My usual practice at least was to pull certain parts of the material together in the analysis and then avoid that in my conclusions, because it dawned on me quite early that that could be a stumbling block, that those who had their fingers on the pulse only read the beginning and end. [Such things were] not politically sensitive, but they ran contra and could be attacked on ideological grounds. So in a case like that, I did the analysis, but kept it out of the conclusions.[22] Then one time, a student, a girl, asked, "but Professor, it follows perfectly from your analysis, so why didn't you put it in?" And I said, "for the simple reason that I knew it would create complications and I'd get myself pointlessly into a conflict I'd no wish to get into."'

He paused briefly, before adding, 'Because the experience of being five years without a job is pretty damn drastic.'

---

[22] Doctor Helianthus articulates what, several years before this interview took place, Chad Bryant argued about 'tendencies among "official" historians writing from the periphery', those that he characterizes as 'grey zone': 'Important among them was a return to positivism, or in Czech terms, a dedication to "factography," which attempted to lay out objective bits of information for the reader without engaging in explicit interpretations of those facts. Put one way, this allowed historians to employ the correct ideological language in order to present their findings, playing a sort of game which allowed them to avoid censorship (and repression) while still having their works published' (Bryant 2000: 40).

His last comment pointed towards the uncomfortable ground of throwing sops to a metaphorical Cerberus in order to get past him.

Professor Stachys seemed to have understood as much when he now said roughly, 'Listen, I've decided, unlike many others who'll keep things back, lie – though I could give you the names of all those who I know for sure will keep from you all the things they wrote – I've decided that I will not lie to you. I wrote one article, an exemplary attempt to salvage as much as possible, and at the same time actually an example of utterly incredible naïvety. Some colleagues and I wrote a joint article for an academic journal at the start [of normalization]. If you read it today, you'd [have no idea] of the situation out of which it emerged. Everything in it, I insist, was written in a cultured, properly argued manner. It was an attempt, I don't know – I really don't know now – if we believed it, or nurtured the belief, that we could convince the inconvincible that sociology should survive institutionally, and we with it. I make no secret of that "and we with it". Another group maintains it was they who salvaged sociology by saving it as an institution. Institutionalized sociology was not abolished after normalization and they claim it as a great positive achievement. With that article we did our last positive deed, in the sense of attempting to salvage the discipline. We simply wished to salvage the discipline, though aware that almost everything that could be lost was already lost, but we were not yet completely lost ourselves.'

In the silence that followed this confession, I reflected how much it must have cost him to make it.

As if Professor SalVia shared my thoughts, she said in a conciliatory tone, 'I said to myself, if it's about words, it doesn't matter, but if it were about people, it would, that's where I drew the line. The minute any statement might be meant to hurt someone, might harm them, that's where the line is. In the case of the odd "successes of socialism", I couldn't have cared less.'

'I don't think [certain subjects] were taboo, it's more that there were more favoured topics,' Professor Stachys turned the issue of writing between the lines around. 'Look, this obviously ranges over a whole panoply of utter crap written about the structure of society, right down to the things some people wrote for no good reason. These were those puke-making articles with which they tried to expiate their past sins.'

'Then came that bout of criticizing bourgeois sociology,' Doctor Sambucus supplied an example. 'And there were people involved who had a pretty good insight into the scholarship in question, including American authors, but they had to go about it in such a way that it sort of had to be critical of bourgeois sociology. As a way to earn a crust, I found this repellent and I thought those people were monsters. Then some of them, one in particular, he surfaced after '89 as a highly intelligent analyst. Quite simply, he stood everything on its head and suddenly became an expert on American sociology. Then he turned up in fairly influential quarters, and finally vanished. So it had suddenly transpired that they might well have been intelligent and perceptive people, but in ethical terms their performance was somewhat problematical.'

'Not once did I quote some panjandrum, no Lenin, nobody, it was just scholarship,' Doctor Hepatica stated firmly. 'I don't know, I've got enough sense to know – but even now, when you write something, you know what's possible and what's not. That inner self-censorship, you know, is always at work, but with me it hasn't been more at work than now.'

'I did assume that someone would definitely be looking at [the manuscript of my book] from the ideological point of view as well,' Doctor LoTus reminded us of the levels of approval through which a piece of writing had to pass. 'So I don't believe I was paying homage to Marxist literary studies, or applying their theories. Though on the other hand there are obviously places where self-censorship is present, or things that I'd like to have said, but didn't. So in terms of self-censorship I avoided certain things. I think my self-censorship resided more in my avoiding things, not in extolling Marxist literary method or, Heaven forbid, even applying it.'

I turned to Professor SorBus, 'You mentioned self-censorship a while ago: Do you think it was always conscious, or had the process become more or less conditioned, got into the bloodstream?'

'It's hard to generalize. I know some people, and unfortunately they included students of mine, who would say: "You'll never come to anything because you don't know how to adapt to the language." They were pursuing their careers and did some excellent things, but I told them: "You'll get it so clogged up with ballast that no one's going to want to read it." They laughed and said that I could think what I liked. So it did exist, but there wasn't much of it. There was self-censorship in the sense we talked about before, that you simply thought three times before using "class struggle" and "socialism" – it really would have to have been about Fourier, or I don't know what.'

'Well, I think something really did get into the bloodstream,' Doctor LoTus said thoughtfully. 'Once you've assimilated a given tactic, I don't mean necessarily in a Schweikian manner, by which you feign loyalty, some of it stays with you even when the need for any such pretence has passed. And then it just looks grotesque.'

He paused and then reflected, 'I don't remember anyone expressly censoring me in the sense that such and such a sentence had to go, things like that, it was more being told [I should place] greater emphasis on Marxism, and so that was there in my book at the beginning.'

'What do you think had a greater effect on the final shape of a text: censorship from outside or self-censorship?' I asked.

'I think it worked from both directions,' Professor Lilius responded. 'External pressure, and then from that arose the self-censorship out of an urge to stave the pressure off somehow. By the end chapters of my second book there are clear signs of me wanting it to come out. It can't be helped when you'd been writing it for so many years, so you might sacrifice certain things – I don't mean any matters of principle – for it to be able to come out.'

'We were a marginalized group, that was one thing,' Professor Sinapis joined in. 'For another, it really was a time when anybody who published things was afraid of getting into hot water. No matter that those editors, the women, might be ever so obliging and ever so kind, and convinced that it would come out, that it had to come out, they were afraid they'd find themselves in hot water. With articles it was a bit different, for example one article took about two years before it came out in a normal journal. I would insist I wasn't going to change anything. So gradually they got about eleven appraisals in and each time I refused and each time made my case for disagreeing. In the end a review was written by an ex-colleague who was embarrassed by the whole thing and who was quite high up, and he simply said, "Yes, nothing needs changing," and the article appeared.'

His response connected censorship with the core principle implied by 'authorship': the authors' control over their own texts. Doctor ForSythia also made that connection, for she said, 'When we submitted an article with the translation of a historical work from German, it had, in those days, to be approved by the head of department, and then the article appeared with his name first and mine second. I'd got my translation in it, and he'd written the preamble, which obviously had a political and ideological slant.'

'Did you know what he was inserting?'

'Not at all! No. I handed the manuscript in and then it came out with his additions.'

'Could anyone tell, in the article, who'd written what?'

'You could never tell. Up until '89 the system was ruled by a kind of vagueness that left everyone with a sense of guilt, without knowing what for. It was that Mao Tse-tung-like way of moulding broken-willed, good collaborators, see? You were always scared, but you didn't know what of. That's what it was like here.'

'My boss also got me to write a whole array of texts for her and never ever put me down as their author,' Doctor SiLena added to that experience. 'She might be doing an article to send somewhere, so she'd have me write eight to ten pages as her source material, took it, used almost the whole thing, just titivating it a bit, then published it under her own name, and that was seen as normal. It used to rile me.'

'So your authorial power to decide about a manuscript was actually seriously curtailed,' I ventured.

'Yes, invariably,' Doctor ForSythia confirmed.

My induction into the nooks and crannies of interferences with scholarly texts in late state socialism was nearing its end. But there was still one more area I wanted to explore: What did the researchers now, at the beginning of the twenty-first century, think of their published efforts during normalization?

'A new edition of my book came out in the early nineties, and I think one of my faculty coursebooks as well,' Doctor LoTus offered the unfinished story of his earlier work.

'And were these texts that came out after 1989 reworked?'

'Apart from the introduction, no, I couldn't see any practical ... ,' he paused for reflection and specified, 'The bit with the [Party] congress, I left that out, 'cos I thought some people might take it as an expression of loyalty [to the Party]. There might be those who'll get upset and, if they don't know their Schweik, might think that Schweik meant what he said, I mean the business with Belgrade. But I don't think I censored anything else out or added any notes to explain what I had or hadn't meant.'

Professor Sinapis said thoughtfully, 'I wasn't the least bit ashamed of texts that I wrote under another's name. With the ones that did carry my name, I was invariably worried that I'd done something that shouldn't have been there.'

He paused briefly, before driving the point home. 'So today, if someone came along asking if the book might be published in a revised edition, I'd have to rewrite it. They're only slight shifts, but it went with the times, which were different.'

'To be frank, reading my things after the passage of time, they strike me as somehow alien, 'cos today I'd write them quite differently, because I wouldn't have to stop and think about every single sentence in case it might get me into trouble. Or then the stereotypical manoeuvring which had taken root in you, that's all gone now,' Doctor LoTus concurred.

'Of the things I revisited, there's not one that was amended. That's to say, of the things that went to press from me [before 1989], all there was in them were things like that these were issues that either continued on into Marx or anticipated Marx,' Professor Fragaria stated, with certainty, her different opinion.

'So that was perhaps as far as I allowed myself to go with something that might be said to be kowtowing to the possibilities that were open. But it was no mere sop, because people were educated in this area, they understood. If you started on about the horizon of the world and transcendental analytics, it meant nothing to them, so [the thing was] to get it across [to them in terms they understood].'

Doctor Hyacintha retorted modestly, 'Recently, I wanted to do a summary report on [some of the things I'd written then] and that came out in a journal. Today they strike me as of no great significance, really and truly quite harmless as texts.'

I wondered how the authors' ex-post assessments resonated with those of their readers.

'After November 1989 did you meet with any responses to your earlier work?'

'People sometimes let drop that they used my coursebooks to study from and I get the feeling they mean it positively, not to have a go at me for what I did or how I'd queered the pitch here,' Doctor LoTus reacted, also with a certain pride, to the mention of passing knowledge to the next generation.

'But that's all pretty much in the past. I reckon that one person who came off rather worse in a sense is Professor Lilius. I expect you know the grounds, because he was like … ,' and he gave me a conspiratorial look, 'and I think that in his case it wasn't really even camouflage. He's of the generation that was perhaps Marxist and meant it, I don't know.'

'I expected it to take longer, didn't I,' Professor Lilius retorted. 'But I didn't avoid anyone, though of course I sort of forced myself into being more critical than perhaps I would today. And what's interesting is that my main work, which is in essence Marxist, a sort of liberal Marxism, is still being read today, I believe.'

'I'm not ashamed of the article I wrote back then even today,' Doctor ForSythia said mildly. 'But when I read the conclusion in my thesis with the bit about Andropov, well, that's horrendous. Horrendous, it's only about half a page, but it's horrendous. It's so obviously just pasted in for its own sake. It's not remotely connected with what the work as a whole was about. There at the end, the bit with Andropov, it's horrendous to read, stomach-churning. Really, it turns your stomach.'

There was a clear note of self-disgust in her words, but that transformed to bitterness as she went on.

'Then there's that article my head of department put his name to as co-author, I can still read it today, my bits of it. It's not that bad. But the fact is that after '89 I had terrible problems. With people at the Faculty. Obviously I wrote from a phenomenological perspective, and there were people working there in the publications office who couldn't understand what I'd written, so they made life terribly difficult for me. I even got something into one journal about philosophy being entitled to be the way it is, that it's actually about the thinking of things thought, and at once there were several ripostes, this was some years ago, extremely nasty ripostes about me having the gall to write in a way nobody can understand.'

She invoked the publishing ghosts of the past in the present. Professor SalVia nodded that it also resonated with her experience.

'In the work I did as the prerequisite to promotion, in a section on the period of normalization, I showed in literally just one or two paragraphs some of the typical words used then, and I had quite a problem with it. I used two named sources and asked a colleague, she's got a good memory, who these men were and if I could use the text, and she said: "They're some ancient professors, long dead." Then it transpired that one was indeed dead, but the other was all too alive and he was even an assessor of the work. He was horribly offended, failed the thesis and got very angry. Then we cleared things up, but it had been a bit insensitive of me because it really was kind of …'

She left the sentence unfinished. 'I expect it was down to those strategies [we've spoken about], and if I'd known he was alive …' She reflected. 'Him being my assessor, that was sheer bad luck. No, it wasn't very nice of me.'

'There were people who had difficulties [with their work from back then],' Doctor Stellaria mused along similar lines, 'including buying up their own books so they wouldn't go any further and couldn't be duplicated. Or there was one chap, and I have the greatest respect for him, a wonderful chap, I'm talking about Professor Stachys, what happened to him was that this girl quoted some nonsense during her entrance examination and he said: "Come off it, you're talking tripe …" That's not how he put it during the exam. She'd no idea who he was and she said: "It was in a coursebook by Professor Stachys." So he buttoned it.' She gave Professor Stachys a mischievous wink.

'It was he himself who told me this had happened, see?'

Professor Stachys looked around apologetically and said, 'I mean, one's basic space was defined according to whether you'd survived at your institution or not. [One colleague] said that he hadn't committed many blunders really – because the temptation hadn't been there much. The difference was in the rate of temptation.'

Everybody seemed subdued after these introspective thoughts. We concluded our session and I hoped the formal farewell lunch that the caterers now began to set up was going to raise people's spirits. While the participants left the room to stretch their legs, I took stock of my quest so far.

We began yesterday on the ground of less than hard evidence. By now we had moved from memories of actions, that is, of institutional practices and of personal experiences with manoeuvring a piece of work through the various stages of approval to publication, to the realm of guesses and perceptions. And increasingly to personal, even intimate regions, for what can be more intimate for authors than questioning them about their relationship to their texts? The last three topics of our discussion – 'sops to Cerberus', self-censorship and post-1989 attitudes to one's earlier texts – required the authors to look deep into themselves and take a stance with decisively moral implications.

We would delve even further into perceptions of authorial decisions taken two or three decades earlier, during lunch. Our attention would turn to the process of scholarly communication and its vehicle, language. The difficulty in establishing 'the facts' during the discussion ahead lay not in the distance in time alone, but also in the nature of written communication. Apart from the real reader and author, an academic text has an implied reader and, arguably, also an implied author, as much as an imaginative narrative text.[23] There is a good deal an author presupposes, imagines and expects of herself or himself in relation to the text and of the audience. All the real authors can do is give an account of this as intentions or perceptions, while any real readers can offer interpretations, not facts.

---

[23] The concepts of implied reader and implied author were developed by narratologists. Rather than any real people, they are both functions of a text and abstract concepts. The implied reader 'can function as a *presumed addressee* to whom the work is directed. (…) In this function, the implied reader is the bearer of the codes and norms presumed in the readership.' It 'functions as an image of the *ideal recipient* who understands the work in a way that optimally matches its structure and adopts the interpretive position and aesthetic standpoint put forward by the work' (Schmid 2009: paragraphs 9, 11). The implied author is not necessarily in any symmetrical relation to the implied reader; the concept 'refers to the author-image evoked by a work and constituted by the stylistic, ideological, and aesthetic properties for which indexical signs can be found in the text. (…) We have the implied author in mind when we say that each and every cultural product contains an image of its maker' (Schmid 2013).

6

The language

Research topics, vocabulary, writing in code

Chapter 3 looked at the censorship of people in the aftermath of the defeat of the Prague Spring reformist movement. The discussion in the previous chapter brought together structural and textual acts of censorship, as remembered by the narrators, with their thoughts on authorship and authoring in state-socialist academia. The natural continuation of the quest leads to the subject of what could be written and how. That is, to the politically acceptable, sensitive and unacceptable research topics and, further, to the preferred and proscribed vocabulary of scholarly texts. This will bring us, finally, to the object of the quest: the elusive 'code' used by the authors either to communicate or to camouflage subversive messages. Little of this can be verified against written evidence: the research topics do, to an extent, make an appearance in the policy documents, but vocabulary preferences cannot be traced to any ideological directives, only to a consensual usage. The 'code', if we consider the lack of clarity in the process towards publication and the often contradictory views on the nature and extent of censorship recorded in the previous chapters, is the stuff legends are made of.

I

The caterers gave us the all-clear sign and we returned to the room to find the table adorned with a colourful array of starters. It was perhaps somewhat mean to ask our Hungarian colleagues to watch us enjoy our rich lunch, but Doctor SzolPi and Professors Szebah, Szandiliah and HorMi said that they didn't mind and would be joining us. Professor Lustani promised to be with us at the beginning, but then would have to leave due to a prior engagement.

I wished everyone *dobrou chuť* and observed that the starters went nicely with the analogous 'hors d'oeuvres' on the programme of our discussion: the research topics of the 1970s and 1980s social sciences and humanities. Immediately, Doctor SiLena reminded me of the overall context of scholarly research.

'Imagine that there were actually various parallel worlds even within sociology. The parallel world at the universities and in science as done at the Academy was miles away from what our applied research institute had to concern itself with. On top of that, ours was run from Slovakia, which of itself played a major role, because that put it sort of out of kilter. There were no particularly radical solutions to people's status there. Some of the people working there didn't even carry a [Party] card.'

Doctor SzolPi took over from her, 'Sociology in the seventies and eighties was a typical occupation for those who wanted to express opposition against the official system. This is, I think, traditionally sociology, that it should be critical.' He gesticulated energetically during his short speech, emphasizing that no internal disciplinary divisions existed in Hungary.

'History had certainly been political since 1918,' Doctor Helianthus compared the sensitive areas within his discipline. 'Practically speaking, if you take, say, *Rudé právo* or *Mladá fronta*, you'll find all the time the selfsame people writing about political history, and on sundry anniversaries: always the same ones.'

Professor Lustani picked up on the issue of sensitive topics and said, 'At the end of the 1960s, the struggle over structuralism took place. Then it was a battle with Marxism, but we won the fight and structuralism was accepted. Well, there were Marxist literary historians and theoreticians, but nobody really cared about those, Marxism didn't exist anymore. After the end of the sixties, only low-quality people, official ones, would claim – although even they wouldn't really say it – that they were Marxist, they were ashamed of it. I was ashamed to be a Marxist.'

'A sort of Western Marxism was popular,' argued Professor HorMi, 'but the main target was not Marxism as such, whether existing in the West [or in the East], but a non-Marxist way of thinking. The French *Annales* social science or structural history looked more important to us than British Marxist history.

The strongest impetus working in us was not to be Marxist and this was to lead ourselves away from Western Marxism as well. That is why, for example, not the history of the working class but the history of the bourgeoisie was the topic, theme, issue which attracted so many younger scholars at that time. So even the thematic orientation of the historians was shaped by our alienism towards Marxism. In the case of the British Marxist historians the great topic was the past of the English working class, a reference point for Marx himself. We wanted to draw ourselves away from these influences. To turn to those segments of the past of our country which were denied by the Marxists and communists, which were underrated, relativized or negatively depicted.'

'We looked out for our disciplines ourselves,' Professor Hedera joined in, stressing the importance of a team or community. 'That's to say, what went on was actually by mutual consent, for the good of the cause, to ensure the discipline didn't perish, to secure its existence. But we could keep things in check, because if we got into, I don't know, something like phenomenology or God knows what special areas, someone would be bound to spot it. Or when institute reports came to be done, you had to know just how to tweak them.'

Doctor Hepatica broke in, somewhat querulously, 'Like I say, industry in the socialist states, [that was] a neutral topic. We did the socialist states, so I wrote it up from statistical yearbooks and statistical data on how many people were in employment and how many not, and in what branches, so I didn't have to compromise or lie about anything. It was all simply based on statistics. Ideologically neutral topics did exist and it depended on you doing ideologically neutral topics, because as soon as anything to do with history cropped up, that probably wouldn't do, because that's why they threw me out, they didn't like my earlier work.'

'Choice of subject was down to me,' agreed Doctor Stellaria. 'I tried to go for topics that didn't touch on politics, though they did anyway. They invariably had something bearing on politics. So you made huge sacrifices for a thing to be able to come out. But I didn't get at all upset by it because I thought: Thank goodness it's coming out, you see?'

'It actually transpired that that kind of pilot studies, surveys with no great scientific ambitions, though they were carried out meticulously, was doable [at my institute]. Nobody made us put any false spin on them in the interpretation of the data, so they could be read as a kind of social critique, as a signal of some phenomenon of crisis,' Doctor Hyacintha said, explaining that even research on officially sanctioned topics could be interpreted as subversive by perceptive readers. She helped herself to a devilled egg and went on.

'Then back in the eighties there was a campaign to do with the construction of housing estates. By participant observation and questioning people we were to find out how these monofunctional units on the urban periphery worked. And again the report on it was quite telling, thought-provoking, and it was impossible [to distribute it] even though people were calling for it, borrowing it, so it did get passed around. Back then, there was a snag with making copies. Xeroxing was entrusted only to comrades who'd been screened and it really was hard for people to get hold of copies of such things. So we heard back that when that kind of a pilot study of a situation was recorded in a credible fashion, they're taken as socially important and politically significant.'

Her account explained how a topic could slide on the scale of acceptability from desirable to sensitive or undesirable. I asked, 'Did you ever get a sense that you were dealing with topics that were awkward from a political perspective, that a given topic was sensitive?'

Doctor Sambucus laughed. 'Well, the entire time of course. The entire time you knew you couldn't go into a particular field, that you'd be exposing yourself to risk, and so this or that area was *de facto* closed off by self-censorship. That apart, I felt no urge to go there, so it didn't cause me any great headaches. I would stick to things involving systematization, relating precisely to such issues as, for the sake of argument, regional planning. Some people might find that kind of thing irksome, but it didn't bother me particularly. So some might agonize about not being able to deal with some sociological theory or social philosophy, but those were areas where I wasn't particularly literate myself. Even later I aimed more towards empirical and applied topics.'

'We didn't actually do any topics in sociology, we did economics topics,' Professor SalVia diagnosed the situation. 'With those anything could be sensitive if it touched on how enterprises operated or, say, on the lead role taken by the *nomenklatura*. I can't think of any other sensitive areas.'

She looked intensely at the salad leaves on her plate for a few moments. Finally, she shook her head, 'I can't think of any politically sensitive subjects ...,' she trailed off, then added, as if she felt she ought to supply an explanation, 'Due to our working group being marginal and they all had such different backgrounds ...'

She seemed lost in thought for a few moments and then spoke aloud what was obviously going through her head.

'One of them was the former head of the institute, now just an ordinary member of staff, and he was a Jew who'd survived Auschwitz, and his wife, but she didn't work there, she was doing sociology of old age somewhere, and when you think of the people her work brought her into contact with, well, much else comes as pretty trivial compared to those questions of life, death and survival, so they took it as a time that was perhaps not entirely pleasant for them.'

She fell silent, as if she thought it inappropriate to compare her experience with that couple's, although the memory of those times was not pleasant for her either.

'It was other pressures,' Doctor ForSythia tackled political sensitivity from another angle. 'My work was forever raising colleagues' suspicions that I was on another planet. It was terribly risky. As if my thinking was a bit far out. It's perfectly obvious in phenomenology, if you've got any inkling about it, then once you get into it, you can no longer be a materialist, because there things are different. The total change of cognitive perspective obviously leads you to a different place ontologically as well. That means you can no longer be the kind of materialist others take you for, doesn't it? And of course some people knew that.'

Professor Sinapis took Doctor ForSythia's argument to sociology: 'If I were to take some text now, it could perhaps be used to show how certain Western theories were treated. Some of them were accepted unequivocally positively, without much being said about them. A case in point is Parsons, structural functionalism. In essence he also supported that kind of view of the socialist world: society is the dominant feature, it's got some kind of structure, function is the determining factor, who does what and how, you know, order, power, and it all suited. Whereas, say, phenomenological theories, not at all. So to use phenomenological sources in the 1980s was like if you turned up at a fish market with a bowl of lettuce hoping to compete. These were two completely different worlds. I was always more interested in alternative theories to the mainstream – including the Western mainstream, which was after all always viewed a bit guardedly, given that there was that chance of possible cooperation. But those alternative or less significant theories of symbolic interaction, there was hardly any of that here. They were bothered by it because the language was different. You couldn't graft the language of ideology onto it because that stemmed from a completely different mind-set.'

'I never wrote about really sensitive topics,' Doctor SzolPi echoed the position of some of the Czech participants.

'The really sensitive topics were social inequalities, stratification, structures of poverty – that was the really sensitive topic.'

'To write on poverty was certainly an issue, or to write on the Roma,' confirmed Professor Szebah.

I asked, 'You couldn't write about these at all? Or was there a way to write about them that was acceptable and a way that wasn't?'

'Both, it depended on all sorts of ... ,' she searched for a better formulation, '[it was] less dependent on the topic: some could write about poverty, others couldn't.'

'In Hungary poverty research had a very important past before the war,' Professor Szandiliah explained the background of this particular area. 'It was nothing really new, it was also known internationally. Maybe between '49 and '55 I didn't have any foreign contacts, but after that I had many. These were active relationships and poverty was one of the things which was, for instance, one of the topics at the '66 congress, at which I met poverty researchers.[1] In '66–'67 we ended a poverty research [project], after having completed research on income. The lowest decile were [identified] as poor and the research was done. That was in '68.'

I recalled that she had mentioned earlier a complication with this research, namely, that one of their team lost his job and I asked her now about the timing, 'When was your colleague fired?'

'In 1968, but the research was already done and some of it was known. Then for over ten years there were no publications on poverty and then it changed again and a colleague, Ágnes Bokor, was probably the third one who published a book, so it sort of came back.'[2]

Doctor Hyacintha nodded her understanding of the peripatetic ups and downs of certain topics.

'It was like this: you heard from someone third-hand that they knew we had such and such a report at our place. This wasn't some kind of functional

---

[1] The 6th World Congress of Sociology was held in Évian-les-Bains, France, from 4–11 September 1966.
[2] Probably (Bokor 1985).

collaboration. It was like when we were delighted at the chance to read reports from the Institute for Economic Forecasting (*Prognostický ústav*) and secretly made copies of, for instance, papers by [Valtr] Komárek.[3] Really and truly, people read those almost like *samizdat*. So those polls and reports were there for anyone interested, and such interested parties could be from some entirely different quarter. A case in point: people would be brought together by Josef Vavroušek, it was called the Ecology Section of the Czechoslovak Biological Association at the Czechoslovak Academy of Sciences, and he would call together people who had some kind of bearing on the environment.[4] That's where I first saw, say, Hana Librová from Brno, or there might be people there interested in healthy nutrition, or there was an important medical man, Dr Anděl from the Thomayer Hospital.[5] There were people from all kinds of professional backgrounds and the meetings would discuss such things as went against a healthy lifestyle, which effectively amounted to criticism of the prevailing conditions, which we understood as criticism of the regime. There was talk of pollution, understood to imply that no one in authority was bothering with desulphurization, with other types of energy, with the burning of poor quality coal.'

She picked up an olive from her plate, and concluded, 'In a nutshell, any signal of some kind of dysfunction, whether it was new high-rise developments or the overemployment of women or wasteful energy consumption, all these signals were seen as politically significant criticism of the regime.'

'And who saw it in those terms, your superiors, or someone else?' I asked.

She waved the olive in the air. 'No, no. I'd go so far as to say people [generally], but our own superiors were fairly critical.'

'I can't now recall, but perhaps during the last five years up to 1989, when topics like [employee] activization took off, it was sort of less than clear,' Professor SalVia mused on the subject of changing boundaries of sensitivity.

---

[3] Valtr Komárek (1930–2013) was a Czech economist. He was involved in the economic reform plans of the Prague Spring and therefore suffered a career setback afterwards. He was the head of the Institute for Economic Forecasting of the Czechoslovak Academy of Sciences since its foundation in 1984. After the Velvet Revolution he was a member of the Czechoslovak government for a few months and a Deputy of the Czechoslovak parliament until the dissolution of Czechoslovakia on 1 January 1993.

[4] Josef Vavroušek (1944–95) was a Czech environmentalist and a pioneer of the movement for sustainable development. He was a member of the government between 1990 and 1992; he died in an avalanche in the Tatras. The Ecology Section was founded in 1978. For more details from one of the co-founders, see (Stoklasa 2004).

[5] Hana Librová (born 1943) is a Czech sociologist and environmentalist. 'Dr. Anděl' refers probably to Michal Anděl (born 1946), a Czech professor of internal medicine, specializing in metabolism.

'Because on the one hand we were expected to come up with descriptions of a kind or something, of reality, but the reality was unfavourable, so I get the feeling that we didn't actually publish them at that time – not till after '89. Because there was some unease over what to do with data that didn't fit in anywhere. And with the Soviet Union things weren't clear either.'

'[My superiors] also claimed I was being critical, that no one had asked me for criticism, that it wasn't constructive criticism, see?' Doctor SiLena added another dimension of sensitivity. 'I never understood it, there was endless arguing. I didn't know what constructive criticism was; I couldn't write within such terms. I thought there was constructive criticism in it.'

'Sensitive topics …,' Doctor Sambucus began thoughtfully. 'Any general theory, obviously, because there was a kind of schematic division between bourgeois sociology and Marxist sociology, so it was a given that the only forays permitted into the banned field of non-Marxist sociology had to be critical of such things. If anybody had wanted to earn a living from writing critiques of, I don't know, Parsons or Daniel Bell or others.'

He paused and then corrected himself, 'Okay, it might have been possible, but I didn't find that acceptable.'

Doctor ForSythia registered the move from merely sensitive to downright undesirable topics and asserted, 'Phenomenology was off limits, phenomenology was not good. If I even began to express slight reservations about functionalism, my supervisor and head of the institute said: "Careful, that could get you a fail, because basically it's the foundation of Marxist philosophical method." He was a philosopher and a very reasonable man, and he'd allowed me to do phenomenology even though for hardline philosophers of a communist stamp it was something akin to an arch-foe. Because "for one thing I can't understand it, and for another I find it insulting", see? It always worked like that. Husserl was always terribly dangerous. And that's where I got into hot water. The first time was when, to an audience consisting of the entire department of the institute's philosophers, I was to speak about Husserl, and I got a terrible drubbing from the hardliners: that phenomenology was only for an elite, that Patočka was just a successor to Husserl, that it was a philosophy that was dangerous, elitist, anti-working-class. So I did have a spot of bother over it and one colleague told me: "You'll never qualify in a lifetime if you go with that topic." But I did. And it was thanks to having that supervisor, so not everyone was so terrible, right?'

'One man with Christian leanings defended a dissertation that we'd concocted so as to be writing about the problem of labour in early Christian philosophy,' Professor Fragaria picked up on the subjects of qualifying works and their supervisors. 'It was excellent. Labour was a sacrosanct Marxist concept and the thesis was untouchable. Labour's important, so if a thing's about labour, it can't be dismissed out of hand, can it? Of course we tried hard to avoid any major conflict, but to ensure that the labour motif was construed in a profoundly humanist, anthropological sense, so that it comported with the Christian concept of the active soul, and then it got through.'

'There were guiding principles,' Professor HorMi summarized. 'Taboos being the Soviet Union, '56 revolution, the Soviet Army – these were permanent taboos – and Trianon was also a taboo.'

'Obviously there were other politically sensitive topics,' Professor Szebah added. 'The foreign relations of this country, the role of the Soviet Union, certain criticism of the Party – you could write about the state, but not about the Party.'

'You knew that the dictatorship of the proletariat was a basic taboo and you shouldn't touch it,' Professor Szandiliah elaborated. 'You knew that the role of the Soviet Union was a basic taboo and you shouldn't touch it, and of course, everything that the power did within the framework of the dictatorial [government] was a taboo.'

'All the other issues constituted objects for negotiations and these negotiations changed,' confirmed Professor HorMi. 'The outcome could not be easily predicted. You submitted an article dealing with an awkward problem, a sensitive issue. You were not sure whether it would be published or not, but there was some room for playing.'

For a while nobody said anything, as people subjected the platters of starters before them to negotiations of what they should transfer onto their own plates. Finally, Professor Stachys returned in time to the consequences the defeat of the Prague Spring had on research topics.

'In the mid-sixties Banka Filipcová wrote her first book about leisure, one of the first books ever [on the subject] in Eastern Europe – then the Russians started, a group of very progressive Soviet sociologists. Then the topic mutated into the socialist way of life. But investigating leisure and the socialist way of life are two entirely different things.⁶ But that was it, right? As if one followed from the other. Social stratification: that mutated into an examination of the social structure of advanced socialist society. Stratification looked at social differentiation, and that mutated into the topic of rapprochement between the working class and the intelligentsia.'

'I'd be interested to know whether the whole period was homogeneous,' I said.

'The period wasn't homogeneous,' Doctor Sambucus declared, 'given it wasn't even socially homogeneous. There was a time of extremely aggressive influence immediately during the first [phase], let's say in the five or six years, up to, I can't say exactly, '76 or '77, when no research was possible and everything was swamped by diatribes against the Prague Spring. Those were extremely unpleasant times, when the Institute was home to some very weird types who later disappeared. Then gradually subjects appeared that had more to do with management, planning, and it was then that I could find a niche for my subject. I won't suggest an exact date, but let's say from '75 on. That's to judge from the fact that in effect it had been legitimated and nobody meddled in what I was up to anymore, so it was a period when I could stick with it, and after that it got gradually easier by fits and starts.'

'History was dismissed at that time,' Professor HorMi made a Hungarian comparison. 'Formerly, historical scholarship, historical consciousness counted as a direct ideological issue. This was the case before the '56 revolution. After that, historical consciousness and history writing lost much of its significance from the ideological point of view. It was not used for legitimizing any more. This gave more room to historians because they were not so much expected to fulfil ideological missions. They were [now] allowed to be more open to Western sciences, because they lost much of their significance from an ideological point of view.'

'Anything written was a hotchpotch,' Professor Stachys countered with a blanket dismissal of Czech sociology, 'but it was possible to rise above that. A few decent research projects did get done, and as time passed …' He checked himself, considering perhaps whether this could have counted as a change, but then said instead, 'Of course, in the mid-eighties sociology was gradually

---

⁶ See the titles of (Filipcová 1966) and (Filipcová 1976), but compare with (Machonin 1967, 1969, 1992).

transforming, the atmosphere of *perestroika* was beginning to show. Suffice it to pick up *Sociologický časopis*.'

Now I became curious what the researchers thought was possible, which areas they thought stood out.

Doctor ForSythia said, 'Topics that were in favour at the time and that I could have happily done my thesis on included dialectical materialism, historical materialism or conceptions of social classes, the character of class conflict through history or the economic characteristics of the development of – for the sake of argument – Albania. All that was straightforward. Anything that was materialist, anything descriptive, anything that tallied with the basic strategy of Marxism–Leninism, that presented no problems.'

Her list of ideologically unproblematic topics obviously held little attraction for her personally. It was Professor SorBus who took the 'personal interest' angle.

'The sociology of the family was being done. That was down to [Ivo] Možný – originally there'd been the sociology of the small town and of the intelligentsia, that had been a grand plan, it started but it never got off the ground – and [Možný] came up with a brilliant idea and said: "Well, the family is the foundation of the state, so said the Pope and Lenin and everybody. And that it's begun to wobble a bit – we all know that." So work on it started and masses of data and private life-stories were collected. The beautiful, if sad, thing was, that the last value that one could take a stand on with a clear conscience was privacy.'

'There were campaigns, as I recall,' Doctor Sambucus said. 'So in 1970, wasn't it, there was a campaign that went back to the Prague Spring in crushing criticism of everything there had been then, including the people involved. Then it somehow burned itself out, to be followed by a kind of campaign that actually went on at the Institute – not so much a campaign, though, more a tendency with some possibly interesting fringes, the science–and–technology revolution tendency. That was [Radovan] Richta and that whole circle around him. Though after '69 Richta *de facto* discredited himself and also ceased being interesting. That was a tragedy, he was a capable man, intellectually and academically, but he went downhill. None the less, the cult of the scientific and technological revolution as a kind of alternative … '

He paused and then reformulated, 'And as a dynamizer of social development, operated by there being the pressure to work on things that were special for the scientific and technological revolution and their social determinants and consequences.'

He went on to dissociate himself from the next 'campaign', the criticism of bourgeois sociology, before he continued with his list of outstanding topics.

'Then came the wave of the socialist way of life as a special topic. Of course it was an ideologized topic, because it embraced the idea of a normative view whereby people ought to live after a socialist model. However, in terms of analysis, what it sought to investigate were certain actual, empirically ascertainable patterns of activity in life and so in this way it could be turned around. And there was "planning of social development" – anyone hearing that today feels revulsion. But it was a kind of digression where many things could be done. It was tied to planning in some sense, so it brought you into contact with a different kind of people and you could do things on the side, I don't know, mainly fluctuation or the problem of wages or working conditions, if it was in industrial concerns, or migration, rates of popular satisfaction with urban infrastructure, siting of activities throughout an urban space and so forth. So under one or other of those headings, provided it wasn't too monstrous, certain things could be addressed.'

I had one last question, before the starters were cleared away, one that looked back to the nature of authorship that we discussed in the morning. I was wondering to whom the power to choose a research topic belonged and how the choice was made.

'I didn't think of a topic, I couldn't have thought of a topic, one was assigned to me,' Doctor SiLena exclaimed. 'These were what were called "state assignments" and I had a topic assigned to me. It was *they* who decided topics. Though not subsidiary topics, they set the basic ones, so you always found your slot. Like "youth": could there be anything broader? Or "leisure": could there be anything broader? Then you found your slot and started searching.'

I turned to the Hungarian researchers for their assessment. Professor Szandiliah said firmly, 'I always followed my own interests and I had great luck of being able to follow it. Very very seldomly did I accept [suggestions on] what I should research.'

II

We had covered a range at least as colourful as the starters, whose leftovers were now being carried off the table: sensitive, undesirable, 'sacred', desirable, acceptable and doable research topics, topics transformed by political circumstances and the author's agency to choose what to research. As the steaming dishes holding the main courses landed before us, we readied ourselves to delve into the 'meaty' subject of our lunchtime conversation: the language in which the authors set down their scholarly efforts.

My first question was similar to the one I posed when we talked about remembered acts of censorship, but this time I was interested specifically in language.

'Do you feel that the rules governing what could and could not be written varied by period or workplace, publisher, journal or type of publication?'

'Of course [it varied],' Doctor Stellaria said promptly. 'Not only in that you had to stick more piffle in …' She broke off, but immediately continued, 'Like if you were doing a CSc. thesis, you had to write a different kind of work, because it was for an academic readership, it didn't have to be so bullshitty. While if you were writing your habilitation or professorial thesis, which you knew was pedagogical – they're teaching [i.e. rather than research] degrees – there had to be more of that communist garbage. And that was known for definite.'

Doctor SzolPi thought of another comparison, 'The Hungarian word for "stratification" you could use without any problem. *Szegénység* [poverty], that depended on where you published it. Not me, but my boss was invited many times to speak on television, or he was interviewed by journalists, or he wrote articles in *Népszabadság*, so there he couldn't use "poverty" or couldn't use "elite" either. You had to be more careful in the media which were available to a broader audience.'

'So you could use the word "elite" in *Szociológia*, an academic journal?'

'Yes I think so. *Elit*.'

' – but not in the media?'

'More than poverty, *szegénység*, but not so much, because we lived in a society of equality, there was no elite in such a society,' he added wryly and laughed.

'[In the media] we probably talked about different types of elites, but we would use the word *vezetők*, leaders. The terms nowadays are "cultural elite", "political elite", in those times we probably used *politikai vezetők, kulturális vezetők*.'

I saw that the Czech participants used the Hungarian interlude to fill their plates, but I drew their attention away from the food by asking, 'Were there, for instance, words that were sort of blacklisted, and then others that were demanded?'

'No, no. I employed economic and statistical methods and there were no banned words,' Doctor Hepatica responded and cut resolutely into a chicken fillet.

Doctor Stellaria challenged her, 'Words like *renta* [annuity] and *důchod* [income; pension]. *Renta* was associated with *rentiér* [person of independent means] and suggested capitalism, so was unusable. But *důchod* could be used. *Penze* [pension] was understood as a bourgeois term, so *důchod* was used instead. These were delicate nuances, but they often came into play and everybody knew what was meant. Or an excellent term that was …'

She stopped, hovering her fork in the air. 'You couldn't use *chudoba* [poverty] – at the time the term used was: *obyvatelstvo s omezenou možností spotřeby* [citizens with a limited capacity for consumption]. These terms were all code, and everyone knew that citizens with a limited capacity for consumption were really the poor, see? How much they could afford to buy and so on.'

'*Szegénység* [poverty] and *alacsony jövedelműség* [low income]. The difference even that time was very clear,' Professor Szandiliah translated into the Hungarian context.

'You had to use a cover language of the time in the late eighties,' Professor Szebah commented.

'What was your cover language?' I asked her.

'"Multiple disadvantages". *Többszörösen hátrányos helyzetű emberek* or *csoportok*. "People with low income" is not the same as writing about "poverty".'

In response to this exchange, Doctor SiLena said slowly, 'You know, it probably never even dawned on me. I came on the scene when these matters had already been researched in this way, so was there any debate concerning certain terms … ?' she asked rhetorically and immediately continued, 'You know what the problem is? Normalization was still going on and actually the whole research environment was approaching the question in such a way that by then it didn't run into much trouble. Doctor Stellaria might have experienced it in 1970. But I only arrived in '78, and by then I'd be hardly likely to ask that kind of question about poverty.'

'Regarding the terminology, the language, there was no expectation to use the genuine Marxist terminology,' Professor HorMi assessed the situation in Hungarian social history. 'Therefore, very many scholarly historical studies were totally independent of any Marxist terminology. This was especially characteristic of the more distant periods, medieval and early modern periods, but even the 19th and, to some extent, the 20th centuries. If you had an interest in these periods you had bountiful opportunities to give an account of the 19th or 20th centuries without engaging in any Marxist paradigms, tenets. Even the use of language could be freed from it.'

'There were magic words,' Mrs Euphrasia reminded us mildly. '"Intelligibility" [*srozumitelnost*], "accessibility to the masses" [*přístupnost masám*] – like that Mayakovsky wasn't remotely accessible to the masses. So that's the way they took it: whether or not he sympathized with the working class and other such bunkum.'

'Can you recall any of the language or types of comments that you got in peer reviews?' I approached the subject from another angle.

Professor Sinapis responded, 'I don't remember very well now. Mostly it was along the lines that "surely Marxism offers a different solution and a different approach" to whatever it was. There'd be formulations of the kind "the morality of socialist man is surely based on different principles, and you can't" – I don't know, if it was to do with, for the sake of argument, egoism – "say that egoism is exactly the same in socialist society as it is in capitalist society, it must always be differentiated". In other words, it was always: "Yes, the problem does exist here, but it's different. You can discuss it, it's good that you're discussing it, but you can't apply what foreign sources say to conditions in this country. You have to say, to show, that we do have the problem, but it's dealt with in a different way and that's better, more positive, it doesn't have capitalist roots because here we don't actually have a morality of self-interest based on exploitation." And that's where words like "exploitation", "bourgeoisie" came in, as part of the thinking of the establishment.'[7]

'Or at one time there was a word that had to be served up in measured doses according to whether you were talking about "internationalism" or "cosmopolitanism",' Doctor Stellaria rushed in. '"Cosmopolitanism" was

---

[7] Compare Professor Sinapis's characterization with the conclusion Eszter Berényi made from her analysis of articles in *Szociológia*, the most significant professional journal of the discipline in Hungary, that were published between 1972 and 1989: 'Whereas "Western societies" or their constituent elements (the Western family; the Western lifestyle; the working classes in the Western societies) were often connected to a narrative of crisis without any further explanation, articles about Eastern European socialist societies did not include a similar crisis narrative. Rather, socialist societies were presented as imperfect but evolving' (Berényi 2018: 270).

repudiated, "internationalism" was tailor-made. But since in the early years of normalization people would sign [declarations] that the entry of Warsaw Pact troops had been international assistance, so when you used the word "international" [as *internacionální*, not the usual Czech word, *mezinárodní*] it was code for "I'm kissing your arse". But then it had to be taken differently again; that "international assistance" was re-interpreted, and by the end of normalization it was more or less on a par with "for eternity".[8] It didn't cut the mustard anymore and was dropped from use. The words had taken on a different flavour and you knew that if you used *internacionální* in the second half of the eighties, it had that association, see? You couldn't use it because by then it would have been meant jocularly, as provocation. That's to say, there's that shift. And the word *internacionální* also couldn't be used because it was linked to the vetting – "international assistance". Or you couldn't use the word "fraternal" either, because that went together with the first period of normalization – "fraternal assistance", "fraternal international assistance".'

Doctor Stellaria changed the flow of conversation from peer reviewers' comments back to general perceptions. Once we were back on that territory, it seemed a good moment to return to the camouflaging language and other means the researchers used to avoid giving offence. Doctor Hepatica seized on the subject.

'All newspapers, magazines and journals were closely monitored, but in, say, *Politická ekonomie* you can find articles that weren't monitored. It was a theoretical journal, with formulae, and some people sheltered behind formulae, others behind statistics. I for one did a lot with figures, and that was my salvation. No one could refute official figures.'

'First and foremost I tried to avoid omitting things,' Professor Lilius defined his strategy.

'Of course that meant my account of, say, [George] Orwell had to be couched in critical terms. And also from that followed the language, how you expressed yourself. My basic principle was not to leave anyone out. Students could read it, I did give a work's title, and so they could then form their own opinion of it. So my view had to be negative, that was perfectly obvious, [those who kept an eye on things] would never have let it go [otherwise].'

---

[8] One of the frequent slogans that communist propaganda used during the normalization period was: 'With the Soviet Union for eternity!' Folk wisdom produced a postscript: 'But not a moment longer!'

'Orwell wasn't banned,' Doctor LoTus explained. 'At most I might have written one sentence to the effect that "a number of left-wing writers" – if I were to write in the manner as I see it today – "previously left-wing writers, such as George Orwell later adopted an anti-Communist stance", and it would be true and that would be an end of it. I wouldn't have said any more on the subject, some clever explanation that they didn't actually mean to criticize Stalin, but only some current trends in the West, I say I wouldn't have written that because it would mean withholding the essential element of the truth of the matter.'

Doctor LoTus made it clear that, unlike Professor Lilius, he preferred omissions to politically more acceptable interpretations.

Doctor SiLena laid her fork down and motioned that she now remembered something about her troubles with language.

'There used to be what were called "state assignments" and I had a topic assigned to me. My topic was to do with the education system, and there I ran into trouble, immediately. Right down the line. My boss returned my paper straightaway, I had to re-do it, and it ran into trouble again. The topic wasn't the problem, I'd been assigned it, but I did have a problem over language. I was reproached for the language being "feminine", and for using euphemisms and words that had no place in it. Never before had anyone said anything of the kind. I can't recall specific words, but then there weren't that many: let's say, if the paper had fifteen pages, there'd be two or three words. But they caused tremendous opposition. To me they were ordinary words, because you could meet any one of them routinely.'

'And were the words described as feminine or unscholarly or something else?' I asked, because she and I had discussed the issue of some language use being labelled as gendered on a previous occasion.

She replied, 'Unscholarly and feminine.'

'[Certain phrases] were even used by the regime. Like capitalism was associated with "and co.", as in "Rikl and Sons" or "Rikl and Co." – "and company" – that branded a thing as capitalist,' Doctor Stellaria reminded us of another use of labelling someone or something by association with particular words.

'All the political trials ran with that "and co.": "Slánský and co.", "Horáková and co.". So there was again an attempt to create the notion that they were capitalists. They used this code word to brand people, "and company" – today you'd say "Co. Ltd". She laughed ironically and added as an afterthought, 'And next time the regime changes, people will be using "Co. Ltd".'

It was probably the sinister implications of Doctor Stellaria's reflections that prompted Doctor ForSythia to an even darker contemplation.

'I was always most afraid of people who simulated philosophy, who only knew the one ghastly version of Marxism that was used to explain things back then. They didn't know Hegel, they didn't know anything. And because they were only half-educated and knew very little, they were the most dangerous ones. Because they always framed the pressure they exerted in a colour scheme of political attacks, but sometimes it was simply that they were affronted by things they didn't understand.'

'Language was pitched at two levels, which means there was considerable ambivalence as regards specialist language, because on the one hand it was perceived as being properly scientific, but on the other because the relevant guardians of ideology didn't understand it very well, so saw it as highly dangerous,' Professor Sinapis confirmed that, indeed, linguistic sophistication could give offence to some in power.

'So if there was talk of "adaptation" [*adaptace*], they preferred to replace the word with something else, because what is "adaptation" really? – Is it *přizpůsobivost* [actually = adaptability] or to do with adapting in moral terms, right? Those people immediately converted it into this kind of language.'

'One danger was fear of an excessive demand for not only conformist, but also accommodating terminology,' Professor SorBus traced the obsessive picking over of words to its origin, fear. 'Authors actually deriving it from the fifties, and that was where they were wrong. They dipped into fifties terminology either from defeatism, or for it to serve as a blanket under which they could retreat and enjoy private life. My feeling is that people often thought that more was not permitted than was permitted, because if you asked no questions and weren't conspicuously provocative, everything was all right.'

Professor SalVia nodded understandingly and spoke in a low tone, 'Human nature contains lots of positives and negatives and the instinct of self-preservation and an ability to justify everything conceivable to oneself may give rise to lots of things. That may even be the reason why I was genuinely afraid to join the Party. That it might do something to me that I wouldn't have wanted. And the seventies revealed in people's characters things that were doubtless there before, but our generation hadn't experienced them and didn't know them. We first encountered them after sixty-eight. That switching of opinions, people doing anything that was to their advantage. In the worse, the ethical sense, that's still with us. The seventies were kind of irksome, dirty, weary. And also the fairly strong fear – though we needn't have had it. We w ... ,' her voice was drowned by a loud scrape against somebody's plate, '... especially us young people who rubbed shoulders with dissidents, one didn't really know. We all had our interrogations at Bartolomějská,[9] which really was unpleasant, but nothing life-threatening, let alone involving physical violence or anything like that. It was kind of ... '

She hesitated what name to put to it, but then merely concluded, 'And we were scared anyway.'

We chewed in gloomy silence for a while. To raise our spirits, I asked everybody, whether they developed some expressions that they preferred to use in place of those perceived as officially required without attracting trouble for nonconformity.

Doctor Stellaria dropped her cutlery as her words gushed forward, 'During the normalization period, you could get away with saying, for instance, "there are major differences", but you weren't going to use "antagonistic differences". Or there was "difference" (*rozdíl*) and "conflict" (*rozpor*). "Conflict" was more telling. That was already like "antagonistic", but because "antagonistic" had Marxist associations, "the antagonistic difference between the exploiters and the exploited", so if you used the word "conflict", the conflict was there, but it didn't have that association; in other words, for an author, in this case me, it was much more acceptable to use "conflict" than "antagonistic difference".'

She picked up the fork again and skewered a potato. 'Look, there really were such things like: "our" society – they wanted it to be "socialist" society. So sometimes I'd write "our" society so as not to have the "socialist" thing, or I might write "the community of socialist nations" or "in socialist systems". They're delicate nuances, but it was in there. [Petr] Fidelius would have had a lot to say about it.[10] He was brilliant at that, he'd say it was a language of attributives, as in: "Our advanced socialist society constructing ... " Then the value of the whole [text] came out of the number of attributives.'

---

[9] The State Security, the secret police, headquarters.
[10] See especially (Fidelius 1983, 1998).

'I may have written "socialist society", Doctor Hepatica admitted, 'It's, I mean ... ,' she trailed off. 'I can't recall, I don't remember if it was on someone's orders. We've all got the same problem even today: we don't say "socialist society", and if I want to write about the past using some kind of shorthand, do I write "the period of socialism" or put "socialism" in inverted commas? Once, when I wanted to put "state socialism", they said: "Fine, but what is it? People don't know." I wanted to avoid "socialism", but back then I didn't avoid it. Because it was also there in the statistics [as a term] and the literature, so I couldn't avoid it.'

I was not willing to give up on the camouflaging yet. 'Did you have your own "translations" to use instead of these expressions?' I asked nobody in particular.

'Like "class struggle"?' Professor Hedera suggested. 'That's something I'd never have written. I might have had to ... ,' she began to explain, but apparently lost her thought.

'No class struggle: people died, people were born and [my topic] was nothing to do with any kind of class struggle. To me class struggle was always ... ,' again she did not finish, but then reflected further, 'And above all else, I knew how nonsensical it was as a term. Then I [couldn't stomach] "socio-economic formations", I avoided them, like there was the slaveholding order and the order of – what was it called? – feudal order. But I did draw a distinction between – what did they call it officially? – "monopoly capitalism" and "free-market capitalism". I did do that, even though it's a Marxist term, but then it's in common use worldwide. I got it from Bourdieu, from the French authors I studied. Though Bourdieu himself was a Marxist, wasn't he? Hobsbawm the same. Marxists do exist and they do their own thing. I recognized the distinction between "free market" and "monopoly". But I didn't see it as some great achievement of Marxism.'

'I avoided those coinages,' Professor SorBus said resolutely. 'I didn't write about class struggles, though today I would, without minding. As applicable, obviously. Today we know since Foucault there's been all-out fighting over discourse, or class struggle since Bourdieu, so what of class struggle? Goodness, in the first half of the nineteenth century, why shouldn't there have been class struggle? I'd happily write that today. But back then it was almost a kind of snobbery, avoiding it.'

'I knew my coursebooks had to be written in a way to avoid the [stigmatizing] excuse that it wasn't Marxist,' Professor Fragaria explained her position as an author.

'In other words, in most works, even in collected volumes up to November [1989], there was always that criterion of the paramount formulation or substantive idea. You'd write "see Marx, page such-and-such", these *topoi* were familiar. There was always that one place, that riposte by Marx on Hegel's *Lectures on the History of Philosophy*, where it was explained what concrete or abstract is in ontological terms. It's an important, interesting area. There were several such places, we always referenced them and that way shielded ourselves. And we'd also shield ourselves by citing world-renowned philosophers on the basis chiefly of Caucasian Soviet philosophers, because there, unlike conditions in this country, phenomenology and existentialism weren't looked down on. This was the only country where such authors couldn't be mentioned. So we'd quote: "one Soviet author says on p. XX that …". And he did say it, but at the same time, within what he said, he was quoting Husserl, Heidegger, Russell and others, so we got the quotes in and that was that.'

The caterers began to clear away the main course dishes. As we were waiting for the desserts, I invited my mentors to assess the overall use of the scholarly language with the hindsight of the intervening years.

I asked, 'Do you think that this practice of using certain authorially preferred or, on the other hand, externally demanded phraseology was always a conscious act, or was it something that had passed so far into the bloodstream as not to register?'

'It was entirely conscious,' Professor Sinapis said without hesitation. 'In my student days I was incapable of accepting the world-view or ideology that existed. So it may have passed into the bloodstream, but I think it was more a kind of indifference to the fact that such phrases were used. They were seen as more or less formal, empty things that were simply put there, like when you get a parcel it's wrapped in padding. Just padding that was of no importance, that got discarded anyway.'

'It was a learning process for all of us,' Professor Szebah confirmed that the situation was similar in Hungary. 'It started in the secondary school: what is the way to describe things? You were socialized into that, and that was the way how you participated. One of the key features of the dissident literature and key aims of participating in underground activities was to learn a different language and to use a different language. Sometimes it was much less about the topic, it was just about how you address a topic.'

She fell silent. Nobody else claimed the floor, so she continued, reflecting, 'I thought about it a lot after the transition, about our language. One very effective tool to stop intellectuals from publishing was depriving them of their language.'

'An "amplifier of terror" didn't apply just to actual "terrorists",' Professor SorBus brought up his earlier metaphor, 'but given how [authors] overused the phraseology, it's understandable this made others feel obliged to follow them. It created a benchmark. For a long time I myself had scruples, but at the very end of that period I did use "Marxist–Leninist".'

'It occurred to me back then that the young generation was so fixated on music, so overrated the importance of musical expression, the language of music, because they were totally disillusioned, totally fed up with the abuse of language,' Doctor Hyacintha offered. 'Because language had lost its credibility. They needed another medium to communicate with others and test whether they saw things the same way and understood one another. It seemed to me – and this still strikes me as basic to the woeful conditions of the eighties, despite *glasnost* and everything – that language was being abused. Words had lost their authenticity, which was why the young generation were so attached to that non-verbal medium, that kind of communication.'

The arrival of a selection of dainty cakes and small glass cups filled with delicious-looking puddings created a powerful distraction for everyone from any further intellectual involvement. It did not matter, because it seemed that we had exhausted the subject of concrete language uses anyway.

III

I waited until everyone seemed happy with their choice of desserts, and as coffees were being poured, I opened the last theme planned for the lunchtime conversation: the very object of my quest, writing in 'code'. Was there some sort of a code shared among the scholarly community of authors and readers that allowed them to speak about ideologically suspicious matters? If so, what did it consist in?

I turned to Doctor LupiNus, 'You mentioned once that, for instance, you left the pronoun out of your translation of "a voice against them" because it could have evoked unfortunate political connotations, and I'd be interested to know if you consciously resorted to what might be called encoding your texts. Did you perhaps select different words or a different tone in your argument, assuming that the readership would understand that you really meant something else?'

'Just so, just so,' he replied animatedly, almost spilling his coffee as he shook his finger in the air. 'Like with those attacks on Austrian censorship. The mass emigration to America due to the wretched economic situation in Austria after the wars it had lost. At the time of [Karel Hynek] Mácha the existence of dual – ecclesiastical and political – censorship and things like that. I expected the reader to grasp the analogy that since Austria–Hungary we'd not … ,' he did not complete his parable, focusing momentarily on settling his cup on the saucer.

'I even put it in my thesis, that any interventions might be down to censorship. And in my articles I simply dropped hints and the intelligent reader would think: "But back then it was …" To the extent that such things were there when I went on about censorship, I was having a go at Austria–Hungary and how they stifled everything.'

I asked the others, 'How far do you think the process of "encoding" was deliberate in you as author and how far had it become so unconscious, so deep-seated that it didn't even need to be deliberate?'

It was Doctor Stellaria who replied. 'Look, I projected it. I'd got double vision, see? And there were probably reflections of it in other authors as well, because for instance I wrote an article for my boss and he put the insertions in. In other words, he had to be reflecting it too, and editors also reflected it. What effect it had on the readership, that I can't say.'

I now noticed that only Professors Szebah and Szandiliah were present in the virtual space and so invited at least them to give us a Hungarian perspective.

Professor Szebah began, 'I can just refer to what I said earlier. You were somehow a part of the language. This tactic that you ask about belongs to a harsh totalitarian rule, then you have this cover language, but that was not much necessary here in the seventies: you used the language that you'd use otherwise and it was not so much a concern. In fact an indication of it is that I recently read some of the things and found them quite OK. Obviously, it's a little bit archaic, it's not the way you'd express the same content [now], but it's more stylistics than anything else.'

'It is quite interesting,' Professor Szandiliah mused, 'I don't know if you know that after '89 everybody expected that lots of literary and scientific work would come out of the drawers which could not be published [during the Kádár regime] but nothing appeared. There was none, except for [István] Bibó, but Bibó is a very special case, and everything he wrote was excellent. But he is really a very very special case. And he was dead by then. Otherwise leading people did not write any manuscripts, which couldn't be published, because after all there was also *Beszélő*, the second *Öffentlichkeit*, and legally or illegally it could [be published]. What was published in *Beszélő* was usually read and known.'

I turned back to my Czech mentors and pressed on, 'Do you think there were ever any universally adopted, but unwritten, rules for communication between authors and readers?'

'As it happens I read many texts that way,' Professor Sinapis confirmed. 'And I think back then our reading culture was quite highly developed. Meaning you passed over some things as unimportant and saw meanings more. On the other hand, I think that in the world of the rather particular kind of readers of specialist literature it didn't play that great a role. There what was of greater interest was the quality of the information they were getting. Meaning the kind of information they were acquiring and, as applicable, the references – the theoretical and other contexts referred to. And then there wasn't so much allegorizing in that type of publication; you got that more in prose and verse, where the language is different, with metaphor and suchlike. There interpreting things becomes something else.'

'So was nothing like that used in the social sciences?' I asked.

'No, I think it was quite slight there.'

'So no agreed code existed?'

'I don't think it did much,' he said sceptically.

Professor Helleborus shook his head, as if he suddenly remembered something and said, laughing, 'I later wrote works more of a fairly popularizing kind, and it became a preoccupation and I definitely meant to write in a kind of code, with a sort of message. It's a book that failed in its message because hardly anyone bought it. It was about the kind of extremist revolutionaries who wanted a totally vanished, beautiful, ideal society, without arriving at its possible realization, because they were, not utopians, but not very close to reality. Then about a year later, a colleague who was in contact with "non-conformists" told me: "Listen, they told me to thank you for that book about dissidents." They sort of saw those people as persecuted dissidents who wanted to change the world. At the time of writing, it would never have occurred to me I could be writing about dissidents, but it was about people who dared, people who had the courage to launch into some great controversy. So that was interesting for the thing about codes.'

Professor Stachys nodded, indicating that he was familiar with the problem of an unintended code and hurried in with his own example, 'Right before the vettings, when it was a life–and–death struggle, my boss became head of the science section at the bureau of an extremely odious, nauseating Party journal. It was terrible. He had us write some article about higher education. A colleague and I did set about it that time, but it took an age, about eight or ten hours. The boss then published it in that journal in two instalments [under his own name]. Then he summoned us and said: "What I'm supposed to make of this I've no idea, the comrades have had a go at me because extracts from it have been read on Radio Free Europe." They'd simply read out certain excerpts from the article – at Free Europe they'd got a good nose for that kind of thing – that we'd let creep in.'

He took a sip of coffee. 'But I insist it hadn't been deliberate, there wasn't a hint of heroism in it. Our thinking had simply been along certain lines, and having tried to mutate ourselves into the spirit of the boss, we apparently hadn't been entirely successful.'

'There might be, say, certain sops to Cerberus, certain wordings I put in,' Professor Sinapis conceded. 'Things like that "socialist society is after all different from capitalist society, and so we must look at it in a different light" or that "the conclusions arrived at by scientists in the West need not be unequivocally applicable to us". But having got one's point across and the readers being able to spot things for themselves, that was the main thing.'

'The criterion was a deeper understanding of what was being talked about,' Professor Fragaria elaborated on this last point.

'A text would be layered. That was, I think, the main way it was resolved. If we wanted to publish, we couldn't set out openly from anti-Marxist postures. If one reads the things one wrote, the conclusion runs: "Thus having due regard to our scientific Marxist theory, this is the key problem that needs to be solved." Whether we were addressing the woman question or some practical issue, like the city or the culture of the construction industry and the like, it made absolutely no difference. For the broadest contexts it always had to have the "Marx says on this that … , and here he says that …". It was a kind of code, and you realized – when you look back at it now, seeing it on TV – that it operated as a magic formula that was taken as something that was therefore irrefutable: if Comenius stands for our progressive tradition, he just has to be published, even if he writes about God, right? There was that sentence: "It's a progressive tradition," they all say it, from Nejedlý right down to goodness knows who, the Soviets say it, so how could anyone conformist harbour doubts about anything so momentous?[11] As a Marxist, you surely can't.'

'My concern was always who was going to read it, so that I didn't look stupid. In other words I wrote it for the book's users, consumers,' Doctor Stellaria looked at the matter from another angle, emphasizing the distinction between the reader-censor and the reader-target audience.

'Did you use certain words that you presumed the reader would understand what you meant by them?'

'Certainly!' she exclaimed. 'I don't remember now, but that's certainly the case. I knew it was code and that the reader would understand. Things like: "in the period preceding the Second World War". Everybody understood this to mean the First Republic. If you used "First Republic", that was associated by the regime with Masaryk and that was unacceptable. You wrote "in the period preceding the Second World War" or "in the period between the two world wars", and then you could say something positive.'

'In my field the concern was more to display facts to the reader in the best possible way,' Professor Hedera dismissed the haggling over language. 'I mean things like average life expectancy, death rates, birth rates and suchlike. The problem with this field is a bit different: to demonstrate that a number says something, that the most convincing proof is in the number. I think that [encoding] applied more to, I don't know, dramatic works and perhaps prose and verse. But in scholarly writing it would really be out of place. More important is not to make things up – for ideological reasons. One historian is castigated for sort of making things up about the urban poor in pre-Hussite times, that for *de facto* ideological reasons he'd misinterpreted the sources. With me there was never any question of possibly misinterpreting a source on voluntaristic grounds, but more because of verbal clumsiness or some methodological failing or other shortcomings. In other words, there was always some ... ,' her voice trailed off. 'Hard to say.'

---

[11] Zdeněk Nejedlý (1878-1962) was an influential communist musicologist and the Minister of Culture and Education in the early state-socialist period.

Hers was a general scepticism about the significance of the code. Professor Stachys seemed to be considering the point and said, 'I was in the pub with the vice-rector of the Political College – we did socialize, sometimes we met at the same pub – and he told me: "Next Wednesday's *Rudé právo* is going to carry a big article on sociology. Read it carefully. You'll see all the things I've got to say." So the next week I read it. We met up in the pub again and I said: "I've tried and tried, but can't find anything but hot air. What's in it?" And then he pointed to one paragraph where he thought he'd said something radical. I couldn't see it. Someone else wrote a book and said: "When you read it, you'll see all the things I've [put in it]." There's absolutely nothing in it, not a thing. This was the self-deception of those people who were part of the "structure", as it used to be called. They kidded themselves they were doing something, but they weren't doing anything. Aesopian language didn't work.'

'I'm not really convinced that things were really encoded like that,' Professor Sinapis joined in on the scepticism. 'Obviously, there are times when one hesitates over how to express something so that it gets across to the reader without entailing some, let's say – in quotation marks – "censorial" intervention. But that's more a matter of stylistics than encoding. Simply ensuring that a thing has the required meaning, without the words somehow debasing the meaning.'

Looking directly to me, Professor Stachys concluded resolutely, 'Listen, my impression is that, if we're talking about the period 1970–89, it wasn't there. In the Soviet Union, there was, among social scientists, an unwritten convention that resided in having an introduction to the effect that "Comrade Brezhnev said such-and-such at the Congress", and then you could move straight on to the Frankfurt School without batting an eyelid. These were those sops to Cerberus that everyone knew how to apply, when it was known exactly what to skip, and it was understood perfectly well. It was visible in the structure of the text. I think that what the Soviets learned to do because it was their only option – and they learned it very well – didn't exist in this country during the period of normalization, which in a sense was a return to a kind of neo-Stalinism.'

With the desserts devoured and the coffee cups drained, the official working time planned for our symposium was up. The conversation over this last meal course was just as 'nutritious' as all the others on this day and the day before. Yet, I did not feel that I had found what I hoped to find at the end of the quest. Over no other issue had there been such an apparently irreconcilable contradiction among the mentors as over the existence of a 'code'. Some had no doubt whatsoever that a code operated, and also that it constituted a part of a sophisticated reading culture, while others dismissed the whole idea and thought it illusory, if not downright self-deceptive.

I *definitely* did not have the object of the quest in my grasp. Admittedly, that was not unusual as far as quests go. I had learned a great deal, but now thought that perhaps I could push it a bit further. The participants were eyeing the wine carafes that appeared on the side table. The plan was to relax with a glass of wine and an informal chat. I wondered if I could coax my mentors into staying a bit longer and talking about the atmosphere in academia since the fall of state socialism.

7

The review

Loss of memory, the ghosts of academia past in the present

The impulse for this entire project came from my early teaching experience in the 1990s, when I realized that the Czech students still studied from many of the same coursebooks as I had a decade earlier, but that they read them differently. The episode narrated by Doctor Stellaria about Professor Stachys's student at the end of Chapter 5 described a situation all too familiar in my classroom. If Professor Stachys had to listen to embarrassing ideological quotes from his own book, I found myself wondering where on earth the student I was examining read such and such thing in this or that book, because I could not remember having read anything of the sort in it myself. So I embarked on a quest to retrieve the 'code' to those texts, which I presumed must have existed in the pre-1989 scholarly community, from their authors and readers. The twenty-eight individual interviews with Czech and Hungarian academics who wrote and read scholarly literature in the 1970s and 1980s and that are presented here as 'imagined conversations' revealed a rich and layered problem, but the key itself remained a mirage. The academics often found it difficult to reconstruct the exact conditions and overall working atmosphere of pre-1989 academia. Moreover, they inevitably projected the public and scholarly discussions current at the time of the interview onto their recollections. This last chapter will explore some of the obstacles time placed in the way of the questing novice. Perhaps the mentors will help her achieve not so much the presumed object of the quest, but an understanding beyond that original goal.

I

Glasses in hand, the participants dispersed around the room and conversed in small groups. The projection screen offered us a blank stare, indicating that none of the Hungarians were connected. I walked over to Professors Hedera and Fragaria who stood next to each other, but did not seem to be involved in conversation. I asked them if they could put themselves in the role of 'reviewers' of the 'text' that we collectively produced and consider the past with the eyes of the present.

Professor Hedera shook her head, 'Look, to be honest, plenty of the kind of people who go on today about being hard done by when it comes to developments in scholarship ... '

She did not complete the sentence to say what these people were or did. She took a sip from her glass.

'Well, we knew them in the days when they were the ones on top. After all, plenty of them were in the Party and, to be honest, we never expected them to produce anything worthwhile in terms of scholarship. So today they'll turn up saying they couldn't because of the harassment, or because they hadn't had access to sources, or they'd been sacked. Well, that might be so, but the way it seems to us ... ,' again she did not say what it seemed like.

'See, it can happen that sometimes emigration itself, or "internal" emigration, might well be why someone runs out of ideas and so turns their mind to other things, like anti-communist politics. Which is to their credit, on the other hand there's no possible claiming that because of that – Dušan Třeštík put it beautifully, some article to mark the 17th November or 28th October, I think, in *Lidové noviny*, that it's hard, that for instance that Catholic ... ,' she looked for the right phrase, 'they think that if the communists' truth ceased to apply in '89, then their own truth has to apply automatically, right?[1] That those who may well have had their problems in the past, they were suddenly rid of them because they'd been anti-communist, and that fact carried some weight with the populace. So once the truth laid down by the communists was scrapped, they got to thinking: "Good, that truth no longer holds, so what does hold is

---

[1] The historian Dušan Třeštík (1933–2007) published numerous articles on the interpretation of history and on 'national truth'. Professor Hedera might be referring, for example, to one of the following (Třeštík 1994, 1995, 1998, 2002).

the truth we had before." Except that even before they had been at loggerheads with all and sundry. Even then they needn't have achieved that much of note, so they can't go blaming their inability on the communists. It's my belief that if you really have something worth saying, a way can always be found to say it.'

Professor Fragaria nodded understandingly throughout this hard assessment that not all resistance turned out to be academically productive and would not stand the test of time. She now said, 'I remember one experience, in eighty-nine or ninety it was, the journal *Pedagogika* arrived – its very last issue, which didn't appear until eighty-nine, though it had gone to press in eighty-eight – so it had a lot of articles that had gone to press before November. The only one that passed muster in the new environment was by – he's dead now – [Vlastimil] Pařízek, writing about the French education system.[2] It had its obvious limitations, not to put too fine a point on it, but it was factually sound and gave a factual account of French education. As for the other articles in it, I looked through them and said to myself: "Good grief, cut out all the Marxist padding, and these articles are totally vacuous." I imagine this shocking impression would have been weaker at an earlier time. It wouldn't have been totally absent, but it would have been weaker than if it had happened before eighty-nine, because in those days you just passed over the waffle and picked up on what interested you, and that was that. Whereas, this time the sheer nonsensicality of it leapt to the eye. Today, when you see this kind of thing in films, all that froth you get in old newsreels and suchlike, you can't help asking; "Goodness, how could we have taken this as background?" Not that we took it as something with a message, but it was there in the background, a cliché that didn't actually irritate us non-stop at the time, provided we had other things to think about than how politics worked and how downright awful it was. But the moment conditions were re-adjusted, it moved to the foreground in all its horror. So in this sense there will have been lots of people who took it like when I was young and everyone crossed themselves as they passed a wayside shrine, though Protestants and atheists wouldn't, but if you did pass a shrine it was in the certain knowledge that anyone from a church happening by would cross themselves.'

Doctor Sambucus and Professor Helleborus must have overheard Professor Fragaria's unsentimental reflections, and joined our group.

---

[2] She refers probably to (Pařízek 1988).

Doctor Sambucus said in wonder, 'I don't know any more. Obviously it's possible that one could become subconsciously immersed in the surrounding sub-culture, where a kind of self-stylization had begun to operate, but I can't now reconstitute my mind-set of twenty-four or twenty-three years ago.'[3]

He contemplated his wine glass for a moment. He obviously thought of those old texts and any 'coding' that may have been taking place in them, because he said, 'Everything's grown a bit hazy, so I probably couldn't do it [decoding] now. It's quite possible, but I'd have to pick up this or that book and have a look at the sections where [text coding] might come into question.'

'Let me put it in another way,' Professor Helleborus offered. 'A certain Scandinavian social scientist – she speaks excellent Czech – who's read and still reads quite a lot of my things, she made herself known to me after 1990 and somehow we got round to what I was writing in the nineties and what I'd written before. And she said: "So you're basically writing the same things, just using different words." Meaning certain words are missing, right? I don't think we actually realize we needn't cover our asses any more by using the right adjectives or quotes and stuff.'

I saw Doctor Stellaria hovering alone nearby and I waved to her. She strolled over just as Professor Hedera began to tell another story.

'There are some very interesting things like about our historians' relations with the *Annales* school and suchlike, but obviously these can go all the way back to the First Republic. And all that's now in those archives. Except there's one very important thing – that anyone working in the archive who hasn't got first-hand experience of such things, who doesn't remember them, whose memory isn't jogged by things, won't get much out of it. There's this young man at my institute, he's doing them there [the relations] and he works at the Academy archive in Prague, but then when you hear him talk – he gave a paper on exiles the other day – you suddenly see that folk like him don't know the period, they didn't know the people, in short, they don't have a clue.'

Professor Helleborus grew animated as she spoke and now interjected, 'Listen, I've got this great story that I love to quote. One doctoral student, a really bright lad who's certainly not way out on the far left, not a bit of it, he

---

[3] This interview was conducted in 2003: not 23 or 24, but 14 years after the demise of state socialism. Doctor Sambucus may have made a simple mistake, but he may also be thinking of the period of normalization as the 1970s, or perceiving the past as more distant than in reality.

wanted to set up a Marxism seminar at the faculty. I'd already had the same idea, but I didn't dare, if the truth were told. Well, they went ahead and it was a great success. And he shows me their syllabus and says: "And I'm putting this here and these ones and here I'm putting British Marxism, so that's perhaps where you'd belong."'

He laughed. 'He already got me pigeon-holed as a has-been, see? He didn't mean it critically, he just meant he'd got me pigeon-holed.' Without pausing, he launched by association into another story.

'Then to my horror I came up against [the different manner those times are interpreted by the young generation] in a completely different way, during an exam one time, when the candidate, she – it was some young woman – took a fancy to some really primitive ideological sop to Cerberus [taken from my own work] and she starts picking it over and sort of going quite deep into it. I don't remember what it was exactly, could have been something about the transition from feudalism to capitalism and then how they were connected, or I don't know, can't remember what it was, but she was *so* very earnest about it and really keen. I wouldn't write it today, see, but that's also relevant, right?'

Doctor Stellaria said brightly, 'Like yesterday, I was in on this debate about minorities and this guy was going on about a refugee camp, and then he says: "Well, the chap running the refugee camp told us that [those people] would be stationed there only temporarily." But you realize, 'being stationed only temporarily' sounded weird in 1990. I looked around at the people there and one was a protestant clergyman and his wife and their two children, and they all cracked a smile. Them and me. For us it carried associations of the Soviet troops who "would be stationed only temporarily [on Czechoslovak soil]", well it would, wouldn't it? Meanwhile, there was this lady from the multicultural centre sitting there – ,' she nodded towards me. 'She must have been about your age or a bit younger – and it never dawned on her that it might be funny. So you could suddenly see that in that hall there was effective communication among five people united by generation, but no real communication with the public.'

Our conversation was interrupted by a sudden movement on the projection screen. To our surprise, four of the Hungarian participants were smiling at us, all gathered in Professor HorMi's study. That is where they had all disappeared to after lunch! They toasted us with glasses of red wine. I regarded the label on the bottle standing on the desk next to them with some envy and looked dispiritedly at my own drink. Well, at least my instinct directed me to the really quite good Moravian white, rather than the red grown under a much colder sun than that lovely Szekszárdi liquid temptingly placed in my line of vision and that I remembered from my time in Hungary.

II

Most of the Czech participants had already left, some were taking their leave now, but I invited the rest back to the table and join Professors Szandiliah, HorMi, Laxi and Lustani for a last bit of talk, one on the ghosts of academia past in the present. How are the works written in the past perceived by the generations that were then too young to write or read them or, indeed, to remember much of the general atmosphere of the time?

Doctor Hepatica grimaced, 'People don't go back to [things published previously]. Look, there was, like, an entire Institute of Economics, and the things they turned out there, and there was me, casting about with my own thing, and they just tossed it out, and the same thing at the [Prague] School of Economics as well. They think that anything written back then was rubbish and has to be got rid of, so they got rid of the whole institute. And it's not there, so I don't delude myself thinking that anyone's going to go looking up my books now. But no one said a word to me. I am highly regarded. I got my readership (*docentura*) after the revolution, so that also tells you that if I my hands were dirty they'd hardly give me a readership at the same institution just so they could give any old kind of honour.'

'I think that it's still in the nature of things here,' Professor Fragaria said flatly, 'especially with those twenty-five or thirty-year-old postgrads – to turn everything upside down. What used to apply was bad; what applies today is anything that goes against what used to be said. And it's my belief that this is due to the particular legacy left to us by the [old] regime. Which has to answer for these limitations: a kind of half-baked intellectualism. Due to not being used to studying the literature from elsewhere in the world and seeing things from various different angles, so taking our opponents' view seriously as well so one could analyze it and appreciate the basis of one's activities in terms of interest, age or paradigm. Until we do appreciate this, we can't understand either ourselves or those other guys. 'Cos it's not a matter of its being good or bad, but very often that it's all completely different. So in my view that's a problem. So you might have students writing an essay or something – but equally it could be postgraduates or researchers – could be about the Roma and their problems, and then they get to wondering what went on in this country between 1950 and 1968 and '69, when Husák made it simple; one third Slovaks, two-thirds Czechs. Which actually affected the Roma's loss of self-awareness, right? What does the literature elsewhere in the world have to say about this? How did they go about solving the problem elsewhere? Are we at all interested in how they went about it anywhere else? All argument is based just on source materials recorded in this country, but any contextuality – even when it's women writing – is missing, because contextuality is no part of what passes for the serious prerequisite for a piece of scholarly writing, right? And that's something that's been taken forward a bit in the world at large, and here we're sort of a bit behind.'

Professor Laxi broke in bitterly, 'What is more important or more complicated is that cultural policy and the lobbyists around it continue to be short-sighted and not a whole lot interests them. Accordingly, they don't support academic publishing, critical publications, they let it all rot. They always want to save on academic journals. The other day a colleague of mine calculated and said it publicly as well: "Do you know how much highway you can build from all the subsidies for all academic journals in a year? 30cm!" And this is what they're saving on. This whole economic-accounting-based outlook, which lacks morals, history, faith and only has idiocy to it, I cannot stand it, I hate it.'

'And it's much the same with publishing houses,' Doctor ForSythia pitched in. 'The patronage system works a treat there – I'll scratch your back, you scratch mine. Some people's things get published and re-published, no matter how rubbishy, while other people can't get anything published at all, so it's all purely formal, just like it used to be. There's no politics in it, but it's the same old thing. I regret to say it, but it's the same old thing all over.'

The strong views on unchanging practices prompted Professor Lustani to musings on unchanging modes of thinking. 'In the history of literature, in historiography, there is not the legacy of Marxism but the legacy of positivism which outlived even Marxism. Under Marxism, many did positivism, and that legacy is still lasting, but Marxism as an ideology or a philosophical orientation ceased.'

I recalled that Doctor ForSythia had complained that she continued to have the same difficulties with the way she expressed her ideas before and after

1989. I turned to her, 'You said that your reviewers in the past targeted not the content but the form, in which your articles were written, and that happens now as well.'

'And indeed it does still go on, nothing's changed,' she confirmed. 'I can't see any major difference. Unfortunately. Imagine this case of mine. I had a book published not that long ago and it got a ghastly review in one of the dailies. It was so dreadful that if I'd read it at the time I might well have jumped out the window. I didn't see it till much much later, 'cos I don't read that particular paper, so it wasn't till someone showed it to me, and I still haven't got over it. It wasn't signed. When I asked the editor who'd written it, he said he wouldn't tell me, not for anything, and that since major international economics journals also carry unsigned reviews, he was going to as well. So it was awful. Now consider this: I had a book due out with an academic publisher, it had had two positive reader's reports, gone through all the approval processes, then out of the blue somebody demanded another report, and that one was so negative that they chucked my book out. So now I'm back in the same old predicament, afraid to publish, a bit, see? I've got two books at home ready to go, but I'm scared to offer them somewhere because they're all in cahoots again, that's my problem. These days it's more to do with money or paying off old scores and stuff, but it's pretty much the same old thing all over again.'

An uncomfortable silence fell that nobody broke, until Doctor ForSythia spoke again, 'Of course the particular discipline can play a part; philosophy isn't a discipline with many women, but I believe that Czech conditions are conditions where any claim to recognition, as human, recognition as women, gets terribly downplayed. I expect you know that, eh? It's so horribly trivialized, not that it's something anyone actually fights against, no, not that, but it does get turned into a kind of farce, so much a farce that any woman is afraid to say that she's got a human right to anything, yes? She's afraid it'll be wrecked in advance by having any significance wiped out of it, by being trivialized and made into a bit of a joke, which gives it a demeaning subtext. So these days almost anybody is afraid to say things like that a woman is a feminist. They really are terrified. Even exponents themselves are apt to say things like: "I do gender studies, but I'm not a feminist." The fear's there all right.'

Doctor ForSythia's diatribe seemed to resonate with Professor HorMi.

He said, 'My firm belief is that many of our current problems originate in the Kádár regime. There is the continuity, permanence of its latent existence. Latent because it isn't explicitly there, but it is latent in the patterns. Especially mentality patterns were established in the course of the long Kádár regime and those guide us even today: the immorality that so much characterizes now not only the political life but the everyday life. I think this is the most important source of our problems, that we were not able to transcend the legacy of the Kádár regime. I would even dare say that Hungary would be in much better circumstances now if the Kádár regime had been worse. The many favourable things in the Kádár regime contributed not to the national but to the social character very common among Hungarians. The Kádár regime is at the background, at every gesture of ours. All those capabilities, all those mental patterns, all those instincts at work are coming from our Kádár past. This turned out to be an important, the decisive factor only after ten or so years, not immediately.'

'It seems to me that you Hungarians are very critical of the present, that you are comparing not what has but what *has not* yet been achieved to the state of things before 1989,' I ventured.

Professor Szandiliah replied, 'Maybe the difference is between the wins and the losses in the Czech Republic and here. I don't know how we will reconstruct our past, but we certainly had limited but greater freedom than my Czech counterparts. The arrival of "real" freedom was not such a shock to us as to them, so as to override every negative aspect of the new reality. We added very little to … '

She did not say to what, but continued from another end.

'This self-censorship we were talking about was very, how could I say it, one could feel that it was now over, but the difference was not so big as in the Czech Republic. Also maybe the critical vein of Hungarians is "better developed". I don't know if social criticism was a genre in the Czech Republic before the war, during the socialist period and now. But in Hungary it always has been. Social criticism has been a well-defined way of thinking and a genre of writing. It has been a social genre. I don't know that everybody was critical, but even before the war censorship was very strong, it was not a democracy [in Hungary] before the war: if you wrote a book on rural poverty, you could, like Géza Féja, be imprisoned for it.[4] Critical social writing and censorship and retribution were not new.'

---

[4] Géza Féja (1900–78) was a Hungarian populist writer and sociographer. Professor Szandiliah probably refers to (Féja 1937).

The pace of the conversation had slowed down and the atmosphere in the room had become more contemplative – or perhaps we were just tired after so many hours of intense revisitings of the past. It was time to raise our glasses in one last toast in a 'thank you' to everyone for their hard work and willingness to guide me through the labyrinth of late state-socialist academic publishing.

Alone with the riches of my mentors' memories, I began to weave them together into an abstract structure. My quest may not have achieved its ultimate objective, but the conversation after lunch had yielded unexpected knowledge: it revealed the possible depths of state-socialist legacy for the post-1989 generations in Czech – and maybe also Hungarian – academia, the tangle of continuities in discourse and in practice. Most importantly, the quest produced the disturbing question whether the legacy survived out of inertia, aided by insufficient resources invested in its analysis and reflection, or because the practices the scholars criticized became so deeply ingrained that they are not even reflected except by a tiny minority, or whether the preservation of the continuities may be serving somebody's interests.

*

In the next chapter, I will take off the garb of a novice on a quest and put on a scholar's gown. The scholar will read the imagined conversations as a 'primary text' and subject it to an analysis, aiming at developing something like a theory of late state-socialist censorship.

Four Sheets of Stories: A visual metanarrative

'The ends'

5. The Prologue
Photo: Jeannette Goehring and Libora Oates-Indruchová.

6. The Inspiration
Photo: Jeannette Goehring and Libora Oates-Indruchová.

7. The Action
Photo: Jeannette Goehring and Libora Oates-Indruchová.

8. Anticlimax
Photo: Jeannette Goehring and Libora Oates-Indruchová.

8

Snakes and ladders

A theory of state-socialist censorship

Institutional personnel strategies and personal strategies of professional survival

Any consideration of scholarly activities during state socialism has to distinguish between the official and the practised. On the one hand, science policies, ideological guidelines and institutional structures determined the overall conceptual and institutional framework. On the other hand, however, when it came to the practical implementation of this framework, institutions and individuals adapted it to their purposes in various, and often subversive, ways. In his anthropological analysis of the cultural meanings produced by the last Soviet generation, Alexei Yurchak demonstrates how a change in relations towards the authoritative ideological discourse by members of this generation enabled the creation of new and diverse cultural forms and meanings, without necessarily resisting or opposing Soviet values expressed in the authoritative discourse (Yurchak 2006). The issue of resistance will be a subject of further discussion below, but Yurchak's observation serves as a good starting point for the conceptualization of scholarly life and publishing in Czecho(slovakia), with a spyglass look at Hungary, between 1969 and 1989.[1]

While the ideological regulatory framework for social sciences and humanities developed and changed over the two decades, and the institutional and personal strategies differed in time, place and by scholarly discipline and research area, three main characteristics of academic life are discernible in the

---

[1] I write 'Czecho(Slovakia)' at this place, because the science policies were applicable to the whole country, although this research focused on academic practice only by *Czech* scholars; however, some of the 'mentors' in Chapters 3–7 also worked and/or published in Slovakia.

period as a whole. The first is the gradual tightening of ideological control from 1969 onwards, all the way to 1989. The Communist Party applied a systematic top-down approach in the application of the control, and from the academic centre to the academic periphery to insure absolute centralization of control. I have sketched the mechanism in the discussion of the science policies of the period in Chapter 2.

The second characteristic concerns the divide in political positions among scholars. These positions were fairly clear in the aftermath of the Prague Spring and the ensuing vetting of all Party members in academic institutions between 1969 and 1970, which resulted in mass dismissals from academic positions, professional blacklisting and other sanctions against the supporters of the Prague Spring reforms and outspoken opponents of the Soviet-led invasion of Czechoslovakia in August 1968. Nevertheless, both the discourse of the Party documents pertaining to the regulation of scholarly life and the interview material suggest a blurring of the boundary by the 1980s, when individual alliances and institutional positions became equivocal.

Finally, the third feature concerns a generational change. The generation with a personal political history of 1968 (Generation 1968) perceived the working conditions in academic institutions as 'being normalized', as being forcefully dispirited – divested of the spirit of the Prague Spring – in the first years after the invasion. It is inevitable, however, that the subsequent age cohorts who began their working academic careers only after the implementation of the policies and changes of early normalization did not perceive the waning of the spirit of the Prague Spring so strongly or not at all. The longer after 1968 they joined the academic profession, the more 'normal' rather than 'normalized' the working conditions in their institutions would seem to them.

Ideological regulatory framework

The policy documents illustrated with clarity that although normalization reached into all areas of academic life and institutions, its pace was uneven. The Communist Party asserted its influence by means of a top-down process. It started with the top layers of institutional hierarchy and gradually spread its controlling directives further down, from the academic 'centre' to its 'significant periphery' by various repressive, preventive and structural means. The main parts of the process were completed within a year (approximately between May 1969 and August 1970) and further substantial measures followed by the mid-1970s. After that and all the way towards the demise of state socialism in 1989, the speed and force of ideological control slackened. Science policies of the time, their echoes in academic or Party media and the narratives of the scholars presented in this book all suggest that the slowing down of normalization was a manifestation of a shift in the Party focus from an emphasis on ideologically correct *content* of research (including its theoretical and methodological grounding) to ideologically correct *form*; that is, a shift from a concern about the *real convictions* of scholars as demonstrated by their *creative* approach to Marxist–Leninist theory and method, to a concern about the *appearance of ideological loyalty*, as demonstrated by their keeping within set doctrinaire boundaries.

According to Vilém Prečan, the vetting (the exchange of Party ID cards) and the following three policy documents issued between May 1969 and August 1970 formed the basis of the ideological regulatory framework of scholarly research and teaching: 'The Executive Directions of the May Plenary of the ÚV KSČ toward Further Party Actions in the Upcoming Period' (Realizační směrnice květnového pléna ÚV KSČ pro další postup strany v příštím období); amendment to the Bill on the Czechoslovak Academy of Sciences; and the amendment to the Bill on universities (Prečan 1994). All three documents aimed at increasing the direct influence of the Party-State institutions over the direction and content of scholarly research, including the power to establish and abolish university departments, and to conclude and terminate employment contracts with academic employees.

The Party began with the leaderships of the Academy and universities. It decided on the continued existence of the research institutes of the Academy and of university departments, called off or appointed directors and department heads. Only afterwards did it reach into the lower levels of academia by reconsidering the employment contracts of all academic staff, and also, for example, the composition of editorial boards of scholarly journals. Gradually, the Party developed a system of communication of its intentions from its central administration to the individual researchers or university lecturers. By the late 1970s the system looked roughly as follows: the Party raised its concerns and demands at Party Congresses and plenary sessions of the Central Committee, these were elaborated into policy documents, which the appointed executives in the research institutes and Party media wrote up into articles published in the appropriate journals and newspapers as guidelines for the scholarly community, while at the same time, the Ideology Commission of the ÚV KSČ made other practical suggestions to influence the institutional process. The system was complemented by a range of prescriptive and restrictive measures and strategies of implementation, such as defining a limited number of research themes for every five-year period, orienting researchers towards other state-socialist countries and away from the West through bilateral cooperation agreements, or organizing obligatory ideological seminars for all scholarly staff.

This framework for ideological regulation of scholarly research, publishing and university teaching was tightly woven and highly restrictive. Nevertheless, from another perspective, the system, with its dependence on central planning, displayed similar signs of *overcentralization* as the Hungarian economist János Kornai described in his work on Hungarian economy (Kornai [1959] 1994). It was inherently inefficient in communicating the Party directives and supervising their implementation in *all* academic institutions by *all* of their employees. This created spaces for flexible interpretations and re-interpretations of the central directives, and an attendant range of processes and strategies employed in different institutions and by different individuals – the development observed by Yurchak in the case of Soviet culture. One significant point of difference has to be mentioned at this stage: Yurchak's account suggests a degree of shared understanding between institutional management and the institution's rank and file about the boundaries within which the new meanings could be created (Yurchak 2006: 77–125). This was certainly also the case in a part of the Czech – and Hungarian – academia, but the Party directives were additionally interpreted in ways aimed at their subversion by academics on the one hand and in ways leading to greater oppression and censorship by institutional managements on the other. I will now outline the institutional personnel strategies as remembered in the 20 Czech and 8 Hungarian researchers' and editors' narratives.

Institutional personnel strategies

The force of personnel repressions in institutions was directed at Communist Party members, but the overall ideological streamlining and control – and that will be the subject of discussion later in this chapter – concerned all academic personnel. Published research has mostly focused on the repressions against the supporters of the reform process from among the Party members (e.g. Hradecká and Koudelka 1998; Tůma 2002; Machonin 2004; Urbášek 2012; Šámal 2015), while the extent to which normalization affected non-Party personnel has not been systematically studied.[2] I deliberately did not ask any of my interviewees questions about their Communist Party membership or involvement in the Prague Spring: I wanted to minimize the need for moral justifications that I expected to arise if I did ask about their political affiliations. This research, then, also cannot provide a systematic analysis of the differences in the treatment of Party and non-Party scholars at the onset of normalization. Nevertheless, many of the narrators supplied information about their Party membership on their own accord.

---

[2] Marie Černá has contributed the first attempt at an analytical perspective on the 1970 screenings of non-members (Černá 2012).

Their accounts allow for two tentative observations. First, those who were in the Party prior to 1968 placed significant emphasis on the post-invasion situation and the persecution of the members of a reformist *group* within their disciplines or institutions after the vetting. These events represent a decisive break in their professional trajectories. Second, for those who were working in academia at the time of the Prague Spring, but were not members of the Party, the early normalization did not create such a major break in their employment situation. Rather, they described the whole period as a delicate *solo* dance in the minefield of political and politically motivated personal sensitivities. They had to negotiate these on their own because they were not associated with a political grouping within their institutions before or after 1968. They were untainted by their political involvement, but also unaided because of it, as I will discuss further.

After the vetting, the Party positioned itself as a gatekeeper of entry into academic positions and publishing venues. It used a variety of gatekeeping strategies to ensure its leading role in society. First of all, it placed duly vetted Party members in leadership positions – department heads, editors-in-chief – and it kept broadening the list of these so-called *nomenklatura* positions, that is, positions for which Party membership was a precondition, from 1969 onwards.[3] The researchers interviewed for this project recount that Party membership was increasingly required not only in decision-making positions, but also to lecture on certain areas of knowledge at universities (Fragaria, LoTus) or to obtain a university position as such (SiLena). They assert that the Party monitored the lists of students admitted to universities (SorBus) and instituted what amounted to a quota system for membership in various academic boards (Hedera).[4] At the same time as the

Fragaria: 'In 1970, after I left ...' p. 76

LoTus: 'I know that they also banned ...' p. 76

SiLena: 'When my department ...' p. 75

SorBus: 'Entrance exams here ...' p. 75

Hedera: 'And even on the committees ...' p. 74

---

[3] The policy to compile a 'blacklist' of undesirable personnel was drafted in 1971 (Hradecká and Koudelka 1998: 221–4), as was the extent of *nomenklatura* (Hradecká and Koudelka 1998: 86–107).

[4] Archival research confirmed the division of applicants for university admission into those with 'red dots', 'black dots' and 'without dots' that Professor SorBus articulated. Several levels of Communist Party hierarchy were involved in ranking the applicants by political criteria into '1. Recommended for admission, 2. No objections, and 3. Not recommended for admission' (Jareš 2009: 45).

Party tried to bring more of its members into academia, it tried to reduce the numbers of non-members by eliminating them through structural measures. The narratives of Fragaria and Euphrasia suggest that as the Party brought in more younger people who had to be Party members in order to even apply for a position, it tried to reduce the proportion of non-members by forcing academics of certain age into retirement around the early 1980s. The latter was enabled by a legislative measure instituted already in the early 1970s (Urbášek 2012: 135) and apparently mobilized as needed. This step followed the logic that the older generation still included a significant number of non-members and people struck off the Party membership list in the vetting, and therefore, eliminating this entire generation by forced retirement would lower the proportion of non-members in academic institutions. The measure was congruent with the Party's findings in 1980 and again in 1986 that its efforts towards increasing membership among academics had been failing (Kašparová 1980; Mokošín 1986).

Fragaria: 'It was all down to ...' p. 77

Euphrasia: 'At my institute ...' p. 77

Hyacintha recollects that, aside from creating *nomenklatura* positions and structural exclusion, the Party changed its priorities in appointing their people to managerial positions from about the mid-1970s, looking for pliable and efficient administrators. The meaning of 'efficient' is not clear from her utterance, but within the context of her narrative it seems to imply lack of interest in professional *or* political principle. This interpretation of the institutional development finds support in Party documents of the time. If, in a 1972 document the Party plenary sets out 'the principled criticism of inimical ideology with simultaneous *creative* development of Marxism–Leninism and *positive solutions* to theoretical problems' as the primary task of social sciences (Hrzal and Matouš 1972; emphasis added), by 1977 a similar document, declares: 'We will gradually increase the extent of the *Party influence* in the social science area' (Majcharčík 1977: 9; emphasis added). The change in the rhetoric suggests a shift in the Party's ideological focus from the content to the form and, by extension, from beliefs to appearances. Also, the Party further

Hyacintha: 'The big break ...' p. 76 and

Hyacintha: 'I can't imagine ...' p. 78

increased its 'influence in the social science area' through direct interventions into the responsibilities of the newly appointed managers by reserving the right to approve employment contracts in their departments as Stachys, Stellaria and Hedera document on their own examples. This combination of strategies kept both the academics in decision-making positions and the rank and file in perpetual suspense and employment insecurity, which placed them effectively in a vassal relationship with each other: a relationship of power, but also of mutual dependence.

Stachys: 'In the last year ...' p. 79

Stellaria: 'My organization ...' p. 80

Hedera: 'You even had to go ...' p. 81

The ideological drive described above and the ways by which it translated into institutional personnel strategies inevitably motivated and even enabled evasive and subversive manoeuvres and solidarity on the one hand, and revenge, punishment and discrimination on the other. One way of lessening the ideological surveillance and creating openings even for politically problematic scholars could have been the absence of information in the personal file that would label one as belonging to a particular milieu and refraining from looking for such information (e.g. the case of Hepatica). Of course, this strategy was not applicable to everyone. The examples of Hepatica, Stachys and Stellaria suggest that lower levels of surveillance in institutions applied to particular – and in other ways disadvantaged – categories of people: pensioners, people with a disability certification and employees on short-term contracts. The partial disability following a heart attack even provided Stachys a degree of relative employment security, although it cannot be established whether he assesses the situation in this way only in hindsight.

Hepatica: 'At one university ...' p. 81

Hepatica: 'They thought long ...' p. 83

Stachys: 'After I'd had a heart attack ...' p. 84

Stellaria: 'So as not to spoil the ...' p. 83

Although Hepatica and Stellaria could take advantage of falling into one of the lower-surveillance categories, they would not be able to avail themselves of the professional opportunities they had without a measure of solidarity on the part of the people in decision-making positions in their institutions. Such solidarity was extended to those who found themselves in a politically compromised position after the vetting by their former colleagues, acquaintances, and even superiors, or by people to whom they were referred as being in need.⁵ This solidarity had at least three aspects: it had structural limits, it could be turned into emotional blackmail and it was not necessarily altruistic. The first aspect was again directly dependent on the level of surveillance in particular academic spaces and on the risks the people authorized to enter them were willing to take. For example, a vetted person could take editorial responsibility for a collected volume and include in it an anonymous article by a politically compromised author (Hepatica). Or, publishers could offer at least translation opportunities to people who could not publish as authors (Sinapis, LupiNus). In another strategy, some institutions 'rotated' an author among them so that one name did not attract attention by its repeated appearance on the payroll of the same institution (Helianthus) and industrial companies could offer intellectual jobs to politically compromised academics under the umbrella of 'rapprochement between the intelligentsia and the workers' (Stellaria). The second aspect, the potential for emotional blackmail, arose from the vassal relationship mentioned earlier: if one acted independently according to one's conscience or needs, these actions could be judged by the colleagues and superiors in terms of whether or not they could expose their fellow scholars to sanctions (SalVia, Stellaria). Finally, what may have looked like solidarity could have been merely self-serving, such as if certain line managers – heads of university or research institute departments – kept someone who could be dismissed on political grounds on their staff as an alibi for the eventuality of a regime change or perhaps to bribe their own conscience (Stachys).

Hepatica: 'They fired us on the instant …' p. 84

Sinapis: 'There were obviously …' p. 84

LupiNus: 'Look, at *World Literature* …' p. 85

Helianthus: 'I was at one institution …' p. 84

Stellaria: 'Factories would give …' p. 85

SalVia: 'In all this the seventies …' p. 86

Stellaria: 'My boss told me …' p. 87 and

Stellaria: 'Though to say …' p. 87

Stachys: 'In essence …' p. 90

---

⁵ Pavel Machonin lists several institutes of empirical social research and sports organizations (Noctua, Technosport and Sportpropag) as workplaces that employed sociologists fired from universities and the Academy of Sciences (Machonin 2004: 645–6). He frames the extension of solidarity in terms of patronage that Maruška Svašek observed in the arts: 'Professional favouritism was used by some artists and Party members with influential positions in the art world to resist official censorship, to increase artistic autonomy and to aid friends' (Svašek 2002: 86). See also (Péteri 2019) for the latest contribution on the subject of patronage in social sciences in Hungary during the Kádár regime. All three accounts imply that the various actors disposed of varying degrees of agency. I will develop this point further in the main text.

If one's political alliances in 1968 could mobilize solidarity in one's favour, they far more systematically produced ongoing discrimination of which the vetting results were only the beginning. Scholars perceived that they were 'labelled' once and for all and that their publishing options depended on their institutional–political belonging. Both SiLena, who was never a Party member, but worked at an institute that employed politically compromised academics, and Stachys, who was struck off the Party membership list but kept his employment, felt that their belonging to a particular group excluded them as authors forever from certain publishing venues. The label carried a stigma that could be summoned by the bearer's line manager at a time of increased ideological pressure, such as after the foundation of Charter 77, for the purposes of almost sacrificial purification. Implementation of further sanctions against a branded person could be seen as a proof of ideological vigilance and such a line manager might think that sacrificing the branded people would save either him or her or the whole workplace from further pressure or even dissolution (Stellaria, Helleborus, Sinapis). The label could also be used to forge serfdom-like relationships going beyond the mere alibi-making mentioned earlier. Stigmatized academics were expected to express their gratitude to their superiors for keeping them employed by providing service ranging from academic exploitation (such as, 'coerced authorship' (Bülow and Helgesson 2018: 4) – Euphrasia, Fragaria, Helianthus) to censoring other colleagues for ideological misdemeanours (Euphrasia). The feudal metaphor of serfdom can be extended even further, to fiefdom: Helianthus and Stachys narrate how some academics in decision-making positions used ideology as a ruse for dismissing their professional rivals at the vetting, while at the same time were willing to keep politically compromised scholars on the staff as long as they were not researching in the same area as themselves. The silencing of rivals is no unique phenomenon in the history of censorship. According to Catherine MacKinnon, '[t]he operative definition of censorship (…) shifts from government silencing what powerless people say, to powerful

---

SiLena: 'It's all about social capital …' p. 90

Stachys: 'My person …' p. 79 and
Stachys: 'We were branded …' p. 79

Stellaria: 'My boss told me …' p. 87
Helleborus: 'There were objective …' p. 89
Sinapis: 'Between '78 …' p. 89

Euphrasia: 'Party members …' p. 90
Fragaria: 'There was this conference …' p. 91
Helianthus: 'I was in that category …' p. 91

Euphrasia: 'The Institute's …' p. 91

Helianthus: 'In some instances …' p. 92
Stachys: 'In my field …' p. 78

people violating powerless people into silence and hiding behind state to do it' (MacKinnon cited in Post 1998: 1–2). Later we will see that this initial division of territory continued throughout normalization by the exclusion of newcomers into the areas of specialization of these powerful individuals.

Whether labelled or not, the rank-and-file academics were selectively 'taxed' by their institutions for the privilege of being allowed to remain in them or of joining them. The vassal relationships and the acts of solidarity required repayment in kind: an (unspoken) request not to write on some topics (Sambucus), a direct request to write on an assigned (political) subject (LupiNus) and public expressions of ideological loyalty (Hepatica, ForSythia).

Sambucus: 'In a way these were ...' p. 90

LupiNus: '[One colleague, ...' p. 92

The interaction of all the components of institutional personnel strategies – structural limitations, ideological oppression and subversion – wove an intricate web of relationships and processes that was difficult to navigate by those outside of, or in the lower spheres of, ideological power. At the same time the web was sufficiently irregular in its pattern for it to leave openings that allowed for manoeuvring. The simultaneous vagueness and far-reaching destructive potential of ideological directives created an atmosphere of suffocating fear. Jonathan Bolton observed that the overall atmosphere in intellectual professions during normalization was such that 'the incongruities of repression were themselves a form of harassment. They gave the state hostages to fortune and room for manoeuver; (...) Inconsistency created uncertainty, which could cause significant stress (...). It was a cheap, reliable, and low-maintenance way to scare people' (Bolton 2012: 87). It also prepared the ground for multifaceted censorship and self-censorship on the one hand, and stimulated the development of a range of personal strategies of professional survival and even profiteering on the other, because '[f]ormal systems are played out in interaction with informal cultures and structures and through the lives and strategies of individuals' (Chamberlayne, Bornat and Wengraf 2000: 9). This would explain the paradoxes of scholarly life of the time revealed in the narratives: ForSythia recounts

Hepatica: 'It all depended on ...' p. 92

ForSythia: 'One place where ...' p. 92

ForSythia: 'You mean if someone ...' p. 93

vividly her incessant fear of sanctions, yet when asked about concrete cases she could not remember any. Others were equally unable to cite concrete examples, or mentioned relatively mild forms of punishment (withdrawal of a monthly salary bonus – ErIgerus; a summons to a discussion with peers to defend a problematic piece of writing – Fragaria, Helleborus) for having written something that offended ideological sensitivities. Only Sinapis mentioned that he feared the loss of employment in one instance following the conclusions of his research that were unfavourable to the state-socialist system. Indeed, it seems that after the vetting of 1969–70 there were few cases of explicit sanctions against someone for a piece of published work. The logical conclusion is that the thing feared was 'being labelled', because that would make one vulnerable to unpredictable and uncontrollable unpleasantness. Hedera says as much in the subtext of her assertion that as long as one did not allow oneself doubts that something was not possible one could function as a professional with relative freedom (see also Helianthus). Freedom in this case does not refer so much to being able to *do* something as to *consider* oneself free, which would include having one's mind free from fearing the being labelled.

The personal history of Hedera suggests another paradox. At the time of the sanctions aimed at transgressing Party members after the vetting, some professional spaces may have become at least temporarily more accessible to non-Party members *because* of the absence of an explicit political misbehaviour. It is, however, impossible to say from the sample how widespread this phenomenon was.

Finally, the third paradox of institutional personnel strategies appears probably in the late 1970s: the efforts of the Party towards increasing ideological control may have backfired due to its structural implementation. Euphrasia recounts how a member of the Central Committee of the Party was placed in her institute to provide censorial supervision. Structurally, his presence was formalized by a part-time employment contract at the institute (presumably, to shield against the appearance of external

---

ErIgerus: 'One bit of unpleasantness …' p. 164

Fragaria: 'In 1974 I was writing …' p. 160

Helleborus: 'General discussion …' p. 159

Sinapis: 'I don't know of any …' p. 164

Hedera: 'The main thing was…' p. 94

Helianthus: 'I failed to get anything …' p. 111

Hedera: 'Even after '69 …' p. 82

Euphrasia: '[Jaromír] Obzina's …' p. 95

interference/censorship) including appropriate remuneration. She further suggests that it was not his only such contract at the Academy of Sciences. This practice may have been systematic, given that in 1980 the Party cells in ten institutes of the Academy of Sciences came directly under the Central Committee (Kubánek and Lacina 1980). It created vested interests for these 'censors' whose loyalties were by definition split between their ideological obligations as Central Committee members and personal material profit. They could be replaced as 'researchers' and lose their additional income should they cause too much trouble. Thus high Party officials also found themselves in a vassal relationship with their 'subjects', which would have yoked their ideological zeal and rendered the Party's measure towards increasing its direct supervision over academia less effective as a consequence.

It is useful at this point to add some contrasting observations about the situation of scholars in Hungarian institutions over the same period of time. Hungarian academia was affected in the long term by the political turbulences related to the 1956 revolution and it also felt the vibrations of the political disturbances elsewhere in the Eastern Bloc. The invasion of Czechoslovakia in 1968 and the Charter 77 produced campaigns of ideological tightening in the early and late 1970s, which resulted in several cases of persecution of scholars whose severity far exceeded that observed among the Czech researchers.[6] HorMi then notes a further 'conservative turn' that included the banning of journals and articles as occurring in the mid-1980s.

> HorMi: 'There were several ...' p. 94

The most significant difference between the approaches of Czech(oslovak) and Hungarian academic institutions to

---

[6] Perhaps the best known is the case of the expulsion of the Lukács philosophical school including Ágnes Heller and her husband Ferenc Fehér (1933–94) from the research institute of the Academy of Sciences in 1972 (see Chapter 5, note 18). In the mid-1970s, the best known cases are those of Miklós Haraszti (born 1945), arrested and tried for distributing his manuscript of *Darabbér* (Piecework; English version *A Worker in the Worker's State*; Haraszti 1977), and whose publication was rejected, and of Iván Szelényi and György Konrád (see Chapter 5, note 5); for details see (Takács 2016). Other cases were mentioned by the Hungarian 'mentors' in the discussion of post-publication censorship.

ideological surveillance derived from a sharper distinction between research institutions, including the Academy of Sciences, and universities in Hungary. Instead of placing the institutes of the Academy under a more direct surveillance by the Party, as was the case in Czechoslovakia, the emphasis was on separating the spheres of the universities and the Academy. On the one hand, György Aczél, the leading cultural politician of the Kádár era, practised the 'policy' of 'three Ts': 'prohibit, tolerate, support' (*tiltani, turni, támogatni*) with respect to the space permitted to researchers (see, e.g., Kornai 2007: 205). The policy allowed the researchers and their institutes more autonomy, but they were also expected to be self-disciplined and not to step over the boundaries of political permissibility. On the other hand, the researchers who belonged to the 'tolerated' group were likely to be kept away from students, so that they did not 'infect' them politically (Sztipoah, Szandiliah).

HorMi, among others, implies another factor that allowed greater agency to researchers in institutes: a different object of solidarity among scholars than in the Czech case. He suggests that the solidarity was motivated by persecution of scholarship, rather than by persecution of a politically defined group (arguably, after the 1963 general amnesty, Hungary did not have a persecuted group of intellectuals linked to a specific historical moment). Indeed, as we have seen in the 'imagined conversations', Hungarian scholars hardly ever spoke about a denouncement from *within* their communities, while the Czech academics mention a whole range of such acts. Intellectual loneliness would have been, apart from fear, an accompanying effect of the lack of professional solidarity among the Czechs. The sociologist Alena Miltová described just that in a letter to a professional friend in 1986: 'I feel like a lonely little petunia in an onion patch when I am supposed to be formulating hypotheses and the only one to discuss them with is my husband' (*Ale snad i pro toto jsme žili, ne?* 2016: 55). In contrast, if the Hungarians exercised their agency by involving themselves in *samizdat* activities, they could rely on the silent complicity,

Sztipoah: 'I was never invited to ...' p. 152

Szandiliah: 'From the sixties on ...' p. 152

HorMi: '[Miklós Szabó] who later ...' p. 86

rather than the surveillance and censorship, of their line managers.

Personal strategies of professional survival

Scholars who expected difficulties because of their political involvement in the Prague Spring or because of their area of research in the reformist 1960s, or who were aware of the continued politicization of academic work, did not passively await a decision from above on their institutional fate or accept it passively even once it was made. Instead, they negotiated the institutional and ideological framework and developed 'a whole series of adaptation mechanisms' (Musil 1993: 63) that would enable them to survive as professionals. Jiří Musil suggested that when these mechanisms went beyond the personal, the 'grey zone' was born: 'to do what was possible within the given constraints, to cultivate the profession, and simultaneously to retire into one's own professional career and avoid political commitments – these people formed the so-called grey zone' (Musil 1993: 64). I argued in the Introduction that most of 'my' narrators could be thus categorized. Depending on the extent of the Prague Spring damage, for some of these scholars the most acute need was to *preserve any* form of professional existence, while for others it was mostly the question of whether they would be able to *continue* in their area of research. In later years, when the questions of basic survival in institutions were more or less settled, the focus of the personal strategies shifted to the possibility of professional *development*. Often the researchers recounted their personal trajectories in the context of responsibility for their professions.

The connection between professional preservation within state-socialist institutions and moral concerns came out as the most intense issue in the narratives. The question of staying in the profession after the vetting or even entering the profession during normalization boiled down to making a decision about how far one could go, how much effort one could direct towards professional self-preservation and still keep one's dignity and an

Sambucus: 'Somehow I managed …' p. 96

Stachys: 'You only need to look …' p. 96 and
Stachys: 'Listen, I've decided …' p. 178

Fragaria: 'Under the past regime …' p. 96

SorBus: 'The burden was …' p. 96

acceptable degree of personal integrity. Sambucus relates that he had to keep his head down and be subjected to institutional procedures that he considered as impositions; Stachys gives an example of his fellow sociologists competing for the publication of a highly pro-regime article in 1970 and his own (desperate) efforts to negotiate a position for himself in the new political–professional conditions with a similar gesture; Fragaria and SorBus considered 'getting soiled by the regime' as being part and parcel of a career in humanities and social sciences. SorBus sees a certain counterbalance to this moral contamination in shifting one's personal priorities from the public to the private sphere: in the absence of self-fulfilment and perhaps also self-respect, intimacy became a refuge of personhood.

These painful moral dilemmas follow from the dual concern about one's personal career and profession, and also from the nature of pedagogical work at universities as a 'helping profession' (Berg and Seeber 2016: 71). Tzvetan Todorov proposed that dignity in itself is not necessarily moral, because it requires only an alignment between conscience and deeds, rather than societal approval. For dignity to be moral, it has to serve good (Todorov [1991] 1999: 67–8). Therein lies the narrators' problem: what was 'good' in their predicament? To stay in the profession and participate in its shaping within the limits set by the regime and in educating the younger generations, but at the cost of complicity with the regime? Or to withdraw from professional life and set a personal example of resistance to the regime, but at the cost of disavowing responsibility for the profession and the young generations? By turning one's back on the profession, one would give up the position of a subject in the sense articulated by Judith Butler:

> [A]n operation of censorship determines who will be a subject, a determination that depends on whether the speech of the candidate for subjecthood obeys the norms that govern what is speakable and what is not. To move outside of the domain of speakability is to risk one's status as a subject; to embody the norms that govern speakability in one's speech is to consummate one's status as a subject of speech. (Butler 1998: 252–3)

In other words, 'living in truth' (Havel 1992), ceasing 'to go through the motions of a ritualized and banal everyday existence' (Bren 2010: 98) was morally problematic for scholars; by satisfying one good, they would be transgressing against another. None of the narrators spoke about their existences under state socialism as if leaving the profession was a serious option – and hence the emphasis on the dilemma between what was moral and what was dignified.

Relatively less morally loaded strategies included, according to the narrators, changing one's professional environment (Hyacintha) and changing one's research topic from a politically sensitive to a politically 'neutral' one or at least one that was not immediately conflictual (Hepatica, Helleborus). Even these, however, contained the underlying moral aspect: Hyacintha decided to leave the university for an applied research institution, because she anticipated greater ideological contamination of the educational environment, while both Hepatica and Helleborus knew that working on certain topics rather than others absolved them of the need to resolve a moral dilemma.

Hyacintha: 'As late as the summer …' p. 97

Hepatica: 'I don't want to appear …' p. 98

Helleborus: 'If I'd insisted …' p. 98

Unsurprisingly, once the institution and the individual decided whether to stay on, ensuring one's continuation within the field was only a matter of gauging the limits of ideological permissibility. SorBus, Hepatica and SalVia listed continued invisibility as the best strategy to avoid further harassment: SorBus prevented his employees with unfavourable political records from contact with sociology's ideologues; Hepatica links attempts at professional advancement to the risk of exposure; and SalVia says that she deliberately marginalized herself by working in a low-profile environment in order to avoid ideological pressure and thus the need for a moral compromise. SiLena elaborates on the varying tensions within disciplines, when she says that empirical sociology was under much less pressure than theoretical. Authors who were themselves active in the sociology of work and industry agree with her when they claim that a number of sociologists who lost work in the vetting and found employment in various institutes of applied research could 'expand and intensify' their work (Havlová

SorBus: 'The first thing …' p. 98

Hepatica: 'We did have problems …' p. 99

SalVia: '[I'd have avoided] …' p. 98

SiLena: 'Sociology got round it …' p. 99

and Sedláček 2004: 653). Since the interview with SiLena, other researchers arrived at this conclusion through document research: quantitative methods and working in applied research institutes 'provided a relatively safe space for low-ideology empirical research' (Skovajsa and Balon 2017a: 75).[7] To identify the areas of ideological friction in order to avoid them, one had to know 'the rules of the game', as Helleborus put it. These could be learned by continuous scanning of the field for openings and closures and maintained by not provoking with anything one wrote. Sambucus adds a political dimension to such scanning: he had to keep himself informed of Party decisions and try to predict their impact on his professional situation. Learning the rules whether by scanning the disciplinary and political horizons or by trial and error (i.e. by testing the thresholds of censorship exercised by one's superiors and editors) inevitably led to self-censorship.[8] I will discuss its dimensions later. At this place suffice it to say that the narrators did not agree on whether it was censorship or self-censorship that affected their work more, and what forms both types of censorship took (Stellaria, Lilius, ForSythia, Stachys, LoTus and SalVia).

If *survival* in an institution after the vetting involved moral dilemmas and *continuation* of one's professional existence appeared morally easier after the dilemmas were negotiated, further personal professional *development* was likely to become a long and frequently forked path up a slippery slope of compromises and trade-offs. A wrong step could mean a professional slither downwards or a fall face forward into sticky political quagmire. The story of LupiNus's professional trajectory serves as a good example of a journey along such a path. He graduated from his first degree, did the ensuing compulsory military service and entered academia just after the vetting in

Helleborus: 'The issue was always …' p. 99
and
Helleborus: 'For a start, a worm …' p. 99

Sambucus: 'Well, there were articles …' p. 99

Stellaria: 'For one thing …' p. 100
Lilius: 'I didn't suppress …' p. 100
ForSythia: 'Censorship …' p. 100
Stachys: 'Self-censorship …' p. 100
LoTus: 'Nobody made cuts …' p. 100
SalVia: 'I don't think so …' p. 101

LupiNus: 'In about four years …' p. 101

---

[7] Michal Kopeček lists urban and environmental sociology, and sociologies of enterprises, youth and education and family as the niches of less ideologically laden research within sociology (Kopeček 2017: 174).
[8] Epp Lauk, Petr Šámal and Teodora Shek Brnardić argue that learning by experience where the limits of permissibility were applied to the East Central Europe in general (Lauk, Šámal and Shek Brnardić 2018: 334).

1970. He did not, therefore, carry the label of involvement in the Prague Spring. His institutional history, however, confirms Hepatica's view of the cost of professional advancement: every rung upwards on the academic ladder was conditioned by a prior, largely political, commitment. In 1974 he was given three options of career development: apply for Party membership, enrol in VUML, or start a PhD. Opting for the latter allowed him to avoid a direct political commitment. To have his PhD examined in 1983, however, another – and entirely political – commitment was required: to enrol in VUML. This time, according to LupiNus, only two options were presented to him: either to enrol and have his PhD examined or to end up without a PhD. He complied and achieved the correct political profile for further promotion. But that also meant that he could be called upon to involve himself politically further still. That happened in 1986 when he was told that since he was the only faculty member with VUML, he could be now appointed the head of the department – but that was a *nomenklatura* position. He gave in to the pressure and entered the Party on the eve of *perestroika*. His case illustrates how, for the age cohort that entered the profession when the normalization regime was already firmly in place, the professional and the political became closely connected and how the political pressure increased all the way towards 1989. Choosing a less politically compromising strategy at one stage enabled a temporary respite, but it was only until one had invested enough in one's profession that one became a target for further demands under the threat of professional stagnation. The institution and the Party gained enough power over one to tighten the screw of political loyalty by another turn.

Hepatica: 'We did have problems ...' p. 99

LupiNus's narrative represents the distilled essence of the situation of an academic with moderate professional ambitions in a normalized institution over an extended period of time. In fact, his story covers almost the entire duration of normalization. It could be just that, a story by means of which he explains the events of his professional life to himself in hindsight, if the chronology of the Party strategies articulated in the science policies did not tell a parallel story.⁹ LupiNus's story is thus entirely plausible, yet he was the only one among the narrators who provided such a clear-cut formulation of a professional trajectory tied to the institutional-political structures. Other narrators fall into the category of either those whose professional lives were governed by their decisions of 1969–70 and they either focused on mere survival or on maintaining their *status quo*, or of those who like LupiNus did not have to make a decision at the time of the vetting (SalVia, ForSythia, LoTus and SiLena in the sample), but nowhere in their narratives suggest an ambition towards career advancement. SalVia even explicitly states that she made a decision not to advance professionally in order to avoid the possibility of political involvement. Both groups then list a number of strategies they used to create opportunities for themselves for non-career-oriented professional development, strategies that would allow them to do scholarly work that they considered worthwhile, but that were not aimed at promotion. The various publishing and textual strategies will be the subject of detailed discussion later. At this point I will only outline their range as it is suggested by the interview material.

SalVia: I'd lived through …' p. 102

The strategies differed in the degree of openness about one's intentions. The most open approach, a direct confrontation with an institution about a publishing ban, was mentioned only once and it referred to a person other than the narrator himself (SorBus). More frequently, researchers approached a professional acquaintance with a request to try and get something published. Such personal relationships were with people in particular positions in publishing (editors, reviewers) who were considered approachable and tried to push through even somewhat controversial texts or authors. Sinapis says that he exploited the bad conscience of such people, their feelings of guilt over their own comfortable career situations in comparison with the

SorBus: 'Tonda [Přidal] went …' p. 111

Sinapis: 'I admit that any manoeuvring …' p. 103

---

⁹ Pavel Urbášek, in his study of Czech universities during normalization, tells a fictive story of a young man's scholarly career to illustrate the system in place after 1977 that is remarkably similar to the personal narrative of LupiNus (Urbášek 2008: 157–67).

professional options of the stigmatized people. He goes as far as calling it a 'peculiar coalition (…) of friends and enemies'. Several other narrators framed this strategy in the context of good will and 'reason': one particular editor from the Party publishing house Svoboda was mentioned repeatedly as someone who managed to get good work published, because apart from her goodwill she had a family connection with a high-ranking Party official (Stellaria and Euphrasia). The rest of the strategies mentioned in the interviews consisted of various kinds of camouflage.

Stellaria: '[One] editor at Svoboda …' p. 103

Euphrasia: 'She was editor-in-chief …' p. 103

Similar to the 'overt' approach, the most 'covert' practice too – publishing under an assumed name either in *samizdat* or abroad – was a rare phenomenon among the narrators. Only Helianthus published once under a pen name abroad and Sinapis began to shift to *samizdat* in the late 1980s. Stellaria moved at the borderline of legality and beyond since 1969, but even she published mostly in the official sphere, although under assumed names, but always in 'coalition' with someone inside the publishing house. Other camouflaging strategies involved a textual compromise between one's own professional loyalty and ideological necessity.

Helianthus: 'I failed to get anything …' p. 111

Sinapis: 'In the second half …' p. 176

Stellaria: 'Look, I had to find …' p. 175

According to the narrators, the widely used strategies were those that could be called 'having learned the language' and 'keeping up appearances'. The first one meant that the researchers used phrases borrowed from the authoritative ideological discourse or policy documents to front their texts and tried to twist their own work into that language, creating a niche for their subject (Helleborus, SalVia, and Stellaria). The second strategy represented an even more covert manoeuvre: research was being reported, but not actually carried out, so that people could do other work instead. Stachys calls one example of this strategy 'Christmas science': sham research reports submitted in time for the Christmas salary bonus.

Helleborus: 'You made the case …' p. 104

SalVia: 'I created my own …' p. 104

Stellaria: 'Well at one time …' p. 104

Stachys: 'People at the institutes …' p. 105

Yurchak uses the phrase 'work with meaning' by means of 'pure pro forma' (Yurchak 2006: 93) to describe this phenomenon in the activities of his Komsomol narrators, although he argues that his narrators understood the 'pro forma' work as a necessary means to meet their ends, which were to do something meaningful.

Nevertheless, that something meaningful was not in contradiction with the official aims of the 'pro-forma' work. The same could be claimed about the Hungarian narrators who were fairly specific in their lists of things that were required and those that were not admissible, but not about the Czechs. A few of the Czech narrators insisted that they did not feel many constraints in terms of having to adjust their research focus or writing style (Hepatica, Hedera, Sambucus), but most pitted their own work more or less sharply against the ideological dictate, which they were trying to avoid or subvert, and from which they clearly dissociated themselves. For them, the authoritative ideological discourse was never a means to do something, but, rather, a ceremonial guard of a solidly positioned enemy who had to be placated or deceived by their own craft.

> Hepatica: 'Not once did I quote ...' p. 179
> Hedera: 'I worked on topics ...' p. 148
> Sambucus: 'In a way these were ...' p. 90

It is important to emphasize that although the interpretation of the camouflaging strategies as appeasement and subversion suggests a dichotomy of one's own work and the ideological dictate, the degree of compromise between one's professional loyalty and ideological necessity differed depending on the level of the institutional and professional hierarchy at which each particular negotiation was taking place. The researchers did some things on sufferance and with the full knowledge that they were compromising their professional conscience (ForSythia), some they could pretend at one stage and remove later (Helleborus), some they included for merely utilitarian purposes to satisfy the supervisory audience, so that they could communicate other things to their intended audience (e.g. Hyacintha), and others they did not consider as being of substantive relevance (SalVia). A more detailed account of these negotiations and the resulting compromises, victories and defeats will again follow later, in the sections that deal with the work, the author and the communication process.

> ForSythia: 'I had to include ...' p. 104
> Helleborus: 'You made the case ...' p. 104
> Hyacintha: 'That narrow circle ...' p. 105
> SalVia: 'I created my own ...' p. 104

I will conclude the part on professional survival with two institutional practices that produced the unintended effects of 'turning adversity into an advantage' and 'internal dissent', both of which furthered the professional development of individual scholars. Stachys and ForSythia narrated how their political (Stachys) and gender (ForSythia) marginalization in effect created space – albeit at a price – for their own academic work, which may not have been possible if they were more mainstream, because then they may not have had the time needed for that work. Arguably, these were two isolated cases among all the narrators of an institutional pressuring that resulted in a positive outcome for the individual. What I termed here 'internal dissent', however, was a series of alternative intellectual spaces in which whole groups of scholars could do meaningful and – according to them, often somewhat subversive – work under the auspices of officially funded activities that developed mainly in the 1980s. Margaret Setje-Eilers observed a similar phenomenon in the GDR in the 1960s: 'Where censorship sought to regulate, it seems also to have simultaneously created blind spots in what it regulated. Some of these spaces developed within a web of personal relationships, while others emerged from issues that existed almost as voids that the party could not directly address' (Setje-Eilers 2009: 386). The seminar series in Brno (*Socialistický životní způsob jako sociální realita* 1982, 1984, 1986, 1988) and Pilsen that Fragaria and SorBus mention (see Chapter 3, note 28) seem to have been such 'voids'. They were funded under the five-year state plan of research and their organizers bypassed ideological surveillance by holding the seminars outside the capital, limiting participation by invitation only, and publishing only low-circulation proceedings from them. This meant that even some of the stigmatized people (such as Stachys, see Fragaria and SorBus), who were not allowed to teach or otherwise participate in the intellectual public sphere of official scholarship, could gather here for professional discussion and presentation of their work. Doubravka Olšáková researched another such seminar series, Comenius Symposia, held in Uherský Brod between 1971 and 1989 (Olšáková 2012) and Chad Bryant and Petr Šámal identify several 'peripheries', as they call them, in history (Bryant 2000: 40) and literary studies (Šámal 2015: 1176). One has to reflect, however, on the darker side of these by-invitation-only seminars: a cultivation of elitism, the formation

Stachys: 'Throughout that time …' p. 106

ForSythia: 'For example, when …' p. 107

Fragaria: 'We would go there …' p. 108

SorBus: 'It could be that …' p. 109

of circles that were not necessarily accessible on scholarly merit, but on social capital. Bolton makes a similar observation of a lack of 'openness to potential new voices' in relation to dissident groupings (Bolton 2012: 97) and Dmitry Kurakin to the sociology of culture in the Soviet Union in the 1970s and 1980s: '[i]ntellectual life as a Soviet academic in the humanities revolved around seminar series which gathered interdisciplinary groups of intellectual *elites and neophytes*' (Kurakin 2017: 403, emphasis added). Professional societies (Sambucus lists the House of Technology in Pardubice and Biological Society, in which he participated) were other such alternative outlets: under the cloak of technological progress that was set as a priority of state-socialist science, these societies helped bring together communities of nonconformist academics from natural sciences and technology as well as from social sciences and humanities.[10]

> Sambucus: 'With various twists …' p. 108

This last point suggests that if the vetting of 1969–70 meant a general closing of spaces for intellectual existence (Louis Aragon used the famous metaphor of the 'Biafra of the soul' to refer to the intellectual famine produced by the early normalization), the 1980s seemed to offer certain openings. Nevertheless, the views on this expressed in the interview material show generational differences that correspond with the development of ideological regulation of scholarly life throughout normalization.

Generational differences

The juxtaposition of the ideological regulatory framework as set in the science policies, guidelines and proclamations of intent issued by the Party, on the one hand, and the narratives of the scholars who were professionally active during normalization, on the

> Laxi: 'I could write for myself …' p. 110
>
> HorMi: 'I met several friends …' p. 109

---

[10] For a study on the House of Technology see (Nešpor 2014a). Among the Hungarians, Laxi and HorMi mention similar alternative spaces: an entirely informal discussion circle in the case of Laxi and a direction intentionally alternative to the mainstream historiography in the case of HorMi. Kornai describes a similar effort towards the institutionalization of a non-Marxist professional circle, the Section of Mathematical Economics within the Hungarian Economic Association, already in the late 1960s (Kornai 2007: 153).

other, reveals an intriguing contradiction: the Party documents testify to increasing ideological control over academic life all the way from 1969 to 1989, while many of the narrators speak of a gradual loosening of ideological surveillance and improvement of conditions for scholarly work and its publication. I propose two contributing factors accounting for this contradiction: a discursive shift that occurred in the Party strategy of academic management and a generational shift.

I characterized the discursive shift at the beginning of this chapter as a shift from a concern with content to a preoccupation with form. Its concrete manifestations were a shift from the examination of the real ideological convictions of scholars (expressed, for example, in their creative approach to Marxism–Leninism) to mere displays of ideological loyalty through the enactment of proper behaviour and use of language (such as attending ideological trainings and using the phrases from the authoritative ideological discourse). Jonathan Larson calls this shift 'hypernormalization', 'the growing importance of reproducing discursive forms rather than communicating meaningful content' (Larson 2013: 111). Hyacintha suggested that the shift in discourse brought a change in institutional management also, that every new cohort of managers was less connected to the subject of research of their institutions and more connected to the Party leadership, to whom they were accountable – which brings us to the generational shift.

Hyacintha: 'I can't imagine …' p. 78

In the immediate aftermath of the vetting, the leaderships of academic institutions were appointed from among their staff that were confirmed as loyal to the new Party leadership. In other words, people who had a personal relationship to the political divisions of 1968 and, more specifically, to those divisions within their disciplines and/or workplaces. As these people either left for different positions or retired, they were gradually replaced by younger people without a personal political history tied with 1968 and who were also new in the given institution and/or discipline. By definition, the relationship of these two age cohorts to the authoritative ideological discourse differed. The Generation 1968 perceived acutely the political division established in the vetting and might even have been genuinely convinced of the new ideology. In contrast, the younger generation did not necessarily have to have such clear loyalties. Their workplace ties were not associated with the political past either and, as both Hyacintha and the policy documents suggest, their appointment would not be made on such strict professional–political grounds as would have been the case in 1969–70. The professional and political emphasis regarding their fitness for the given position would have shifted. Consequently, they would tend to focus on the discursive propriety of their institutions as a whole, rather than on the knowledge substance in the publications of every single scholar under their management. Moreover, the examples from the narratives showed that the supervisors and line managers might themselves have had vested material interests that took priority over their ideological loyalty. The farther from 1968, the less clear-cut the loyalties of the managers were. The line between 'us' and 'them' grew fuzzy.

A similar generational shift applied to the rank-and-file scholars also. The narrators from both age cohorts agree on the turning points in the conditions for scholarly work during normalization – around 1974–5, post-Charter 77 and *perestroika* years – but differ in their characterizations of the phases between the points. Some narrators say that things began to loosen up roughly in 1974–5, when even the previously persecuted people could find some form of professional existence and publishing opportunities (such as Helianthus and Hepatica). This is also echoed in Šámal's content analysis of the journal *Česká literatura*, in which he observes that after 1975 a number of the authors who had disappeared by 1970 began to publish again (Šámal 2002: 240). At the same time the narrators (for example, Hyacintha and SorBus) say that the substance of scholarly pursuits began to matter less, while the semblance of ideological propriety began to matter more. Slackening in the dogged examination of post-1968 loyalties began to open spaces for those sanctioned in the vetting, while more emphasis on ideological compliance made the professional lives of those who managed to remain in their institutions and those who started their careers after 1968 more insecure. This younger age cohort was not likely to perceive ideological relief for themselves. Thus Stachys remained in his teaching position at the university (we can say that he was kept there as an alibi for the new management) and avoided more severe professional ostracism until 1975 despite being struck off the Party membership list. The new emphasis on the general ideological performance of institutions, rather than on purging them of Prague Spring elements, placed him at the front line of vulnerability and he lost his job when his boss needed to demonstrate the loyalty (or 'efficiency', in the words of Hyacintha) of his department. The scholars at the beginning of their careers, most notably ForSythia, then speak of constant insecurity and fear or at least of the overall disorienting atmosphere in academia (SalVia).

The short window of respite for some was followed by a further overall ideological tightening, quite understandably, after Charter 77 (Stellaria, Sinapis, Laxi), while the *perestroika* years from the mid-1980s onwards emerge as the last distinct phase. Some narrators talk about these last years of state socialism as a period of relative relaxation, but that does not seem to refer to any improvement in institutional processes related to publishing. Rather, the characterization is linked to the creation of the alternative spaces for intellectual exchange that I discussed earlier. Sinapis's account is exemplary in this respect: he began to enjoy academic freedom through publishing in *samizdat* and around the same time he was threatened with losing his job due to his ideological unreliability.

The generational shift was manifest also in personal strategies of professional survival: different ones were available to, and needed by, the different age cohorts. The strategies that the narrators associated with the period immediately after the vetting included dignified compromise, change of environment or topic, invisibility or non-conflictual orientation. By definition these applied primarily to the Generation 1968. The narrators continued to define invisibility and non-conflictual orientation also in relation

Stachys: 'My person …' p. 79 and
Stachys: 'We were branded …' p. 79 and
Stachys: 'In essence …' p. 90

Hyacintha: 'I can't imagine …' p. 78

ForSythia: 'One place where …' p. 92

SalVia: 'In all this the seventies …' p. 86 and
SalVia: 'In the seventies it was like …' p. 153

Stellaria: 'According to the year …' p. 127
Sinapis: 'There were watershed …' p. 144
Laxi: 'I was a committed …' p. 165

Sinapis: 'There were watershed …' p. 144

to the later years of normalization, but a host of new strategies appear: self-censorship, having learned the language, keeping up appearances, entering the Party, turning adversity into advantage and creation of alternative spaces. The two age cohorts were able, or needed, to adopt these in different measures.

The Generation 1968 could sometimes gain professional opportunities through solidarity of their former colleagues or by serving as an alibi for their vetted supervisors. Someone might lend their name to a compromised author (ghost-authoring), publish a compromised author under the auspices of 'et al.' (see the personal examples of Stellaria and Hepatica) or under a pen name. Members of this older cohort were also able, under certain conditions, to gradually work their way back into official academic structures. If they were, for example, retired or on disability pension, they could be given some opportunities, because their category of employment was under lesser surveillance. The cohort without a 1968 past did not have to resort to some of these strategies, but it also did not have others – such as solidarity – available to it. SiLena articulates clearly that young people lacked the social capital of the cohort affected by 1968: the 'normalizers' of sociology were willing to offer small opportunities to some of their erstwhile colleagues, but not to others.

The lack of social capital had the clear consequence of increased pressure towards moral and political compromises. Such would be the case, if the requirement to demonstrate ideological loyalty accompanied aspirations to professional development. For example, if one were asked to apply for Party membership before being granted the permission to defend one's PhD. That the pressure was there follows logically from the development of ideological regulation and monitoring described in Chapter 2 and earlier in this chapter. According to Stachys, a member of the Generation 1968, the younger cohort had fewer moral options: 'The generation that embarked on its professional career after '68, that was the most problematical group of course. They didn't have a choice, did they? Basically, we did have a choice, given us by the Party in 1970, when the vetting process was on.' We could say that

Stellaria: 'In our environment ...' p. 137

Hepatica: 'With the very first ...' p. 137

SiLena: 'It's all about social capital ...' p. 90

Stachys: 'The generation that ...' p. 93

for this age cohort, the institutional environment was no longer 'being normalized', but was simply 'normal'. This lies at the crux of how the younger narrators viewed themselves even in hindsight as authors and how they engaged with the ideologized language of social sciences and humanities of the time.

Before turning to these further concerns, let me summarize the main conclusions regarding the institutional personnel strategies and personal strategies of professional survival: (1) The Party exerted more ideological control over life in academic institutions from 1969 onwards, but its directives were progressively less concrete with regard to scholarly content; (2) If there were two opposing ideological sides in 1969, there was no clear 'us' and 'them' by 1989; and (3) The extent of agency and the strategies needed or available for professional survival differed by generation. The younger age cohort, in particular, was exposed to the gradual erosion of resistance to the ideological dictate. Indeed, the 'grey zone' was hardly of a uniform shade, but was diversified into a greyscale.

The highway code for getting published

The previous section looked at the physical *bodies* in state-socialist academic institutions; this one will deal with the physical *objects* produced by those bodies in those institutions. It will follow the journey of scholarly texts from a manuscript to a printed and published text. If today's academia is ruled by the maxim 'publish *or* perish', pressuring authors towards cranking out one publication after another and competing for a high impact factor, the dynamics in state-socialist academia could be summarized as 'publish *and* perish'. Any publication meant a potential risk to one's standing within the institution and to one's future publication opportunities. Every step along the manuscript's journey through institutional structures was regulated by so many written and unwritten rules, supplemented with numerous exemptions and complications that the metaphor of an intricate highway code is brought to mind. Who, and under what

The driving licence: Who could publish?

Sometime in the early 2000s the Czech Republic introduced new regulations concerning driving licences: instead of the previously unlimited validity of the document, now all licences had to be exchanged for new ones marked with an expiration date. The new rule also prescribed that all holders of long-term residence permit in the Czech Republic had to exchange the licences issued by their countries for Czech driving licences. And here was the catch: drivers from countries that signed one of the international highway code conventions which were also signed by the Czech Republic could obtain a Czech licence simply by turning in their foreign licence, but drivers who were long-term Czech residents from other countries, such as the United States, had to start the process of obtaining a Czech driving licence from the beginning. They had to enrol in a driving school, attend all the theoretical lectures and driving lessons that any beginner had to take, and then pass the written examinations and the practical driving test. The trust in the driving competence of the first group of drivers was conferred by virtue of their belonging to a community of nations subscribing to a shared set of rules, while in the latter case that trust had to be earned by demonstrating their individual compliance with those rules.

This sequence of procedures could be read as an uncanny allegory of state-socialist authorship. There, too, the figurative 'licences' to write and publish were renewed in the vetting process of 1969–70 and the trust to publish was conferred on those who remained members of the certifying community (i.e. Party members). Those with an insufficient licence (e.g. those who were struck off the Party membership list, as Euphrasia suggests) had to earn the trust to publish just like those yet without a licence (i.e.

Euphrasia: 'People who'd been ...' p. 115

conditions, could drive (write/publish), where and at what speed, who supervised the traffic regulations, to whom and under what circumstances the regulations did not apply, and how were 'traffic violations' approached? These are the issues I will now consider.

those who entered academia only after the vetting, or non-Party members – see the testimony of LupiNus). Moreover, just like the new driving licences, the 'licences' to publish were only a prerequisite to participation in scholarly production, but not its unlimited guarantee: the holding of a 'licence' was conditional upon compliance with the rules – whatever those might be. And this is where the allegory ends, for both the rules for keeping one's 'licence' and the series of tests one had to pass in order to earn it changed over time or were not ever formally set down, or only partially, as we have seen from the archival holdings of the Editorial Board of the Academy of Sciences. In the rest of this section I will try and outline at least a partial typology of the rules, procedures and strategies entailed in the process of achieving the publication of one's work as can be assembled from the interview material.[11]

LupiNus: 'At the outset …' p. 114

Highways and byways: The levels of approval

When planning a motoring trip, one opens a map and considers whether to take a fast and straight highway or a slower winding country road to reach one's destination. It is clear from the narratives of state-socialist academics that there were figurative highways and byways in the publishing process also. Unfortunately, the various roads did not seem to have a marked or stable classification, if, indeed, there even was a map rather than just the sun to aid orientation like in a desert, where any tracks are erased by a gust of wind. The memories of the scholars are patchy and full of uncertainties, so it is not possible to say exactly what levels of approval a manuscript had to pass through to get published.[12] The records of the Editorial Board confirm what the scholars' recollections imply: the rules kept changing over time and depended on who wanted to publish and where. Nevertheless, the

---

[11] The oral material seems to be an adequate source for this purpose, as it did not contradict the written record of the Editorial Board of the Academy of Sciences in a single point.
[12] The Czech case was certainly not unique regarding the non-transparent hierarchies of decisions. Siegfried Lokatis found the situation in the GDR scholarly publishing similar in this respect (Lokatis 1996: 46).

gaps in the narratives are revealing in themselves. They add further pieces to the puzzle of how scholars represent their 'knowledge of power' (Jansen 1991: 8) to negotiate their professional existence.

It can be safely established that any manuscript had to pass through the gates of one's workplace, where it was directed either to the fast lane, that is, the line manager either did not want to see it at all or merely passed it on, or into one of the slower lanes. In that case the author had to obtain a publication permit from the superior, the superior insisted on co-authorship (see the accounts of their frustration with the practice by SalVia and ForSythia) or the work had to be discussed and approved in a forum of one's colleagues. The Hungarian narrators mentioned this last procedure as usual and entirely professional. Reporting obligations about publishing intentions to one's line manager was not consistently required in Hungary, and, according to Szebah, it was dropped altogether in the 1980s. If the manuscript was merely a research report, no further approval was needed. In case of an article or book publication, the two next levels were peer reviews (in the Czech case, not in the Hungarian, it seems – SzolPi) and the editorial office or board in the publishing house. Finally, the last level was a peer review for ideological purity (sometimes requested from the Institute of Marxism–Leninism), which was emphasized or at least alluded to by the Czech scholars, and almost not at all by the Hungarians. Only Szebah says that occasionally there was some political reviewing, but she never learned about its content, only the final 'yes' or 'no'. Unsurprisingly, publication abroad was accompanied by a stricter approval process. That led the authors (together with their editors and/or superiors) to inventing games of keeping up appearances (Helleborus, Szandiliah), in order to avoid administrative protractions.

The awareness about the existence of the level of ideological reviewing differed dramatically among the narrators. As would be expected, the two Czech narrators-editors described it in great detail, but the authors spoke about it vaguely. The assumption by the authors that such a thing existed, but that at the same time they did not know how it worked, is the most prominent gap in the

---

Margin notes:

SalVia: 'We carried out sociological ...' p. 135
and
SalVia: 'Actually, the main ...' p. 150
ForSythia: 'Connected with one ...' p. 135

Szebah: 'In the 1970s ...' p. 115

SzolPi: 'At that time it was ...' p. 114

Szebah: 'It wasn't formalized ...' p. 118

Helleborus: 'I was on the editorial ...' p. 133
Szandiliah: 'I don't think there were ...' p. 114
and
Szandiliah: 'If you sent something ...' p. 115

sequence of publishing procedures in the narratives, but one that allows several deductions. First and the most obvious is that awareness of surveillance with the simultaneous ignorance of its mechanisms creates conditions for self-censorship (see Hyacintha). Second, the enigma of the ideological review, together with what we already know about the ideological regulatory framework of academic life, gives it a superior status to that of the scholarly content of manuscripts. Several of the narrators say that the professional peer reviews were a mere formality, that they did not affect publication (ErIgerus, Lilius, Helleborus, Euphrasia). Thirdly, the importance of the ideological review and the relative unimportance of the scholarly content make every publication a potential risk to the author and the line managers approving the manuscript. Publishing in such an environment was not a professional necessity, but a privilege. Finally, under these circumstances, on the one hand, the concern of the line managers was not so much the publication of research results conducted under their helm or scholarly originality of their staff, as the anxiety that none of them stepped out of line and drew undesirable attention to their workplace (comp. Helianthus). On the other hand, however, the editors in the publishing houses, whose interest even in the non-market economy was to publish things that would find their readers, had to mobilize informal resources to push manuscripts through the levels of approval. And here is perhaps the most important reason for not having the highways and byways clearly classified on the publishing map: the editors relied on personal relationships with the ideological reviewers (ErIgerus, Euphrasia) and with the authors and vice versa, rather than on the professionalism of the reviewing process (Hepatica).

Hyacintha: 'Surprisingly not ...' p. 114

ErIgerus: 'It all started with ...' p. 118

Lilius: 'I was writing ...' p. 118

Helleborus: 'There were two ...' p. 119

Euphrasia: 'Look, [the manuscript ...' p. 119

Helianthus: 'Institutes and institutions ...' p. 121

ErIgerus: 'The way the system ...' p. 120

Euphrasia: 'Thing is, institutions ...' p. 121

Hepatica: 'Getting up and ...' p. 116

Fast lanes, bypasses, speed ramps and roadblocks: Accelerators and obstacles to publication

The importance of the ideological review created an obstacle in the path of a manuscript towards publication. It either slowed down or blocked the progress of the journey, or needed to be bypassed by the author's textual craft (it will be the subject of discussion later) or by means of personal relationships. If we now remember the discussion of the regulatory framework and the conclusion that the focus of ideological surveillance gradually moved from the content to the form, to the appearance of ideological compliance, it is logical that both the textual craft and the personal relationships worked to meet this end first of all. To obtain a recommendation from a politically suitable reviewer was essential, but *all* that really mattered, as ErIgerus, Helianthus, Sambucus and Sinapis agree. This double bind, in which the actual scholarly content is not a part of the argument, however, opened the way for exploitation and various power games: for example, impeding publication by insisting on a review from one particular person (Euphrasia), humiliating politically compromised scholars by appointing their junior colleague as, in effect, their censor (SalVia), or taking advantage of the general fear of a blot on one's ideological image by telling tales about a rival, labelling him as an ideological risk to the publishers (Hedera).

The centralization of ideological surveillance was another factor producing roadblocks. Its main effects were division of publishing spaces to what could be called 'gated communities' (or, consistent with the metaphor of this section, 'restricted access roads') and barriers in the form of distribution quotas that in turn produced shortages of various resources in the publication process.

The division of publishing spaces was motivated by the ideological surveillance, but also by personal gain and rivalry, as well as by subversion of the surveillance. The narrators agreed that the types of publications with the highest degree of ideological surveillance (such as academic journals) attracted and invited authors endowed with political and institutional power ('normalizers' and compliant Party members, people holding *nomenklatura* positions – SiLena, Sambucus, Helleborus). It is also possible that in some cases, as SiLena argues, the right to publish grey literature that required only a lower-level authorization, such as student texts and lecture notes (*skripta*) published by individual faculties, was guarded within a closed group of people endowed

ErIgerus: 'The way the system ...' p. 120

Helianthus: 'In the eighties ...' p. 120

Sambucus: 'In my own case ...' p. 121

Sinapis: 'Obviously, things varied ...' p. 122

Euphrasia: 'I phoned the reviewer ...' p. 123

SalVia: 'We would read ...' p. 125

Hedera: 'One time, the editorial ...' p. 124

SiLena: 'I never tried placing ...' p. 128

Sambucus: 'For my part, I wasn't ...' p. 128

Helleborus: 'There were journals ...' p. 176

SiLena: 'No sociology textbooks ...' p. 126

with institutional (i.e. Party) power. In both cases – scholarly journals and internal publications – the combination of ideological surveillance and institutional power in the hands of particular people could serve as a strategy to keep any professional rivals out. Similarly, publishing houses, in which there was less ideological surveillance according to the narrators, could discriminate among authors on the basis of their social capital: Were they 'friends', 'foes' or with unknown alliances (Hedera, Sambucus, Helleborus, Stellaria, Helianthus)? Counterbalancing this formation of 'gated communities' from above, a similar process was happening simultaneously from below: Fragaria recollects that she belonged to a community of scholars who had an agreement among themselves as to where it was (morally) acceptable for them to publish. Sambucus says that most of his publication output was in proceedings from workshops organized again by distinct academic communities, alternatives to the mainstream.

Hedera: 'The Academy of Sciences ...' p. 126

Sambucus: 'In my own case ...' p. 121

Helleborus: 'It was better ...' p. 127

Stellaria: 'According to the year ...' p. 127

Helianthus: 'The Nakladatelství ...' p. 127

Fragaria: 'I never tried to publish ...' p. 127

Sambucus: 'For my part, I wasn't ...' p. 128

Material barriers to publication have been described by scholars working on state-socialist publishing before. Jiřina Šmejkalová lists paper quotas to publishing houses and increasing the size of print-runs rather than the number of published titles as the main impediments to publishing in the late period of state socialism (Šmejkalová-Strickland 1994; Šmejkalová 2011: 119). The narrators for this research listed other material limitations also: long production times and moving a book back a year or longer in the publishing plan, which could have served as an excuse for not publishing something instead of rejecting it right away (ErIgerus and Sinapis), quotas on content (LupiNus recalls that a literary journal had a content policy of one-third originating in the socialist bloc, one-third in the developing countries and one-third in the West), or a related policy of making the publication of a book from the West conditional to also publishing another from the Soviet Union (ErIgerus). Yet another kind of restriction presented more access to scholarly literature to some institutions and lesser to others (SiLena).

ErIgerus: 'It all started with ...' p. 118

Sinapis: 'There were production ...' p. 131

LupiNus: 'At the time, [the journal] ...' p. 130

ErIgerus: 'Then of course ...' p. 130

SiLena: 'Paradoxically ...' p. 129

Needless to say that both the existence of the 'gated communities' and the shortages of resources further enhanced the importance of personal connections, because those could move one's manuscript up the line or open access to a restricted space. They could take the form of either favouritism (ErIgerus) or collegial solidarity: SorBus and Lilius recall instances of favourable reviews written explicitly to enable the publication of a politically sensitive text or an objectionable author.

ErIgerus: 'What got published ...' p. 135

SorBus: 'I did a rave review ...' p. 136

Lilius: 'On the verge ...' p. 136

Highway patrols and lollipop ladies: Editors-in-chief and editors

The favourable reviews and personal recommendations served as 'access permissions', so to speak, to an otherwise restricted area, but manuscripts accompanied by these were still subject to inspection at checkpoints: by editors and editors-in-chief. I have already mentioned the editors' ambivalent and, to a degree, crucial role in the highway code of state-socialist publishing, as facilitators and gatekeepers at the same time. The narrators associated editors more with the facilitating function and the editors-in-chief with gatekeeping. They would disagree with Robert Darnton's categorization of editors as censors in his older study of GDR literary publishing (Darnton 1995) and would be pleased to read that in his more recent work he presents editors as actors in the system of censorship, with whom authors could negotiate and therefore exercise agency (Darnton 2014: 191). The scholars reserved the word 'censor' or a concept to that effect for the ideological reviewers, for their line managers (SiLena), for some unspecified and even unknown personality lurking somewhere in the wings, or for the editor-in-chief (Sinapis). They never applied it to the editors assigned to a particular manuscript, although the clause ErIgerus quotes from his employment contract making him 'responsible for linguistic, factual and ideological correctness' gave editors the status of censors. The narrators referred to editors either as people who, just like in democratic publishing, corrected a mistake here and there or, first of all, as people who were the author's allies. They were perhaps not quite the guardian angels,

SiLena: 'I switched to ...' p. 135

Sinapis: 'The manuscript ...' p. 134

ErIgerus: 'Well, according to ...' p. 132

but, rather, the nice lollipop ladies, as the majority of the narrators refer to them in the feminine, who looked out for the safe moment to cross the road – or publish something or somebody who may have been deemed difficult (ErIgerus, Laburnus, Helleborus, Hepatica). Of course, the division of roles between the editor-in-chief and the other editors could have been of the bad cop–good cop arrangement to keep the authors placated, but the interview material and the science policies discussed in Chapter 2 suggest another explanation. Editors-in-chief were probably always in *nomenklatura* positions. Their loyalty and obligation would have been first of all to the Party discipline and they would be personally accountable for any ideological misbehaviour. They would have known that all the editors-in-chief whose journals published material supportive of the Prague Spring reform ideas lost their jobs at the beginning of normalization. Indeed, they may have been themselves their replacements.

ErIgerus: 'Well, according to …' p. 132

Laburnus: 'It's interesting that …' p. 132

Helleborus: 'The English translation …' p. 132

Hepatica: 'My book sold out fast …' p. 133

Epp Lauk, Petr Šámal and Teodora Shek Brnardić's argument that the personalization of responsibility made the whole system 'much more efficient than institutionalized and bureaucratic censorship because loyalty had to be proved if one sought to keep one's position' (Lauk, Šámal and Shek Brnardić 2018: 341) would certainly apply to the editors-in-chief, but perhaps not so much to the lower-level editors. These were not always Party members, they worked closely with the authors rather than with the Party, and they were responsible for *getting* things published, although they would still be responsible if they let through something ideologically unsound. This last point meant that however loyal to their profession rather than to the Party the editors may have been, they were bound in a vassal relationship with their authors and had to nurture their trust. Here such a relationship meant that authors applied self-censorship in order not to put their editors, or their relationship with the editors, into jeopardy or place them in the embarrassing situation of having to censor. I will discuss the range of acts of censorship in the next section, but first I will briefly consider two 'appendices' to the rules of traffic in state-socialist publishing: reasons for staying 'off the road' and not to publish, and general approaches by authors and publishing authorities to 'highway code violations', that is, attempts to publish ideologically unsound texts.

Wintering the vehicle: Why NOT to publish?

Given all the 'regulations' of the 'highway code' discussed so far, it is not surprising that some scholars published little or hardly at all. There were those without a 'licence' to publish, but also others who could publish, but for one reason or another did not. The division of spaces that excluded some individuals or whole communities from certain publication venues was one reason. Hyacintha says that she and her institute did not make another attempt to publish in an academic journal after they were rejected on the grounds that they cooperated with politically compromised researchers. ForSythia recounts another form of exclusion from publication opportunities: informal exclusion on the basis of gender, when her male colleagues made publication plans after work in a pub, where she could not always go with them due to her family obligations.

Several reasons for refraining from publication that were mentioned by the narrators are connected with the points I made earlier: not being seen as stepping out of line and publishing being a potential risk and therefore a privilege, rather than a professional necessity. Helleborus, for example, explains that he never even tried to publish in the West, because he did not dare and did not want to draw attention to himself.[13] SiLena says clearly that in hindsight the low production at an academic institution was because 'the greater your output, the more problems you had', and SorBus thinks that publishing did not bring any professional advantage, because professional discussion was absent. Euphrasia

Hyacintha: 'In the seventies ...' p. 141

ForSythia: 'I always sensed ...' p. 140

Helleborus: 'I didn't have anything ...' p. 142

SiLena: 'These days I understand ...' p. 141

SorBus: 'Scholarly writing ...' p. 141

Euphrasia: 'I was at the Academy ...' p. 142

---

[13] It is unclear how Helleborus defines publishing abroad, because he is one of the few narrators who actually did publish in the West, but this publication was mediated by the official Czech agency, Dilia, that existed for this purpose and he goes into detail about the circumstances of this publication in his narrative.

describes perhaps the most absurd situation produced by these circumstances: her institute had considerable funds for a major publication, but the director, aware of the sensitivity of the subject matter that was certain to draw criticism after the work was published, successfully avoided publication for ten years.

Highway code violations: Overstepping the line and getting away with it, or not

The final points to consider with regard to 'driving' one's manuscript on the roads of state-socialist publishing are how authors succeeded with manuscripts that may have gone beyond the line of ideological permissibility and how they were told that it was not going to work. The safest eventuality in getting away with going too far was to avoid being discovered. That would be the case if the text did not fall into the hands of any objecting reviewers, for example, because it covered a topic that did not attract political attention or in which only few specialists were interested (Sambucus). Helianthus gives details of another evasive strategy, which he claims was more common: he satisfied the reviewers' objections in the pre-publication phase and obtained the permission to publish – and then he reverted the text to the original in the page proofs.

Sambucus: '*De facto* I had …' p. 143

Helianthus: 'In the eighties, or …' p. 143

Rejecting a manuscript on ideological grounds is a tricky matter, if the officially maintained fiction is that there is no censorship and that the scholarly content is what matters above all. Various restrictive strategies and punitive procedures are possible, but there is a limit to the degree to which they can be formalized. Several narrators agreed on the uneasiness the responsible personnel at the publisher's displayed when they were to issue a formal rejection on the grounds that could be seen as censorship. ErIgerus says that the ideological reviews from the Institute of Marxism–Leninism merely stated 'recommended for publication' or 'not recommended for publication', but without giving reasons, Hedera describes the embarrassing 'pass-the-buck' manoeuvring with returning a manuscript to a politically

ErIgerus: 'They never made …' p. 138

Hedera: 'At *Český časopis historický* …' p. 139

compromised former colleague, and Stachys recollects the impossibility of obtaining a written rejection statement from the publishing house.

<small>Stachys: 'Somewhere about 1985 ...' p. 140</small>

The main consequences of the 'highway code' of state-socialist academic publishing could be summarized as follows: (1) The authors could not publish just by virtue of being scholars, but they had to be regarded as politically trustworthy. Either trust could be conferred on them (i.e. it followed from their Party membership) or they had to earn the trust of their line managers and publishers by demonstrating their ideological loyalty or at least by establishing a record of trouble-free publishing. (2) The ideological, rather than the scholarly peer review carried decisive importance, but its mechanisms were not necessarily clear to the authors. (3) This made publishing into a privilege, rather than a professional necessity. Every publication was a potential political risk to the author and his or her institution. (4) Together, the need for the ideological review, the lack of transparency of how it worked and publishing being a privilege elevated personal relations with the ideological reviewers and also between authors and editors to prime importance. Personal contacts helped build relations of trust, but also vassal relationships and relations based on institutional and political power. This led to the creation of publishing communities that invited some and excluded others. (5) Authors considered editors as facilitators rather than gatekeepers, although they were formally responsible for what amounted to censorship. (6) The pretence of not having censorship in academia meant that rejection procedures on political grounds were not formalized and lacked due process.

Acts of censorship, authors and their texts

It is only logical that if a complete rejection of a scholarly manuscript that could be perceived as political censorship was an uncomfortable affair for publishers, a range of measures would be developed and 'dispersed' (Burt 1998: 17) throughout the publishing process to render this extreme solution redundant or the very last resort. These measures varied throughout the period in response to the political climate: the ideological mobilization following the publication of Charter 77 resulted in tighter surveillance that may have prolonged publishing delays, as Sinapis suggests on his own example, while the *perestroika* years may have lifted some restrictions. The conditional mode underscores the vagueness of the 'regulations' against which the authors made their assumptions and also the generational discrepancy in the political positioning towards publishing restrictions and opportunities. The Hungarian researchers reported similar ups and downs affecting their opportunities for publication of less conformist views (Szandiliah, HorMi). I will now try and reconstruct the range of possible acts of censorship from the authors' narratives, as well as how these may have affected the relationship between authors and their texts.

Sinapis: 'There were watershed ...' p. 144

Szandiliah: 'There were waves ...' p. 144

HorMi: 'There was a cyclical ...' p. 144

Acts of censorship

The acts of censorship experienced by authors could be divided into four types: no censorship, preventive censorship, post-publication censorship, and – the most elusive of them all – self-censorship.[14] Incredible as it may sound, some authors actually did claim to have experienced no censoring restrictions. One way of explaining such statements is reading them as refusals to accept the victim status, as James Mark argues about some post-1989 autobiographical narratives of people who actually were subjected to pressure: 'They coped with Communism by refusing to accept the persecution they had suffered as being central to their identity. For them, "becoming a victim" was the real sign that one had "given in" to the regime' (Mark 2010: 192-3). Another way of reading the 'no censorship' claims is to consider them in the larger context of the accounts in which they occur. It will become

---

[14] Self-censorship will be discussed in the subsection on the relationship of authors and texts below.

apparent that the narrators either add a qualification to the claim or contradict themselves later in the narrative. Hedera, for example, says that she was not constrained in her writing *once she had decided which topic* would be unproblematic. Of the other types of censorship, preventive censorship is the most intriguing, because it had to take place in the absence of any official censoring body. It was dispersed (Burt 1998: 17) into four areas: censorship of people (i.e. particular *names*), material and structural barriers, restrictions on subject matter, and lastly (and relative to the other areas, minimally) textual censorship.

Hedera: 'I worked on topics ...' p. 148

The censorship of people extended to both new authorship and bibliographic citations of past works. SorBus insists that 'censorship was practically non-existent. It did exist, but in the sense that it was people who were censored, not what they wrote. That if you mightn't write, you mightn't. You might pen a paean to Stalin, but it would get you nowhere.'[15] Euphrasia lists the grounds for silencing of published authors: 'This one was a pessimist, that one was a bourgeois historian, this one was an anti-Semite, that one had emigrated, and so on. Mostly it was the Chartists, if anyone did append their name [to a civic proclamation].' Censoring people thus followed Foucault's 'logic of censorship':

SorBus: 'Self-censorship ...' p. 151

Euphrasia: 'The problems ...' p. 156

> [The] interdiction is thought to take three forms: affirming that such a thing is not permitted, preventing it from being said, denying that it exists. (...) one must not talk about what is forbidden until it is annulled in reality; what is inexistent has no right to show itself, even in the order of speech where its inexistence is declared; and that which one must keep silent about is banished from reality as the thing that is tabooed above all else. (Foucault 1990: 84)

We will see later that such erasure did not occur in the other traditional domains of censorship: subject matter and language. The oral testimonies suggest that those two areas appear to have

Sztipoah: 'There was this policy ...' p. 151

Lustani: 'From the ideological ...' p. 152

Szandiliah: 'From the sixties on ...' p. 152

[15] Some of the Hungarian researchers classified themselves as 'tolerated', as opposed to 'prohibited' or 'supported', authors (Sztipoah, Lustani, Szandiliah).

been open to a host of modification and evasion strategies, as well as to negotiation. The limits of Butler's 'unspeakability' thus extended to persons. Their very names were banished to the realm of the unspeakable, but their activities not entirely: 'Since to name authors expelled from their field for (…) mistakes in the past would have been an equally grave mistake, the criticisms and condemnations of their opinions and work were usually condensed in short and neutrally-sounding labels' (Skovajsa 2011: 24). Marek Skovajsa then gives an example of the approach of Pavel Machonin's team as being labelled 'empiricism', thus marking it as undesirable (Skovajsa 2011: 25). Even in these contexts, however, the authors emphasized the role of personal relations and of the institutional power of some individuals: a person could be censored because of his or her being known in particular circles or for having encroached into the research territory of somebody occupying a position of power (Hedera, Helianthus). The latter could sometimes take the opposite form, a sort of 'positive' censorship in pursuit of personal gain, such as 'coerced authorship' (Bülow and Helgesson 2018: 4) (SalVia).

As in the case of shepherding a text through the publishing stages, material and other structural barriers were present in the research process also. Some of the more common ones included restricted access to professional literature, funding (Sztipoah), archival resources and the scholarly community by limiting contacts with international scholars from the East or West. Miloslav Petrusek writes on the normalization period in sociology:

> [After 1970] Contacts with world sociology were disrupted. Interaction with Western and Polish sociology was completely severed, and contacts with Russian sociology were strictly monitored and required Party approval. In addition, from 1971 to 1989, not a single translation of any sociological book of Western origin was published. Translations of works by Eastern Bloc authors were carefully censored. (Petrusek 2003: 51)

Recent content analysis of *Szociológia*, the main Hungarian sociology journal, certainly implies that Petrusek's latter assessment

Hedera: 'One time, the editorial …' p. 124

Helianthus: 'What mattered …' p. 78

SalVia: 'We carried out sociological …' p. 135 and

SalVia: 'Actually, the main …' p. 150

Sztipoah: 'That's an interesting …' p. 155

may have applied also to translations of Hungarian production. The analysis found a prevalence of Western material among the international material in the journal, rather than articles about and from other state-socialist countries, for most of the period between 1972 and 1989 (Berényi 2018). The Czech institutional vigilance against contamination by 'bourgeois' thought would most likely have meant heightened surveillance of Hungarian scholarship.

From among the narrators, Helianthus, for example, recounts that he could only access those archival collections that were relevant to the research topic for which he was contracted, but not any others. SalVia says that foreign travel was sometimes not encouraged only because it meant administrative work for people in the institution. The Hungarian paradox seems to have been that travel to the West gradually became available to wider circles of academics, while travel to the East was reportedly more anxiously supervised for ideological purity (SzolPi, HorMi). Circulation of scholarly texts published in low print-runs was also constrained by limiting access to photocopying facilities (Hyacintha). Some examples of structural barriers reveal tragicomic ingeniousness on the part of the gatekeepers, such as in the anecdote told by Euphrasia about her colleague who tried, in vain, to borrow a book from a library in China and always received a polite apology either that the book was on loan or that the library was being refurbished and the book was thus temporarily inaccessible. Other forms of this censoring mechanism were less humorous, such as when LupiNus was asked to report to the State Security for having received a copy of a cultural magazine published by the US cultural centre in Prague.

Politicization of certain research subjects and approaches led to a more openly ideological censorship. Phenomenology is a typical case in point as ForSythia documents, although she also suggests that even here the political reasons were used at least in part as a ruse to mask injuries to professional egos or personal relations. She stresses that this strategy for discrediting someone was not specific to state socialism, but that the situation in state-socialist publishing created favourable circumstances for such personal

---

Helianthus: 'No, no.' p. 155

SalVia: 'In the seventies it was …' p. 153

SzolPi: 'I started to travel …' p. 154

HorMi: 'In the 1970s, we wanted …' p. 154.

Hyacintha: 'It actually transpired …' p. 189

Euphrasia: 'With China …' p. 155

LupiNus: 'Through the entire …' p. 155

ForSythia: 'The problems …' p. 150
and
ForSythia: 'Phenomenology …' p. 194

reasons to be presented as de-personalized and made political. Apart from phenomenology and several other cases (such as post-1918 history or structuralist approaches – see Helianthus, Lustani), the politicization of research topics was rarely specific. Rather, it was perceived by the narrators as a general fear of articulations of critical perspectives on socialism or socialist society as a product of the socialist system (Helleborus, SiLena, SalVia). Szebah suggests that objections concerning topics may have been a little more specific in Hungary, where a measure of criticism was tolerated. The editors perceived what exceeded that measure and the authors kept testing the boundaries.

Helianthus: 'History had certainly …' p. 188

Lustani: 'At the end of the 1960s …' p. 188

Helleborus: 'For a text to be published …' p. 150

SiLena: '[My superiors] also …' p. 194

SalVia: 'I can't now recall …' p. 193

Szebah: '[In the 1980s] I discovered …' p. 148

Finally, the last form of preventive censorship – textual censorship – focused, surprisingly and at least according to the narrators, not so much on omissions (i.e. cuts in texts) as on additions: on supplementing suitable bibliographic citations and Marxist–Leninist phrases and vocabulary (Sinapis, ForSythia, LupiNus, Helleborus, LoTus) that would preempt potential accusations of ideological deviation. This relative insignificance of textual censorship, and cuts in particular, in the narratives can be explained by pervasive self-censorship (whether internalized or intentional) that rendered external imposition redundant. This has been argued as a distinct feature of censorship in other state-socialist countries also, such as, in the GDR (Klötzer and Lokatis 1999: 256) and Yugoslavia (Lauk, Šámal and Shek Brnardić 2018: 341), while Matthew Little considers self-censorship constitutive of expression in general: 'most censorship is self-imposed, a voluntary discipline and acceptance of the realities and demands of the institution in which one works' (Little 2001: 717). SorBus points out the snag in Little's perspective in the state-socialist context, when he calls the self-imposed discipline 'an amplifier of terror': 'when you're scared, you'll put the empty phrases in yourself.' Nevertheless, others disagree that fear would be such an overwhelming motivator of pretended loyalty and emphasize the possibility of negotiations and creating spaces (Mervart 2017: 56).

Sinapis: 'Yes, yes …' p. 157

ForSythia: 'The supervisor …' p. 157

LupiNus: 'I'd finished …' p. 157

Helleborus: 'I was lucky in that …' p. 158

LoTus: 'I don't recall …' p. 158

SorBus: 'No, no …' p. 159

I will conclude the discussion of preventive censorship with a liminal form of censorship – (un)friendly censorship: a form that is perhaps endemic to a publishing environment characterized by foregrounding personal relationships, developing closed peer communities and lacking formalized censoring procedures. It is liminal because it borders on both preventive censorship and self-censorship. If preventing a professional rival from publication by inventing a political difficulty around the person could be called 'unfriendly censorship', then the opposite, advising an author from the position of a peer or an editor not to publish something or to suggest cuts in the text, could be seen as an instance of 'friendly censorship' (Fragaria, Sambucus, Stellaria, SzolPi).[16] Friendly censorship and again its vassal quality is symptomatic of state-socialist publishing conditions, although not unique to it: For how many of us have avoided making unfavourable criticism of a friend's or superior's work? What is specific about it in state socialism is that it formed an organic part of the whole system, connected to and following from its structures: (non)-compliance with a suggested textual change was not an independent and individual course of action, but could have consequences beyond the particular author. It is for this reason that Stellaria categorizes her complicity with friendly censorship as voluntary. Similarly, the Romanian writer Marin Sorescu recollects:

Fragaria: 'I gave a paper ...' p. 148

Sambucus: 'Where it was articles ...' p. 149

Stellaria: 'For instance I couldn't ...' p. 149

SzolPi: 'Self-censorship in Hungary ...' p. 149

Stellaria: 'Hungarians were okay ...' p. 156

> But the censor often happened to be a friend. He would come to you complaining that his career would be destroyed if you did not get rid of this passage or that one. When an official edited my text, I got terribly angry. But when the same person came begging that he would be ruined if I did not change something, asking me to understand him, saying that those things might be published later, in a better context, then I found it very hard not to give in and give up the passage in question. This was in a way complicity with censorship. (Sorescu in Vianu 1998: 92)

As authors the world over depend on relations with their editors, friendly censorship would have had a particularly disarming effect on state-socialist scholars. Still, authors were not always and not

---

[16] Richard A. Zipser uses the term *sanfte Zensur* for the negotiations between the editor and the writer (Zipser 1990b: 111–12).

entirely helpless against acts of censorship. Like any participants in a discourse they had agency as individuals and they could turn to supportive peer communities. Helleborus and Fragaria suggest that a public peer discussion could sometimes overcome a censoring attempt. Pavel Janoušek documented exactly such a case from the correspondence between an editor and an author threatened with post-publication censorship in the early 1980s (Janoušek 1996: 83). Szebah argues that negotiation based on professional reasoning was possible and Sinapis gives examples of actions by a peer community to bypass censorship. These options applied as long as the authors remained discursive participants, as long as they were not excluded or did not break away from the institutional and the discursive structures of state-socialist publishing. They had to take seriously any censoring recommendations, however informal or 'friendly', because compliance with disciplining discursive practices could be rewarded by solidarity and protection from exclusionary discursive practices. The authors retained their status as subjects (Butler 1998: 253).

Friendly censorship is liminal also because its aim was not a prevention of publication in order to protect some abstract principle, but, rather, a very practical protection of the author and/or a particular community against post-publication censorship and its potential larger consequences (Hedera). The Czech narrators supplied details of acts of post-publication censorship, although the range of those acts was of a smaller scale than in the Hungarian case. The physically documented acts listed by the Czechs included reporting by a person unknown to the Ideology Commission of the Party that could result in the publication of the so-called 'critical review' – a condemnation of the work and its author (Sinapis, Helianthus, SorBus) – or in a tightening of surveillance (Helianthus), suspending a developing scholarly discussion in a journal, if that discussion was found to be ideologically deviant (Fragaria), banning the reprinting of a successful book (ErIgerus) and taking away a salary bonus in case the author or editor was found guilty of giving offence by a piece

Helleborus: 'General discussion ...' p. 159

Fragaria: 'In 1974 I was writing ...' p. 160

Szebah: 'If they required ...' p. 159

Sinapis: 'To my mind ...' p. 172

Hedera: 'We looked out for ...' p. 189

Sinapis: 'I wrote an article ...' p. 161

Helianthus: 'Hmm, for a long time ...' p. 163

SorBus: 'The review of that ...' p. 163

Helianthus: 'I always met ...' p. 161

Fragaria: 'We had a motley company ...' p. 164

ErIgerus: 'One bit of unpleasantness ...' p. 164

of writing (ErIgerus, Sinapis). Šámal documented the latter form of sanctions as a measure implemented by the government in 1972: 'In case the system of dispersed censorship despite all precautions failed, an official reprimand, or financial or career-related sanctions against directors or editors-in-chief followed' (Šámal 2015: 1182). All the other acts of post-publication censorship listed by the Czech academics belong to the realm of perceptions: suggestive and scary remarks by colleagues (ForSythia), fear of 'the unseen and unexpected bombshell' at the sight of one's printed text (ForSythia) and fear of job loss (Sinapis).

In contrast, the Hungarian academics reported several cases of actual job losses as direct results of having published a controversial piece. I have already mentioned the well-known case of the short-term imprisonment of Iván Szelényi for having published *The Intellectuals on the Road to Class Power* together with György Konrád (Konrád and Szelényi 1979) abroad without permission. Considering the gravity of these acts of post-publication censorship, their accounts by the narrators are sparse on the details of their circumstances and the narrators' personal responses to them. The narratives are dispassionate and matter-of-fact, while several of the Czech narratives emphasize bouts of fear and communicate an intense sense of wrong being done to the narrators. Moreover, several of the Hungarian researchers give accounts of their small gestures of protest, such as letters to their superiors, against the cases of post-publication persecution of their peers. It suggests either that they felt secure enough to do that or that their manifestations of protests were considered appropriate in their scholarly communities as parts of a professional discussion, even though negative consequences sometimes did and sometimes did not follow (HorMi, Szebah, Sztipoah).

Despite the broad knowledge of repeated fairly severe post-publication censorship, several of the Hungarian narrators (Szebah, Sztipoah, Lustani, Laxi) continued to test the boundaries of permissibility in their research topics or by publishing in *samizdat* and thus attempted to expand the space for intellectual

---

ErIgerus: 'One bit of unpleasantness ...' p. 164

Sinapis: 'I don't know of any ...' p. 164

ForSythia: 'Before it was published ...' p. 162

ForSythia: 'Yes, and I was scared ...' p. 162

Sinapis: 'I don't know of any ...' p. 164

HorMi: '[Miklós Szabó] who later ...' p. 86

Szebah: 'There were ups ...' p. 167

Sztipoah: 'We demonstrated ...' p. 168 and

Sztipoah: 'To the Academy ...' p. 168

Szebah: In a somewhat ...' p. 166 and

Szebah: 'Yes. But clearly ...' p. 166

Sztipoah: 'There was great ...' p. 166

Lustani: 'All three ...' p. 167

Laxi: 'So let me list ...' p. 167

discussion. Barbara Falk observed about dissident authors in Hungary that they often tried to publish in the official sphere first, and only if they were unsuccessful they resorted to *samizdat* (Falk 2003: 130). Several of the narrators mentioned this strategy, too, which shows that it was also practised within the official sphere. None of the Czech researchers published simultaneously in the official sphere and under their own names in *samizdat*. Apart from the clear distinction between official publishing and *samizdat*, their experience indicates a narrower circle for intellectual discussion, marked by smaller gains and, indeed, the perception that more modest ambitions were realistic. The Hungarian testimonies seem to be indicative of a more dynamic discussion, carried out within a larger intellectual circle.[17]

The overview of the forms of censorship shows, for the Czech case, systematic surveillance that corresponds to the strategy of control apparent from the policy documents outlined in Chapter 2. Excluding politically compromised people was the first and the coarsest filter, material and structural barriers the second and finer one, with the politicization and tabooing of certain subject matters and textual censorship being the finest filters. The lack of clear dos and don'ts kept everybody on tiptoes, so that the uncertainty would keep them alert to the possible political significance of every word and purge their texts of any hint of ideological non-compliance. Under these circumstances, post-publication censorship was not needed. If it was used, no dramatic punishments were necessary, the occasional raised finger was enough to restore obedience. At least that would be the logic of this system and, as the interview material suggests, it was, indeed, self-perpetuating – up to a point, as we will see in the section on research subjects and language, in which I will outline

---

[17] Bolton argues convincingly how the post-1968 repressions of intellectuals in Czechoslovakia created a large community of outsiders to the system, whose common grievances predisposed them to form a variety of dissident initiatives (Bolton 2012: 64–5). The non-exclusive relationship between official and *samizdat* publishing in Hungary might present an additional explanation why the intellectual circles within the official sphere were perhaps more and dissident 'membership' less numerous there than in the Czech case.

further possibilities created as a consequence of this system that appeared to pay close attention to every word. At this point, I will propose for consideration two additional phenomena to the so far dyadic model of state-socialist censorship (i.e. external pressure paired with resistance to it): the few isolated claims by the Czech researchers that they were not hampered by censorship at all, and the Hungarian narratives that emphasize academic freedom with regard to preventive censorship, but record frequent occurrence of post-publication censorship.

Even if we allow for memory distortions or self-stylization, the denial of any effects of censorship may also mean that there, indeed, were some authors who happened to fit into the niche of subjects and approaches permitted by the state-socialist publishing structures and thus may not even have been aware of the larger context and of the effects on other writers. The work of such academics could even today be considered as having decent scholarly value, rather than being subject to ideological distortions. Nevertheless, another explanation, and one whose implications I will discuss later, could be that the claim of no censorship is indicative of the state of scholarly discussion and critical reflection in some disciplines or subjects at the time – and, unfortunately, also at the time of the interviews in the early 2000s.

It has been argued that 'Hungary was "the happiest barracks in the socialist camp." Intellectual freedom was greater than anywhere in the Eastern bloc' (Mihály 1993: 57). The Hungarian narratives certainly suggest that a less systematic surveillance and less intense attention to every word in academic publishing produced conditions in which scholarly discussions could and did develop. Several of the narrators emphasize productive peer discussions in their *subjects*, as opposed to the Czech narrators who mention productive discussions exclusively in the context of particular peer *communities*. The reverse side of the relative freedom seems to have been that, consequently, the system occasionally 'needed' to restore boundaries of permissibility in a dramatic act of post-publication censorship.

As 'the history of censorship and the history of authorship (…) are (…) intimately bound together' (Coetzee 1996: 42), the relationship of authors to their texts follows logically as the next subject of discussion.

Authors and their texts

The lack of clarity about what was and what was not permissible to write begs the question of how the authors knew and how they oriented themselves towards the boundaries delimited by – most relevantly, textual – censorship. Related issues to discuss include balancing of the authors' various professional roles in response to the censoring pressures, the concept of authorship under state socialism, textual strategies and self-censorship, and finally, the authors' present reflection on their work.

As to the sensitization of authors towards boundaries, only Sambucus was able to locate its source: 'official social science'. He had no problem distinguishing what it required, because it used language that did not belong to his scholarly discipline, sociology. He was aware of the articles on the role of social sciences published by their ideologues – presumably the representatives of the 'official social science' – in scholarly journals, but skimmed through them only for the purpose of gauging his personal position of a non-Party member. He was trying to uncover the 'hidden transcript of the powerful' by making inferences 'from the text of power presented to [the subordinate groups] in the public transcript' (Scott 1990: 67). Sue Curry Jansen pointed out that '[a]ccording to Marx, (…) the worst tyranny would be a tyranny of concealed rules' (Jansen 1991: 95) and that is certainly the drive of most of the answers by the Czech narrators. They ranged from '[a]ctually that was an advantage – us not knowing exactly [where the boundaries were]' (Helianthus), through the acknowledgement that it was not rational, but one knew that there was pressure (Lilius), and that one got the idea what was 'in' from colleagues and published texts (LoTus), to characterizations that it was internalized, that it 'was in the air'

Sambucus: 'Official social science …' p. 170

Helianthus: 'Actually that was …' p. 169

Lilius: 'That's a very hard question …' p. 169

LoTus: 'I kept an eye on …' p. 171

and that one knew intuitively (SalVia, Stachys, LupiNus). The latter voices echo Annabel Patterson's observation that 'one of the cardinal principles of the hermeneutics of censorship [is] that the institutionally unspeakable makes itself heard inferentially' (Patterson 1984: 63). Only HorMi identifies a concrete benchmark – the relatively liberal Hungarian journal *Valóság* – but then he takes that as the outer limit of 'speakability', publishing something without ensuing persecution, *including samizdat* publications. The range of answers further confirms what has been said so far. There was a basic framework that was a given, but its interpretation, and therefore implementation at various levels, entailed guesswork: comparing one's writing to others' regarding suitable political tone and language or, as Jiřina Šmejkalová observed, trying to guess the objections raised at the next level of approval. Thus authors tried to predict what their superiors would object to, the boss tried to gauge what the editor would not permit, the editor made similar guesses about the editor-in-chief and so on (Šmejkalová-Strickland 1994: 204). By this process everybody was, albeit at different stages of the publishing process, censored and a censor, or at least 'the boundaries between author and censor were less than clear-cut', as Silvia Klötzer and Siegfried Lokatis observed about the GDR censorship (Klötzer and Lokatis 1999: 257). ForSythia says that 'the system was ruled by a kind of vagueness that left everyone with a sense of guilt, without knowing what for. It was that Mao-Tse-tung-like way of moulding broken-willed, good collaborators, see?' Her characterization makes a perfect fit with Renata Salecl's observation that '[f]or a successful political system, the mechanisms at work on the hidden micro-level of power must be capable of translating Party decisions into popular 'obedience'. (...) Normalization succeeds as long as people accept the discourse of power, even if they do not believe in the official ideology and maintain a cynical distance from it' (Salecl 1994: 39). The mechanism placed everybody regardless of institutional or even Party hierarchy into the precarious position of a player in the snakes and ladders board game: what spin to put on the rolling

SalVia: 'I think it must have been ...' p. 170

Stachys: 'Intuition told us ...' p. 170

LupiNus: 'It was in the air ...' p. 171

HorMi: 'There was not a fixed border ...' p. 170

ForSythia: 'You could never tell ...' p. 181

die, so that one lands on a ladder and gets ahead, rather than landing on a snake and slithering down. On the one hand, it necessitated the vassal relationship and/or solidarity, and on the other, generated the fear so many of the narrators mentioned, and thus created the conditions at every level for proactive censorship, that is, censoring more than was perhaps necessary. The authors 'for their own self-preservation, vainly [tried] to guess at the almost daily changing wishes of the authorities' (Blyum 2003: 17):

> That nothing was publicly banned [in Czechoslovakia after the Prague Spring], while everyone 'knew' what was not allowed, imposed a most sophisticated kind of terror on intellectuals. They were silenced precisely because they were forced to guess what the desire of the government was. Self-censorship thus became a prerequisite for intellectuals' survival; they knew that they had to be quiet and do nothing in order not to provoke the government. (Salecl 1994: 42–3)

Because everybody's position was precarious, everybody feared 'the unseen and unexpected bombshell' (ForSythia), and I should add, a bombshell of unknown impact, because of the lack of evidence of post-publication censorship in the narratives. Helianthus characterizes this unknown bully as someone trying 'to stir things up'. His diagnosis illustrates that the censorship dispersed in the various stages of the publication process worked in concert with the decentred character of the censoring power: it could be anybody – acting defensively or offensively – because anybody could be threatened.

ForSythia: 'Before it was published ...' p. 162

Helianthus: 'Goodness ...' p. 171

On the one hand, the insecurity of one's authorial position and the need for caution would discourage authors from attempts towards scholarly originality, as that could draw unwanted attention to them (LupiNus, Hedera, SorBus). On the other hand, the looseness of interpretation of the boundaries would open spaces for negotiation within texts and with one's various professional roles (Fragaria). Both circumstances together would put into question the very category of authorship. The authors regarded different types of their own texts with different scholarly seriousness and

LupiNus: 'Well, I haven't lost ...' p. 173

Hedera: 'Not that I couldn't ...' p. 172

SorBus: 'That self-censorship ...' p. 172

Fragaria: 'You have to accept ...' p. 173

chose when and where to negotiate. Sinapis, for example, points out the absurdity of trying to marry empirical results with the ideological speak in research reports and says that he and his colleagues treated them as 'fun', while he paid careful attention to how he used that same ideological language in his scholarly articles. The negotiation extended beyond textual content and into one's other professional activities. It would be easy to see the justification of ideological compromises or low academic production by prioritizing the role of the teacher as a self-romanticizing alibi claimed after the demise of the regime, if it were not a real possibility under the existing circumstances. Placing more emphasis on educating the younger generations is at least as legitimate a strategy of maintaining professional self-respect as treating one's scholarly articles with greater caution than research reports with respect to the deployment of the ideologized language. If these narrators were banned from teaching, teachers whose primary loyalty lay with the Party or with their own advancement, rather than with their disciplines, would have been likely to take their place. I suggest that prioritizing teaching over research, or writing something that one did not know would ever be possible to publish, but that one considered important (Sinapis), can be seen as service to one's profession. Service that did not necessarily bring recognition to the individual as an author and that could require moral compromises elsewhere. Regardless, it was work that carried real value – or 'work with meaning' (Yurchak 2006: 93–8).

The narrators labelled some of the compromises as 'libations' or 'sops to Cerberus' (Stellaria, LupiNus, Sinapis, Stachys). They included mostly textual compromises or trade-offs, such as having to write some texts to order (Stachys, Sambucus). Generally, the narrators agreed that they were willing to throw 'sops to Cerberus', but only up to a certain point of acceptability, which they tried to define for themselves (Euphrasia). Outside that they devised various evasions: researching in non-controversial areas (Helianthus), avoiding certain journals on principle (Helleborus, LoTus), avoiding certain topics (Stellaria, LoTus) or trying to find

---

Sinapis: 'To my mind …' p. 172

Sinapis: 'I also ran out of energy …' p. 174

Stellaria: 'For instance I couldn't …' p. 149 and
Stellaria: 'It took huge libations …' p. 174
LupiNus: 'I'd finished …' p. 157
Sinapis: 'There might be …' p. 211
Stachys: 'Listen, my impression …' p. 213

Stachys: 'Listen, I've decided …' p. 178 and
Stachys: 'I don't think …' p. 178
Sambucus: 'Then came that bout …' p. 178

Euphrasia: 'You have to realize …' p. 177
Helianthus: 'I think it was second …' p. 177
Helleborus: 'There were journals …' p. 176
LoTus: 'Before the nineties …' p. 176

Stellaria: 'For instance I couldn't …' p. 149
LoTus: 'I don't recall …' p. 158

ways to avoid the ideologized language (SorBus and more on this in the next section). Helianthus lists among his textual strategies a particular way of structuring his argument: he included his potentially controversial conclusions in the middle of his text instead of in their proper place at the end of the article, because he expected the ideological reviewers to read the beginning and the end but not the middle. Kornai details how he opted for that strategy in his book *Economics of Shortage* (Kornai 1980): he ended the book without drawing the conclusions that would have followed logically from what went before, namely, 'that the cause of the general, intense, and chronic shortage economy was the Communist system and that a change of system was required before the shortage could be ended for good' (Kornai 2007: 244). Some authors reached more radical solutions, namely, publishing abroad or in *samizdat* under a pen name (Stellaria, Sinapis, Stachys). Only a few mentioned resistance on their part within official publishing. Of these few, Sinapis describes his near-Sisyphean effort of refusing to make changes to one of his articles. It took eleven consecutive peer reviews over two years before the text was finally accepted for publication. It is significant that the last two approaches – pen name and resistance – were mentioned only by the narrators belonging to the Generation 1968 (Stellaria, Stachys, Sinapis, Helianthus).

Apart from the libations, another aspect – and one originating clearly in the generational difference – brings us to the key issues of authorship and authorial control over text. The narrators belonging to the Generation 1968 mention the practice of publishing under an allonym, or 'ghost-authoring' (*psaní s pokrývačem*).[18] If one wanted to publish, one could use one's social capital and make an arrangement with a publishing house, providing some other physical person whose name was not compromised communicated

SorBus: 'It's hard to generalize ...' p. 179

Helianthus: 'I don't think it was ...' p. 177

Stellaria: 'I published both ...' p. 176
Sinapis: 'In the second half ...' p. 176
Stachys: 'Obviously, those were ...' p. 176

Sinapis: 'We were a marginalized ...' p. 180

---

[18] 'Allonym' is a general term covering a range of ways and reasons for the practice of fronting a text; I chose the term 'ghost-author' to distinguish the particular usage when the ghost-author is the person physically involved in the practicalities of the publishing process, but not in creating the given text.

with the publisher in the official capacity of the author. If the actual author featured as a co-author at all, then it would be under a pen name (Stellaria). Šámal identifies the use of allonyms as a frequent strategy in the humanities (Šámal 2015: 1191), but one might ask why a scholar would write without the possibility to be recognized as the author. A simple answer could be that the practice was used for economic reasons. The narrators report that it was used not only for original work but for translations as well and an honorarium was certainly part of the arrangement. Another reason, however, could be again a service to one's profession, which overrode the importance of individual authorship.[19] The testimony of the Czech sociologist, Jaroslav Kapr (1933–2003), points in that direction. He recounts an episode of meeting a student in the library, looking for a book to which Kapr had contributed, but from which his name had been removed: 'At that moment, I felt a peculiar satisfaction that he will never know that the person whom he met at this time and place was the author of the book. Moreover, he will never know, but will live his days assuming that the book that he either liked or disliked, found useful or not, was written by somebody else' (Konopásek 1999: 306).

Yet another explanation, however, may lie in the already undermined concept of authorship. That resulted from limited authorial control over the text and reduced the status, and thus the importance, of authorship in the discourse on writing and publishing. ForSythia relates how her article could only be published with her line manager as the lead author and she had no say in either the co-authorship per se or in the content of the co-authored parts, or, indeed, even in the decision whether to publish her text or not. Another Czech sociologist, Miloslav Petrusek (1936–2012), told in a letter from 1987 a story he had heard second-hand of how the dean of the Faculty of Arts, Antonín Vaněk, insisted that a bibliographic reference to the sociologist

---

Stellaria: 'Look, I had to find ...' p. 175 and
Stellaria: 'Yes, a proposal ...' p. 175 and
Stellaria: 'Yes, about the proposal ...' p. 175

ForSythia: 'When we submitted ...' p. 180 and
ForSythia: 'Not at all! ...' p. 181

Lustani: 'I published translations ...' p. 174

[19] Lustani implies by his own case that even the ideological watchdogs had an unorthodox idea of authorship as creating *original* work, which included one's own ideas and translation of somebody else's ideas, but not the transmission of ideas, that is, scholarly editing.

Dragoslav Slejška (1923–96) who carried the label of a 'revisionist' had to be excluded from an article written by a lecturer from his own department. He would also not allow the author to withdraw the article, because that would be 'a scandal' (*Ale snad i pro toto jsme žili, ne?* 2016: 128).[20] These extreme examples of lack of authorial control merely complement the range of censoring pressures on authors to adapt their texts to the sometimes absurd or arbitrary ideologically motivated requirements. Lilius says plainly that if one wanted to publish, one had to make adjustments and these may have been in response to explicit external pressure, or implicit – that is, self-censorship. The trouble is that neither must have been necessarily always conscious and thus under authorial control. The problem in identifying self-censorship in hindsight, when 'it is difficult to differentiate and separate exactly what constituted the speak of the times, what among the scholar's words was a strategy and what was an organic part of his thought' (Janoušek 1996: 86), adds another layer of complication. Mark Cohen points out the problem of distinguishing between self-censorship and editing even in democracies:

Lilius: 'I think it worked …' p. 180

> The motivation in the first case is political or ideological (…), while in the second it is aesthetic. But poststructuralist critics have suggested that there is no pure, objective, aesthetic realm, that aesthetic judgments do not exist independent of the ideological forces (economic, social, historical, etc.) that shape them. Ideological foundations can affect judgments of style no less than they do other kinds of aesthetic judgments (such as 'quality'). (Cohen 2001: 14)

Samantha Sherry observed precisely this difficulty when researching literary translations into Russian: 'It is sometimes difficult to distinguish which specific examples of manipulation in translation are conscious censorship and which are the result of an unconscious internalisation of discursive norms' (Sherry 2015: 60). LoTus also suggests that the game of keeping up appearances may

LoTus: 'Well, I think something …' p. 180

---

[20] Letter of Miloslav Petrusek and Alena Miltová to Martin and Zora Bútora of 29 August 1987.

at some point cease to be a game, because some of that 'assimilated' strategy, 'by which you feign loyalty, some of it stays with you even when the need for any such pretence has passed.'

The question that cannot be satisfactorily answered is whether such loss of control over one's text was shared by the Generation 1968, as well as by the age cohort without the personal political history of 1968 (to which LoTus belongs), or whether it characterizes only this latter one. It is possible that the younger age cohort is the one that *reflects* the loss of authorial control because of their generational experience of no respite from ideological pressure, of dwindling options of evasion and of the erosion of their own resistance that I proposed in the section on personal strategies of professional survival. As to the members of the Generation 1968, on the one hand, they make frequent comparisons between what they or their peers wrote before 1968 and how that had changed afterwards, but on the other, they do not reflect any generational change and exchange post-1968, the mind-set of their historical orientation remains frozen in 1968. What can be concluded from the evidence so far is that scholars managed to avoid or minimize censorship by creating alternative spaces, whether peer communities within the official sphere or *samizdat*, in which (relatively) free thought could develop, but scholarly expression outside of these spaces was heavily constrained. Valuable academic work was certainly possible, if the only yardsticks for 'measuring' its quality are not scholarly imagination and critical thinking in the sense these concepts are used under democratic conditions, because techniques of textual evasion and the ability to identify researchable topics also require those same qualities. This would pertain to *authors*; whether and with what limitations these qualities could also be cultivated in the *readers* outside of the immediate peer communities of the authors will be the subject of discussion in the next section.

The final point to consider at this place concerns the authors' relationship to their texts written during state socialism from the perspective of more than a decade after the regime's end. Given the range of views expressed by the narrators on the issues discussed so far, it is not surprising to find a great diversity also in the post-1989 reflection: from the texts not needing any changes (this also from authors who did republish their pre-1989 work – LoTus) to having to rewrite them entirely if they were to be published today (Sinapis); and from the texts appearing 'alien' once the internalized 'stereotypical manoeuvring' had disappeared (LoTus), to asserting that self-censorship is not any weaker today than at that time (Hepatica), or that some motivations to censorship, such as when one writes on a subject that others do not understand, have remained the same (ForSythia).

One can consider these views defensive and self-justifying, but they are also indicators of the different positioning towards discourse, because the authors stepped out of one discourse and into another. The Yugoslav writer Danilo Kiš observed that when writing in the context of censorship, 'you attribute to this imaginary censor faculties which you yourself do not possess, and to the text a significance, which it actually does not have' (Kiš 1986: 44). So the narrators looked at their texts with a distance of years since the demise of state socialism: with a different set of discursive assumptions about it and about scholarly work carried out during its time. They assessed them with today's criteria of scholarly work and with perceptions of themselves as possibly wearing the unflattering label of state-socialist academics. From the perspective of the new discourse, Hyacintha sees the past texts as 'of no great significance' and 'quite harmless', the past concerns appear as much ado about nothing. Helleborus was told by a 'Western' scholar that he was writing the same things after the demise of state socialism as before, but in different words. The 'different words' probably refer to the then mandatory Marxian vocabulary and conceptual apparatus. Fragaria adds an important perspective on this vocabulary by pointing out that its use was necessary for communication with readers, because Marxism was the theory in which they were educated. The other thing that the narrators' post-1989 views reflect is their general sensitivity towards influences on the writing process and author–reader communication, which will be relevant for the discussion of text coding in the next section.

The relationship of authors and texts shows that in a system in which everybody involved in scholarly publishing was censored

LoTus: 'Apart from the introduction …' p. 181

Sinapis: 'I wasn't the least bit …' p. 181

LoTus: 'To be frank …' p. 182

Hepatica: 'Not once did I quote …' p. 179

ForSythia: 'The problems …' p. 150

Hyacintha: 'Recently, I wanted …' p. 182

Helleborus: 'Let me put it …' p. 218

Fragaria: 'Of the things I revisited …' p. 182

at one level and a censor at another, the authors were perhaps over-sensitized to the eventuality of giving offence with a piece of academic writing. That resulted in pervasive but elusive self-censorship: it is clear that research subjects, publication venues and linguistic formulations were all chosen with a bow to political constraints, but that the choice was not necessarily conscious. Nevertheless, even if the authors could not always determine whether their textual or research choices were deliberate, they were aware of the existence of general boundaries, within which they had to negotiate their professional existences. They were willing to 'throw sops to Cerberus' to accommodate these constraints with the intention to maintain a self-defined equilibrium between their professional and moral principles. The 'sops' included compromises dependent on one's professional goal: whether one's primary aim was to do academic work in a broader sense or to publish it. If one saw one's main contribution to scholarship in teaching one's discipline, rather than in publications, publishing was deposed from the pedestal of primary importance among academic activities, and one's relationship with one's texts may have become less intense. It may not have involved any dramatic sacrifice for, as I discussed in the section on the 'highway code' of state-socialist publishing, publication was not a professional necessity and there were distinct disadvantages and risks associated with being visible in print. If, however, one's goal was to get one's work published, the libations could include dissolving or undermining the category of authorship for the same reasons. That occurred on the part of the authors themselves and by external interference. The authors undermined the notion of 'author', for example, by publishing under the umbrella of 'et al.', the use of pen names, and the practice of ghost-authoring. External interference then reduced or took away authors' control over their texts. A byproduct of the over-sensitization to the general censoring pressures and the consequent attrition of the category of authorship might have been, paradoxically, a reduced or distorted sensitivity to the various influences on the writing process and the dynamics of author–reader communication, which I will discuss further.

In conclusion, if we now survey the relationship between acts of censorship and authors' relationship to their texts, we can say: (1) The systematic surveillance in all phases of the publishing process in the Czech case had a mostly preventive function and made textual censorship relatively insignificant and post-publication censorship minimal. (2) The surveillance made all participants in the publication process (authors, editors, line managers) over-sensitized to textual content, despite the actual minimal interference in texts, and execute proactive censorship (i.e. predicting censorship at the next level of approval). (3) 'Friendly' censorship was an organic part of the publishing process, contributing to discursive deal-making: it required willing compliance from its addressees in exchange for peer protection against discursive exclusion on the one hand, and it increased sensitization to textual content and self-censorship on the other. (4) The surveillance mechanisms together with the authors' resistance against them contributed to the attrition of the category of authorship.

The comparison between the Czech and the Hungarian situations showed the following main differences: (1) The Czech narratives frequently alluded to the atmosphere of fear, while the Hungarian ones tended to emphasize academic freedom. (2) The much less systematic preventive censorship in Hungary made post-publication censorship more frequent and more dramatic than in Czech academia. (3) Intellectual discussion tended to develop in self-contained communities in the Czech case, while in the Hungarian context it seemed to have a broader, disciplinary reach.

Politicization of research subjects, ideologized language and text coding[21]

The political over-sensitization to the content of scholarly texts concerned two main areas: the subjects of research and the

---

[21] An earlier version of this section provided the basis for (Oates-Indruchová 2018). This text is here used with the permission of *The Slavonic and East European Review*.

language employed to write on them. The former were acceptable, sensitive or desirable topics, while the latter concerned concepts, terms and word choice.²² The need to write only on some things and in a particular way, by definition, produced a debate in the interviews on the possible existence of a certain *code* of communication between the author and the reader. It is to these concerns that I will now turn.

Politicization of research subjects

It is not surprising that both the Czech and the Hungarian narrators spoke of the existence of parallel academic worlds not only in terms of different communities, but also in relation to the research subjects and the language of scholarly texts. These worlds differed in the degree of permissibility: the wider and less specialized the audience, the greater the need for caution. The main dividing lines ran between the Academy of Sciences and universities on the one hand and applied research institutes on the other (SiLena) in the Czech case,²³ and between the Academy of Sciences and universities in the case of Hungary (HorMi, Lustani, Sztipoah, Szandiliah, Szebah). Other lines separated the academic venues of expression from the broader public. When this separation was made more official, greater continuity of scholarly discussions could be preserved, as the documentation we have available on Poland shows. Sensitive subjects could be discussed and politically compromised researchers, for example, Zygmunt Bauman, could be relatively freely cited in scholarly publications but not in publications with a wider circulation (Schöpflin 1983: 32–102). When it was not formalized, such as in Hungary, scholars could expect sanctions, if they crossed the expected boundary.

SiLena: 'Imagine that there were …' p. 188

HorMi: 'Personally I didn't …' p. 110 and

HorMi: 'No, there was none …' p. 110

Lustani: 'I was publishing …' p. 148

Sztipoah: 'I was never invited to …' p. 152

Szandiliah: 'Let's say, we revolted …' p. 153

Szebah: 'No, it's quite …' p. 165

---

²² Ivo Bock compiled a list of general principles for censoring or promoting certain topics and perspectives (Bock 2011: 76–103). A detailed comparison would deserve a separate study. Suffice it to say that there is a significant overlap between his list that relates to the media and the perspectives expressed by the scholars in this research.

²³ Other researchers have reached this conclusion through the study of memoir literature and contemporary published research (Nešpor 2014a; Kopeček 2019: 234).

Szandiliah suggests as much about the case of the sociologist István Kemény, who used the word 'poverty' (*szegénység*), instead of an acceptable euphemism for the phenomenon, outside academia and lost his position at a research institute as a consequence.[24] In the Czech environment, in which the responsibility of scholars towards ideology was repeatedly emphasized in Party policy documents, the narrators may have disagreed on whether there were any non-politicized subjects or not, but they expressed active engagement with defining the borders of 'safety' in their thematic areas with respect to their own professional survival and moral acceptability (Helianthus, Hedera, Hepatica, Stellaria, Sambucus). Only the researchers employed in institutes of applied research (SiLena, Hyacintha, SalVia) observed relatively lesser political pressure concerning the subject matter and language of scholarly texts. They explained it by the overall objective of their research, its usability in practice. In Hungary, Szandiliah points out that, contrary to the general expectations, no reams of unpublished texts emerged from various 'bottom drawers' after 1989, because authors could resort to *samizdat* without serious sanctions during the Kádár regime and, therefore, there were no insurmountable obstacles to publication.

Even at the institutes of applied research the researchers hit the limits of publishability at times. SalVia gives an example from the very end of the 1980s when her team's empirical research that was to describe 'reality' could not be published because the reality was 'unfavourable' and the data 'didn't fit in anywhere'. Hyacintha's observation that 'criticism of the state of things' was understood by the readership of the texts as 'criticism of the regime' puts SalVia's account into a larger ideological context. Criticism of the regime would be synonymous with criticism of the state-socialist system, which was, by definition, a taboo no matter who the

Szandiliah: 'When the term poverty …' p. 168

Helianthus: 'History had certainly …' p. 188

Hedera: 'We looked out for …' p. 189

Hepatica: 'Like I say …' p. 189

Stellaria: 'Choice of subject …' p. 189

Sambucus: 'Well, the entire time …' p. 190

SiLena: '[Final reports …' p. 148

Hyacintha: 'It actually transpired …' p. 189

SalVia: 'We didn't actually …' p. 190

Szandiliah: 'It is quite interesting …' p. 209

SalVia: 'I can't now recall…' p. 193

Hyacintha: 'It was like this: …' p. 192

Szandiliah: 'In Hungary poverty …' p. 192

SzolPi: 'The Hungarian word …' p. 199

Szebah: 'You had to use …' p. 200 and

Szebah: '"Multiple disadvantages" …' p. 200

---

[24] Several of the Hungarian sociologists described how poverty was always a sensitive issue: research on it began in the 1960s, but there were waves when it was not desirable to research it and waves when replacement terms had to be used even in scholarly literature (Szandiliah, SzolPi, Szebah).

audience were. Moreover, it could be easily extended to the criticism of the leading role of the Party in society, a taboo explicitly listed by both Czech and Hungarian researchers.

This suggests that even applied research could reach an impasse: if unfavourable empirical data could not be published, what spaces were left for scholarly inquiry? Yet, other researchers said they were able to find researchable topics from a certain period onwards. For Sambucus, that period began approximately in 1975, for Stachys, in the mid-1980s. The Hungarian researchers then report occasional difficulties with getting funding for this or that project (Sztipoah), but on the whole their narratives are ones of active and continuous research. One obvious explanation is that the different perspectives reflect differences between disciplines, between research areas within the same discipline and differences in theoretical and methodological approaches. Another explanation, however, lies in the general approach towards the interpretation of the taboos and political sensitivities that I have already discussed earlier. The Czech researchers either spoke about their particular disciplines or research areas, or derived an outline of the development of sensitive topics over the normalization period from their own experience in publishing. In contrast, several of the Hungarian researchers provided fairly concrete, itemized lists of untouchable topics, applicable, according to them, across disciplines. These included the 1956 revolution, friendship with the Soviet Union, Hungarian international relations, and the leading role of the Party in society (HorMi, Szebah, Szandiliah). The difference between the Czech and Hungarian narratives suggests that the Czech academic environment was subject to *volatile* interpretations, with a vague understanding of the taboos, which gave rise to the proactive censorship. SiLena expresses the situation in a hyperbole: 'It was explained to me that a banal sentence like "A person is walking along a street" could imply some political problem, and I was not inclined to accept that, seeing it as paranoid.' In comparison, the Hungarian environment was more *literal* in its interpretations of the taboos. According to the narrators, the few taboos were

Sambucus: 'The period wasn't ...' p. 196
Stachys: 'Anything written ...' p. 196
Sztipoah: 'That's an interesting ...' p. 155

HorMi: 'There were guiding ...' p. 195
Szebah: 'Obviously there were ...' p. 195
Szandiliah: 'You knew that ...' p. 195
SiLena: 'In various ways ...' p. 151

understood in their literal political context and there was no effort to see them lurking behind remote research subjects (comp. HorMi).

Thus, the Hungarians gave the impression that they could orient themselves more easily in the political sensitivities and, by extension, in their research arenas, which also generated the perception of greater academic freedom. Moreover, Lustani and HorMi offer the observation that there was a definite and conscious tendency towards looking for an alternative, non-Marxist research orientation within disciplines. HorMi says that in history it was because 'historical consciousness and history writing lost much of its significance from the ideological point of view. It was not used for legitimizing any more'. SzolPi then adds that the whole field of sociology was seen as a site of resistance. His observation ties in with Sztipoah's statement that sociology was suspicious to the regime.

Overall, the Czech narratives show that the taboos and sensitivities concerning both the research topics and the language of academic texts mirrored not one, like in Hungary, but two kinds of binaries: the Cold War binaries of the world divided into socialist and 'bourgeois' and the divisions resulting from the Prague Spring positionings. This, together with the tendency to look for political meanings everywhere, produced two effects in the treatment of research subjects and language: conceiving of *any* research subject in terms of the two binaries and only in binaries, and devising ways of transforming the research subjects on the 'wrong' side of the binary oppositions, so that they could be co-opted into the 'right' side.

By this logic, any approach or topic that could not be clearly attached to one side of the binary was *à priori* suspect. ForSythia, for example, talks about the aversion to phenomenology, which as a non-Marxist philosophical school clearly belonged to the 'wrong' side of the binary. Nevertheless, the implications are broader, as Sinapis suggests in his account of the unacceptability of alternative theoretical approaches, such as symbolic interactionism, in the Czech environment: 'They were bothered by it because the

HorMi: 'All the other issues …' p. 195

Lustani: 'At the end of the 1960s …' p. 188
HorMi: 'A sort of western …' p. 188

HorMi: 'History was dismissed …' p. 196

SzolPi: 'Sociology in the seventies …' p. 188

Sztipoah: 'Sociology was always …' p. 79

ForSythia: 'Phenomenology …' p. 194

Sinapis: 'If I were to take …' p. 191

language was different. You couldn't graft the language of ideology onto it because that stemmed from a completely different mindset.' If Butler observed that the 'implicit operations of power (…) rule out the unspoken ways what will remain unspeakable' (Butler 1998: 249), Sinapis diagnoses what these 'unspoken ways' in the Czech context were: any language other than the discursively established binaries. He points to the need for an ideological underpinning of all scholarly pursuit that was systematically cultivated through binaristic thinking. Such thinking always requires a clear labelling of right and wrong and cannot admit the existence of a third, fourth or any other way. Any research conducted within such a framework has to relate to the two known paradigms, which means that its scientific method is not governed first of all by logical reasoning, but by relating to recognizable, value-carrying markers. It is hard to assess to what extent this thinking continued to affect Czech academia at the time of the interviews, but the difficulties and sometimes hostility encountered by new scholarly directions and disciplines, be it qualitative approaches, poststructuralism or feminist theory, are suggestive indicators of its lasting influence.

The latter effect, transformation and co-optation of research subjects, was most straightforwardly manifest in a negative prefix attached to anything that had to do with the 'West' or 'bourgeois', such as criticism of non-Marxist theoretical directions (Sambucus).[25] When applied to the Prague Spring binaries, however, this method could not work, or at least, not throughout the entire normalization, because it would mean complete uprooting of intellectual traditions carried by researchers still active in academia despite the institutional purges. While a complete break with these traditions was certainly the intent of the promoters of normalization, it was not realistic to achieve. The research subjects and approaches that belonged to the reformist discussions of the 1960s and that were thus moved to the 'wrong'

Sambucus: 'Sensitive topics …' p. 194

---

[25] Kurakin reports the practice of 'camouflaging one's interest in theory via a special genre, the "criticism of bourgeois sociology"' (Kurakin 2017: 405) as existing also in the Soviet Union from the 1970s onwards.

side of the binary after the defeat of the Prague Spring were subjects of hostile criticism in the first years of normalization. Sambucus ends that period in 1976–7, which corresponds to the findings in the archival materials. Articles attacking concrete people and subjects gradually cease to appear around that time. In later years, the subjects reappear under different headings or adorned with appropriately Marxist contexts. Stachys gives examples of such transformation: research on 'leisure' was later turned into 'socialist way of life', 'social stratification' turned into 'social structure of advanced socialist society', or 'social differentiation' turned into 'rapprochement of the working class and the intelligentsia'.[26] Fragaria recollects the case of a religious student who wanted to write his final paper in philosophy on Christian philosophy. This would not have been possible without a suitable Marxist context, so the topic was phrased in terms of 'labour', which 'was a sacrosanct Marxist concept', hence a discussion of labour in early Christian philosophy made for a politically acceptable topic. It can be argued that such transformations and contextualizations must have caused distortions and limited perspectives on the studied subjects. As a counterargument, they were ways of maintaining a degree of continuity with previous intellectual traditions and possibly also of subverting the directions of the five-year plans of state-funded

Sambucus: 'The period wasn't ...' p. 196

Stachys: 'In the mid-sixties ...' p. 195

Fragaria: 'One man with Christian ...' p. 195

---

[26] For published examples of the change in terminology, see the following book titles: *Člověk, práce, volný čas* (*Humankind, Work, Leisure*) (Filipcová 1966) and *Různoběžky života: Zápas o socialistický životní způsob* (*Divergencies of Life: The Struggle for the Socialist Way of Life*) (Filipcová and Filipec 1976), but compare with *Sociální struktura socialistické společnosti: Sociologické problémy soudobé čs. společnosti* (*Social Structure of Socialist Society: Sociological Problems of Contemporary Czechoslovak Society*) (Machonin et al. 1967), *Československá společnost: sociologická analýza sociální stratifikace* (*Czechoslovak Society: A Sociological Analysis of Social Stratification*) (Machonin et al. 1969) and *Sociální struktura Československa v předvečer Pražského jara 1968* (*Social Structure of Czechoslovakia at the Dawn of the Prague Spring 1968*) (Machonin 1992). Eszter Berényi found an article by the Soviet scholar G. E. Glezerman from 1974, in which he 'argued that the concept of "way of life" is far richer than that of "lifestyle" used by bourgeois sociologists' (Berényi 2018: 276). Hungarian scholars recently pointed out that '[l]ifestyle was the topic of the first large-scale, complex empirical studies among different social groups after the Second World War in Hungary' and propose that '[i]n a sense, lifestyle research was pioneering in Eastern European gender studies and the sociology of material culture and of the family' (Filipkowski et al. 2017: 153 and 156). Other Hungarian scholars then argue that in the 1960s 'replacement of "class" with "stratification" also helped to eradicate class analysis from Hungarian sociology in the long term' (Gagyi and Éber 2015: 600).

research, because the researchers learned to adjust the declared topics to their own needs. Some of these adapted topics became pivotal for the creation of the alternative intellectual spaces existing within the official institutional structures (SorBus, Sambucus, SiLena).

SorBus: 'The sociology of the family ...' p. 197
Sambucus: 'There were campaigns ...' p. 197
SiLena: 'I didn't think of a topic ...' p. 198

Ideologized language

The existence of the parallel academic worlds divided by what could be researched also implied differences in the language of scholarly texts, depending on how large and specialized the expected audience was. Stellaria provides an illustrative example of qualifying theses: according to her, a PhD was considered 'only' a scholarly matter; therefore, its language could be much less ideological than a habilitation or a professorial thesis. Those were defined as pedagogical degrees and their authors as teachers had to demonstrate greater ideological loyalty. But not all narrators showed such awareness of linguistic nuances. With the exception of a few events and concepts, for which a euphemism sometimes had to be used, the Hungarian researchers did not speak of any special treatment of language. HorMi even says that the whole Marxian conceptual apparatus was not *required* in scholarly writing. The Hungarian interviews also suggest that, as in the case of the research subjects, the narrators perceived more clearly than their Czech counterparts that the required or undesirable language extended only to relatively few terms and phrases. The Czech narrators take three positions on language: (1) They had to pay attention to the ideologized language in their work. (2) They did not have to make ideological compromises in their language use. (3) They now reflect that they were not aware of it then.

Stellaria: 'Of course [it varied] ...' p. 199

HorMi: 'Regarding the terminology ...' p. 200

I will set the most interesting, the first, position aside for the moment and comment on the other two. The second position was infrequent and expressed by scholars whose research area could be called 'descriptive' or perhaps 'quantitative': describing sociological, historical or demographic phenomena on the basis of statistical data and not necessarily requiring theoretical reflection. The Hungarian economist János Kornai wrote about the usefulness of mathematical language for hoodwinking the censor in his autobiography:

> Mathematical language was incomprehensible to commissars, party officials, and all who kept watch on institutes, publishers, and journals. Having seen a few equations in a manuscript, they put it down with a shiver. (…) Mathematical formalism gave an impression of political neutrality – rightly, to some extent, as a formula, equation, or geometrical figure has no inherent party allegiance. […] No one ever objected on political grounds to research of mine that used mathematical methods. I can say that watchful as the commissars were, I outwitted them with this choice of subject. (Kornai 2007: 152–3)

In the Czech context, the historians Hepatica and also Hedera, to an extent, hold the same view on the power and ideological neutrality of numbers. However, this strategy might also be considered as the next-door neighbour to Slava Gerovitch's diagnosis of what Soviet censorship did to historical narrative: it became 'internalist [i.e. not including context], factological, and discussion-avoiding' (Gerovitch 1998: 203). Jiří Musil goes even further when, without even a nod of acknowledgement in the direction of numbers, he pronounces his judgement on sociology:

Hepatica: 'No, no. I employed …' p. 200

Hedera: 'In my field …' p. 212

> I see two traditional weaknesses of Czech sociology. The first among them is descriptivism, the hereditary sin of Czech social science work, including economics, and that has its origins in the positivist tradition. In recent years it was down to the situation that people wanted to avoid public confrontation with Marxism, because that was suicidal, and consequently, it practically killed theoretical thinking. (Musil in 'Kulatý stůl "Dluhy sociologie"' 1991: 5)[27]

Hepatica and Hedera, both of whom spoke at least about some of their work as relying on the neutrality of statistical data and never

Hepatica: 'No, no. I employed …' p. 200 and

Hepatica: 'All newspapers …' p. 202

Hedera: 'Like "class struggle"?' p. 206

---

[27] Šámal observed a similar disappearance of theoretical work in literature in the 1970s. His content analysis of the journal *Česká literatura* showed that compared to the 1960s, the ratio of literary-historical articles increased five-fold. He explains it by a number of literary theorists being censored out, but also by historical topics being seen as less politically sensitive than theoretical discussions (Šámal 2002: 237–8).

mentioned theory as their preoccupation, also expressed less concern about language use. They tended to regard terms, such as 'socialist society' or 'bourgeois' as denoting established categories and the fact that they belonged to the Marxian conceptual apparatus was secondary.

The third position on the use of the ideologized language, the reflection that the authors were not aware of it then, appeared only among the members of the younger age cohort of researchers, those who entered academia in the 1970s, and is phrased the most explicitly by SiLena: 'You know, it probably never even dawned on me. I came on the scene when these matters had already been researched in this way, so was there any debate concerning certain terms...?' Her statement articulates my earlier point about the generational difference: for this age cohort, the situation in academia was not being normalized, but merely normal – and that extended also to language use.

If we now return to the first position, having to pay attention to the ideologized language, the metaphor of the 'Big Axe' used for the Cold War linguistic binaries by Petr Fidelius in his analyses of the language of the main Party daily, *Rudé právo*, is appropriate here:

> According to this principle, humankind lives in two 'radically different' worlds, which have nothing in common. This severance is of 'class' origin, that is, it has its roots in the socio-economic sphere; from there it transfers into all other planes of human existence: *the class axe reaches also into the political, cultural, ethical and other spheres. There are not and cannot be either shared legal principles or shared morality.* (...) The inevitable consequence of the mental divide of reality is the severance of language. (...) And so, each of the 'worlds' will speak a different 'language'; the same words will become mutually incomprehensible to both sides. Any dialogue is then principally and theoretically impossible. (Fidelius 1998: 172–3; emphasis in the original)

The narrators testified to the need to emphasize the difference between the two worlds in scholarly texts also by using different

SiLena: 'You know, it probably ...' p. 200

language, depending on whether they wrote about the state-socialist or the capitalist context. Sinapis illustrates the practice on a hypothetical example of 'egoism': 'You have to say, to show, that we do have the problem, but it's dealt with in a different way and that's better, more positive, it doesn't have capitalist roots because here we don't actually have a morality of self-interest based on exploitation.' He illustrates a practical application in social science of the promotion of the advantages of socialism over capitalism that Ivo Bock tracked as a general Party directive from 1986 (Bock 2011: 91).

Sinapis: 'I don't remember …' p. 201

Three features of this language use are discernible in the researchers' narratives. The first one was the need to use the Marxian conceptual apparatus across social sciences and humanities. Authors could sometimes negotiate this by supplying a Marxist introduction to their texts and then minimize the use of the Marxian vocabulary in the rest of the text.[28] The second one was a deliberate choice of 'magic words' (Euphrasia), ideologically laden terms, words or phrases, in order to provide legitimization for one's argument. The dual need for the Cold War binaries and for the legitimizing terms together created a *language of attributives* (Stellaria with reference to Fidelius). Věra Majerová characterized the language of the 1970s aptly: 'The poverty of vocabulary was camouflaged by rich use of comparatives and embellished with lofty expressions, such as, "unprecedented", "massive", "ever-increasing", "exclusive", "dynamic" and "qualitatively different"'

Euphrasia: 'There were magic words …' p. 201

Stellaria: 'Look, there really were…' p. 205

---

[28] A derivative strategy was the politics of bibliographic references. Citing the classics of Marxism and Soviet authors was either required by supervisors and editors, or thought by authors to be a requirement. This by extension produced a subversive strategy of citing Western thinkers who may not have been acceptable if cited directly, by citing not their names, but their thoughts from Soviet translations or compilations (see Fragaria). Kurakin confirms that selected Soviet scholars had privileged access to the Institute of Scientific Information on Social Sciences (INION) and were, therefore, able to study and mediate professional literature that was otherwise unavailable (Kurakin 2017: 402). It follows that through the publications of this Soviet elite, international discussions became available to a larger community of state-socialist scholars. Annabel Patterson describes a similar strategy of authors to 'limit [their] authorial responsibility for the text' in the conditions of censorship as existing already in early modern England. There, the authors drew on translations from classics and other historical texts to express subversive ideas and displace the authorship from themselves (Patterson 1984: 57).

Fragaria: 'I knew my coursebooks …' p. 207

(Majerová [1994–5] n.d.).²⁹ Such language use amounts to Scott's 'consistent risk-averse use of language by the powerless – an attempt to venture as little as possible, to use stock formulas when available, and to avoid taking liberties with language that might give offense' (Scott 1990: 30). The practice could have two contrary effects: an increased sensitivity to language and a loss of attention to language. Stellaria gives nuanced examples of the first effect, almost a personal writer's battle of attributives: according to her, there was a difference of political significance if one wrote 'antagonistic differences', 'conflict' or 'major differences'. Szandiliah and Szebah describe this struggle over terminology in the case of 'poverty' (*szegénység*), when the regime preferred 'low income' (*alacsony jövedelműség*), which Szandiliah insisted was not the same. Szebah used 'people with multiple disadvantages' (*többszörösen hátrányos helyzetű emberek*) to avoid using either term, but still capture the substance of the concept. The second effect, the loss of attention to language, has to do with the fact that the language embellished with superfluous words became citational, as Yurchak observed on socialist authoritative discourse: whole phrases and blocks of text could be implanted here and there to impart the weightiness of an utterance through impression, while the words would be emptied of meaning (Yurchak 2006: 59–75). In the researchers' narratives the traces of this effect are present through their awareness that there were set phrases, but at the time of the interview they were unable to recall the exact words.

Finally, the third feature is the 'reversed' stigmatization of certain words and phrases as a result of their ideological overuse in particular contexts. Stellaria cites the example of *internacionální* (international) as connoting 'the Soviet occupation', for which the official propaganda used the term 'international assistance'. Hence the word first became unusable if one did not want to be seen as complicit with the regime, but later its use became precarious,

Stellaria: 'During the normalization …' p. 205

Szandiliah: '*Szegénység* [poverty] …' p. 200
Szebah: '"Multiple disadvantages" …' p. 200

Stellaria: 'Or at one time …' p. 201

---

²⁹ Lokatis found out that in the GDR scholarly publishing, the copy editors employed the reversed process, removing the attributives, if a book was to be published in West Germany (Lokatis 1996: 60).

because it could be interpreted as a provocation. Stellaria's is a rare example in the Czech context of a transformation of the formulaic language by its users that Yurchak sees as a widespread and ultimately a creative phenomenon in the late Soviet Union: 'the performative reproduction of the form of rituals and speech acts actually *enabled* the emergence of diverse, multiple, and unpredictable meanings in everyday life, including those that did not correspond to the constative meanings of authoritative discourse' (Yurchak 2006: 25). Contrary to Yurchak's argument, the Czech scholars do not at any point speak about the practice as creative or as enriching existing meanings. Stellaria merely notes the change as something to which she, as an author, had to adapt. Also, this stigmatization has had lasting influence on language use. Some words and phrases laden with ideological baggage fell into disuse and were replaced by other expressions, others that were more difficult to replace, still produced ideological unease in the early 2000s (e.g. it was still problematic to translate 'exploitation', a frequent word in British cultural studies, as *vykořisťování* due to its association with the 'bad', that is, capitalist side according to the principle of the 'Big Axe').

The divisions in language, by definition, produced further consequences. Authors had to learn to navigate this linguistic minefield, because they were faced with the dilemma whether to say something at all, in order to avoid saying it in a certain way, or attempt some camouflaging manoeuvre (Lilius, LoTus). The language with negative ideological connotations (i.e. connoting 'capitalist') could be used to label and discredit somebody's work or opinion (Stellaria illustrated this on an example of journalistic propagandist usage, but the same could occur also in academia). Using unusual language could earn the author ideologically motivated criticism for being 'different' (e.g. elitist), because the less educated ideologues who may have been reading the text at one of the levels of approval understood only the divided language (some language could offend by being too sophisticated – ForSythia, Sinapis; some could be labelled as 'feminine' and therefore 'unscholarly' – SiLena). Finally, the need to express

Lilius: 'First and foremost …' p. 202

LoTus: 'Orwell wasn't banned …' p. 203

Stellaria: '[Certain phrases] …' p. 203

ForSythia: 'I was always …' p. 204

Sinapis: 'Language was pitched …' p. 204

SiLena: 'There used to be …' p. 203 and

SiLena: 'Unscholarly and feminine …' p. 203

ideological allegiance by using particular language generated fear of language, so that some authors may have used more strongly polarized expressions proactively to hide behind them, as SorBus suggests about the renewed use of the 1950s linguistic repertoire after 1968. He calls the unnecessary overuse of such language an 'amplifier of terror' (SorBus), because in effect it created a benchmark for others to which they felt they had to raise their own texts.

Some authors opted for avoidance or ellipses; others negotiated with their own conscience and with the editors in publishing houses their personal preferences for formulations that they found politically acceptable. Yet others tried to keep their texts as neutral as possible by stating facts and not elaborating on them, if they felt it would require an act of ideological conformism. Still others, such as LupiNus and Helleborus, attempted allegories. They wrote about a neutral subject, but hoped that the reader would understand that they were writing about something else. All these accounts of strategizing, however, raise the issue discussed already in the subsection on self-censorship: Was such language use always conscious or did it become second nature and not always a conscious choice? Sinapis articulates the ambivalence: '[i]t was entirely conscious', but it also 'may have passed into the bloodstream' as 'a kind of indifference'. Readers saw the ideological phrases 'as more or less formal, empty things', as packaging or 'padding that was of no importance, that got discarded anyway'. Sinapis implies two things: that authors were conscious of their ideologically relevant linguistic choices and that readers were able to distinguish between the 'padding' and the real content. The mention of indifference, nevertheless, also suggests that the attention to the words on a page became blunted: Can one control to which words and meanings one will always be attentive and to which not? Does this practice cultivate Jonathan Culler's 'experienced reader' capable of discerning nuances and decoding meanings (Culler 1997: 62–3)? Hyacintha identifies a turning away from words altogether as a consequence of the ideologization of language. According to her, the young people during

---

SorBus: 'One danger was ...' p. 204
SorBus: 'An "amplifier of terror" ...' p. 208

LupiNus: 'Just so, just so ...' p. 209
Helleborus: 'I later wrote works ...' p. 210

Sinapis: 'It was entirely conscious ...' p. 207

Hyacintha: 'It occurred to me ...' p. 208

normalization 'so overrated the importance of musical expression, the language of music, because (…) language had lost its credibility. They needed another medium to communicate with others and test whether they saw things the same way and understood one another.' If Sinapis at the same time suggests a communication code through language between authors and readers and the precariousness of its sustainability, Hyacintha suggests an almost total loss of verbal language and its communicative function. A loss that Aviezer Tucker argues has carried over into post-socialism: '[t]he most long-lasting legacy of late-totalitarian ideology has been the decoupling of language from experience and reality' (Tucker 2010: 139). Szebah says that 'one very effective tool to stop intellectuals from publishing was depriving them of their language' and that in Hungary one of the 'key aims of participating in underground activities was to learn a different language and to use a different language'. The possibility of the existence of a coded language among the scholarly community within the official sphere will be the final consideration in this section.

Szebah: 'I thought about it …' p. 208 and

Szebah: 'It was a learning process …' p. 207

Text coding

Before we proceed with discussing whether text coding could have worked or not, we have to consider the evidence for the existence of an author–reader 'compact' that would provide a basis from which a code could be traced. After all, the origin of this whole project was in that I, as a lecturer in the 1990s, was alarmed to find that my students were losing the code for reading books published during state socialism whose existence I took for granted, because *I*, as a student in the 1980s, was constantly looking for coded messages in both scholarly and fictional texts. This already alludes to the main problem with finding any evidence: that the reading experiences are so individual and 'are not easily traced and are nearly impossible to inspect retroactively' (Lishaugen and Šmejkalová 2019: 183). We have seen in the discussion so far that the narrators differed in their approach to and conditions of writing by age cohort, by discipline and research orientation, by specific intellectual communities, and by audience and publication venue. One may then question the meaningfulness of the archaeological effort for the retrieval of something so elusive and volatile. Scott offers justification of the search for what he calls 'the hidden transcript' of the powerless in terms of the depth of theoretical understanding:

> I argue that a partly sanitized, ambiguous, and coded version of the hidden transcript is always present in the public discourse of subordinate groups. Interpreting these texts which, after all, are designed to be evasive is not a straightforward matter. Ignoring them, however, reduces us to an understanding of historical subordination that rests either on those rare moments of open rebellion or on the hidden transcript itself, which is not just evasive but often altogether inaccessible. (Scott 1990: 19)

In the case at hand, the discourse around the 'code' brings to the foreground the complexity of the author–text–reader communication matrix in state-socialist scholarship. If we accept Scott's argument, we need to ask: What *kind* of evidence is there? There are certainly numerous accounts of personal linguistic strategies noted during this project and in published literature.[30] These testify to the already discussed sensitivity to certain language use and to efforts of the *producers* of texts (authors and editors, as well as peer reviewers) to construct or unmask a code. However, we do not have similar evidence from and about readers other than those who were authors at the same time, such as those interviewed for this research, and they do not say much about how they read other texts, or placed themselves in one of the 'censoring' positions (editors, peer-reviewers). In other words, we do not have much evidence of the functioning of the dialogic principle:

> Orientation of the word toward the addressee has an extremely high significance. In point of fact, *word is a two-sided act*. It is

---

[30] See, for example, the detailed testimonies by Romanian writers and scholars of their coding efforts and their disclosures by vigilant editors in Vianu's book *Censorship in Romania* (Vianu 1998).

determined equally by *whose* word it is and *for whom* it is meant. As word, it is precisely *the product of the reciprocal relationship between speaker and listener, addresser and addressee.* Each and every word expresses the 'one' in relation to the 'other'. I give myself verbal shape from another's point of view of the community to which I belong. A word is a bridge thrown between myself and another. If one end of the bridge depends on me, then the other depends on my addressee. A word is a territory shared by both addresser and addressee, by the speaker and his interlocutor. (Voloshinov cited by Pearce 1994: 43; emphasis in the original)

The other side of the 'bridge' dissolves in fog and we do not know who stands there, when state-socialist academic censorship is concerned. Stellaria says that not only she, but also her boss reflected the language, because when she wrote an article for him, he added the 'insertions' he deemed necessary. What her statement implies, however, is a difference between particular words or set phrases used as mere legitimizing signposts and a code proper, that is, meanings encoded in those 'insertions' and understood by the reader at the other end of the 'bridge'. The text would not mean the same, if the signposts were removed. Stellaria's account implies that the placement and the variety of the signposts may have been shared between authors and readers due to their shared knowledge of the authoritative discourse. However, it does not tell us if the readers shared in the understanding of the meanings intended by the author through the employment of various other textual strategies. I propose that in the narratives of researchers this distinction between 'signposts' and 'code' is often confused and that is the snag in finding evidence of the author–reader compact. I will return to the implications of this confusion for the overall argument about intellectual communication under state socialism in the concluding section.

That censorship cultivates reading abilities is one claim often made about intellectual communication under repressive conditions (Strauss 1952). When the scholars referred to this concept in their narratives, they really spoke of the ability to

Stellaria: 'Look, I projected it ...' p. 209

recognize the signposts and weed out the additions: 'You passed over some things as unimportant and saw meanings more' (Sinapis). As to the actual coding or Aesopian language, however, if they admit its existence at all, they largely disagree as to its importance in academic texts as opposed to fictional genres or poetry (Sinapis). Szebah concurs by saying that upon rereading, the past texts sound 'a little bit archaic', but otherwise the language does not seem to her distorted by political pressures. Most importantly, however, if the reader was expected constantly to employ the practice of focusing on some things and passing over others, readings unintended by the author were bound to occur. Certain readers – ideological zealots, nonconformists or even the regime's dissidents (Helleborus, Stachys) – could find meanings in the texts due to unique intersections of their personal or group experience with the imagined censoring potential of the words and their connotations (an object of the proactive censorship discussed earlier).[31] In other words, the texts were also read by people other than their implied readers,[32] which either frustrated the planted code or created a coded text where none was intended. The Romanian poet Ștefan Augustin Doinaș (1922–2002) appreciated the value of the opening to multiple interpretations, 'because it brought us all closer to the essence of poetry, which is plurisemantic language,' but he also acknowledged its risks: 'I was positive that I had said what I had meant to say, but objectively, the text did not convey those things. (…) When the reader approached

Sinapis: 'As it happens …' p. 210

Sinapis: 'As it happens …' p. 210

Szebah: 'I can just refer to …' p. 209

Helleborus: 'I later wrote works …' p. 210

Stachys: 'Right before the vettings …' p. 211

---

[31] Kornai tells of another peril of readers interpreting a text written under state socialism. In his case, it may have been an instance of a correct interpretation – or, possibly, decoding – of his text by his old friend and colleague, the sociologist Péter Kende, when he cited from Kornai's pre-1956 work after his own emigration to France: 'Then, too, [Péter Kende] may have thought that authors, on the whole, are gratified to be quoted. And I *am* gratified – unless the quotations are made by Péter Kende and appear around 1957. (…) In a somewhat far-fetched manner, therefore, I included language distancing myself from Péter Kende in the article. It protested against the way he was reading the failure of socialism into my book, adding self-critically that faulty wording in *Overcentralization* made it possible to draw such a conclusion' (Kornai 2007: 129).

[32] 'The implied reader is a function of the work, even though it is not represented in the work. (…) [T]he implied reader can function as a *presumed addressee* to whom the work is directed and whose linguistic codes, ideological norms, and aesthetic ideas must be taken into account if the work is to be understood. In this function, the implied reader is the bearer of the codes and norms presumed in the readership' (Schmid 2009: para 9 and 11; emphasis in the original).

my text, he could not go back on my tracks, nor could he reach the same conclusions I thought I had expressed' (Doinaş in Vianu 1998: 31–2). He emphasizes the community-building, rather than communicative aspect of the significance of Aesopian language even in poetry. In scholarly communication clarity of expression and unambiguous meanings are of a far greater, indeed, crucial significance.

Some of the narrators, however, did insist that there was a real and even functioning code between authors and readers. They located it in two textual strategies: in creating multiple textual layers (Fragaria) and in stylistics (Sinapis). The layers in a text meant that one could not write in a straightforward manner about some subjects but 'wrap' the text in appropriate contexts, vocabulary, citations, while keeping the substantive message in focus (Fragaria). This strategy relied on a holistic approach to texts and their subject matter, which must have increased its potential for miscommunication, even though authors might have practised it with utmost care. Stachys points out its pitfall if deployed by less skilled – or educated – authors in the environment of such heightened ideological sensitivity as was Czech normalization: an eventual loss of perception of what was and what was not a politically necessitated code, because these authors became absorbed by the ideological discourse around them. They thought they were being subversive, but a reader positioned differently, like Stachys, considered such self-assessment a delusion.

Fragaria: 'The criterion was …' p. 211

Sinapis: 'It was entirely conscious …' p. 207

Fragaria: 'The criterion was …' p. 211

Stachys: 'I was in the pub …' p. 213

Writers and scholars have repeatedly pointed out the ambiguity of Aesopian language. The writer Anatoly Kuznetsov, for example, commented that 'by reading between the lines, the Soviet reader is able to discover things that the author never meant to say, while even the experienced reader can miss the point of an allusion' (Dewhirst and Farrell 1973: 33). Irina Sandomirskaja traced the doubting voices from Lenin to Bourdieu and added her own valuation. The former left nobody in doubt as to what he thought about the method: 'An accursed period of Aesopian language, literary servility, slavish speech, and ideological serfdom! The proletariat has put an end to this infamy which stifled everything living and fresh in Russia'

(Lenin quoted in (Sandomirskaja 2015: 78)). Sandomirskaja finds that Bourdieu's argument runs in a similar direction: 'All subjects involved in the political economy of symbolic domination adapt to it, and thus contribute, even through subversive euphemisms, to the further legitimation of the hegemonic language' (Sandomirskaja 2015: 79). Nevertheless, she also introduces Deleuze and Guattari's perspective of the importance to speak in the language of the establishment, rather than in a 'minor' language, if the speakers of that language are to have any potential to institute a change in the establishment (Sandomirskaja 2015: 81). She summarizes that

> Aesopian language is a fundamentally ambiguous phenomenon, in the understanding of which one has to deal with multiple uncertainties. It is uncertain as a (communicative) action with uncertain political and aesthetic intentions; underlying it is an uncertain subjectivity vacillating between the opposed poles of resistance and conformity; it is uncertain whether its ambiguity achieves the double purpose of deceiving the foe while appealing, at the same time, to the solidarity of the friend; it is equally uncertain whether the friend responds to its message with a reciprocal gesture of solidarity. (Sandomirskaja 2015: 12)

Sandomirskaja goes beyond the contemplation of the nature of Aesopian language and in the direction that interests us here: the achievement of Aesopian communication in scholarship. She illustrates it on the example of the Soviet literary critic and historian Lydiya Ginzburg (1902–90) who consciously employed the method in her work. According to Sandomirskaja, Ginzburg concedes in her memoirs that 'the dominant language (…) consumes its resistant opponent and digests its resistant meanings' (Sandomirskaja 2015: 84). She concludes that Aesopian writing opened to its practitioners 'a space for manoeuvring in the short run, but led to a necrosis of language in the end' (Sandomirskaja 2015: 83). This pessimistic assessment casts a different light on the entire discussion of the 'code' in the 'imagined conversations'. Whether the code existed or not, whether it did or did not bring communities of scholars together, the core issue becomes the ultimate effect of censorship – the central question of this book.

The practice and perception of text coding may have contributed to the atmosphere of creativity and solidarity among academics and that helped them persevere in their pursuits. Nevertheless, none of the voices represented here suggests in the slightest that the Aesopian method would move their disciplines as such ahead. They speak of professional survival, of being able to find a meaning in their work or to keep a professional discourse in their disciplines going. They are more or less proud of their work, but they frame all their efforts as emergency solutions.

The other strategy mentioned by the researchers, coding by means of stylistic devices, plays into the argument of the 'necrosis of language' even more strongly. It is simpler than the 'text layering', because it relies only on a shared understanding of particular and concrete phrases, not the text as a whole. Ernest Andrews lists a whole typology of these in the Soviet case: 'epithetical phrases, laudatory for the *good* side of reality (…), derogatory for the *bad* side (…) slogans (…), jingles (…) and quotations from the "classics" of socialist/communist ideology' (Andrews 2011: 3). Stellaria gives an illuminating example of 'the period preceding the Second World War' being used to imply 'the First Czechoslovak Republic', because the latter 'was associated by the regime with Masaryk and that was unacceptable'.[33] Were she to use it, she would have to write about the period in negative terms, while the alternative phrasing enabled her to write in a positive tone. Incidentally, Robert Darnton gives an account of how GDR editors scanned manuscripts for expressions that could trigger an allergic reaction in the political watchdogs and replaced them with very similar phrases that Stellaria mentioned: 'She would change "opponent of Stalinism" to "contradictor of his time"; and even replaced "the 1930s" with a safer, vaguer expression: "the first half of the twentieth century"' (Darnton 1995: 54). This similarity between two countries and two different actors in the publishing process – author and editor – suggests, that at least as far as particular words and expressions were concerned, there seemed

Stellaria: 'Certainly!' p. 212

---

[33] Comp. with Kevin Moss's 'code' 'Ancient Russian music' to mean 'church music' (Moss 1995: 131).

to have existed, analogously to early-modern England by the way, 'conventions that both sides accepted as to how far a writer could go in explicit address to the contentious issues of his day, how he could encode his opinions so that nobody would be *required* to make an example of him' (Patterson 1984: 11; emphasis in the original). Provided this practice existed and was understood by readers, however, it still does not mean that it cultivated reading abilities in any sense of honing attention to nuanced textual meanings or sharpening critical thinking. This strategy would require only learning a specific and limited vocabulary – and translating/transposing accordingly.

To summarize, the main theoretical concepts concerning research subjects, language and text coding are as follows: (1) The Czech academic environment was specific in that apart from the Cold War binaries, it developed also a dualism reflecting the Prague Spring academic and political divisions that affected the choice of and approach to research subjects and the language of scholarly texts. (2) The need to emphasize the two sets of binaries in scholarly work led, over time, to the emptying of language of meaning and to a generational erosion of language use. (3) In terms of the discussion over the possible existence of a coded language of academic texts, the previous two points and the overall development discussed in this section suggest that coding consisted in developing a particular (and possibly more or less stable) vocabulary of 'official' and alternative expressions, euphemisms and shades of meaning that could be shared between authors and readers, rather than a code that would require a more complex production of textual meanings.

The ghosts of academia past, their spectres haunting the present

In this section I would like to propose how the intricate system of relations in and contexts of state-socialist academic publishing appeared from the distance of time to the generations that participated in it, what consequences their reflections may have for the later generations, and, most importantly, how that system may still have had effects on scholarly publishing – and academia as such – in the early 2000s, when I conducted the interviews, and perhaps even at present. At the very last I will suggest how the system of state-socialist publishing relates to both the main arguments on the effects of censorship – that it is either conducive or detrimental to critical thinking – in contemporary censorship debates.

The ghosts of academia past

The unimaginability of the past was a frequently occurring theme in the interviews. It was implied by responses to my questions, such as 'I don't know anymore', '[e]verything's grown a bit hazy' (Sambucus), 'I've suppressed it since and forgotten all about it' (Stachys), or to the effect that 'you are asking about unpleasant things that we are trying to forget'. Apart from the underlying considerable active and passive memory work that could be analysed from the perspective of memory studies, the responses also fit within the framework of the argument about state-socialist publishing presented so far. Once the authoritative ideological discourse was removed, its citationality was disrupted: because the phrases and text blocks were empty of their original meanings, they were neither usable in the newly forming academic discourse(s) to communicate information, nor needed as signposts. If the scholars who separated the language of academic texts into two registers – the signposts and the parts with meaning – learned not to see the 'padding' made of the ideological language, they did not miss this language – these 'insertions' – in the messages they hoped to communicate through their texts. It is quite possible that in the changed discursive conditions they discarded it and were unable to recall it afterwards. This process can also produce another effect, however, as Fragaria illustrates.

Sambucus 'I don't know any more …' p. 218 and

Sambucus: 'Everything's grown …' p. 218

Stachys: 'But of course …' p. 173

Fragaria: 'I remember one experience …' p. 217

For her, the 'padding' came to the foreground with the discursive change and the duality of the language and the meaninglessness of one of its registers became more visible.

It follows that if the generations of the participants cannot really replicate the 'code', the generational divide between them and the later age cohorts with regard to the continuity of intellectual discussions deepens, because the 'code' is not communicated across generations, as several of the researchers observed (Hedera, Helleborus, Stellaria). Yet, the participants called for the authority of experience at the same time (see Hedera), claiming that the younger generations could not understand the past because they did not live in it.[34] It further follows that this rupture in communication is likely to have far-reaching consequences for research on state socialism. Having lost the 'code', the younger generations interpret the state-socialist texts differently from the original audiences. They cannot distinguish the 'padding' from the nuggets of meaning couched in it, the two registers of language merge into one. While the amalgamation can produce interesting new interpretations, it is also likely to produce distortions and a loss of interpretative sensitivity (the dualistic approach criticized by Yurchak). Finally, the generational divide together with some of the discursive practices that continued to operate after the fall of state socialism – and may still be in place in the present – have the potential for lasting effects in the academic community.

The spectres haunting the present

The 'alpha spectre' from the past haunting the post-socialist academic present of the early 2000s and today is undoubtedly ideologically based dualistic thinking. It allows, on the one hand, the validity, the legitimacy and the experience of the past to be

---

Hedera: 'There are some ...' p. 218

Helleborus: 'Listen, I've got this ...' p. 218

Stellaria: 'Like yesterday ...' p. 219

Hedera: 'There are some ...' p. 218

---

[34] It is interesting how often East Central European historians, in particular, raise this objection. It has also been my experience in the course of this research project. An exceptionally striking instance came when, after a conference presentation, a *medievalist* questioned my findings on the grounds of a lack of my own lived experience with the environment that I was researching. I was tempted to respond: 'You don't look *that* old yourself.'

discarded by the present and, on the other, ideologically motivated judgements to take precedence before scholarly criteria. James Mark points out the damage 'to a deeper form of liberal democratic development' in society at large that is a consequence of the carrying over of the 'same politicized and divisive' tropes in narrating about the communist era in the effort to 'take revenge on the past' (Mark 2010: 221). Hedera and Fragaria define the post-1989 academic – and social – discourse as a simple reversal of whose truth now applies: 'What used to apply was bad; what applies today is anything that goes against what used to be said' (Fragaria). She frames this view in terms of a legacy from state socialism: 'half-baked intellectualism' that does not require international context and awareness of other perspectives as a standard of good scholarship.

Hedera: 'Look, to be honest …' p. 216

Fragaria: 'I think that it's still …' p. 220

In Slovakia, Bohumil Búzik and Eva Laiferová identified a similar problem as hampering Slovak scholarship: 'This lack of theoretical pluralization [i.e. the legacy of the Marxian paradigm being the only one] (…) resulted in a theoretical vacuum in sociology and the social sciences. The result has been the lack of a conscious and critical reflection on the social world' (Búzik and Laiferová 2003: 156).[35] The Czech sociologist Hynek Jeřábek remarked laconically that 'Czech sociology as a whole does not care much about world sociology' (Jeřábek 2002: 43). Fragaria's account implies still broader consequences than these for post-socialist scholarly work. She says that the reversal of whose truth prevails does not necessarily indicate any changes in *processes*. This research cannot answer to what extent the processes of academic work or in institutions have or have not changed since 1989, but it can point to some of the challenges of a transformation of state-socialist academia that have their origin in the system of relations and practices established before 1989. I will return to these at the close of this chapter. At this place I would like to propose an explanation of why perhaps the system may not even have been challenged to transform by any movement from the inside.

---

[35] Adam Hudek also observes a continuity in theoretical and methodological approaches in Slovak historiography from normalization (Hudek 2013: 97).

Unlike the younger age cohort, the Generation 1968 researchers related their narratives to 1968 as a landmark not only in their professional development, but also in the development of their disciplines. Further, their narratives related to the post-1989 times as the time of professional freedom and revival. In contrast, articulations of perceptions of personal professional insecurity in post-1989 times occurred exclusively among the younger age cohort. Szandiliah, a member of the older generation, adds an interesting observation from the Hungarian perspective: due to the relatively greater academic freedom in Hungary than in Czechoslovakia, '[t]he arrival of "real" freedom was not such a shock to us as to them, so as to overwrite every negative aspect of the new reality'. The disparate post-1989 recollections by the two Czech generations indicate that as the Prague-Spring-generated ideological divisions affected academia throughout normalization, the reversal of power in 1989 maintained the divisions: not only the divisions in terms of 'whose truth', but the divisions of which subjects, what language, which people can publish and what. Lustani illustrates a similar process when he suggests that some approaches, such as positivism in the case of literary history, continued under the guise of Marxism and at the time of the interview they came out in the open. That implies no real change or broadening of approaches, but merely a change of terminology. The Prague-Spring divisions that were ideological, not scholarly, in their origin became endemic to Czech academia and even attained a symbolic significance of oppression and resistance already during normalization and also in the years following the political overthrow, thus leaving little space for other discourses to develop outside this powerful dualism.

This is not to equate the post-1989 or current academic environment with the authoritarian, state-socialist one, but to point out that the conditions in the 1990s were favourable to enabling the preservation of certain pockets of residues. If some of the scholars claimed that they encountered little censorship during normalization, because their research was non-controversial,

Szandiliah: 'Maybe the difference ...' p. 223

Lustani: 'In the history of literature ...' p. 221

it is also probably the case that a number of (or perhaps most) researchers in the 1990s – or today – do not meet with constraints.

The interesting, because symptomatic, group consists of those researchers who did and do encounter barriers in getting their work recognized, because it falls on the wayside of the dominant discourse – or networks. Feminist approaches are an illustrative case in point: 'Even exponents [of feminist research] themselves are apt to say things like: "I do gender studies, but I'm not a feminist." The fear's there all right' (ForSythia). Her observation is traceable with almost comical consistency in published works on women's history. Pavla Horská insists in her important early contribution to the history of the Czech nineteenth-century women's movement that these women were 'emancipists' and not 'feminists' (Horská 1999: 90), but leaves the distinction between the two for the reader to decide. Similarly, Marie Bahenská praises the 'non-violence' of the Czech women's movement in contrast with the 'violent' aspects of its counterparts in France and Great Britain. She explains that it was because 'the public learned about women's demands one by one and had enough time to come to terms with them' (Bahenská 2005: 144), a striking conclusion for anyone familiar with the long history of the first wave of the women's movement in Western Europe. She makes the comparison although the book's bibliography does not list any works on the English, American or French women's movements and neither does the author discuss the nature of these movements earlier in the text. Instead, her textual strategy is reminiscent of that practised by normalization scholars: one expected the conclusion to be read by 'censors', so one made sure it pressed all the right stops. Analogously to the authors of normalization, Bahenská may have felt that her academic environment tended to discredit research informed by feminist approaches, regardless of its scholarly rigour. Musil's unflattering assessment of immediately post-1989 Czech sociology carried on in a similar vein:

> To the changes, which are more recent and more surprising in the context of Czech culture, belongs the growing antiscientism, (...). The anti-theoretical and anti-scientific bias

ForSythia: 'Of course the particular ...' p. 222

is beginning to have negative effects on the social sciences, or at least on some of their parts; in sociology shallow empiricism, onesided stress in quantitative methods, surveys, and public opinion polls predominate, underestimating the importance of sociohistorical approaches, qualitative methods, observations and the like. (Musil 1993: 69)

Feminist theory and qualitative methods were, like poststructuralism, postmodernism, postcolonial theories or oral history, not a part of the ideological divisions of normalization and were thus viewed with suspicion for long years after the change of the regime. They just did not carry the clear labels indicating 'which side they were on', a suspicion that has not been fully overcome to this day. Ten years after Musil and roughly at the time I conducted the interviews for this research, Petrusek saw the relationship between quantitative and qualitative sociologists in Czech academia as a 'conflict' that '[i]n Western sociology (…) withered away long time ago. In addition, it was only within the framework of this dispute that the issue of postmodernism entered Czech sociological discourse' (Petrusek 2003: 58). Still almost a decade later, Skovajsa's content analysis of the flagship of Czech sociology, *Sociologický časopis* reveals a surviving, and certainly not commendable, continuity with normalization:

> The matter of fact is that this type of article [highly technical discussions of methodological approaches or narrow empirical analyses of (quantitative) sociological data] survived the end of communism and continues to appear in *Sociologický časopis*. Their characteristic features are an aversion to theory or any broader contextualization, a preference for descriptive and straightforward statements, and scant use of metaphorical or figurative language. (Skovajsa 2011: 34)

Part of this whole discussion has to do with the legitimation of new approaches within an established discourse and one can argue that it is not an issue particular to post-socialism, that it is always a difficult process also in democratic academia. What is particular about the problem in the post-socialist environment, however, is that the politically charged – and for the most part unreflected – residual dualism is only too easily at hand. All the more so because by now public discourse and social memory on state socialism have developed that reinforce the dualistic vision of victims and perpetrators and equate it with moral right and moral wrong. When Michal Pullman argued for a more nuanced perspective on normalization in his book *Konec experimentu* (The End of an Experiment) (Pullmann 2011), he was attacked at conferences and social media by a certain section of historians for relativizing the evils of communism.

The strength of the lasting ideological sensitivities potentially renders less visible other residual processes that (have) affected post-socialist academia. In Hungary, HorMi proposes that 'mentality patterns' inherited from the Kádár regime continue to plague Hungarian society. In the Czech Republic, ForSythia goes as far as to say that things did not change: judgements motivated by revenge and rivalry can be made by some peers to cause professional damage to others, because they now occupy a higher moral ground and therefore a position of power. She also suggests that favouritism in publishing persists, which need not be taken at face value, but considered within the framework of state-socialist publishing discussed so far, it would be logical if it did continue. Academic communities then depended on personal relations that were built around solidarity with those who were persecuted and on trust. Once the cause of the need for solidarity and trust was removed, but the ideologically based dualistic mind-set remained, it should cause no surprise if post-socialist academic communities around publishers, journals or university departments continued to operate largely on personal relations, and were divested of the grace of the other two features – solidarity and trust.

HorMi: 'My firm belief is …' p. 222

ForSythia: 'And indeed it does …' p. 222 and

ForSythia: 'And it's much the same …' p. 221

Conclusion

In the Introduction I foregrounded the two contrary arguments about the effect of censorship that are prominent in theories of censorship. One argument goes that censorship encourages creative and critical thinking, the other that it stifles it. I then asked why *both* these arguments echoed in the testimonies of such a relatively homogenous group as the participants in scholarly publishing of the Czech normalization and Kádárist Hungary was. The discussion of the oral history interviews, supplemented by the framework of science policies and the archive of the Editorial Board of the Czechoslovak Academy of Sciences, presented in this book now allows me to offer an explanation.

The presence of multiple censoring filters was felt – to varying degrees and in various periods of the regimes – by all who participated in the production of scholarly texts, despite the non-existence of formal censoring institutions in academia in either country. In the Czech case this led to the creation of an overall atmosphere of fear of unspecified retributions for something one had said or written. The list of taboos and ideological improprieties was unclear and thus everything was subject to interpretations. This applies to a lesser extent to Hungary, where the authors were able to define the taboos with greater precision and felt they were working in an environment less prone to volatile interpretations of scholarly texts. In the absence of a clear list of proscriptions, the attention of Czech academic writers focused on prescriptions regarding phrasing and contextualizing of their thoughts on the one hand, and on avoidance of anything potentially controversial on the other. Such conditions were not conducive of originality in scholarly work and of publishing in general, because every text carried a potential risk.

Such conditions produced two main effects that one might see as repressive and productive at the same time: formation of intellectual communities based on mutual trust, which then contained intellectual discussion within these circles, and attention to every word of scholarly texts by both writers and readers, especially the readers with a censoring function. The creation of intellectual communities was obviously productive, because it allowed academics professional existence, to exercise agency in the face of the oppressive regime and even subvert some of its dictates.

The activities of these communities created intellectual value for their members and their readers. That value was, nevertheless, limited in its outreach, because the communities were more or less self-contained, and thus their impact in a broader context – disciplinary or international – was limited, even doubtful. In a sense, the communities also had a repressive function, because they invited some and excluded others. Moreover, some of it seemed to have survived the demise of state socialism, as Pavel Machonin observed on sociology as being fragmented, with little interest among individuals or teams in a dialogue across narrow specializations or different approaches (Machonin 2002: 53).

The attentiveness to language had a productive function in that having learned to use the ideologized language academics could adapt the state-declared research topics to their needs and to communicate intellectual thoughts even in the repressive environment. However, I argued that this attentiveness did not necessarily mean greater sophistication of textual interpretation and, therefore, neither the cultivation of critical readers nor the development of critical thinking on the part of the writers. In this the effect was repressive, because the attention was directed merely at the presence of particular – and the textual record of the time as well as the interview material seem to suggest that limited – vocabulary. Coetzee's metaphorical reflection on his own writing under the censorship of the apartheid seems to capture the ultimate effect of normalization's dispersed and hierarchical censoring mechanisms: 'Working under censorship is like being intimate with someone who does not love you, with whom you want no intimacy, but who presses himself in upon you. The censor is an intrusive reader, a reader who forces his way into the intimacy of the writing transaction' (Coetzee 1996: 38). The weight of scholarly communication in such conditions may have shifted more towards the sphere of the oral. Kurakin identifies a similar shift in the mode of communication in the Soviet Union in the early 1970s (Kurakin 2017: 395) and Petrusek reported in a letter to a professional friend in 1988 the diagnosis of 'oral sociology' formulated by the Polish sociologist Antoni Sulek

(*Ale snad i pro toto jsme žili, ne?* 2016: 233–4). The emergence of several seminar series in Czech academia in the 1980s suggests that it, indeed, may have been the case. The first consequence of this 'oral sociology', that is, a sociology that does not write and publish, is that 'the level of scholarly communication decreases, spoken word is less binding, it does not make one to look for precise formulations' (*Ale snad i pro toto jsme žili, ne?* 2016: 233–4). In other words, the attentiveness to language narrowed down, rather than broadened one's creative approach to verbal expression: the written ideologized language was reduced to a few phrases and bibliographic references. Moreover, this language emptied of meaning, became citational and filled the function of signposts, symbolically marking the ideological propriety of the text. The sensitivity to this language use was likely to have eroded in time and the younger, post-1968 age cohort of researchers did not express it as strongly as the older generation with personal political histories related to 1968.

The dual consequence – productive and repressive – of these two effects explains the simultaneous occurrence of both the beneficial and the detrimental functions of censorship found, particularly, in the Czech narratives. The participants in the scholarly life of state socialism could legitimately feel active as professionals, because they actively negotiated the discourse of the oppressive regime and were involved in peer communities. Nevertheless, intellectual communication was atomized into these narrow circles, with few overlaps between them, which precluded a broader discussion. They were largely isolated from wider Czech and international scholarly communities, not only in terms of not having access to the state of the art of social science and humanities disciplines, but also in terms of academic processes.

The regime change of 1989 thus arrived in a research culture, in which relying on personal relations for one's professional development, drawing intellectual inspiration from self-contained communities, and perfecting politically necessitated evasions rather than cultivating scholarly discussion became ingrained in the practice of intellectual interaction. Political circumstances rather than scholarly merit often decided if one climbed up or slithered down the career path. Professional ethics and due processes in reviewing and publishing likewise took the second place to political criteria. The legacy and challenges for the post-1989 academic research environment are apparent: a weedy garden, albeit with fertile soil, that would be hard to toil and cultivate into a research culture based on achievement rather than allegiances; a culture that finds intellectual inspiration through cross-pollination in the orchards of the world, instead of gazing into its own flowerbeds; a culture in which the need for the skill of hedging arguments against ideologically motivated censorship is replaced with mechanisms for 'censoring the censors' (Jansen 1991: 44), and which grows a diversity of species rather than a monoculture.

Postscript:

I recorded the last Czech interview in December 2003. Then, in 2007, the Institute for the Study of Totalitarian Regimes and the Security Services Archive were founded and gradually made available online the ledgers of the Security Services. These contain the lists of all the individuals on whom the Security Services kept a file, whether as agents, persons marked as potential collaborators or 'inimical persons' (*nepřátelská osoba*), as one category was called. The existence of files bearing the names identical to eleven out of the twenty narrators included in this book, together with reasonably corresponding dates of birth, is recorded in the ledgers. The classifications range from 'inimical person' to 'agent', from those monitored to the monitors.

As the ledgers contain only the name, code name and birth date of each person, a full identification is not possible. However, I am fairly confident that only one or two of the names could perhaps belong to somebody other than the narrators in this book. In a sample that I selected by the criterion of professional respect among peers at the time of the interview, the high proportion of persons in whom the Security Services took interest is an indication of the heightened surveillance to which the state subjected academia.

9

Coda

A good number of the narrators have passed away; others have retired from active scholarly life since I talked to them and are thus unable to reflect on their experience with state-socialist publishing from the perspective of today. How would they regard today's academia by comparison, I wonder? Would they see the same disquieting parallels that some of us do when reading current debates on neoliberal or corporate university, the future of humanities, threats to academic freedom in Hungary, or, indeed, on Czech and international politics?

It seems that whether the subject is North America, Western, Northern or East Central Europe, writers agree that scholarly research and university education are changing and that the change, although it may have been in process for a while, has sped up in the years just after the turn of the millennium (Linková and Stöckelová 2012; Cidlinská and Vohlídalová 2015; Cannella and Koro-Ljungberg 2017; Kováts, Heidrich and Chandler 2017; Suoranta and FitzSimmons 2017). Martha Nussbaum calls the change unreservedly 'a worldwide crisis of education' and predicts that it will be 'far more damaging to the future of democratic self-government' than the economic crisis (Nussbaum 2010: 2) that was just then gripping the world. She writes, of course, about the creeping cuts in the humanities subjects across the American educational system and elsewhere in the world – most recently in Brazil. The newly elected President Jair Bolsonaro 'tweeted that the government was considering withdrawing public funding for philosophy and sociology courses. Instead, it would concentrate its spending on areas that create "immediate return for the taxpayer," such as veterinary science, engineering and medicine' (Barbara 2019). Nussbaum argued that by making monetary profit the leading criterion for education efficiency, nations of the world are casting off skills indispensable for the survival of democracies: 'the ability to think critically; the ability to transcend local loyalties and to approach world problems as a "citizen of the world"; and, finally, the ability to imagine sympathetically the predicament of another person' (Nussbaum 2010: 7). Instead, they are producing 'useful machines' rather than 'complete citizens' (Nussbaum 2010: 2).

Bolsonaro condemns scholarly disciplines for their low direct monetary value, and state-socialist countries purged their universities of subjects like sociology and philosophy in the 1950s for exactly the potential described by Nussbaum. It was not until the 1960s that these disciplines experienced a revival in the Eastern Bloc (Péteri 1998; Voříšek 2012), followed, in the Czech case, by renewed constraints and tight state control during normalization. Maybe the orchestrators of normalization deserve credit for recognizing the dangers critical scholarship posed to authoritarian power. If they had to suffer these disciplines at all, they kept the student numbers low and developed the system of dispersed censorship over academic life and publishing described in this book. Hungarians were luckier as far as funding was concerned, because the Kádár government recognized that it needed scholars to develop and advance economic reforms.

Not any longer. Scholars have noted that the Hungarian system of higher education, which through legislative reform began, by 1985, to depart from the Soviet system, then 'started to swing back to a state-dominated system' in 2011 (Kováts, Heidrich and Chandler 2017: 570). The new governmental reforms include restrictions on international labour mobility of the university graduates who obtained state funding for their degrees (i.e. did not pay tuition fees), binding them contractually to employment within Hungarian borders for an extensive period of time (Füzessi (2013) cited by Tarlea 2017: 677). The measure, by extension, constrains the exchange of ideas across borders, an aim pursued by state-socialist educational policies. Brain drain, rather than the spread of foreign ideologies, was probably the target of Viktor Orbán's government in this instance, but the new university law passed in the spring of 2017 signals that those fears also drive 'the "illiberal" U-turn that was taken in 2010' (Kováts, Heidrich and Chandler 2017: 569). The law includes several stipulations limiting the ongoing operation of Central European University (CEU), a privately funded, graduate, largely social science institution accredited in Hungary and the United States. CEU is known for the liberal direction of its curricula and its faculty body is, for the most part, international. After almost two years of fruitless negotiations, CEU's US-accredited legal entity was pushed out of Hungary and began its relocation to Vienna in the summer of 2019.

The Hungarian government now also approves the list of academic disciplines permitted to be taught at universities – public *and* private. As of 2018 gender studies is not among them, ostensibly due to the lack of employment prospects for the graduates. Alas, how the government reached this conclusion remains a mystery, as the two-year master's degree at Eötvös Loránd University had opened only a year earlier. It rather appears that the discipline was removed on ideological grounds, as the simultaneous emergence of a new discipline on the list, 'family studies', suggests. CEU's programmes in gender studies will be run from Vienna from October 2019.

The latest move towards governmental control over academic life is the placement of the Academy of Sciences institutes into a newly established state research network (Eötvös Loránd Kutatási Hálózat) approved by the Parliament just this month. The network will be supervised by a board, whose members will be appointed by the prime minister and it will have the authority to 'decide on funding and appoint directors for each research institute' (Gall 2019). Not even the Communist government dared to go that far in Hungary – in contrast to Czechoslovakia in 1970. The official rhetoric says that it is in the name of higher international competitiveness and efficiency of Hungarian research, but it looks very much like the measures taken by the Communist Party of Czechoslovakia at the onset of normalization 'to renew the leading role of the Communist Party in society'.

Would the Czech narrators from this book express compassion for their Hungarian colleagues? Would they feel a little jab of satisfaction that now their fortunes seem to have changed, that it is now the Hungarians who have to struggle with more limitations to their scholarly pursuits? Maybe. But they might also remember that the 'Central European' in the name of the university originally referred to the intention of the founder, George Soros, to have one faculty each in Czechoslovakia, Hungary and Poland. They might further remember that for a few years in the early 1990s, one of those faculties and the main seat of the university resided in Prague and that its closure was a result of 'a political and financial battle between its founder and the Czech government' (Durcanin 1993), that is, the right-wing government of Václav Klaus. The Prague faculty finally closed in 1996 and by the time of the imagined conversations presented here, it was history and none of the narrators alluded to it in their reflections on post-1989 academia.

They did, however, speak about the state-socialist legacy of binary and insular thinking and about economic pressures in society in general, although not yet in education and research. At about the time of my interviews with the Czech narrators, the sociologist Jiřina Šiklová coined the term 'neonormalization'.[1] She defines 'normalization' as 'the petrification of power held by the communists after the 1968 invasion' (Šiklová 2003: 97), which in due course produced resistance in the form of various dissident groupings. She goes on to draw a parallel with the 1990s. James Krapfl contrasts the revolution in 1989 that 'set off an avalanche of discourse' (Krapfl 2013: 76) with the next phase that set in already in the early 1990s. By then the discursive openness was gradually replaced with ideologies that 'increasingly advocated the forceful exclusion of individuals and groups who represented a danger to the pure social system they envisioned, even at the risk of violating explicit or implicit rules' (Krapfl 2013: 218). I argued elsewhere for a similar periodization on the example of the openness of the media and the publishing industry to feminist and gender perspectives: a short period of openness was followed by a period of a media witch-hunt from about 1992, while receptive spaces began to open again towards the end of the 1990s (Oates-Indruchová 2016: 938). Šiklová terms this development 'neonormalization', a petrification of the new, post-1989 establishment that, however, gave rise to 'new civic disobedience' (Šiklová 2003: 100), organized initiatives by intellectuals and students that, according to her, began in 1999.

Šiklová is not the only scholar drawing parallels with normalization. The Czech philosopher Václav Bělohradský uses the term 'neonormalization' to describe the public discourse in the first decade of the new millennium that resulted from the stunted education in critical thinking and world citizenship. This discourse excludes alternative views and thus a further development of democracy (Bělohradský 2007). The narrators from this book would probably see it as a direct descendant of the binary thinking of normalization – and it does not seem to be waning. Normalization-like labelling of undesirables is being resurrected for that same old purpose of ostracizing nonconformist voices. The media attacks against Muriel Blaive, a French specialist in

---

[1] I am indebted to James Krapfl for directing me to the origin of the term in the Czech context.

contemporary Czech history and the advisor for research and methodology to the director of the Institute for the Study of Totalitarian Regimes (ÚSTR), in the summer and autumn of 2017, are prime examples of this discourse.

Blaive gave an interview to the online paper *A2larm*, in which she said that by including 'totalitarian' in the name of the institute, its founders already provided the answer to a research problem that should have been posed as a question (Pehe 2017). It is a question historians all over the world had been asking not only in the light of empirical evidence, but also as an epistemological concern. A serious scholar has to approach any subject by questioning available concepts before applying them, in order to move the critical discussion ahead and, in this case, to a more nuanced understanding of the past. A certain segment of the media unleashed a hate campaign accusing Blaive, among others, of 'relativizing' history by questioning the appropriateness of the term (Sezemský 2017). The label connotes uncomfortably the familiar normalization condemnation of a dissenting opinion as 'revisionist', that is, questioning the orthodoxy of the Marxist–Leninist doctrine. As we have read in the imagined conversations, being labelled a 'revisionist' meant silencing by a publishing ban or dismissal from employment. Also in this case certain media were calling for the cleansing of ÚSTR of these 'relativist' views. They display a '(neo)normalization mentality' that understands 'criticism as an attack, a manifestation of disloyalty, or collaboration with the enemy' (Škabraha 2008: 7). One has to wonder if that implies that the Czech public discussion is governed by a 'doctrine' of totalitarianism that scholars may not critically examine, if they are to remain in their professions. Michael Holquist calls such discourses 'monologic' and itself essentially totalitarian, for they 'abhor difference and aim for a single, collective self': 'the more powerful the ideology, the more totalitarian (monologic) will be the claims of its language' (Holquist 2002: 52–3). The good news is that rebuttals also appeared (e.g. Smlsal and Stachová 2017). This would hardly have been an option during normalization. The not so good news is that the counKervoices were considerably fewer. That is also a consequence of the neglect to cultivate 'the ability to think critically; the ability to transcend local loyalties' in the Czech academia of the present.

Does this extensive discussion of one word perhaps seem a trivial example in the larger scheme of today's world? The Yale historian Timothy Snyder would have disagreed, as in one of his 'twenty lessons from the twentieth century, adapted to the circumstances of today' he encourages readers to watch for particular words in political speeches because their 'expansive use' is likely to signify an ulterior agenda (Snyder quoted in desmoinesdem 2016). The political scientist Kieran Williams adds his own comment, making an explicit comparison with Czechoslovak normalization, 'the process by which a country is sidetracked from having a government responsive to the preferences and needs of the people' and which 'involves a shocking moment – an Event with a capital E' (Williams 2016). He goes on to list behaviours that aided and abetted Czechoslovak normalization. Several of them involved rhetorical acrobatics, such as an interpretation of 'all events before the Event (…) as steps in a vast imaginary conspiracy, to deflect attention from the actual conspiracy between Moscow and Czechoslovak collaborators' (Williams 2016). Both US scholars and specialists on East Central European twentieth-century history wrote in the immediate aftermath of the election of Donald Trump as the US president. They wrote before 'fake news' and 'post-truth' became household names.

In 2016, it was individual words and twists of argument that stole the political show. Today expressions like 'some very good things may come out of that', 'that is very very bad', or 'we have to get those illegals, those bad guys' have become commonplace in the US political scene. It very much reminds one of the normalization language emptied of content, in which words that used to have meanings degraded to signposts marking ideological correctness of the message.

Communist regimes recognized the political importance, and therefore the danger to themselves, of social sciences and humanities. That is why – and the normalization policies could not be more explicit about it – they elevated them to the order of utmost societal importance, but chained them to the ruling ideology. They were to provide service, to describe rather than critically analyze, to generate data rather than theories, to use predefined paradigms in interpretations rather than look for new methods and approaches, and to bow to haloed concepts and definitions rather than question and redefine them. The instrumentalization of scholarly pursuits was to steer scholars and students towards becoming 'useful machines' and away from becoming 'complete citizens'. Viktor Orbán learned well the lesson that social sciences and humanities do matter. He makes good use of it in this age of new party dictatorships that feed their populations propaganda, rather than foster dialogue, reward adherents, encourage conformism and punish dissidence.

July 2019

Bibliography

Archives

Ediční rada ČSAV [Editorial Board of the Academy of Sciences; referred to as EBAS in the footnotes] (Dílčí fond), Prague, Archive of the Czech Academy of Sciences, holdings 1970–1989, boxes 9–17.

Radio Free Europe/Radio Liberty Research Institute holdings, Budapest, Open Society Archives (OSA); the items that were published in print (e.g. in journals or magazines) and cited in the text are listed in the references below.

References

Adams, Tony E., Stacy Holman Jones and Carolyn Ellis (2015), *Autoethnography*, Oxford and New York: Oxford University Press.

Alasuutari, Pertti (1995), *Researching Culture: Qualitative Method and Cultural Studies*, London: Sage.

Ale snad i pro toto jsme žili, ne? Výber z korešpondencie Milana Petruska a Aleny Miltovej s Martinom Bútorom a Zorou Bútorovou 1985–1989 [We Have Lived Also for This, Have We Not? Selected Correspondence of Milan Petrusek and Alena Miltová with Martin Bútora and Zora Bútorová, 1985–1989] (2016), Prague: Sociologické nakladatelství.

Andělová, Kristina (2019), 'Czechoslovak Generational Experience of 1968: The Intellectual History Perspective', *East European Politics and Societies and Cultures*, 33 (4): 881–98.

Anderson, Benedict (1991), *Imagined Communities: Reflections on the Origin and Spread of Nationalism*, rev. edn, London and New York: Verso.

Andrews, Ernest (2011), 'Introduction', in Ernest Andrews (ed.), *Legacies of Totalitarian Language in the Discourse Culture of the Post-Totalitarian Era: The Case of Eastern Europe, Russia, and China*, 1–13, Lanham, MD: Lexington Books.

Andrews, Molly (2000), 'Texts in a Changing Context: Reconstructing Lives in East Germany', in Prue Chamberlayne, Joanna Bornat and Tom Wengraf (eds), *The Turn to Biographical Methods in Social Science: Comparative Issues and Examples*, 181–95, London and New York: Routledge.

Andrle, Vladimir (2000), 'Neither a Dinosaur Nor a Weathercock: The Construction of a Reputably Continuous Self in Czech Postcommunist Life Stories', *Qualitative Sociology*, 23 (2): 215–30.

Badley, Graham Francis (2019), 'Post-Academic Writing: Human Writing for Human Readers', *Qualitative Inquiry*, 25 (2): 180–91.

Baets, Antoon de (2002), *Censorship of Historical Thought: A World Guide, 1945–2000*, n.p: Greenwood Publishing Group.

Bahenská, Marie (2005), *Počátky emancipace žen v Čechách: Dívčí vzdělání a ženské spolky v Praze v 19. století* [*The Beginnings of Women's Emancipation in Bohemia: Education for Girls and Women's Associations in 19th-Century Prague*], Prague: Libri and Slon.

Barbara, Vanessa (2019), 'Who Needs the Humanities When You Have Jair Bolsonaro?' *The New York Times*, 12 June. Available online: https://www.nytimes.com/2019/06/12/opinion/education-cuts-brazil-bolsonaro.html (accessed 1 July 2019).

Bareš, Ivan (1979), 'Na naší nejstarší univerzitě: Výměny členských legitimací [At Our Oldest University: The Exchange of the Party IDs]', *Život strany*, November 1979: 24–5.

Bates, John Michael (2001), 'Poland', in Derek Jones (ed.), *Censorship: A World Encyclopedia*, 1882–95, London and Chicago: Fitzroy Dearborn.

Bělohradský, Václav (2007), *Společnost nevolnosti: Eseje z pozdější doby* [*A Society of Nausea: Essays from the Later Days*], Prague: Sociologické nakladatelství.

Bence, György et al., eds (1980), *Bibó emlékkönyv*, 3 vols, Budapest: [samizdat].

Berényi, Eszter (2018). 'International Influences in the Hungarian Sociological Profession, 1972–1994', in Adela Hîncu and Victor Karady (eds), *Social Sciences in the Other Europe since 1945*, 249–79. Budapest: Pasts, Inc. and Central European University.

Berg, Maggie and Barbara K. Seeber (2016), *The Slow Professor: Challenging the Culture of Speed in the Academy*, Toronto: University of Toronto Press.

Blium, Arlen (1998), 'Censorship and Public Reading in Russia, 1870–1950', *Libraries & Culture: A Journal of Library History*, 33 (1): 17–25.

Blyum, Arlen (2003), *A Self-Administered Poison: The System and Functions of Soviet Censorship*, trans. I. P. Foote, Oxford: Legenda and European Humanities Research Centre, University of Oxford.

Bock, Ivo, ed. (2011), *Scharf überwachte Kommunikation: Zensursysteme in Ost(mittel)europa (1960er–1980er Jahre)*, Münster: LIT Verlag.

Bokor, Ágnes (1985), *Deprivació és szegénység: Műhelytanulmány* [*Deprivation and Poverty: A Working Paper*], Budapest: Kossuth Kiadó.

Bolton, Jonathan (2012), *Worlds of Dissent: Charter 77, The Plastic People of the Universe, and Czech Culture under Communism*, Cambridge, MA and London: Harvard University Press.

Bourdieu, Pierre (1991), *Language and Symbolic Power*, trans. Gino Raymond and Matthew Adamson, Cambridge: Polity.

Bren, Paulina (2010), *The Greengrocer and His TV: The Culture of Communism After the 1968 Prague Spring*, Ithaca and London: Cornell University Press.

Bryant, Antony and Kathy Charmaz (2007), 'Grounded Theory Research: Methods and Practices', in Antony Bryant and Kathy Charmaz (eds), *The SAGE Handbook of Grounded Theory*, 1–28, London and Thousand Oaks, CA: Sage.

Bryant, Chad (2000), 'Whose Nation?: Czech Dissidents and History Writing from a Post-1989 Perspective', *History & Memory*, 12 (1): 30–64.

Bugge, Peter (forthcoming), 'A Western Invention? The Discovery of Czech Dissidence in the 1970s', *Bohemia*, 59 (2).

Bülow, William and Gert Helgesson (2018), 'Hostage Authorship and the Problem of Dirty Hands', *Research Ethics*, 14 (1): 1–9.

Burget, Eduard (2013), *Slovník české literatury*. Available online: http://www.slovnikceskeliteratury.cz/showContent.jsp?docId=1743 (accessed 27 February 2017).

Burt, Richard (1998), '(Un)Censoring in Detail: The Fetish of Censorship in the Early Modern Past and the Postmodern Present', in Robert C. Post (ed.), *Censorship and Silencing: Practices of Cultural Regulation*, 17–41, Los Angeles, CA: Getty Research Institute for the History of Art and the Humanities.

Butler, Judith (1998), 'Ruled Out: Vocabularies of the Censor', in Robert C. Post (ed.), *Censorship and Silencing: Practices of Cultural Regulation*, 247–59, Los Angeles, CA: Getty Research Institute for the History of Art and the Humanities.

Búzik, Bohumil and Eva Laiferová (2003), 'In Search of Its Own Identity: A Decade of Slovak Sociology', in Mike Forrest Keen and Janusz L. Mucha (eds), *Sociology in Central and Eastern Europe: Transformation at the Dawn of a New Millennium*, 153–63, Westport, CT: Praeger.

Cannella, Gaile S. and Mirka Koro-Ljungberg (2017), 'Neoliberalism in Higher Education', *Cultural Studies ↔ Critical Methodologies*, 17 (3): 155–62.

'Celostátní aktiv pracovníků společenských věd' (1974), *Nová mysl*, 11 November, OSA 300-30-6, box 44.

Černá, Marie (2012), 'Náš nepřítel oportunista: Prověrky roku 1970 v Československu [Our Enemy, the Opportunist: The 1970 Screenings in Czechoslovakia]', in Marie Černá, Jaroslav Cuhra et al., *Prověrky a jejich místo v komunistickém vládnutí: Československo 1948–1989*, 72–93, Prague: Ústav pro soudobé dějiny AV ČR.

Černá, Marie, Jaroslav Cuhra et al. (2012), *Prověrky a jejich místo v komunistickém vládnutí: Československo 1948–1989* [Screenings and Their Place in the Communist Rule: Czechoslovakia 1948–1989], Prague: Ústav pro soudobé dějiny AV ČR.

Češka, Zdeněk (1976), 'Jaký učitel, takový student' [Like the Teacher, Like the Student], *Rudé právo*, 16 June: 3.

Chamberlayne, Prue, Joanna Bornat and Tom Wengraf (2000), 'Introduction: The biographical turn', in Prue Chamberlayne, Joanna Bornat and Tom Wengraf (eds), *The Turn to Biographical Methods in Social Science: Comparative Issues and Examples*, 1–30, London and New York: Routledge.

Charmaz, Kathy (2006), *Constructing Grounded Theory: A Practical Guide Through Qualitative Analysis*, Los Angeles: Sage.

Choldin, Marianna Tax (1998), 'Russian Libraries and Readers after the Ice Age', *Libraries & Culture: A Journal of Library History*, 33 (1): 26–33.

Cidlinská, Kateřina and Marta Vohlídalová (2015), 'Zůstat, nebo odejít? O deziluzi (začínajících) akademických a vědeckých pracovníků a pracovnic [To Stay or to Leave? On a Disillusionment of (Young) Academics and Researchers]', *Aula*, 23 (1): 3–36.

Clare, Janet (1990), *'Art Made Tongue-Tied by Authority': Elizabethan and Jacobean Dramatic Censorship*, Manchester and New York: Manchester University Press.

Coetzee, J. M. (1996), *Giving Offense: Essays on Censorship*, Chicago: University of Chicago Press.

Cohen, Mark (2001), *Censorship in Canadian Literature*, Montreal and Kingston: McGill-Queen's University Press.

Connelly, John (2000), *Captive University: The Sovietization of East German, Czech, and Polish Higher Education*, 1945–1956, Chapel Hill and London: University of North Carolina Press.

Connelly, John (2000), 'The Sovietization of Higher Education in the Czech Lands, East Germany, and Poland during the Stalinist Period, 1948–1954', in Michael David-Fox and György Péteri (eds), *Academia in Upheaval: Origins, Transfers, and Transformations of the Communist Academic Regime in Russia and East Central Europe*, 141–77, Westport, CT: Bergin & Garvey.

Corbin, Juliet (2009), 'Taking an Analytic Journey', in Janice M. Morse, Phyllis Noerager Stern, Juliet Corbin, Barbara Bowers, Kathy Charmaz and Adele E. Clarke, *Developing Grounded Theory: The Second Generation*, 35–53, Walnut Creek, CA: Left Coast Press.

Corbin, Juliet and Anselm Strauss ([1990] 2015), *Basics of Qualitative Research: Techniques and Procedures for Developing Grounded Theory*, 4th edn, Thousand Oaks, CA: Sage.

Costabile-Heming, Carol Anne (1997), 'Censorship and Review Processes: The Case of Günter Kunert', in Marc Silberman (ed.), *What Remains? East German Culture and the Postwar Public*, 52–74, Washington DC: American Institute for Contemporary German Studies.

Culler, Jonathan (1997), *Literary Theory: A Very Short Introduction*, Oxford: Oxford University Press.

Curry, Jane Leftwich, ed. (1984), *The Black Book of Polish Censorship*, New York: Vintage.

Dąbrowski, Jakub (2017), 'A Few Remarks on the Mechanisms of Censorship in the PRL and the Third Republic of Poland', *Acta Universitatis Lodziensis: Folia Litteraria Polonica*, 45 (7): 209–24.

Darnton, Robert (1995), 'Censorship, a Comparative View: France, 1789–East Germany, 1989', *Representations*, 49: 40–60.

Darnton, Robert (2014), *Censors at Work: How States Shaped Literature*, London: The British Library.

Demszky, Gábor (1989), 'The Trouble with NOT Having Censorship', *Index on Censorship*, 18 (10): 19–21.

desmoinesdem (2016), 'Weekend Open Thread: Preparing for the Worst Edition', *Bleeding Heartland* [blog], 26 November. Available online: https://www.bleeding heartland.com/2016/11/26/weekend-open-thread-preparing-for-the-worst-editio n/ (accessed 1 July 2019).

DeVault, Marjorie (1996), 'Talking Back to Sociology: Distinctive Contributions of Feminist Methodology', *Annual Review of Sociology*, 22: 29–50.

Dewhirst, Martin and Robert Farrell, eds (1973), *The Soviet Censorship*, Metuchen, NJ: Scarecrow Press.

Dobrenko, Evgeny (1997), *Social and Aesthetic Contexts of the Reception of Soviet Literature*, trans. Jesse M. Savage, Stanford, CA: Stanford University Press.

Durcanin, Cynthia (1993), 'Central European University to Leave Prague', *The Prague Post*, 20 January. Available online: https://web.archive.org/web/20141225155451/ http://www.praguepost.cz/archivescontent/13126-central-european-university-to -leave-prague.html (accessed 22 October 2017).

Dutton, Richard (1991), *Mastering the Revels: The Regulation and Censorship of English Renaissance Drama*, Basingstoke: Macmillan.

Dutton, Richard (1999), 'Licensing and Censorship', in David Scott Kastan (ed.), *A Companion to Shakespeare*, 377–92, Oxford and Malden, MA: Blackwell.

Ellis, Carolyn and Leigh Berger (2003), 'Their Story / My Story / Our Story: Including the Researcher's Experience in Interview Research', in Jaber F. Gubrium and James A. Holstein (eds), *Postmodern Interviewing*, 157–83, Thousand Oaks: Sage.

Falk, Barbara J. (2003), *The Dilemmas of Dissidence in East-Central Europe: Citizen Intellectuals and Philosopher Kings*, Budapest: Central European University Press.

Féja, Géza (1937), *Viharsarok: az Alsó Tiszavidék földje és népe* [*Viharsarok: Land and People of the Rural Lower Tisza Region*], Budapest: Athaneum.

Fidelius, Petr (1983), *Jazyk a moc* [*Language and Power*], Munich: Arkýř.

Fidelius, Petr (1998), *Řeč komunistické moci* [*The Language of the Communist Power*], Prague: Triáda.

Filipcová, Blanka (1966), *Člověk, práce, volný čas* [*Humankind, Work, Leisure*], Prague: Svoboda.

Filipcová, Blanka and Jindřich Filipec (1976), *Různoběžky života: Zápas o socialistický životní způsob* [*Divergencies of Life: The Struggle for the Socialist Way of Life*], Prague: Svoboda.

Filipec, Jindřich and René Rohan (1973), 'Ideologický boj a společenské vědy [Ideological Struggle and the Social Sciences]', *Nová mysl*, 7: 1000–12.

Filipkowski, Piotr, Judit Gárdos, Éva Kovács and Vera Szabari (2017), 'Culture over Structure: The Heritage of Lifestyle Research in the 1970s in Hungary and Poland', *Stan Rzeczy* [*State of Affairs*], 2 (13): 147–70.

Fojtík, Jan (1972a), 'Situace na společenskovědním úseku a úkoly společenských věd po XIV. sjezdu KSČ [The Situation in the Social Science Sector and the Tasks of the Social Sciences after the 14th Congress of the CPCS]', *Nová mysl*, 2: 147–69.

Fojtík, Jan (1972b), 'Věda a společnost [Science and Society]', *Tvorba*, 12 April: 3, 5.

Fonow, Mary Margaret and Judith A. Cook, eds (1991), *Beyond Methodology: Feminist Scholarship as Lived Research*, Bloomington: Indiana University Press.

Fonow, Mary Margaret and Judith A. Cook (2005), 'Feminist Methodology: New Applications in the Academy and Public Policy', *Signs*, 30 (4): 2211–36.

Fontana, Andrea (2003), 'Postmodern Trends in Interviewing', in Jaber F. Gubrium and James A. Holstein (eds), *Postmodern Interviewing*, 51–65, Thousand Oaks: Sage.

Foucault, Michel (1990), *The History of Sexuality: Volume I, An Introduction*, trans. Robert Hurley, New York: Vintage.

Freshwater, Helen (2004), 'Towards a Redefinition of Censorship', in Beate Müller (ed.), *Censorship and Cultural Regulation in the Modern Age*, 225–45, Amsterdam: Rodopi.

Füzessi, Károly (2013), 'Higher Education under Threat in Hungary', *openDemocracy*, 11 February. Available online: https://www.opendemocracy.net/can-europe-make-it/károly-füzessi/higher-education-under-threat-in-hungary (accessed 22 October 2017).

Gagyi, Ágnes and Márk Áron Éber (2015), 'Class and Social Structure in Hungarian Sociology', *East European Politics and Societies and Cultures*, 29 (3): 598–609.

Gall, Lydia (2019), 'Hungary Renews Its War on Academic Freedom', Human Rights Watch, Available online: https://www.hrw.org/news/2019/07/02/hungary-renews-its-war-academic-freedom (accessed 6 July 2019).

Gerovitch, Slava (1998), 'Writing History in the Present Tense: Cold War-era Discursive Strategies of Soviet Historians of Science and Technology', in Christopher Simpson (ed.), *Universities and Empire: Money and Politics in the Social Sciences during the Cold War*, 189–228, New York: The New Press.

Gruntorád, Jiří (2011), 'Poznámka ke zveřejnění dosud neznámých jmen signatářů Charty 77 [A Note on Making the Names of the So Far Unknown Signatories of

Charter 77 Public]', *Libri Prohibiti*. Available online: http://www.libpro.cz/cs/a rchiv/charta77/nezverejneni (accessed 9 March 2017).

Gruša, Jiří (1982), trans. Paul Wilson, 'In Praise of Aunt Censorship', *Index for Censorship*, 11 (4): 4–5, 10.

Haraszti, Miklós ([1975] 1977), *A Worker in a Worker's State: Piece Rates in Hungary*, trans. Michael Wright, Harmondsworth: Penguin.

Haraszti, Miklós ([1981] 1987), *The Velvet Prison: Artists under State Socialism*, trans. Katalin and Stephen Landesmann and Steve Wassermann, New York: Basic Books.

Haraway, Donna J. (1991), *Simians, Cyborgs, and Women: The Reinvention of Nature*, London: Free Association.

Havel, Václav (1992), 'The Power of the Powerless', in Paul Wilson (ed.), *Open Letters: Selected Writings 1965–1990*, 125–214, New York: Vintage.

Havlová, Jitka and Oto Sedláček (2004), 'Sociologie práce a průmyslu v letech 1965–1989 [The Sociology of Work and Industry 1965–1989]', *Sociologický časopis / Czech Sociological Review*, 40 (5): 651–64.

Hodrová, Daniela (1993), *Román zasvěcení* [*The Novel of Initiation*], Jinočany: H&H.

Holquist, Michael (2002), *Dialogism: Bakhtin and His World*, 2nd edn, London: Routledge.

Horská, Pavla (1999), *Naše prababičky feministky* [*Our Great-Grandmothers, the Feminists*], Prague: Lidové noviny.

Hradecká, Vladimíra and František Koudelka (1998), *Kádrová politika a nomenklatura KSČ 1969–1974* [*Personnel Policy and Nomenklatura of the Communist Party of Czechoslovakia, 1969–1974*], Prague: Ústav pro soudobé dějiny AV ČR.

Hroch, Miroslav (1999), *Na prahu národní existence: touha a skutečnost* [*On the Threshold of National Existence: Dream and Reality*], Prague: Mladá fronta.

Hrzal, Ladislav (1974), 'Vývoj, současný stav a úkoly společenských věd v ČSSR [The Development, Current State and the Tasks of Social Sciences in the CSSR]', *Sociologický časopis*, 10 (5): 449–54.

Hrzal, Ladislav and M. Matouš (1972), 'Společenské vědy po ideologickém plénu [Social Sciences after the Ideological Plenary]', *Tvorba*, 29 November: 3, 4.

Hudek, Adam (2013), 'Totalitno-historické rozprávanie ako dedičstvo normalizačnej historiografie [Totalitarian-Historical Narrative as a Legacy of Normalization Historiography]', *Forum Historiae*, 7 (1): 92–105.

Hudek, Adam (2015), 'Perception of Slovak Academy of Sciences as an Institution of National Science', in Florian Bieber and Harald Heppner (eds), *Universities and Elite Formation in Central, Eastern and South Eastern Europe*, 169–83, Zürich: LIT Verlag.

Husitská kronika [*The Hussite Chronicle*], (1979), Prague: Svoboda.

Ingram, Peter G. (2000), *Censorship and Free Speech: Some Philosophical Bearings*, Aldershot: Dartmouth and Ashgate.

Janáček, Pavel (2004), *Literární brak: Operace vyloučení, operace nahrazení, 1938-1951* [Literary Trash: An Operation of Removal, An Operation of Replacement, 1938-1951], Brno: Host.

Janoušek, Pavel (1996), 'Spor o Lukeše: Kapitola z historie české literární kritiky počátku osmdesátých let [A Dispute over Lukeš: A Chapter from the History of Czech Literary Criticism of the Early 1980s]', in Jan Wiendl (ed.), *Normy normalizace*, Opava, Czech Republic 11-13 September 1995, 82-90, Prague: Ústav pro českou literaturu AV ČR and Opava: Slezská univerzita.

Janovský, Julius (1979), 'Poslání společenskovědního vzdělání v rozvinuté socialistické společnosti [The Mission of Social Science Education in a Developed Socialist Society]', *Společenské vědy ve škole*, September: 2.

Jansen, Sue Curry (1991), *Censorship: The Knot That Binds Power and Knowledge*, Oxford: Oxford University Press.

Jareš, Jakub (2009), 'Přijímací řízení na vysoké školy v období normalizace: Příklad Filozofické fakulty UK [University Entrance Examinations during Normalization: An Example of the Faculty of Arts of Charles University]', in Katka Volná, Jakub Jareš, Matěj Spurný and Klára Pinerová, *Prověřená fakulta: KSČ na Filozofické fakultě UK v letech 1969-1989: Edice dokumentů*, 35-84, Prague: Ústav pro soudobé dějiny AV ČR.

Jeřábek, Hynek (2002), 'Sedm slabin české sociologie – osobní pohled jednoho sociologa [The Seven Weaknesses of Czech Sociology: The Personal Viewpoint of One Sociologist]', *Sociologický časopis / Czech Sociological Review*, 38 (1-2): 37-47.

Jones, Sara (2011), *Complicity, Censorship and Criticism: Negotiating Space in the GDR Literary Sphere*, Berlin: de Gruyter.

Kabele, Jiří (2011), 'Sportpropag – nepravděpodobné místo pro studium společnosti: Osobní pohled [Sportpropag – An Unlikely Place for the Study of Society: A Personal View]', *Sociální studia*, 8 (1): 17-35.

Kaplan, Karel and Dušan Tomášek (1994), *O cenzuře v Československu v letech 1945-1956* [Censorship in Czechoslovakia, 1945-1956], Prague: Ústav pro soudobé dějiny AV ČR.

Kašparová, Stanislava (1980), 'Komunisté na vysokých školách [Communists at Universities]', *Život strany*, 15 December: 28-9.

Kelly, Catriona (1995), '"Thank You for the Wonderful Book": Soviet Child Readers and the Management of Children's Reading, 1950-75', *Kritika: Explorations in Russian and Eurasian History*, 6 (4): 717-53.

Kenney, Padraic (2002), *A Carnival of Revolution: Central Europe 1989*, Princeton and Oxford: Princeton University Press.

Kis, Danilo (1986), 'Censorship/Self-Censorship', *Index on Censorship*, 15 (1): 43-5.

Klötzer, Sylvia and Siegfried Lokatis (1999), 'Criticism and Censorship: Negotiating Cabaret Performance and Book Production', in Konrad H. Jarausch (ed.),

Dictatorship as Experience: Towards a Socio-Cultural History of the GDR, 241–63, New York and Oxford: Berghahn.

Kocka, Jürgen (1998), 'Wissenschaft und Politik in der DDR', in Jürgen Kocka and Renate Mayntz (eds), *Wissenschaft und Wiedervereinigung: Disziplinen im Umbruch*, 435–59, Berlin: Akademie Verlag.

kol. (1971), *Rybízy, angrešty, maliníky a ostružiníky* [Currants, Gooseberries, Raspberries and Blackberries], Prague: Academia.

Komárek, Valtr (1992), *Mé pády a vzestupy: Paměti ředitele prognostického ústavu za normalizace* [My Rises and Falls: Memoirs of the Director of the Prognostic Institute during Normalization], Prague: Nadas.

Konicková, Mária (1978), 'Stranická práce na vysokých školách [Partisan Work at Universities]', *Život strany*, 27 February: 20–2.

Konopásek, Zdeněk, ed. (1999), *Otevřená minulost: Autobiografická sociologie státního socialismu* [An Open Past: Autobiographical Sociology of State Socialism], Prague: Karolinum.

Konopásek, Zdeněk and Zuzana Kusá (2006), 'Political Screenings as Trials of Strength: Making the Communist Power/Lessness Real', *Human Studies* 29 (3): 341–62.

Konrad, George (1983), 'Censorship and State-Owned Citizens', *Dissent*, 30 (Fall): 448–55.

Konrád, György and Iván Szelényi (1979), *The Intellectuals on the Road to Class Power: A Sociological Study of the Role of the Intelligentsia in Socialism*, San Diego: Harcourt Brace Jovanovich.

Kopeček, Michal (2017), 'From Scientific Social Management to Neoliberal Governmentality? Czechoslovak Sociology and Social Research on the Way from Authoritarianism to Liberal Democracy, 1969–1989', *Stan Rzeczy* [State of Affairs], 2 (13): 171–95.

Kopeček, Michal (2019), 'Kritika, řízení, byznys: Sociální výzkum a sociologie jako nástroje vládnutí v Československu po roce 1969 [Criticism, Management, Business: Social Research and Sociology as Instruments of Governmentality in Czechoslovakia after 1969]', in Michal Kopeček (ed.), *Architekti dlouhé změny: Expertní kořeny postsocialismu v Československu*, 217–65, Prague: Argo, ÚSD AV ČR and FF UK.

Kornai, János (1980), *Economics of Shortage*, Amsterdam: North Holland Press.

Kornai, János ([1959] 1994), *Overcentralization in Economic Administration: A Critical Analysis Based on Experience in Hungarian Light Industry*, trans. John Knapp, Oxford: Oxford University Press. Hungarian original 1957.

Kornai, János (2007), *By Force of Thought: Irregular Memoirs of an Intellectual Journey*, trans. Brian McLean, Cambridge, MA: MIT Press.

Kostlán, Antonín, ed. (2002), *Věda v Československu v období normalizace (1970–1975)* [Academic Research in Czechoslovakia during Normalization (1970–1975)], Prague: Výzkumné centrum pro dějiny vědy.

Kováts, Gergely, Balázs Heidrich and Nick Chandler (2017), 'The Pendulum Strikes Back? An Analysis of the Evolution of Hungarian Higher Education Governance and Organisational Structures since the 1980s', *European Educational Research Journal*, 16 (5): 568–87.

Krapfl, James (2013), *Revolution with a Human Face: Politics, Culture, and Community in Czechoslovakia, 1989–1992*, Ithaca and London: Cornell University Press.

Kubánek, Vladimír and Karel Lacina (1980), 'Stranická práce ve společenskovědních ústavech [Partisan Work in Social Science Institutes]', *Život strany*, 11 August: 42–4.

'Kulatý stůl "Dluhy sociologie" [Roundtable: "The Debts of Sociology"]' (1991), *Sociologický časopis / Czech Sociological Review*, 27 (1): 5–12.

Kurakin, Dmitry (2017), 'The Sociology of Culture in the Soviet Union and Russia: The Missed Turn', *Cultural Sociology*, 11 (4): 394–415.

Kutnar, František (1973), *Přehledné dějiny českého a slovenského dějepisectví 1: Od počátku národní kultury až po vyznění obrodného úkolu dějepisectví v druhé polovině 19. století* [Survey of the History of Czech and Slovak Historiography 1: From the Beginning of National Culture to the Fulfilment of the Goals of the Awakening in the Second Half of the 19th Century], Prague: SPN.

Kutnar, František (1978), *Přehledné dějiny českého a slovenského dějepisectví 2: Od počátků pozitivistického dějepisectví na práh historiografie marxistické* [Survey of the History of Czech and Slovak Historiography 2: From the Beginning of Positivist Historiography to the Threshold of Marxist History-Writing], Prague: SPN.

Larson, Jonathan L. (2013), *Critical Thinking in Slovakia after Socialism*, Rochester, NY: University of Rochester Press.

Lauk, Epp, Petr Šámal and Teodora Shek Brnardić (2018), 'The Protean Nature of Communist Censorship: The Testimony of Collections', in Balázs Apor, Péter Apor and Sándor Horváth (eds), *Handbook of COURAGE: Cultural Opposition and Its Heritage in Eastern Europe*, 329–49, Budapest: Institute of History, Research Centre for the Humanities, Hungarian Academy of Sciences.

Linková, Marcela and Tereza Stöckelová (2012), 'Public Accountability and the Politicization of Science: The Peculiar Journey of Czech Research Assessment', *Science and Public Policy*, 39 (5): 618–29.

Lishaugen, Roar and Jiřina Šmejkalová (2019), 'Reading East of the Berlin Wall', *PMLA*, 134 (1): 178–87.

Little, Matthew (2001), 'Editors', in Derek Jones (ed.), *Censorship: A World Encyclopedia*, London: Fitzroy Dearborn.

Lokatis, Siegfried (1996), 'Wissenschaftler und Verleger in der DDR: Das Beispiel des Akademie-Verlages', *Geschichte und Gesellschaft*, 22 (1): 46-61.

Loseff, Lev (1984), *On the Beneficence of Censorship: Aesopian Language in Modern Russian Literature*, Munich: Otto Sagner.

Macherey, Pierre (1978), *A Theory of Literary Production*, trans. Geoffrey Wall, London: Routledge and Kegan Paul.

Machonin, Pavel et al. (1967), *Sociální struktura socialistické společnosti: Sociologické problémy soudobé čs. společnosti* [*Social Structure of Socialist Society: Sociological Problems of Contemporary Czechoslovak Society*], Prague: Svoboda.

Machonin, Pavel et al. (1969), *Československá společnost: Sociologická analýza sociální stratifikace* [*Czechoslovak Society: A Sociological Analysis of Social Stratification*], Bratislava: Epocha.

Machonin, Pavel (1992), *Sociální struktura Československa v předvečer Pražského jara 1968* [*Social Structure of Czechoslovakia at the Dawn of the Prague Spring 1968*], Prague: Karolinum.

Machonin, Pavel (2002), 'Je čas k zásadní diskusi [It Is Time for a Serious Discussion]', *Sociologický časopis / Czech Sociological Review*, 38 (1-2): 49-54.

Machonin, Pavel (2004), 'K sociologii v období normalizace [Sociology During the Period of Normalization]', *Sociologický časopis / Czech Sociological Review*, 40 (5): 643-50.

Mahler, Zdeněk (1989), *Nekamenujte proroky: kapitoly ze života Bedřicha Smetany* [*Do Not Stone the Prophets: Chapters from the Life of Bedřich Smetana*], Prague: Albatros.

Mahler, Zdeněk (2004), *Nekamenujte proroky: kapitoly ze života Bedřicha Smetany* [*Do not Stone the Prophets: Chapters from the Life of Bedřich Smetana*], Prague: Primus.

Majcharčík, Jan (1977), 'Úkoly společenských věd po XV. sjezdu [The Tasks of Social Sciences after the 15th Congress]', *Život strany*, 29 August: 7-9.

Majcharčík, Jan (1979), 'Stranická práce na vysokých školách [Partisan Work at Universities]', *Život strany*, 8 October: 12-14.

Majerová, Věra, n.d. [approx. 1994-5], 'Normalizace vědeckého života, 1969-1970 [Normalization of Academic Life, 1969-1970]', habilitation [digital file].

Mark, James (2010), *The Unfinished Revolution: Making Sense of the Communist Past in Central-Eastern Europe*, New Haven and London: Yale University Press.

McCorkel, Jill A. and Kristen Myers (2003), 'What Difference Does Difference Make? Position and Privilege in the Field', *Qualitative Sociology*, 26 (2): 199-231.

McRobbie, Angela (1982), 'The Politics of Feminist Research: Between Talk, Text and Action', *Feminist Review* 12: 46-57.

Merton, Robert K. ([1945] 1973), 'Paradigm for the Sociology of Knowledge', in *The Sociology of Science: Theoretical and Empirical Investigations*, ed. and with an Introduction by Norman W. Storer, 7–40, Chicago and London: University of Chicago Press.

Mervart, Jan (2017), 'Rozdílnost pohledů na československou normalizaci [Different Perspectives on Czechoslovak Normalization]', in Kamil Činátl, Jan Mervart and Jaroslav Najbert (eds), *Podoby československé normalizace: Dějiny v diskusi* [*The Faces of Czech Normalization: History in a Discussion*], 40–78, Prague: Ústav pro studium totalitních režimů and Nakladatelství Lidové noviny.

Mihály, Gábor (1993), 'The Dual Nature of Censorship in Hungary, 1945–1991', in Ilan Peleg (ed.), *Patterns of Censorship Around the World*, 49–63, Boulder: Westview Press.

Miko, František (1981), 'Obnova princípov marxismu–leninizmu v literárnej vede a kritike [The Restoration of Marxist–Leninist Principles in Literary Theory and Criticism]', *Slovenská literatúra*, 28 (6): 536–42.

Míšková, Alena (1990, unpublished), 'Ediční rada ČSAV 1962–1989: Soupis dílčího archivního fondu [Editorial Board of the Czechoslovak Academy of Sciences, 1962–1989: The Inventory of the Archival Holdings]', in Ediční rada ČSAV [archival holdings], Archiv AV ČR, Prague.

Míšková, Alena (2002), 'Proces tzv. normalizace v Československé akademii věd (1969–1974) [The Process of the So-Called Normalization in the Czechoslovak Academy of Sciences (1969–1974)]', in Antonín Kostlán (ed.), *Věda v Československu v období normalizace (1970–1975)*, 149–67, Prague: Výzkumné centrum pro dějiny vědy.

Mokošín, Vladislav (1986), 'Hlavní úkoly společenských věd [The Main Tasks of Social Sciences]', *Život strany*, 2: 17–20.

Morkeš, František (2002), 'Vysoké školy v letech normalizace [Universities during Normalization]', in Antonín Kostlán (ed.), *Věda v Československu v období normalizace (1970–1975)*, 61–73, Prague: Výzkumné centrum pro dějiny vědy.

Morse, Janice M., Phyllis Noerager Stern, Juliet Corbin, Barbara Bowers, Kathy Charmaz and Adele E. Clarke (2009), *Developing Grounded Theory: The Second Generation*, Walnut Creek, CA: Left Coast Press.

Moss, Kevin (1995), 'The Underground Closet: Political and Sexual Dissidence in East European Culture', in Ellen E. Berry (ed.), *Postcommunism and the Body Politics*, 229–51, New York and London: New York University Press.

Možný, Ivo (2004), 'Brněnská anomálie? Brněnská sociologie 1963–1989 – subjektivní historie [The Brno Anomaly? Sociology in Brno 1963–1989: A Subjective History]', *Sociologický časopis / Czech Sociological Review*, 40 (5): 609–22.

Müller, Beate (2004), 'Censorship and Cultural Regulation: Mapping the Territory', in Beate Müller (ed.), *Censorship and Cultural Regulation in the Modern Age*, 1–31, Amsterdam: Rodopi.

Musil, Jiří (1993), 'Education and Research in the Czech Republic: Burden of the Past and Hope for the Future', *East European Politics and Societies*, 7 (1): 59–73.

Nešpor, Zdeněk R. (2014a), '"Šedá zóna" v éře tzv. normalizace: Dům techniky ČSVTS Pardubice v dějinách české sociologie [The House of Technology in Pardubice: The "Grey Zone" between Official and Dissident Sociology in Czechoslovakia in the 1970s and 1980s]', *Sociologický časopis / Czech Sociological Review*, 50 (1): 107–30.

Nešpor, Zdeněk (2014b), *Dějiny české sociologie*, Praha: Academia.

Nisonen-Trnka, Riika (2012), *Science with a Human Face: The Activity of the Czechoslovak Scientists František Šorm and Otto Wichterle during the Cold War*, Tampere: Tampere University Press.

Nussbaum, Martha (2010), *Not for Profit: Why Democracy Needs the Humanities*, Princeton and Oxford: Princeton University Press.

Oates-Indruchová, Libora (2003), 'The Ideology of the Genderless Sporting Body: Reflections on the Czech State-Socialist Concept of Physical Culture', in Naomi Segal, Roger Cook and Lib Taylor (eds), *Indeterminate Bodies*, 48–66, Basingstoke: Palgrave Macmillan.

Oates-Indruchová, Libora (2008), 'The Limits of Thought? The Regulatory Framework of Social Sciences and Humanities in Czechoslovakia (1968–1989)', *Europe-Asia Studies*, 60 (10): 1767–82.

Oates-Indruchová, Libora (2016), 'Unraveling a Tradition, or Spinning a Myth?: Gender Critique in Czech Society and Culture', *Slavic Review* 75 (4): 919–43.

Oates-Indruchová, Libora (2018), 'Self-Censorship and Aesopian Language of Scholarly Texts of Late State Socialism', *The Slavonic and East European Review*, 96 (4): 614–41.

Oates-Indruchová, Libora (2019), 'Between Censorship and Scholarship: The Editorial Board of the Czechoslovak Academy of Sciences (1969–1989)', in Muriel Blaive (ed.), *Perceptions of Society in Communist Europe: Regime Archives and Popular Opinion*, 177–87, London: Bloomsbury Academic.

Olšáková, Doubravka, ed. (2012), *Niky české historiografie: Uherskobrodská sympozia J.A. komenského v ofenzivě (1971–1989)* [*Niches of Czech Historiography: J. A. Comenius Symposia in Uherský Brod on the Offensive (1971–1989)*], Červený Kostelec: Pavel Mervart.

Otáhal, Milan (2002), *Normalizace 1969–1989: Příspěvek ke stavu bádání* [*Normalization 1969–89: The State of Research*], Prague: Ústav pro soudobé dějiny AV ČR.

Otáhal, Milan, Alena Nosková and Karel Bolomský, eds (1993), *Svědectví o duchovním útlaku (1969–1970): Dokumenty.* [*A Testimony of Spiritual Oppression (1969–70): Documents*], Prague: Maxdorf and Ústav pro soudobé dějiny AV ČR.

Ottlová, Marta, Milan Pospíšil and Roman Prahl, eds (1991), *Proudy české umělecké tvorby 19. století: Smích v umění* [*Trends in Czech 19th Century Art: Laughter in Art*], Pilsen, Czechoslovakia, 16–18 March 1989, Prague: Ústav pro hudební vědu ČSAV, Ústav dějin umění ČSAV and Český hudební fond.

Pařízek, Vlastimil (1988), 'Problémy odborného vzdělání v USA [The Problems of Vocational Education in the USA]', *Pedagogika*, 38 (1): 71–80.

Patterson, Annabel (1984), *Censorship and Interpretation*, Madison, Wisconsin and London: University of Wisconsin Press.

Pearce, Lynne (1994), *Reading Dialogics*, London: Edward Arnold.

Pecen, Jaroslav (1977), 'Jednotný program společenských věd po XV. sjezdu KSČ [The Unified Program of Social Sciences after the 15th Congress of the CPCS]', *Tvorba*, 27 July: 3.

Pehe, Veronika (2017), 'ÚSTR: Od totalitarismu ke komplexitě minulého režimu [ÚSTR: From Totalitarianism to the Complexity of the Previous Regime]', A2larm, 15 August. Available online: http://a2larm.cz/2017/08/ustr-od-totalitarismu-ke-komplexite-minuleho-rezimu/ (accessed 22 October 2017).

Péteri, György (1998), *Academia and State Socialism: Essays on the Political History of Academic Life in Post-1945 Hungary and Eastern Europe*, Highland Lakes, NJ: Atlantic Research and Publications.

Péteri, György (2002), 'Purge and Patronage: Kádár's Counter-revolution and the Field of Economic Research in Hungary, 1957–1958', *Contemporary European History*, 2 (1): 125–52.

Péteri, György (2016), 'Contested Socialisms: The Conflict between Critical Sociology and Reform Economics in Communist Hungary, 1967–71', *Social History*, 41 (3): 249–66.

Péteri, György (2019), 'By Force of Power: On the Relationship between Social Science Knowledge and Political Power in Economics in Communist Hungary', *History of Political Economy* 51 (annual suppl.): 30–51.

Petrusek, Miloslav (2003), 'Sociology in the Czech Republic after 1989', in Mike Forrest Keen and Janusz L. Mucha (eds), *Sociology in Central and Eastern Europe: Transformation at the Dawn of a New Millenium*, 49–60, Westport, CT: Praeger.

Petrusek, Miloslav (2004), 'Výuka sociologie v čase tání a v časech normalizace (1964–1989) [The Teaching of Sociology in the Times of the Thaw and Normalization (1964–1989)]', *Sociologický časopis / Czech Sociological Review*, 40 (5): 597–608.

Pillow, Wanda S. and Cris Mayo (2012), 'Feminist Ethnography: Histories, Challenges, Possibilities', in Sharlene Nagy Hesse-Biber (ed.), *Handbook of Feminist Research: Theory and Praxis*, 187–205, Thousand Oaks, CA: Sage.

Post, Robert C. (1998), 'Censorship and Silencing', in Robert C. Post (ed.), *Censorship and Silencing: Practices of Cultural Regulation*, 1–12, Los Angeles, CA: Getty Research Institute for the History of Art and the Humanities.

Potůček, Martin, ed. (1995), *Normalizace ve společenských vědách – Můj život v normalizaci* [*Normalization in the Social Sciences – My Life during Normalization*], Prague: ISS FSV UK.

Prečan, Vilém (1994), 'Společenské vědy ve svěráku "konsolidace" [Social Sciences Gripped in the Vice of "Consolidation"]', in Vilém Prečan, *V kradeném čase: Výběr ze studií, článků a úvah z let 1973–1993* [*In the Stolen Time: A Selection of Studies, Articles and Essays from 1973–1993*], 272–301, Prague: Ústav pro soudobé dějiny AV ČR and Brno: Doplněk.

Prokůpek, Ladislav (2002), 'Normalizace v Ústavu pro filosofii a sociologii ČSAV [Normalization in the Institute for Philosophy and Sociology of the Czechoslovak Academy of Sciences]', in Antonín Kostlán (ed.), *Věda v Československu v období normalizace (1970–1975)* [*Academic Research in Czechoslovakia during Normalization (1970–1975)*], 201–17, Prague: Výzkumné centrum pro dějiny vědy.

Pullmann, Michal (2011), *Konec experimentu: Přestavba a pád komunismu v Československu* [*The End of an Experiment: Perestroika and the Fall of Communism in Czechoslovakia*], Prague: Scriptorium.

Pynsent, Robert B. (1994), *Questions of Identity: Czech and Slovak Ideas of Nationality and Personality*, Budapest and New York: CEU Press and Oxford University Press.

Rapport, Nigel (1987), *Talking Violence: An Anthropological Interpretation of Conversation in the City*, St. John's: Institute of Social and Economic Research, Memorial University of Newfoundland.

'Recordings of Miklós Szabó's Lectures Donated to OSA' (2013), Budapest: Blinken Open Society Archives. Available online: http://www.osaarchivum.org/press-ro om/announcements/Recordings-Mikl%C3%B3s-Szab%C3%B3s-Lectures-Dona ted-OSA (accessed 21 March 2017).

Reinharz, Shulamit (1992), *Feminist Methods in Social Research*, New York: Oxford University Press.

Richta, Radovan et al. (1966), *Civilizace na rozcestí: Společenské a lidské souvislosti vědeckotechnické revoluce* [*Civilization at the Crossroads: Social and Human Implications of the Scientific and Technological Revolution*], 1st edn, Prague: Svoboda.

Richta, Radovan et al. (1969), *Civilization at the Crossroads: Social and Human Implications of the Scientific and Technological Revolution*, trans. Marian Šlingová, 3rd edn, Prague: International Arts and Sciences Press.

Rimmon-Kenan, Shlomith (1983), *Narrative Fiction: Contemporary Poetics*, London: Routledge.

Romek, Zbigniew (2010), *Cenzura a nauka historyczna w Polsce 1944–1970* [*Censorship and Historiography in Poland, 1944–1970*], Warszawa: Neriton and Instytut Historii PAN.

Sabrow, Martin (2002), 'Consensus and Coercion: The Third Reich and the German Democratic Republic in Comparative Perspective', in Jörn Leonhard and Lothar Funk (eds), *Ten Years of German Unification: Transfer, Transformation, Incorporation?* 69–80, Birmingham: University of Birmingham Press.

Salecl, Renata (1994), *The Spoils of Freedom: Psychoanalysis and Feminism after the Fall of Socialism*, London: Routledge.

Šámal, Petr (2002), '"Normalizace" literární vědy v zrcadle časopisu *Česká literatura* ["Normalization" of Literary Studies through the Perspective of *Czech Literature*]', *Česká literatura*, 50 (3): 229–41.

Šámal, Petr (2009), *Soustružníci lidských duší: Lidové knihovny a jejich cenzura na počátku padesátých let 20. století (s edicí zakázaných knih)* [*Turners of Human Souls: Censorship of Libraries in the Early 1950s (Including the Lists of Proscribed Books)*], Prague: Academia.

Šámal, Petr (2015), 'V zájmu pracujícího lidu: literární cenzura v době centrálního plánování a paralelních oběhů [In the Interest of the Working People: Literary Censorship in the Era of Central Planning and Parallel Circulations]', in Michael Wögerbauer, Petr Píša, Petr Šámal, Pavel Janáček et al., *V obecném zájmu: cenzura a sociální regulace literatury v moderní české kultuře 1749–2014*, 1097–223, Prague: Academia and Ústav pro českou literaturu AV ČR.

Sandomirskaja, Irina (2015), 'Aesopian Language: The Politics and Poetics of Naming the Unnameable', in Petre Petrov and Lara Ryazanova-Clarke (eds), *The Vernaculars of Communism: Language, Ideology and Power in the Soviet Union and Eastern Europe*, 63–87, London and New York: Routledge.

Schmid, Wolf ([2009] 2013), 'Implied Reader', in Peter Hühn, Jan Christoph Meister, John Pier and Wolf Schmid (eds), *The Living Handbook of Narratology*, paragraphs 1–32, Hamburg: Hamburg University Press. Available online: https://www.lhn.uni-hamburg.de/node/59.html (accessed 17 July 2019).

Schmid, Wolf (2013), 'Implied Author', in Peter Hühn, Jan Christoph Meister, John Pier and Wolf Schmid (eds), *The Living Handbook of Narratology*, paragraphs 1–26, Hamburg: Hamburg University Press. Available online: https://www.lhn.uni-hamburg.de/node/58.html (accessed 17 July 2019).

Schöpflin, George, ed. (1983), *Censorship and Political Communication in Eastern Europe: A Collection of Documents*, New York: St. Martin's Press.

Scott, James C. (1990), *Domination and the Arts of Resistance: Hidden Transcripts*, New Haven: Yale University Press.

Sedm pražských dnů 21.–28. srpna 1968: Dokumentace [*Seven Prague Days, August 21–28, 1968: Documents*], Prague: Historický ústav ČSAV.

Setje-Eilers, Margaret (2009), '"Wochenend und Sonnenschein": In the Blind Spots of Censorship at the GDR's Cultural Authorities and the Berliner Ensemble', *Theatre Journal*, 61 (3): 363–87.

Sezemský, Jiří (2017), 'Poradkyně ředitele ÚSTR Blaive: Archivy nesvědčí o zlu minulého režimu [Blaive, Advisor to the Director of ÚSTR: Archives Do Not Give Evidence of the Evil of the Former Regime]', *Forum24*, 26 August. Available online: http://forum24.cz/poradkyne-reditele-ustr-blaive-archivy-nesvedci-o-zlu-minuleho-rezimu/ (accessed 22 October 2017).

Shepherd, David (1989), 'Bakhtin and the Reader', in Ken Hirschkop and David Shepherd (eds), *Bakhtin and Cultural Theory*, 91–108, Manchester: Manchester University Press.

Sherry, Samantha (2015), *Discourses of Regulation and Resistance: Censoring Translation in the Stalin and Khrushchev Era Soviet Union*, Edinburgh: Edinburgh University Press.

Šiklová, Jiřina (1983), 'Save These Books', *Index on Censorship*, 12 (2): 37–9.

Šiklová, Jiřina (1992), 'The "Gray Zone" and the Future of Dissent in Czechoslovakia [September 1989]; Epilogue [1990]', in Marketa Goetz-Stankiewicz (ed.), *Good-bye, Samizdat: Twenty Years of Czechoslovak Underground Writing*, 181–92, Evanston, IL: Northwestern University Press.

Šiklová, Jiřina (2003), 'Everyday Democracy in the Czech Republic: Disappointments and New Morals in a Time of Neo-Normalization', in Grażyna Skąpska, Annamaria Orla-Bukowska and Krzysztof Kowalski (eds), *The Moral Fabric in Contemporary Societies*, 93–101, Leiden and Boston: Brill.

Siniavski, Andrei (1989), 'Censoring Artistic Imagination', in Marianna Tax Choldin and Maurice Friedberg (eds), *The Red Pencil: Artists, Scholars, and Censors in the USSR*, 94–100, Boston: Unwin Hyman.

Škabraha, Martin (2008), 'Naše dnešní (neo)normalizace: Přizpůsobit se dějinám – nebo se k nim přiznat? [The (Neo)normalization of Our Present Days: To Adapt to History – Or to Own Up to It?]', *A2*, n.d.: 1–11. Available online: https://www.advojka.cz/archiv/2008/22/nase-dnesni-neonormalizace (accessed 29 August 2017).

Skovajsa, Marek (2011), 'The Absent Past: The Language of Czech Sociology Before and After 1989', in Ernest Andrews (ed.), *Legacies of Totalitarian Language in the Discourse Culture of the Post-Totalitarian Era: The Case of Eastern Europe, Russia, and China*, 15–38, Lanham, MD: Lexington Books.

Skovajsa, Marek and Jan Balon (2017a), '1969–1989: The Long Hour of Party Ideologists', in *Sociology in the Czech Republic: Between East and West*, 73–95, London: Palgrave Macmillan.

Skovajsa, Marek and Jan Balon (2017b), *Sociology in the Czech Republic: Between East and West*, London: Palgrave Macmillan.

Šmejkalová, Jiřina (2000), *Kniha (k teorii a praxi knižní kultury)* [*A Book: Theory and Practice of Book Culture*], Brno: Host.

Šmejkalová, Jiřina (2011), *Cold War Books in the 'Other' Europe and What Came After*, Leiden and Boston: Brill.

Šmejkalová-Strickland, Jiřina (1994), 'Censoring Canons: Transitions and Prospects of Literary Institutions in Czechoslovakia', in Richard Burt (ed.), *The Administration of Aesthetics: Censorship, Political Criticism and the Public Sphere*, 195–215, Minneapolis and London: University of Minnesota Press.

Smith, Dinitia (1998), 'Philosopher Gamely in Defense of His Ideas', *The New York Times*, 30 May: B7, B9.

Smlsal, Jiří and Monika Stachová (2017), 'To my ne, to režim [It Wasn't Us, It Was the Regime]', *A2larm*, 12 October. Available online: http://a2larm.cz/2017/10/to-my-ne-to-rezim/ (accessed 22 October 2017).

Socialistický životní způsob jako sociální realita: pracovní texty sympozia [*Socialist Way of Life as a Social Reality: Conference Proceedings*] (1982, 1984, 1986, 1988), Brno: Univerzita J. E. Purkyně v Brně, Filozofická fakulta, Katedra marxisticko–leninské sociologie.

Sociologický časopis / Czech Sociological Review (2004), 40 (5).

Sommer, Vítězslav (2011), *Angažované dějepisectví: Stranická historiografie mezi stalinismem a reformním komunismem (1950–1970)* [*Committed Historiography: Party Historiography between Stalinism and Reform Communism (1950–1970)*], Prague: Nakladatelství Lidové noviny and FF UK.

Sommer, Vítězslav (2015), 'Forecasting the Post-Socialist Future: *Prognostika* in Late Socialist Czechoslovakia, 1970–1989', in Jenny Andersson and Eglė Rindzevičiūtė (eds), *The Struggle for the Long-Term in Transnational Science and Politics: Forging the Future*, 144–68, New York and Abingdon: Routledge.

Sommer, Vítězslav (2016), 'Towards the Expert Governance: Social Scientific Expertise and the Socialist State in Czechoslovakia, 1950s–1980s', *Serendipities*, 1 (2): 138–57.

Stoklasa, Jaroslav (2004), 'Jak jsme zelenali v Ekologické sekci [How We Turned Green in the Ecological Section]', *Nika: časopis pro ochranu přírody a životního prostředí*, 25 (1). Available online: https://stuz.cz/index.php?option=com_content&view=article&id=146:jak-jsme-zelenali-v-ekologicke-sekci&catid=56&Itemid=56 (accessed 17 July 2019).

Strauss, Anselm L. and Juliet M. Corbin (1990), *Basics of Qualitative Research: Grounded Theory Procedures and Techniques*, Newbury Park, CA: Sage.

Strauss, Leo (1952), *Persecution and the Art of Writing*, Glencoe, IL: Free Press.

Suoranta, Juha and Robert FitzSimmons (2017), 'The Silenced Students: Student Resistance in a Corporatized University', *Cultural Studies ↔ Critical Methodologies*, 17 (3): 277–85.

Svašek, Maruška (2002), 'Contacts: Social Dynamics in the Czechoslovak State-Socialist Art World', *Contemporary European History*, 2 (1): 67–86.

Takács, Ádám (2016), 'The Sociological Incident: State Socialism, Sociology and Social Critique in Hungary', *Divinatio*, 42–3: 241–99.
Tarlea, Silvana (2017), 'Higher Education Governance in Central and Eastern Europe: A Perspective on Hungary and Poland', *European Educational Research Journal*, 16 (5): 670–83.
Todorov, Tzvetan ([1991] 1999), *Facing the Extreme: Moral Life in the Concentration Camps*, trans. Arthur Denner and Abigail Pollack, London: Weidenfeld & Nicolson.
Tomášek, Dušan (1994), *Pozor, cenzurováno!, aneb, Ze života soudružky cenzury* [*Attention, Censored!, or, From the Life of Comrade Censorship*], Prague: Vydavatelství a nakladatelství ministerstva vnitra České republiky.
Trávníček, Jiří (2015), '"Ózetefka" a jejich "elpéčka": Prohibita a oddělení zvláštních fondů v době normalizační [Banned Books and Special Collections during Normalization]', in Michael Wögerbauer, Petr Píša, Petr Šámal, Pavel Janáček et al., *V obecném zájmu: cenzura a sociální regulace literatury v moderní české kultuře 1749–2014* [*In the Public Interest: Censorship and Social Regulation of Literature in Modern Czech Culture, 1749–2014*], 1309–19, Prague: Academia and Ústav pro českou literaturu AV ČR.
Třeštík, Dušan (1994), 'Ta naše morálka česká [That Our Very Own Czech Morality]', *Lidové noviny*, 30 September: 8.
Třeštík, Dušan (1995), 'Dějiny jako arbitráž? Dějiny jako vetešnictví [History as Arbitration? History as a Brick-a-Brack Shop]', *Lidové noviny*, 21 April: 9.
Třeštík, Dušan (1998), '28. říjen aneb Umíme ještě slavit? [28 October, or Do We Still Know How to Celebrate?]', *ZN zemské noviny*, 27 October: 6.
Třeštík, Dušan (2002), 'Svátek, se kterým nevíme, co si počít [A Public Holiday We Do Not Know What to Do with]', *Lidové noviny*, 26 October: 1, 11.
Tucker, Aviezer (2010), 'Jamming the Critical Barrels: The Legacies of Totalitarian Thinking', *Angelaki: Journal of Theoretical Humanities*, 15 (3): 139–52.
Tůma, Oldřich (2002), 'Společenské a politické souvislosti termínu normalizace [Social and Political Background of the Term Normalization]', in Antonín Kostlán (ed.), *Věda v Československu v období normalizace (1970–1975)* [*Academic Research in Czechoslovakia during Normalization (1970–1975)*], 17–24, Prague: Výzkumné centrum pro dějiny vědy.
Urban, Otto (1978), *Kapitalismus a česká společnost: K otázkám formování české společnosti v 19. století* [*Capitalism and Czech Society: On the Formation of Czech Society in the 19th Century*], Prague: Svoboda.
Urban, Otto (1982), *Česká společnost 1848–1918* [*Czech Society, 1848–1918*], Prague: Svoboda.
Urbánek, Eduard (1970), 'Lenin a sociologie [Lenin and Sociology]', *Sociologický časopis / Czech Sociological Review*, 6 (3–4): 221–31.

Urbášek, Pavel (2002), 'Diskontinuita jako určující faktor vývoje českých vysokých škol v letech 1970-1975 [Discontinuity as the Determining Factor of the Development of Czech Universities between 1970 and 1975]', in Antonín Kostlán (ed.), *Věda v Československu v období normalizace (1970-1975)*, 81-8, Prague: Výzkumné centrum pro dějiny vědy.

Urbášek, Pavel (2008), *Vysokoškolský vdělávací systém v letech tzv. normalizace* [*The University System during the So-called Normalization*], Olomouc: Univerzita Palackého v Olomouci.

Urbášek, Pavel (2012), 'Čistky na českých vysokých školách v letech 1945-1990: Pokus o zobecňující pohled [Cleansings at Czech Universities between 1945 and 1990: An Attempt at a Generalizing Perspective]', in Marie Černá, Jaroslav Cuhra et al., *Prověrky a jejich místo v komunistickém vládnutí*: Československo 1948-1989, 121-38, Prague: Ústav pro soudobé dějiny AV ČR.

Vianu, Lidia (1998), *Censorship in Romania*, Budapest: Central European University Press.

Vohlídalová, Marta (2018), 'Vědkyně v době pětiletek a v době soutěže: ženské vědecké dráhy před rokem 1989 a po něm [Women Researchers in the Age of the Five-Year Plan and in the Age of Competition: Women's Research Careers before and after 1989]', *Sociologický časopis / Czech Sociological Review*, 54 (1): 1-33.

Voříšek, Michael (2008), 'Antagonist, Type, or Deviation? A Comparative View on Sociology in Post-War Soviet Europe', *Revue d'Histoire des Sciences Humaines*, 18: 85-113.

Voříšek, Michael (2012), *The Reform Generation: 1960s Czechoslovak Sociology from a Comparative Perspective*, Prague: Kalich.

Voslensky, M. S. (1986), 'Officially There Is No Censorship ...', *Index on Censorship*, 15 (4): 28-30.

'Vývoj, současný stav a úkoly společenských věd: z materiálu předsednictva Ústředního výboru KSČ' [The Development, Current State, and the Tasks of Social Sciences: from the Document of the Central Committee of the CPCS] (1974), *Rudé právo*, 20 June: 3, OSA 300-30-6, box 44.

Wichner, Ernest (1993), '"Und unverständlich wird mein ganzer Text": Anmerkungen zu einer zensurgesteuerten "Nationalliteratur"', in Ernest Wichner and Herbert Wiesner (eds), *'Literaturentwicklungsprozesse': Die Zensur der Literatur in der DDR*, 199-216, Frankfurt: Suhrkamp.

Wichterle, Otto (1996), *Vzpomínky* [*Memoirs*], Prague: Ideu Repro.

Wiendl, Jan, ed. (1996), *Normy normalizace: Sborník referátů z literárněvědné koference 38. Bezručovy Opavy, 11.-13.9.1995* [*The Norms of Normalization: Proceedings of the 38th Bezruč's Opava Literary Conference, 11-13 September 1995*], Prague: Ústav pro českou literaturu AV ČR and Opava: Slezská univerzita.

Williams, Kieran (2016), 'The "Normalization" Playbook', *Bleeding Heartland* [blog], 27 November 2016. Available online: https://www.bleedingheartland.com/2016/11/27/the-normalization-playbook/ (accessed 1 July 2019).

Wögerbauer, Michael, Petr Píša, Petr Šámal, Pavel Janáček et al. (2015), *V obecném zájmu: cenzura a sociální regulace literatury v moderní české kultuře 1749–2014* [*In the Public Interest: Censorship and Social Regulation of Literature in Modern Czech Culture, 1749–2014*], Vol. 2: 1938–2014, Prague: Academia and Ústav pro českou literaturu AV ČR.

XYZ (Praha) (1977), 'Čeští filosofové po 30 letech: Současný stav "normalizované" filosofie [Czech Philosophers after 30 Years: The Current State of "Normalized" Philosophy]', *Studie (Roma)*, 49: 4–22.

Yarim-Agaev, Yuri (1989), 'Coping with the Censor: A Soviet Scientist Remembers', in Marianna Tax Choldin and Maurice Friedberg (eds), *The Red Pencil: Artists, Scholars, and Censors in the USSR*, 71–4, Boston: Unwin Hyman.

Yurchak, Alexei (2006), *Everything Was Forever Until It Was No More: The Last Soviet Generation*, Princeton, NJ: Princeton University Press.

Zbraslavská kronika [*The Zbraslav Chronicle*], (1976), Prague: Svoboda.

Ze starých českých kronik [*From Old Bohemian Chronicles*], (1975), Prague: Svoboda.

Zhuk, Sergei I. (2013), '"Academic Détente": IREX Files, Academic Reports, and "American" Adventures of Soviet Americanists during the Brezhnev Era', *Cahiers du monde russe*, 54 (1–2): 297–328.

Zipser, Richard A. (1990a), 'Literary Censorship in the German Democratic Republic: Part Two: The Authors Speak', *The Germanic Review*, 65 (3): 118–29.

Zipser, Richard A. (1990b), 'The Many Faces of Censorship in the German Democratic Republic 1949–1989: Part One: A Survey', *The Germanic Review*, 65 (3): 111–17.

Index

Academia (publishing house)   53, 84, 117
    n.4, 126 n.11, 129 n.14, 131 n.16
  editorial policies in   116 n.3, 133 n.18,
    138 n.23
academic freedom   12, 20, 242, 257
  in Hungary   38–9, 40–1, 94, 223, 280,
    291, 295, 316, 325
academic production   10, 61, 96, 261,
    268, 274, 284
Academy of Sciences   42, 49, 51–4, 56–8,
    60, 95, 233–4, 244, 292
  employment in   79, 88, 92, 122 n.6,
    140–1, 142, 243
  publishing in   126–8, 151
acceptability   132, 190, 284, 293, 295
accessibility to the masses   201
access to literature/resources   62, 77, 107,
    109, 111, 113, 129, 153–6, 216,
    265, 273–4, 322
actors   6–7, 9, 11, 13, 25–6, 37, 39, 43, 61
    n.26, 266, 311, *see also* agents
Aczél György   151, 151 n.1, 244
additions   4, 40, 143, 181, 275, 308, *see
    also* insertions
advantage   90, 91, 106–7, 128, 169,
    238–9, 252, 258, 268, 281
Aesopian language   8, 13, 42, 43 n.18,
    213, 308–11
agency   2, 9, 10, 13–15, 26, 40, 169, 199,
    244, 259, 266, 277, 320
agents   14–16, 19, 33, 63, *see also* actors
Alasuutari, Pertti   26–8, 31
alibi, alibism   112, 239, 240, 257,
    258, 284
alliance   40, 77, 90, 95, 232, 240, 265, *see
    also* coalition
allonym   41, 285, 285 n.18, 286, *see also*
    ghost-author
alternative spaces   40, 62, 106, 108–10,
    253–4, 257–8, 265, 288, 298, *see
    also* niches of relative freedom;
    opening of intellectual space

amend, amendments   103, 120,
    132, 148, 182
ancien regime   7
Anděl, Michal   205, 205 n.5
Andrews, Ernest   311
Andrews, Molly   33
Andropov, Yuri   104, 104 n.18, 183
Annales   154, 188, 218
anonymization   35, 41, 137, 149, 174, 239
antagonistic differences   205, 302
Anticharta, *see* Anti-Charter
Anti-Charter   76, 76 n.1, 86–7
anti-communism, anti-communist   53,
    60, 165, 203, 216–17
anti-Marxist   167, 211
anti-socialist   50
appearance of (ideological) loyalty, *see*
    loyalty, appearance of
appearances   58, 105–6, 237, 242–3, 251,
    258, 263, 287
appeasement   106, 252
applied research   42, 108, 140–1, 188,
    190, 247–8, 292–4
approval   81, 84, 222, 273
  levels of   37, 95, 114–19, 130–3,
    261–3, 282, 291
archival, archives   6, 21, 24–5, 58, 77,
    141, 155, 218, 323
assessment of the past   29, 34, 44, 45,
    182, 217, 317–18
attribution   135, 141, *see also* authorship
attributive   42, 205, 301–2
audience   33, 42, 53, 194, 199, 212, 252,
    292–4, 298, 306, 314
author, relationship to text   4, 19, 26, 37,
    184, 272, 288–91
  blacklisted   6, 7, 51, 199–200, 232
  compromised   52, 73, 82, 238–40,
    258, 264, 266, 268–70, 279,
    285–6, 292
authorial control   4, 41, 169,
    180–1, 285–8

authorial intention   17
authoritarian   4, 15, 57, 59, 316, 326
authority   5, 14–15, 21, 53, 76,
    121, 145, 327
author–reader compact/contract   17–18,
    42–3, 208–10, 289, 305–7
authorship   4, 19, 41, 145, 169, 174–5,
    180, 260, 273, 281, 283, 285–6,
    291, *see also* attribution
  collective (*see* et al.)
autobiography   12, 271, 299
autonomy   4, 11, 126, n.11, 244

Bahenská, Marie   317
Bakhtin, Mikhail   31, 42
ban   77, 94, 102, 107, 109, 165–7, 194,
    203, 243, 283, *see also* ostracism
  publishing   47, 61, 79–80, 85, 129,
    165–7, 250, 277, 329
  teaching   76, 77, 165–7, 284
barriers to publication   22, 264–5,
    272–4, 279
Bauman, Zygmunt   292
Bělohradský, Václav   328
benchmark   208, 282, 304
Berend Iván   152
Beszélő   210
Bibó István   167, 210
Bill on Universities   233
binary   41–2, 295–7, 300–301, 312, 328,
    see also dualism
Biologická společnost, *see* Biology
    Association
Biology Association   108
Black Book of Polish Censorship   6, 10
blacklisting   6, 7, 11, 20, 51, 61, 200, 232,
    236 n.3, 320
Blaive, Muriel   328–9
Blyum, Arlen   7–8, 18, 283
Bock, Ivo   301
bodies (*orgány*)   1, 10, 49, 105, 117
    n.4, 138 n.23
Bokor Ágnes   192
Bolsonaro, Jair   325–6
Bolton, Jonathan   3 n.1, 241,
    254, 279 n.17
book industry   11, 53, 328
book manuscripts   25, 113–45, 179
boss, the   78–9, 86–92, 110–11, 125, 163
  exploitation by   135, 150, 181, 211

the power of   3–4, 129, 203,
    209, 257, 307
boundaries   9, 39–40, 48, 77, 93–4,
    134, 193–4, 233, 235, 244, 275,
    278–83, 290
Bourdieu, Pierre   9, 14, 129, 208, 309–10
bourgeois   60, 136, 150, 156, 200, 272,
    274, 295–6, 300
  sociology   47, 79–80, 170, 178–9, 194,
    198, 296 n.25, 297 n.26
branded   79–80, 203, 240, *see also* stigma
Bryant, Chad   177 n.22, 253
bullying   106, 283, *see also* harassment
Burt, Richard   15–16
Butler, Judith   14–15, 246, 273, 296
Búzik, Bohumil   315

camouflage   8, 74–5, 77, 171, 182, 187,
    202, 206, 251–2, 296 n.25,
    301, 303
campaign   94, 161–3, 190, 197–
    8, 243, 329
capitalism, capitalist   52, 200–203, 206,
    211, 219, 301–3
career advancement   50, 61, 103, 249–50
censor   13–18, 91, 134, 212, 264, 276,
    282, 289–90, 321–3
censoring body   1, 5, 10, 272
censoring guidelines   10
censoring practices   6, 9, 11, 38
censoring pressures   9, 13, 281, 287, 290
censors   2, 7–10, 18, 25, 41, 119, 243,
    266, 317, 323
censorship, constitutive   14–15, 275
  corrosive effect of   18–19
  definition of   14–17
  denial of   280
  dispersed   5, 7, 10, 15–16, 270–2, 278,
    283, 321, 326
  displaced   5, 15–16
  domains of   272–3
  editorial   7, 10, 104, 132–4, 148,
    222, 276, 282
  effects of   18–19, 37, 310–13, 319–20
  Elizabethan   5 n.2, 17, 39, 132
  formalized   5, 10, 20, 37, 80, 118,
    269–70, 276, 292, 320
  friendly   7, 40, 100, 148, 149, 275–7,
    291 (*see also sanfte* Zensur)
  library   3, 7, 62, 77, 107, 155, 274

literary   7–9, 11–12, 266
multilevelled   20–1
New (*see* New Censorship)
of people   20, 151, 187, 272
post-publication   23–4, 40–1, 101, 143, 162–8, 277–83, 291
preliminary   8
pre-publication   101, 269
prescriptive   4, 8, 234
preventive   40–1, 48, 233, 271–6, 280, 291
proactive   41, 283, 291, 294, 304, 308
proscriptive   8, 15
punitive   8, 269
regulative   14
restrictive   4, 61, 234, 269
system of   5–6, 10–11, 15–19, 266, 278, 326
textual   40, 101, 187, 272, 275, 279, 281–7, 291
theoretical models of   6–8, 15–16, 280
theories of   13–19, 319–20
top-down, view/perspective of   11, 15–17
Censorship in Romania   6, 21
Central European University   326–7
centralization   11–12, 51, 232, 264
Česká literatura   256, 299 n.27
Český časopis historický   55, 121, 139, 163 n.12, 176
Český úřad pro tisk a informace (ČÚTI), *see* Czech Office for Press and Information
Charmaz, Kathy   26–9, 31
Charter   77, 40, 89, 108, 127, 156, 165 n.15, 173–4, 240, 243, 256, 271–2
checkpoints   129, 143, 156, 266
Choldin, Marianna Tax   7
chronological, chronology   11, 16, 19, 24–5, 249–50
citations   40, 104–5, 272, 275, 309, *see also* references
Clare, Janet   17
class struggle   50, 179, 206
coalition   90, 103, 251, *see also* alliance
co-author   4, 92, 137 n.22, 183, 262, 286
code   2, 8, 16–19, 37, 42–3, 200–203, 208–14, 215, 292, 305–12, 314, *see also* text coding

coding (a qualitative method)   26–9, 34–5
coerced authorship   240, 273
coercion   137
Coetzee, J. M.   281, 321
Cohen, Mark   13–14, 17, 287
cohort   23, 38, 70, 71, 232, 249, 255–9, 288, 300, 306, 314–16, 322, *see also* generation
Cold War   13, 41, 295, 300–301, 312
collaboration   8, 16, 84, 87, 100, 140, 156, 181, 192–3, 282, 323, 329–30
collective publication   128–9, 135, 137 n.22, 173, *see also* authorship, collective
colloquium   89, 148, *see also* seminar
Comenius   80, 212
Comenius Symposium   253
communication   8, 16–19, 37, 42–3, 53, 56, 208, 219, 234, 252, 310, 314, 321
 intellectual   5, 13, 36, 62, 184, 307, 309, 321–2
 written   184
communication with the reader   8, 13, 18, 42–3, 184–5, 210, 289, 290–2, 305–9, 310
Communist Party   2, 24, 26, 38, 44, 47–63, 75, 81, 101, 104, 232–3
 Central Committee of   48–9, 54–60, 74, 79–81, 90, 95, 118–19, 134, 139, 155, 161, 234, 242–3
 Congress   53 n.12, 55–7, 92, 98, 158, 181, 213, 234
 leading role of   49, 52, 59, 73, 236, 294, 327
 members/membership   23, 25, 50–1, 74, 102, 124, 139, 152, 235, 240 (*see also* non-Party members; struck off)
community   260, 270, 278–80, 306, 307, 319–22
 alternative   109, 127, 254, 265, 288
 closed   150, 276, 291, 322
 effect on   162, 309–10
 exclusion by/of   43, 98, 103, 244
 gated (*see* gated communities)
 imagined (*see* imagined community)
 Party control of   54–8, 234
 in period vocabulary   205

resistance by   88
size   19
supportive   40, 277
competition   78, 125, 158 n.9, 246, 327
complicity   8, 16, 36, 244–6, 276, 302
compromise   101, 159, 168–9, 189, 247–9, 251–2, 257, 258, 284, 290, 298
conceptual apparatus   157, 170, 289, 298, 300–301
concessions   17, 137, see also libations
conclusion (of a piece of writing)   104, 143, 157, 177, 183, 211, 242, 285, 308 n.31
conditions, repressive   2, 5, 7, 26, 233, 307, 320–2
conference proceedings   12, 109, 253, 265
conferences   89, 91, 99, 109, 110, 124, 148, 154, 164
conform, conformity   8–9, 77, 90, 138 n.23, 204, 212, 271, 304, 310, 330, see also nonconformist
confrontation   109 n.27, 120, 250, 259
Connelly, John   10–11, 62 n.27
conscience   87, 103, 197, 239, 246, 250, 252, 304
continuity   20, 222, 224, 292, 297, 314, 315 n.35, 318
control, centralized   25, 37, 48–9, 53, 59–60, 62–3, 232–3, 279
   of access to resources   155
   of discourse   13–15, 79, 206, 304
   ideological   37, 59, 232–3, 242, 255, 259
   state   326–7
control over text, authorial, see authorial control
convictions   38, 48, 59, 82, 95, 157, 233, 255
copyrights   133 n.18, 137
Corbin, Juliet   26–9
corporate university   325, see also neoliberal university
cosmopolitanism   201–2
courage, courageous   78, 90, 167, 211
coursebook   126, 157, 160, 181, 182, 184, 207, 215, see also textbook
creative, actors   13, 25
creative expression   1, 12
creative process, autonomy of   4

creativity   17–18, 42, 59, 156, 311
critical analyses   24, 55–6, 166
critical reading   42–3
critical thinking   17–18, 43, 223, 288, 312–13, 320–1
criticism, constructive   194
   of alternative views   80, 157, 162, 197–8, 273, 297, 303
   of inimical ideology   58, 60, 237, 296
   of the Party   195
   of the regime (see regime, criticism of)
   social   223
   tolerance of   275, 329
CSc., see PhD
Culler, Jonathan   304
cuts   15, 100, 129, 275–6, 325
Czech Office for Press and Information (ČÚTI)   131 n.16

Darnton, Robert   7, 15, 266, 311
decentralization   12, 170
decision-making   62 n.27, 105, 126 n.11, 140, 236, 238, 240
delegitimation   16, 21
demography   83, 298
deviant, deviation   275, 277
dialectical materialism   157, 197
dialogic   42
dialogic principle   306–7
dictatorship of the proletariat   196
dignified, dignity   96–7, 112, 245–7, 257
Dilia   133, 268 n.13
directives   44, 48, 53–5, 57, 233–5, 301
   vagueness/knowledge of   6, 38–9, 77, 169, 241, 259
   and vocabulary   187
disability, disabled   83–4, 238, 258
disadvantage   106, 128, 140, 200, 238, 290, 302
disciplines   1, 9, 19, 50, 56–8, 326–7
   difference by   222, 231, 247, 280, 294–6
   discursive limits of   99, 170
   institutional conditions in   12, 144 n.26, 171, 255
   leaders of   23
   loyalty to (see loyalty to the discipline)
   personal advancement in/of   77, 107, 113, 161, 189, 290, 311, 316
discourse   224, 277, 289, 315–16, 322

authoritative ideological   24, 28, 42, 231–2, 251–2, 255, 302–3, 307, 309, 313
  control of (*see* control of discourse)
  dominant   18, 282, 317
  policy   38
  political   100, 172
  public   21, 30, 33, 63, 306, 319
  scholarly   129, 170, 286, 311, 315, 318
  variety of   31, 43, 316
discrimination, discriminatory   75, 106, 107, 140–1, 238, 240
discursive participants   277
discursive practices   277, 314
discursive shift   255
dispersal and displacement   15
dissent, dissenting   134, 328–9
  internal dissent   252–3
dissertation   82, 138 n.23, 157, 195, *see also* thesis
dissident   6, 18–22, 86, 165, 210–11, 279, 308
  circles/groups   23, 159, 205, 207–8, 254
Division of Book Culture   53, 118, 119, 123
docentura, *see* habilitation
Doinaș, Ștefan Augustin   308–9
dominant   18, 33, 37, 62–3, 310, 317
dualism   312, 316, 319, *see also* binary
dualistic approach   43, 314, 319
due process   39, 270, 323
Dům techniky, Pardubice   108
Dutton, Richard   132 n.17

Eastern Bloc   1, 5, 6, 243, 273, 280, 326
Ediční rada ČSAV, *see* Editorial Board of the Czechoslovak Academy of Sciences
Editorial Board of the Czechoslovak Academy of Sciences   21, 24–6, 29, 116–44 (notes), 261, 320
editorial boards   54, 57, 116, 124, 133, 139, 161, 234, 262
editor-in-chief   54, 103, 123–5, 132–6, 139, 144 n.26, 266–70, 278, 282
editors   132–4, 170, 262–3, 266–70
  cooperation with authors   3, 82–3, 85, 122, 136, 137, 161, 180, 251, 304, 306, 311
  position of   17, 39–40, 149, 250
efficiency   48, 78, 234, 237, 257, 267, 325, 327
elite   90, 94, 128, 154, 199, 254
  elitist   150, 194, 253–4, 303
ellipses   43 n.18, 304
emigration   137 n.22, 138 n.23, 156, 209, 216, 272, 308 n.31
empirical research   109, 135, 141, 190, 198, 247–8, 284, 293–4
empiricism   273, 318
employment contract   52–4, 75, 81–4, 132, 165, 233–4, 238, 266
  for Central Committee members   95
  for peer reviewers   122–3
  short-term/part-time   83–4, 91–2, 238, 242–3, 274
encyclopaedia   3, 12, 119, 129 n.14, 130, 177
enemy   10, 83, 87, 103, 161, 174, 251, 252, 329
entrance examinations (university)   75, 184
Eötvös Loránd Tudomány Egyetem (ELTE)   152, 165, 327
et al.   41, 135, 258, 290, *see also* authorship, collective
ethical, ethics   26, 30, 35, 179, 205, 300, 323
euphemism   203, 293, 298, 310, 312
evasion, evasive   238, 269, 273, 284, 288, 306, 322
Evening School of Marxism-Leninism, *see* VUML
evidence   3, 6, 17, 20–1, 81–2, 184, 187, 283, 305–7
exclusion   14, 75, 91, 237, 240–1, 268, 270, 277, 279, 287, 291, 321, 328
Executive Directions   52, 233
exile   6, 218, *see also* emigration
existentialism   207
expectations   90, 101, 200, 293
expelled (from the Party)   51, 77, 79, 83, 91, 97–8, 111, 116, 124, 153, 156, 273
experienced reader   304, 309
expertization   11, 12
exploitation   91, 95, 201, 240, 264, 301, 303

expressions 43, 157, 169, 176, 205–6, 301, 303–4, 311–12, 330, *see also* vocabulary; word choice; words

factography 177 n.22
factology 9, 299
faculty, of Arts 88, 89, 93, 219, 286
Falk, Barbara 59, 165 n.15, 279
family, sociology of 197
favouritism 239 n.5, 266, 319
favours 91, 136
fear 38, 87, 162, 241–2, 257, 275, 278, 283, 291, 320
   and conformity 125, 159, 204
   fear of being labelled 242
   of job loss 242, 278
   of language 304
   locations associated with 92–3
   memories of 40
   post-1989 222, 317
   of publishing 22–3, 37
   taking advantage of 264
   without cause 153, 181, 205
Fehér Ferenc 243 n.6
feminist 3, 222, 296, 317–18, 328
   methodology 30
Fidelius, Peter 41 n.17, 205, 300–301
fields of censoring interaction 16
Filipcová, Blanka 195–6
Filozofický časopis 55, 141
First (Czechoslovak) Republic 212, 218, 311
Fojtík, Jan 55–9
Foucault, Michel 14, 206, 272
Frankfurt School 213
freelance 85
Free University 86
Freshwater, Helen 15
Fromm, Erich 104, 175
functionalism 191, 194
funding 53, 108, 152, 173, 253, 297–8, 325, 326–7
   unavailability of 148, 154, 155, 168, 273, 294

gated communities 39, 264–5
gatekeeping, gatekeepers 120 n.5, 135, 236, 266, 270, 274

GDR censorship 6, 7, 9–10, 253, 261 n.12, 266, 275, 282, 302 n.29, 311
gender 12, 75, 106, 140–1, 203, 253, 267, 268, 303, 328
   studies 222, 297 n.26, 317, 327
generation 93, 208, 231, 237, 254–9, 300, 312, 313–16, *see also* cohort
   post-1989 219, 224, 313–14
   young, accountability to 30, 61, 246, 284
Generation 1968 38, 39, 232, 255–8, 285, 288, 316, 322
generational change/shift 37–9, 78–9, 232, 255–7
Gerovitch, Slava 9, 299
ghost-author 41, 157, 175, 258, 285, 290
Ginzburg, Lydiya 310
give offence 39, 169, 202, 204, 277, 290
glasnost 8, 208
Glavlit 7
grey literature 3, 129, 264, *see also* in-house prints
grey zone 8, 22–3, 103, 177 n.22, 245, 259
grounded theory method 22, 26–7
guidelines 10, 55, 231, 234, 254
guilt 87, 181, 250, 282
GUKP 10, *see also* Office for Control of the Press, Publication and Public Performance

habilitation 99, 199, 220, 298
habitus 9
harassment 3, 110, 216, 241, 247, *see also* bullying
Haraszti Miklós 18, 243 n.6
Havel, Václav 38, 59, 247
Hegedüs András 156, 168
hegemonic, hegemony 24, 52, 61, 310
Heller Ágnes 168, 243 n.6
hidden transcript 37, 63, 281, 306
hierarchization, hierarchy 10, 15–16, 48, 52–3, 57, 103, 114, 119, 126 n.11, 169, 233, 252, 261 n.12, 282, 321
historical materialism 197
Historical Society (Hungary) 110, 131
history 27, 92, 116, 133, 188, 196
   of censorship 240, 281

of class conflict 197
of the Communist Party 129 n.14
cultural history 155
economic 120–1, 124, 143,
    154, 155, 197
history, oral 21, 24, 27, 318, 320
history department 78
history writing 9, 196, 295
intellectual 13
interpretation of 43
labour 109, 129 n.14
literary 221, 316
political 52, 171, 188
post-1918 275
social 83, 109–10, 131, 200
of unfreedom 12
urban 154
women's 317
of working class 189
Hodrová, Daniela 32, 124 n.9
Holquist, Michael 14, 329
honorarium 25, 128, 128 n.13, 286
Horská, Pavla 317
Hrbek, Jaromír 97
Hrzal, Ladislav 57–8
Hudek, Adam 20, 315 n.35
Hungarian 11, 38, 42, 110, 153, 167–8,
    244, 292, 327
    Slovak 20
Husák, Gustáv 92, 98, 221
Husserl, Edmund 107, 150, 194, 207
Hussite 148, 164, 212
hypernormalization 255

ideas 2, 4, 17, 38, 49, 73, 160, 162,
    221–2, 267, 286 n.19, 326, see
    also thoughts
ideological compliance 11, 59, 105, 256,
    264, 279, 291
ideological content 38, 39, 48, 58, 130
    n.16, 233, 237, 264
ideological control 37, 48, 59, 62, 232–3,
    235, 242, 255, 259
ideological dictate 22, 252, 259
ideological form 48, 58, 233,
    237, 255, 264
ideological relaxation 40, 144 n.26, 257
ideological review, see review
ideological sphere 1, 52 n.10
ideology, state-socialist 2–4

Ideology Commission 49, 54–5, 100,
    163, 234, 277
illegal 167, 210, see also samizdat
imagined community 33
imagined conversations 26–9, 31, 33–6,
    44–5, 63, 215, 224, 310
immorality 223
implied author 185,
implied reader 184, 308
imprimatur 126
income 85, 95, 136, 168, 192, 200, 243,
    302, see also salary
Index on Censorship 6, 9
indulgencies 96
inequality 192
in-house prints 3, 121, 129, see also grey
    literature
INION 107, 301 n.28
initiation narrative 32, see also quest
insertions 4, 40, 143, 181, 275, 308, see
    also padding
Institute for the Study of Totalitarian
    Regimes (ÚSTR) 323, 329
Institute of Economic
    Forecasting 114, 193
institution, censoring 5, 20, 23, 37, 320
institutional context 2, 13, 16, 26, 37,
    108, 231–59
institutional hierarchy 48, 52, 233, 252
institutionalization 19, 110, 178,
    254 n.10, 267
institutional power 11, 26, 233, 241, 249,
    264–5, 270
institutional practices 184, 252
institutional processes 6, 13, 55, 129,
    234, 241, 246, 257, 270
institutional structures 44, 77, 231, 250,
    259, 277, 298
instrumentalization 13, 15, 36, 330
integrity 36, 76, 122, 246
intellectual communication, see
    communication, intellectual
intellectual life 94, 170, 254
intellectuals 23, 47, 50, 55, 153, 208, 244,
    279 n.17, 283, 305, 328
internalization, internalize 6, 18, 275,
    281, 287, 289
internationalism 201–2
interpretation 30, 185, 314, 321
    plurality of 13, 308

political   151, 203, 330
  volatile   40, 43, 234, 282–3,
    294, 320–1
intimacy   36, 44, 184, 246, 321
intuition   170, 282
invasion of Czechoslovakia (August 1968)
    20, 23, 47–8, 53, 137, 139 n.24,
    156 n.8, 168 n.18, 232,
    236, 243, 328
invisibility   247, 257

Jeřábek, Hynek   315
job loss   47, 278
Jones, Sara   8–9
journals   54–7, 171, 221, 234, 267, 281
  banning of   94, 243
  editorial policies of   130, 169
  new   131, 144 n.26
  publishing in   118, 121, 176, 199–202,
    256, 268, 284
  quality of   83
  samizdat   110
judgement   14, 32, 287, 299, 315, 319

Kaplan, Karel   11, 19
Kapr, Jaroslav   286
Kemény István   152–3, 168, 293
Kende Péter   308 n.31
Kenney, Padraic   31
Kiš, Danilo   289
Klaus, Václav   327
Klötzer, Silvia   282
knowledge, production of   1, 26, 44, 129
Komárek, Valtr   193
Konrád György   7, 9, 19, 153 n.5,
    243 n.6, 278
Kopeček, Michal   248 n.7
Kornai János   62, 152, 234, 244, 254 n.10,
    285, 299, 308 n.31
Kotek, Ludvík   133–4
Krapfl, James   328
Kurakin, Dmitry   5 n.3, 254, 296 n.25,
    301 n.28, 321
Kutnar, František   163
Kuznetsov, Anatoly   309

label   91, 160, 203, 238, 240–2, 249,
    264, 273, 284, 287, 289,
    296, 303, 318, 328–9, *see
    also* stigma

labour   109, 195, 297
Laiferová, Eva   315
language   187–214
  abuse of   208
  to adapt to   179, 303, 310, 321
  Aesopian (*see* Aesopian language)
  attention to   9, 42, 284, 298,
    300–304, 321
  citational   42, 302, 313, 322
  cover   200, 209
  divided   42, 295, 300, 303, 314
  emptied of content   312, 330
  fear of (*see* fear of language)
  feminine   203, 303
  ideologized   28, 105, 192, 284–5, 296,
    298–305, 321–2, 329
  language use   41, 201–3, 255, 298,
    300–306, 312, 322
  learn the language   27, 104, 207–8,
    251, 258, 305, 312, 321
  mathematical   299
  of music   208, 305
  necrosis of   311
  register   313–14
  sensitivity to   42, 302, 306, 314, 322
Larson, Jonathan   20, 255
layering (of text)   32, 42–3, 211,
    309, 311
legacy   9, 33, 43, 220–1, 223–4, 305,
    315, 323, 328
legal deposit   3
legal procedures   124
legislation, legislative   1, 20, 55, 237, 326
legitimation, legitimization   15–16,
    30, 43, 84, 131, 196, 295, 301,
    307, 310, 314, 318, *see also*
    delegitimation
leisure   195, 198, 297
lektorský sbor, see College of
    Peer Reviewers
Lenin, V.I.   96, 171, 179, 197, 309–10
Lessons Learned from the Crisis
    Development   55
libations (*also referred to as* sops to
    Cerberus)   149, 158, 174, 178,
    184, 211, 213, 284–5, 290
libraries   2–3, 7, 11–12, 20, 62, 77,
    107, 155, 274
Librová, Hana   193
lifestyle   42, 193, 201 n.7, 297 n.26

literary journals 94, 130-1, 176, 265, 299 n.27
literary studies 6-9, 30-2, 136, 158, 171, 253, 310, 316
  literary censorship (see censorship, literary)
literary theory 76, 101, 158
  Marxist (see Marxist literary theory)
literary translations 85, 114, 130-1, 287
literature 42, 57, 76, 167
Little, Matthew 275
living in truth 247
Lokatis, Siegfried 9-10, 261 n.12, 282, 302 n.29
loophole 90, 112, 174
Loseff, Lev 8, 43
loyalty 243, 249, 251-2, 256-8
  appearance of 38, 48, 105, 180-1, 233, 241, 255, 264, 270, 275, 288, 298
  to the Communist Party 33, 59, 113, 267, 284
  to the discipline 2, 22, 61
Lukács School 167, 168 n.18, 243 n.6

Macek, Josef 139-40
Mácha, Karel Hynek 209
Macherey, Pierre 4
Machonin, Pavel 80, 141, 239 n.5, 273, 321
Mackinnon, Catherine 240-1
managers 25, 40, 78, 86, 94-5, 237-40, 245, 255-6, 262-3, 266, 270, 286, 291
manoeuvre 38, 48, 59, 87, 103, 143, 147, 182, 214, 238, 251, 269-70, 289, 303, 310
manuscript, see also book manuscript
  proposal 25, 116-17, 124 n.9, 138 n.138
  submission of 4, 25, 116-17, 122-4, 126, 133 n.18, 149, 181
  trajectory 113-45
marginal, marginalized 98, 180, 190, 247, 253
Mark, James 271, 315
Marx, Karl 59, 76, 150, 182, 207, 281
Marxian 289, 298, 300-301, 315
Marxism 109, 157, 167, 170, 180, 188, 197, 201, 204, 206, 221, 289, 299, 316
  liberal 183
  Western/British 188-9, 219
Marxism–Leninism 171
  Evening University of (see VUML)
  institute/department of 52, 92, 97, 119-20, 138, 164, 262, 269
  teachings of 49, 52
  theory development 58, 104, 237, 255
Marxist 1, 110, 124 n.9, 143, 182-3, 188-9, 212, 297, 301
  classics 40, 53 n.12, 158, 301 n.28
  literary theory 101, 158, 179, 188
  sociology 194
  vocabulary 40, 200-201, 205-6, 275
Marxist–Leninist 208
  doctrine 57, 329
  theory 48, 59, 194, 211, 233
Master of the Revels 39, 132
meaning 210, 231, 235, 295, 303-4, 308, 310-13, 330
  empty of 42, 302, 314, 322
  intended 8, 18, 307
  precise 43, 213, 309
  work with meaning (see work with meaning)
meaningful 102, 251-3, 255, 306, see also work with meaning
memory 29, 33, 215, 218, 280, 313, 319
mentality 223, 319, 329
merit 44, 75, 254, 323
metanarrative 44-5, 65, 225
metaphors 13, 14, 210, 240, 254, 259, 300, 318, 321
methodology, feminist (see feminist methodology)
Miltová, Alena 244
Ministry of Culture 53, 118, 119, 123
miscommunication 309
Míšková, Alena 24-5, 51, 52 n.9, 57 n.19
Mladá fronta (publishing house and/or newspaper) 126, 127, 188
Mlynář, Zdeněk 80
monologic 329
moral compromise 258, 284
moral dilemma 5, 246-8, 319
moral position 29, 76, 77, 184, 221, 223, 235, 265, 290, 293
moral support 84
Moss, Kevin 8
Možný, Ivo 109 n.27, 197

Müller, Beate   16–17
Musil, Jiří   245, 299, 317–18

narrative   12, 31–2, 36–7, 39, 201 n.7,
   299, 315
narratology   45, 185 n.23
narrator   31–3, 70
natural sciences   88, 96, 254
necessity   39, 106, 109, 251, 252, 263,
   268, 270, 290, 309, 322
negotiation   1, 7–8, 13–16, 63, 112,
   266, 322, 326
   personal   159, 170, 195, 245–
   52, 301, 304
   space for   10, 39–40, 273, 275–7, 283–4
Nejedlý, Zdeněk   212
neoliberal university   325
neonormalization   328
Népszabadság   199
New Censorship   8, 14–15
niches of relative freedom   12, 77, 105,
   196, 248 n.7, 251, 280, *see also*
   alternative spaces
Nisonen-Trnka, Riika   12
nomenklatura   190, 236, 237,
   249, 264, 267
non-conformist   23, 205, 210–11,
   254, 308, 328
non-Marxist   188, 194, 254 n.10, 295–6
non-Party members   60, 76, 82, 119 n.5,
   148, 160, 168, 235, 237,
   242, 261, 281
normalization (definition of)   19, 21,
   24–5, 37–9, 282–3
normalizing executive (the
   'normalizers')   50, 51, 57, 78,
   82–3, 91, 113, 126, 258, 264
nostalgia   29, 176
Nová mysl   55, 57
November 1989   79, 109, 123, 182, 207,
   217, *see also* revolution 1989
Nussbaum, Marta   325–6

Oborská, Jarmila   140
Obzina, Jaromír   95
Odbor knižní kultury, *see* Division of
   Book Culture
Office for Control of the Press,
   Publication and Public
   Performance (GUKP)   10

Olšáková, Doubravka   253
omissions   40, 100, 203, 275
omnicensorship   7
opening of intellectual space   39,
   144 n.26, 248, 254, *see also*
   alternative spaces
Open Society Archives   24, 58
Open Society Foundation, *see* Soros
   Foundation
opponent   78, 220, 232, 310, 311
opportunism, opportunist   49, 51, 57
opportunities   91, 95–6, 112, 136, 154,
   238–9, 256, 258–9, 271
   exclusion from   78, 268
   for non-Party members   82, 250
opposition   9, 23, 85, 167 n.17, 188
oppression   15, 43, 235, 241,
   316, 320, 322
Orbán, Viktor   326, 330
originality   96, 114, 173, 263,
   283, 286, 320
Orwell, George   100, 202–3
ostracism   257, 328, *see also* ban
Otáhal, Milan   19
overcentralization   38, 62 n.27, 234
over-senzitization   41, 290, 291

padding   207, 217, 304, 313–14, *see also*
   insertions
paper quota   11, 39, 53, 61, 117 n.4, 131
   n.16, 136, 265
paradigm, totalitarian, *see*
   totalitarian paradigm
parallel worlds   42, 188, 292, 298
Pařízek, Vlastimil   217
Parsons, Talcott   191, 194
Party members/membership, *see*
   Communist Party members/
   membership
Patočka, Jan   107–8, 150, 173–4, 194
patronage   11, 221, 239 n.5
Patterson, Annabel   282, 301 n.28, 312
pay   76, 136, *see also* salary
pay grade   128 n.13, *see also* honorarium
Pedagogika   217
peer   10, 276, 278, 288, 291, 319
   community   2, 40, 276–7,
   280, 288, 322
   discussion   242, 277, 280
   respect of   22, 24, 73, 106, 113, 323

peer review 114, 116–18, 122 n.7,
    123 n.9, 124 n.9, 201, 262, 263,
    270, 285,
peer reviewers 120, 122 n.7, 144 n.26,
    157, 202, 306
  College of 119 n.5, 122, 126 n.11
pen name 106, 251, 258, 285, see
    also pseudonym
pension, pensioner 81, 83–4, 99,
    200, 238, 258
perceptions 5–6, 13, 24, 37, 62, 106,
    159, 184–5, 202, 278, 289, 295,
    309, 311, 316
perestroika 40, 89, 102, 144, 164, 176,
    197, 249, 256, 257, 271
periodization 90, 144, 328
periphery 48, 58, 62, 177 n.22, 190,
    232, 233, 253
permissibility 10, 22, 39, 244, 247, 248,
    269, 278, 280, 281, 292
permissions 2, 115–16, 155,
    258, 266, 269
persecuted 39, 168, 210, 244, 256, 319
persecution 22, 39, 95, 152, 236, 243,
    244, 271, 278, 282
personal experience 21, 24, 29, 36, 40,
    74, 184, 308
personal relations 3, 39, 43, 81, 83, 91,
    103, 106, 250, 253, 263–4, 270,
    273–6, 319, 322
personnel politics 75, 77, 113, 145,
    155
personnel strategies 231, 235–44, 259
Péteri György 10–11, 153 n.7
petition 168
Petrusek, Miloslav 273, 288, 287
    n.20, 318, 321
PhD 23, 60, 101–2, 104, 138 n.23, 157,
    199, 249, 258, 298
phenomenology 150, 157, 162, 174, 189,
    191, 194, 207, 274–5, 295
philosophy 58, 150, 162, 173, 183, 190,
    204, 222, 325–6
  Christian 195, 297
  institute/department of 51 n.8, 52, 60
    n.23, 80 n.3, 93, 148
  medieval 91, 148
photocopying, see Xeroxing
phraseology 159, 207–8, see also
    vocabulary

phrases 8, 42, 203, 251, 255, 275, 298,
    301–4, 307, 311, 322, see also
    vocabulary
  empty 159, 177, 275, 304, 313
planning of social development 198
plot 43 n.18, 45
pokrývač, see ghost-author
Poland 5, 6, 10, 156, 292, 327
policy 81, 221, 330
  context 13, 16, 47–63
  discourse 38, 113
  documents 37, 38, 105, 112–13,
    145, 187, 231–5, 251,
    256, 279, 293
  editorial 125 n.11, 130, 265
  science 19, 20, 151, 231–2,
    250, 267, 320
Polish censorship 6, 10
political affiliation 235
political and personal 3, 93, 236,
    274–5, 276
Political College 57, 122, 129, 213
political involvement 23, 98, 235–6,
    245, 249, 250
politically compromised (author), see
    author, compromised
Politická ekonomie 82, 202
polyphony 31–2, 33
positioning 32, 37, 42, 271, 289,
    295
positivism, positivist 143, 157, 177 n.22,
    221, 299, 316
post-academic writing 29–30
postgraduate 82, 220, 221
post-socialism, post-socialist 43,
    305, 314–19
Potůček, Martin 108
Poučení z krizového vývoje, see Lessons
    Learned from the Crisis
    Development
poverty 152 n.5, 168–9, 172, 192, 199,
    200, 223, 293, 301
power, petrification of 328
  political 43, 137, 145, 166, 233,
    241, 265, 270
  position 43, 48, 52, 79, 80,
    136, 273, 319
  relations 30, 37, 238, 270
  state/Party, 9, 11, 15, 26, 37
powerless 14–15, 140, 240–1, 302, 306

Prague Spring 5, 12, 37–9, 42, 73, 195, 197, 232, 236, 245, 257, 267, 283, 295–7, 312
Prečan, Vilém 50, 52 n.11, 54 n.13, 233
pressure 83, 87, 110, 164, 169, 180, 191, 204, 240, 247, 249, 258, 288
  censoring (*see* censoring pressures)
  on institutions 73, 78, 81–2, 86
Přidal, Antonín 111
primary text 31, 44, 224
principles (moral) 78, 87, 290
printing house 117 n.4, 142–3, 156
prioritizing of roles 284
privacy 97, 123, 142, 197, 204, 246
privilege 7, 11, 30, 129, 155, 241, 301 n.28
  publishing and 39, 113, 263, 268, 270
processes, regulatory 13, 16
  institutional 6, 55, 241, 257, 315, 319
  publishing 117, 118
professional association/society 74, 77, 94, 254
professional development 39, 108, 112, 245, 248–50, 252, 258, 316, 322
professional existence 39, 51, 77, 111, 245–8, 256, 262, 290, 320
professional roles 281–4
professional standards 39, 59
professional trajectory 19, 89, 248, 250
profit, personal 95, 112, 241, 243
pro-forma work 252
Prognostický ústav ČSAV, *see* Institute of Economic Forecasting
Progress Report 49–54
prohibit, tolerate, support (Aczél's policy) 151, 244, 272 n.15
promotion 183, 249–50
proofreading 91
proofs 124, 142–3, 157, 269
propaganda 4, 7, 8, 24, 58, 73, 130, 330
proposition 28, 31
proscribed books 11
protest 171, 278, *see also* revolt
provĕrky, *see* vetting
province 88–9, 166–7
pseudonym 35, 111, 174–5, *see also* pen name
publication output 61, 265, 268–9
publication venues 16, 22, 39, 77, 113, 268, 290

publish *and* perish 39, 259
publishing abroad/in the West 111, 115, 142, 167–8, 176, 251, 262, 278, 285, 302 n.29
publishing house 60, 132, 138 n.23
  differences between 92, 126–7, 133
  procedures in 117, 122 n.6, 148–9, 285
publishing plan 16, 117 n.4, 118, 136, 265
publishing proposal 25, 104, 116–17, 124 n.9, 128 n.13, 138 n.23, 144 n.25, 175
Pullmann, Michal 319
punishment 238, 242, 279
purge 3, 21, 38, 79 n.2, 296, 326, *see also* vetting
purification of observations 27

qualitative methods 28, 30, 33, 35, 296, 318
quantitative methods 28, 90, 248, 298, 318
quest 13, 31–2, 36, 73, 145, 184, 187, 208, 214–15, 224
quota 39, 138 n.23, 144 n.25, 236, 264, 265
  paper (*see* paper quota)

Radio Free Europe/Radio Liberty Research Institute (RFE/RL) 24, 211
rapprochement between the intelligentsia and the workers 85, 196, 239, 297
reader, *see* author–reader compact/contract
reader's report 114, 122–5, 132, 138, 222, *see also* review
reading between the lines 177, 309, *see also* writing between the lines
Realizační směrnice, *see* Executive Directions
reception 13, 18, 22, 37, 163
reception theory 4
recommendation 7, 82, 116, 122–3, 157, 173, 264, 266, 277
references 53 n.12, 149, 171, 207, 286–7, 301 n.28, 322, *see also* citations

reflection   29, 33, 45, 280, 288–9, 298–9, 300, 313–19
reform process   37–8, 50, 52, 73, 235, *see also* Prague Spring
regime   62, 87, 96, 246, 249, 320
  Ceauşescu   6
  communist   8, 330
  criticism of   188, 193, 293
  fall of   43, 51, 284
  Kádár   110, 144, 210, 222–3, 293, 319
  regime change   107, 113, 239, 318, 322
  state-socialist   15, 36
rejection (of a publication)   39, 124 n.9, 131 n.16, 138 n.23, 140, 265, 268–70
removal and replacement   15
remuneration   96, 136, 243
repression   6, 12–13, 47, 235, 241
repressive   2, 7–8, 26, 95, 307, 320–2
research assignment   116, 121, 155, 173, 198, 203
research culture   322–3
research institute   52, 239, 293, 327
  applied   141, 188
research pedagogy   44
research process   30, 36, 45, 273
research reports   104–5, 114, 128, 135, 141, 148, 150, 173, 190, 251, 262, 284
research subjects   150, 255, 290, 299, 312, *see also* research topics; subject matter
  politicization of   41–2, 274, 291–8, 329
research topics   61, 138 n.23, 188–98, 208, 241, 275, 321, *see also* research subjects
  choice of   9, 148, 155, 203, 247, 272, 288
  favoured   105, 131 n.16, 178–9
  sensitive   119, 278
  unacceptable   79
resistance   8, 14, 43, 95, 176, 217, 280, 285, 291, 295, 310, 328
  act of   54, 62, 77
  erosion of   259, 288
restrictions   1, 5, 47, 62, 73, 265, 271, 326
retirement age   237
revenge   88, 238, 315, 319

review   121, 133, 159, 171, 180, 222, 266, 323, *see also* reader's report
  book   84, 89, 136, 142–3, 176
  critical   163, 277, 285
  ideological   39, 118, 150, 262–4, 269–70
  peer (*see* peer review)
reviewer   122–4, 127, 149, 269
  peer (*see* peer reviewers)
revisionism, revisionist   57, 60, 160, 287, 329
revolt   153, 168, *see also* protest
revolution   31
  1956   23, 114, 152 n.5, 156 n.8, 167 n.17, 168, 195, 196, 243, 294
  1989   82, 109, 193 n.3, 220, 328
risk   39, 81, 120, 163, 174, 190, 191, 239, 247, 259, 263, 268, 270, 302, 320
ritual   38, 247, 303
rival, rivalry   112, 124, 150, 240, 264–5, 276, 319
Roma, the   192, 221
romanticization   29, 36, 284
royalties   136, *see also* honorarium
Rudé právo   55, 57, 89, 103 n.16, 165, 188, 213, 300
rules   14, 38, 99, 114, 119, 199, 248, 261
  communication   210
  methodological   28, 33
  unclear   41, 44, 281–2
  written and unwritten   5, 10, 259

salary   85, 95, 103, 166
salary bonus   242, 251, 277
Salecl, Renata   282–3
Šámal, Petr   11–12, 16, 51, 53, 253, 256, 267, 278, 286, 299 n.27
samizdat   6, 16, 23, 244, 282, 293
  distribution   110
  publishing in   144, 148–9, 176, 251, 257, 278–9, 285
  sanctified *samizdat*   129, 193
sample   28, 37, 43, 323
  sample saturation   29
sanction   39–40, 47, 54, 93, 101, 164–5, 167–8, 232, 239–40, 278, 292–3
Sandomirskaja, Irina   8, 309–10
sanfte Zensur   7, *see also* friendly censorship
scholarly value   2, 143, 280, 288, 321, 326

scientific and technological
 revolution   53, 197
Scientific Committees of the Czechoslovak
 Academy Sciences   25, 57, 119
 n.5, 124 n.9, 126 n.11
Scott, James C.   37, 63, 281, 302, 306
second *Öffentlichkeit*   210
secret police   7, 88, 96, 156, 205, *see also*
 State Security
Security Services, *see* State Security
Sedm pražských dnů   139 n.24
self-censorship   7, 15–18, 38, 40,
 149, 172, 180, 223, 258, 263,
 275–6, 283
 acts of   148, 159, 179, 267
 effect on writing   14, 151, 248
 elusiveness of   287, 290
self-deception   213–14
self-respect   246, 284
self-stylization   29, 218, 280
seminars   1, 40, 89, 108–9, 128–9, 161,
 174, 253–4, 322
 political   57–8, 60, 234
sensitization, sensitized   27, 169,
 281, 291
service to the profession   174, 284, 286
Setje-Eilers, Magaret   253
Sherry, Samantha   8–9, 15, 287
shortage of resources   39, 264, 265
signposts   30–8, 313, 322, 330
Šiklová, Jiřina   22–3, 328
Skovajsa, Marek   53 n.12, 61
 n.26, 273, 318
Slejška, Dragoslav   287
Slovakia   4, 20, 82, 109, 175,
 176, 188, 315
Šmejkalová, Jiřina   10–12, 41
 n.15, 265, 282
Smetanovské dny   109 n.28
snakes and ladders (a board game)   37,
 38, 39, 44, 231, 282
Snyder, Timothy   329–30
social capital   90–1, 254, 258, 265, 285
social control   15
social differentiation   196, 297
socialist society   104, 105, 158, 201,
 205–6, 211, 300
socialist way of life   42, 109, 195, 198, 297
social sciences and humanities, roles/tasks
 of   14, 56–8, 113, 171, 237, 281

Society for Science and Technology   108
socio-economic formations   206
*Sociologický časopis / Czech Sociological
 Review*   12, 53 n.12, 55, 57, 96,
 109, 128, 141, 171, 318
sociology   126, 141, 197, 247, 273, 299,
 315, 317–18, 326
 bourgeois   79, 170, 178–9, 194, 198,
 296 n.25, 297 n.26
 empirical   99, 141, 247
 institute/department of   52, 90, 135
 Marxist (*see* Marxist sociology)
 oral   321–2
 status during state-socialism   47, 57–8,
 79, 170, 178, 188, 295
solidarity   39, 54, 83, 88, 137, 240–1,
 244, 266, 311
 with persecuted scholars   84, 85, 86,
 136, 239, 258, 319
Sorescu, Marin   276
Soros, George   327
Soros Foundation   154–5
Soviet, *see* Soviet sociology
 language of   170, 281
Sovietization   11, 53 n.12, 61 n.27
Soviet sociology   153, 213, 254
Soviet Union   52, 102, 153, 154, 213, 254,
 265, 303, 321
 relationship to   194, 195, 294
speakability, speakable   246,
 273, 282, 296
speech acts   303
speeches, ideological/political   97, 169,
 330
spying   81, 95, 161
Stalinism   38, 213, 311
Stalinist   7, 11
state-owned citizens   7
State Plan of Basic Research   52, 58, 126,
 138 n.23, 253
State Security   205, 274, 323, *see also*
 secret police
state-socialist ideology   2–3, 7
state-socialist system   242, 293
Statistical Office (Hungary)   152 n.5,
 153, 168
statistics   59, 83, 206 (method)   143,
 189, 200, 202, 298–9
Státní plán základního výzkumu, *see* State
 Plan of Basic Research

status   10, 22, 23, 263, 266, 271, 286
    as a subject   246, 277
StB, *see* secret police
stereotype   36
stigma   79, 80-1, 85, 240, *see also* label
stigmatization   81, 207, 302-3
stigmatized   111, 165, 251, 253
story   30-1, 34, 36, 37, 45, 62
strategies, discursive   9
    institutional   94, 234-45, 259
    personal   26, 38, 111, 231, 241, 257, 259, 288
    textual   19, 33, 42-3, 103, 111, 250-1, 281, 285, 306-7, 309, 312, 317
stratification   80 n.3, 170, 192, 196, 199, 297
Strauss, Leo   17
stress   101, 241
struck-off (the Party membership list)   23, 50 n.7, 79, 90-1, 111, 115-16, 125, 237
structural barriers   272-4, 279
structural factors   117
structuralism, structuralist   133-4, 159, 174, 188, 275
students   75, 77, 100, 153, 162, 215, 236, 244, 305, 326, 328, 330
    generations of   1, 61
stylistic devices   8, 43, 311
stylistics   42-3, 209, 213, 309
subject matter   3, 269, 272, 279, 293, 309, *see also* research subjects
subversion   235, 241, 252, 264
subversive   187, 197, 238, 301 n.28, 309, 310
Sulek, Antoni   321-2
superior   17, 39, 121, 194, 282, *see also* boss, the
    exploitation by   87, 91, 135, 150, 240, 262
supervision   242, 243
    authority   15, 21, 54
    supervisory   55, 252
supervisor (of a dissertation or a thesis)   157, 162, 194-5
surveillance   41, 93, 165, 239, 244, 263-5, 279-80, 291
    heightened   47, 75, 89, 271, 274, 277, 323
    lesser   74, 238, 255, 258, 265

subversion of   95, 253
survival   142, 191, 325
    in institutions   96, 102, 248
    professional   26, 38, 112, 231, 241, 245-54, 257, 259, 283, 288, 293, 311
Svašek, Maruška   239 n.5
Světová literature, *see* World Literature
Svoboda (publishing house)   82, 85, 103, 127, 129 n.14, 133, 137, 140, 251
symbolic interactionism   191, 295
Szabó Miklós   86
Szelényi Iván   152-3, 153 n.5, 243 n.6, 278
Szociológia   199, 201 n.7, 273-4

taboo   105, 141, 178, 195, 272, 279, 293-5, 320
tactic   180, 209, *see also* strategy
teaching at universities   24, 38, 52, 61, 81-2, 97, 106, 152, 165-6, 233-4
terminology   79, 159, 200-204, 297 n.26, 302, 316, *see also* vocabulary
territorial divisions   53, 129, 241, 273
testimony   6-9, 17-18, 51, 286, 306 n.30
textbooks   2-3, 126, 132, 148, 158
text coding   22, 42-3, 209, 213, 218, 304, 305-12, *see also* code
text production   5, 13, 17, 320
textual presentation   29-36, *see also* written presentation
theoretical sampling   23
thesis   2-3, 101, 104, 124 n.9, 183, 195, 197, 199, 209, 298, *see also* dissertation
thought(s)   2, 50, 274, 288, 320, 321
    detriment of   17, 37
    schools of   41, 43
tiltani, turni, támogatni, *see* prohibit, tolerate, support
Todorov, Tzvetan   246
Tomášek, Dušan   11, 19
totalitarian   8, 38, 209, 305, 329
    paradigm   21
trade unions   61 n.26, 76
transcript, hidden, *see* hidden transcript
transgression   14, 39, 40, 242, 247
translating   81, 149, 239, 282
translation (process)   132, 135, 180
    of expressions   43, 206, 208-9, 303, 312

translations   85, 92, 114, 129, 130, 136, 174, 273–4, 286, 287, 301 n.28
translators   8–9, 61, 85
Trávníček, Jiří   62
Třeštík, Dušan   216
Trianon   195
Tribuna   55
Trump, Donald   330
trust   39, 107, 114, 129, 161, 260, 267, 270, 319–20
Tucker, Aviezer   305
Tůma, Oldřich   50–1
turning points   144, 256, *see also* periodization
Tvorba   55, 57, 171, 176
typology   22, 27–9, 31, 34, 43 n.18, 261, 311

universities   38, 42, 52, 60, 75–6, 153, 236, 244, 246, 292, 326
unriddling   27–8, 31
Urban, Otto   133, 163
Urbášek, Pavel   25 n.7, 250 n.9
utterance   42, 302

vague, vagueness   38, 49, 138 n.23, 181, 241, 262, 271, 282, 294
Valóság   170, 282
Vaněk, Antonín   286
vassal   90, 238–43, 267, 270, 276, 283
Vavroušek, Josef   193
Večerní univerzita marxismu-leninismu, *see* VUML
vědecká kolegia ČSAV, *see* Scientific Committees
Vědecko technická společnost, *see* Society for Science and Technology
vědecko-technická revoluce, *see* scientific and technological revolution
vested interests   29, 243, 256
vetting (1969–70)   50–4, 61, 88, 240
   generational aspects of   78, 232, 254–5, 258, 261
   of libraries   62
   survival after   96, 248, 257
   vocabulary associations with   202
Vianu, Lidia   6, 18, 21–2, 29

victim   87, 271, 319
vocabulary   40–3, 104, 275, 289, 301, 309, 312, 321, *see also* expressions; word choice; words
voice, dissenting   134, 254, 328, 329
   legitimate   43
   polyphony of voices   29, 31–3, 36
VUML   60, 83, 101–2, 249
výměna stranických legitimacy, *see* vetting
Vysoká škola politická ÚV KSČ, *see* Political College
vysokoškolský zákon, *see* Bill on universities

Williams, Kieran   330
woman   30, 75, 106–7, 136, 140, 149, 211, 222
women   23, 30, 85, 96, 107, 180, 193, 221–2, 317
word choice   35, 42, 292, 301, 304, *see also* expressions; vocabulary; words
words   8, 42, 123, 132, 178, 183, 200–214, 289, 301–4, 307, 311–12, 330, *see also* expressions; vocabulary; word choice
work with meaning   251, 284
World Literature   85, 130
writing between the lines   17–18, 177, 178, *see also* reading between the lines
writing process   13, 289–90
written presentation   29–36, 44

Xeroxing   190

young people   75–81, 91, 105, 152, 158, 174, 205, 237, 255, 258, 304–5
youth   166, 198, 248 n.7
Yurchak, Alexei   42, 231, 235, 251, 284, 302–3, 314

Zaslavskaya, Tatyana   153
Zipser, Richard A.   7
Život strany   55, 59–60
Zpráva o plnění realizační směrnice, *see* Progress Report

www.ingramcontent.com/pod-product-compliance
Lightning Source LLC
Chambersburg PA
CBHW072119290426
44111CB00012B/1705